From Disrupter to Achiever

Creating Successful Learning Environments for the Self-Control Classroom

James Levin, Ph.D.

Pennsylvania State University

John M. Shanken-Kaye, Ph.D.

Associates for Counseling and Educational Services

KENDALL/HUNT PUBLISHING COMPANY
4050 Westmark Drive Dubuque, Iowa 52002

0335854

Book Team

Chairman and Chief Executive Officer Mark C. Falb
Vice President, Director of National Book Program Alfred C. Grisanti
Editorial Development Supervisor Georgia Botsford
Developmental Editor Liz Recker
Prepress Project Coordinator Sheri Hosek
Prepress Editor Carrie Maro
Design Manager Jodi Splinter
Designer Suzanne Millius
Senior Vice President, College Division Thomas W. Gantz
Managing Editor, College Field Paul Gormley
Associate Editor, College Field Chip Noonan

For information on professional inservices and workshops
focusing on the Self-Control Classroom Model, please
visit http://www.selfcontrolclassroom.com

Cover image © Copyright Comstock, Inc. 2002

Copyright © 2002 by Kendall/Hunt Publishing Company

ISBN 0-7872-7239-6

All rights reserved. No part of this publication may be reproduced,
stored in a retrieval system, or transmitted, in any form or by any means,
electronic, mechanical, photocopying, recording, or otherwise,
without the prior written permission of the copyright owner.

Printed in the United States of America
10 9 8 7 6 5 4 3 2 1

DEDICATION

THIS BOOK IS DEDICATED TO THE WOMEN WE LOVE

ANDY

CAROLYN

HEIDI

SARAH

SOMMER

Contents

0335854

About the Authors

James Levin, Ph.D. is an Associate Professor in the Graduate School of Education, Director of Advising for the Eberly College of Science at Penn State University, and an educational consultant. Dr. Levin has consulted with hundreds of school districts, alternative schools, and treatment centers nationwide on the management of disruptive behavior and effective instruction. He is a nationally recognized expert in methods of influencing appropriate behavior, motivation, and self-esteem. He teaches graduate and undergraduate courses on classroom management, effective instruction, self-esteem, and motivation.

Dr. Levin is co-author of the books *The Principles of Classroom Management: A Professional Decision Making-Model* and *The Self-Control Classroom: Understanding and Managing the Disruptive Behavior of All Students Including Students with ADHD.* In addition, he has published numerous articles on classroom management and effective instruction.

Dr. Levin's dynamic presentation style makes him a sought after speaker. He previously taught mathematics and science at the secondary level in inner city, suburban, and residential schools for disruptive youth.

John Shanken-Kaye, Ph.D., is a PA licensed psychologist, Director of Associates for Counseling and Educational Services, and an educational consultant in private practice in Doylestown, PA. He has for many years worked effectively with children, adolescents, their families, and teachers. Dr. Shanken-Kaye is a nationally recognized expert in methods of influencing appropriate behavior, motivation, and self-esteem. A Diplomate in Forensic Psychology and Counseling (ACFE, AAFC), he is a therapist for the Bucks County Juvenile Court, as well as a consultant to many school districts, alternative schools, and treatment centers on the topics of behavior management, treatment of Oppositional-Defiant Disorder, Conduct Disorder, and ADHD.

Dr. Shanken-Kaye is co-author, with Dr. James Levin, of the book *The Self-Control Classroom: Understanding and Managing the Disruptive Behavior of All Students Including Students with ADHD*. He brings a new understanding to the behavioral and emotional difficulties of all children, adolescents, and adults.

A sought after speaker, Dr. Shanken-Kaye has provided inservice education across the country to thousands of teachers and parents on the topics of classroom management, the causes of disruption, violent and delinquent behavior, effective parenting, self-esteem, and motivation.

Acknowledgments

The authors gratefully acknowledge the patience, understanding, and support of their wives, Carolyn and Andy, and their children Sommer, Heidi, and Sarah. Please look at our pictures; we have changed little during our time away writing, and promise to be home soon.

The authors owe a debt of gratitude to Dr. Andrea Commaker, without whose sagacious editing it is doubtful the reader would be able to understand much beyond this page.

Our thanks to our team from Kendall/Hunt: Chip Noonan, Georgia Botsford, Liz Recker, and Carrie Maro for their understanding and forbearance while a one-year project became a two and one half year endurance event.

There are many people who have embraced the Self-Control Classroom model as an alternative to traditional authoritarian and coercive models of classroom management. Hopefully, students, parents, teachers, and administrators have derived benefit from the vision that the use of teacher expertise and respectful relationships increases the probability that students will learn to be accountable and to control their own behavior.

Colleen Qaseem, Bellefonte School District; Paul Eakin, Bristol Boro School District; Richard Coe, Ted Davis, Chuck Miller, and Warren Smith, Bucks County Intermediate Unit; John Herb, Center for Juvenile Justice Training and Research; Bruce Taylor and Bruce Hechman, Central Bucks School District; Lori Steele, Chester County Intermediate Unit; Dave Hrach and Dianne Hrach, Cochise County Schools; Maxine Reardon, Deer Valley School District; Susan Weeks, Eastern School District; Kitty Kaczmarek, Glendale School District; Ann Mellot, Hanover School District; Cindy Goldsworthy, Lancaster Lebanon Intermediate Unit; Deb Montplasir, Mesa School District; Kevin Gentilcore, Montgomery County Youth Center; John Gould, Frank Kawtoski, and Kathryn Taylor, Morrisville School District; Mary Ann Evans-Patrick, National School Conference Institute; Bernie Hoffman, Neshaminy School District; Bill Curley and Beth Gill MacDonald, Penn State University; Mark Dowling, Roosevelt School District; Phil Hemphil (deceased), Southwestern School District; Bill Beisel, University of Akron; Dave Campbell, Upper Moreland School District; Steve Iovino, Larry Zeamer, and Michael O'Hara, Warwick School District; Jeff Bair, West Branch School District; John Hoffman, York City School District; Nina Bone, Yuma Educational Opportunity School; and Walt Jones, Littlestown School District.

Preface

The Self-Control Classroom model challenges the beliefs and practices of many educational professionals. The model presents a new paradigm of how to influence students to develop and exhibit self-control. The model is not about management, not about rewards, and not about punishment. It is about the development of personal accountability, integrity, and duty to others.

Because the model challenges many everyday classroom practices, as well as traditional wisdom about the relationship between teachers and students, many readers may experience significant cognitive dissonance. Cognitive dissonance is often described as a "pain in the brain"; it is the uncomfortable feeling that occurs when one is presented with information or experiences which contradict what the individual believes to be true or correct. It is an uncomfortable feeling of disequilibrium that individuals seek to resolve.

Cognitive dissonance may be resolved in two ways. The first is to disregard the new information. By ignoring the input, the individual stays with what is familiar and comfortable and ceases to trouble themselves with learning something new and possibly having to change their behavior. The second way to resolve cognitive dissonance is to critique the new information. This is, of course, the way that new knowledge is analyzed, refined, and ultimately accepted or rejected. In the most positive circumstances, the critique is founded upon empirical research and/or professional consensus and experience. It is our hope that readers will grapple with the information presented in this book, and that they will be persuaded that the old way of doing business—that is, attempting to manage the behavior of students—is not as effective in helping students develop self-control and accountability as is the approach presented in the Self-Control Classroom model.

A teacher who resolved her cognitive dissonance and began practicing the Self-Control Classroom model said, "In today's schools, a teacher cannot base her feelings of competency on how students achieve or behave. Instead she must base her feelings on what she does each day to encourage achievement and appropriate behavior. Everyday I ask myself, "Am I proud of the way I taught today?" and "Would I want my own child to be in a classroom taught by a teacher like me?" If I answer yes to both questions, I know I've done a good job. If I answer no to either question, well I know tomorrow is a new day and I can try again.

Notes about the Structure of the Book

This book has five major sections. They are: 1) Introducing a New Paradigm (Chapters 1–2), 2) Foundations (Chapters 3–7), 3) Establishing Successful Learning Environments (Chapters 8–12), 4) Maintaining Successful Learning Environments (Chapters 13–17), and 5) Reestablishing Successful Learning Environments for Students Who Exhibit Common or Chronic Discipline Problems, While Protecting the Learning Environment for All Students (Chapters 18–26).

The activities used throughout the book are designed to encourage readers to develop their understanding of the philosophies and concepts discussed. These activities are similar to those we use in our workshops. Participants at these workshops indicate that the activities are very helpful, and we therefore encourage you to take the time to complete them.

Studying the many tables, charts, and figures will help readers gain a deeper understanding of the relationships among the various concepts explored in this book.

Each chapter ends with "Where We've Been," "Where We're Headed," a Concept Map, and "Questions for the Study Team." "Where We've Been" summarizes each chapter. "Where We're Headed" provides an advanced organizer for the next chapter.

The concept maps are visual representations of how the major concepts in each chapter are interrelated. Your understanding of the conceptual relationships in each chapter may be different from the authors', so we encourage you to try your hand at developing your own concept maps. This exercise will yield a far deeper understanding of the concepts developed in each chapter.

The "Questions for the Study Team" were culled from submissions of participants at our workshops and from students in our courses. Schools and districts around the United States have found that an understanding of the Self-Control Classroom model is greatly enhanced when teams of teachers, administrators, and other professionals meet to study and discuss the book. These questions may serve as excellent entry points to the discussion of the model.

Chapters 24 and 25 tackle the difficult issue of students who exhibit chronic disruptive behavior. Chapter 26 helps teachers and administrators develop curricula to teach all students how to control themselves and behave appropriately so that the information in Chapters 24 and 25 will no longer be necessary.

There are five appendices at the end of the book. Appendix A, Components of a Successful Learning Environment, summarizes the requisite outcomes to help disrupters become achievers. Appendix B, The Professional Decision Making Matrix, is a tool to help teachers diagnose deficits in a successful learning environment and plan future interventions to enhance a successful learning environment. Appendix C, The Teacher Individual Management Action Plan, is an instrument that helps teachers to prepare to intervene with students who exhibit chronic disruptive behavior. Appendix D, The Anecdotal Record Keeping Form, is a simple way for teachers to record the everyday behaviors of students, as well as the teachers' responses to that behavior. Appendix E, Hierarchy of Interventions, is a chart that lists, in a hierarchical fashion, the strategies and interventions to create, maintain, and reestablish successful learning environments.

To foster equality without being cumbersome, gender pronouns are alternated by chapter. Chapter 1 has female pronouns; Chapter 2, male; Chapter 3, female; and so forth.

Section 1

Introducing a New Paradigm

This section describes the vision of the Self-Control Classroom model and highlights the differences between this model and traditional models of classroom management.

Educators do not need another text on classroom management. Over the years, hundreds of texts have been published, most with the purported goal of helping teachers control their students' behavior and therefore get on with the job of imparting important content to these same students. In the models these texts embrace, disruptive student behavior calls for "management" to ensure a steady supply of compliant students, much as livestock requires management to ensure an orderly processing of animals for food.

The underlying assumption of traditional models of classroom management is that students are like other animals, amenable to the same rewards and punishments to shape their behavior. Therefore, when teachers are faced with ongoing disruptive behavior, these models assume that either the teacher doesn't understand effective behavior management (or herd control), or the teacher is dealing with a "bad kid." If the teacher doesn't seem to possess a high degree of competence, then he or she is referred for additional instruction in behavior management (or, to torture the analogy further, animal husbandry). On the other hand, if the conclusion is that the teacher is dealing with a "bad kid," then that student is targeted for ever more aggressive interventions. This most often culminates in academic failure, and in many cases, results in an early exit from public education, either through referral to an alternative school or by dropping out. Given the fact that over 14% of high school students drop out of school prior to completion (U.S. Department of Education, 1999), this "culling of the herd" has been highly effective.

In a democracy most people believe the job of public education is not merely to impart content knowledge to students, but also to impart social norms, respect for self and others, integrity, and honor—in sum to prepare students to become pro-social citizens. If this outcome is desired, then it is apparent from the rates of juvenile detention that the traditional method of punishing inappropriate student behavior and providing incentives for appropriate student behavior in public schools, with the goal of more positive student behavior and citizenship is a failure.

The Self-Control Classroom model of adult/student interaction offers a new paradigm for influencing the behavior of young people. It is a model of prevention of inappropriate behavior, rather than a reaction to or management of inappropriate behavior. The model is predicated upon the mutual accountability of adults and students for their actions. It stresses the importance of both respectful relationships and instructional expertise in creating an environment where students can and desire to behave appropriately and are positive citizens of their school and outside communities. By recognizing the unique characteristics of each teacher, each student, each classroom, and each school, the Self-Control Classroom model is not a "one size fits all" approach. The model encourages teachers and administrators to recognize these differences and account for them when devising school-wide and classroom strategies to influence student behavior.

CHAPTER 1

Avoiding a Disciplinary Nightmare

". . . almost all U.S. schools have goals or mission statements on preparing students to be independent learners and to participate in a democratic way of life. But when we look at how most classrooms are managed, few schools actually promote this goal." (Mann, 1998)

A Disciplinary Nightmare

The New Horizons Middle School
Class Roster

Teacher: Ms. Mellot	Chavez, Caeser	Mandella, Nelson
Room: 213	Christ, Jesus	Meir, Golda
Fall Term	Darwin, Charles	Mohammed
	Geronimo, Chief	Moses
	Ghandi, Indira	Parks, Rosa
Abzug, Bella	Goodall, Jane	Roosevelt, Eleanor
Ali, Mohammed	Huerta, Dolores	Sadat, Anwar
Anthony, Susan	Jefferson, Thomas	Steinem, Gloria
Bolivar, Simon	Jones, Mother	Teresa, Mother
Buddha, Gutama	King, Martin Luther	Wiesenthal, Simon
Bull, Sitting	Kyi, Aung San Sou	Winnemucca, Sarah
Carson, Rachael	Lincoln, Abraham	

School begins in three days. This is your seventh grade class roster. Are you looking forward to the school year? Do you believe this will be an obedient, easily managed group of students? These students are likely to be noncompliant, question your authority, think independently, disrespect the status quo, quarrel, and some may be hyperactive. In short, this class is likely to be a disciplinary nightmare for many teachers.

These same individuals, as adults, are admired by most of us. Why? Every one on the class list grew up and, as adults, made significant contributions to society. To accomplish this, these men and women broke rules, defied authority, disregarded precedent, and stood against injustice, often to their personal detriment.

If these were your students, would your classroom environment allow them to question rules and your authority, to develop new ways of doing things, and to attempt to change those situations that they believed were unjust? Sadly, in most classrooms the answer would be "no." In schools today there is an increasing emphasis on the use and adaptation of instructional and management models designed to encourage compliance and obedience. If your classroom conforms to these models of compliance and obedience, these students probably would receive detentions, be suspended, expelled, or placed in emotional support classes in order to curb their non-compliance and disobedience.

The Self-Control Classroom model helps to prevent disruptive, delinquent, and violent behavior, and to encourage accountability, achievement, integrity, and duty to others through adult/youth interaction, emphasizing trusting, caring, and respectful relationships and the use of effective, expert instruction.

What is the common factor that enabled the members of our hypothetical class to become great leaders and figures of admiration? When these individuals upset the status quo, all were willing to accept the consequences of their actions. In other words, they were personally accountable.

What is the preferred outcome for your students or indeed, for your own children? Do you prefer that your students and children grow up to be compliant and obedient, not questioning authority, always supporting the status quo, and ever fearful of punishment? Or, is it that these children become independent thinkers, questioning authority, having the courage to stand up for injustices and for what they believe, and willing to accept the consequences for their behavior? All Western democracies embrace the latter outcomes for their citizens. In spite of the philosophical position of Western democracies, the majority of schools today embrace models which encourage a contrary outcome—that is, compliance and obedience. The reasons given are to ensure safe schools, to teach respect for authority, to protect the learning environment for all students, and to improve academic performance.

This book presents a model of adult interaction with students, which:

- ensures safe schools,
- teaches respect for authority,
- protects the learning environment for all students,
- improves academic performance, and
- insists that all individuals accept responsibility for their behavior.

At the same time, the model:

- encourages students to engage in independent thought,
- to question authority, and
- to develop the courage to stand up for injustices and for what one believes—in sum, to assist these children and young adults in becoming accountable, productive, achievement-oriented individuals, prepared to accept the challenges of becoming pro-social citizens in a twenty-first-century democracy.

The Self-Control Classroom Vision Statement

The Self-Control Classroom model helps to prevent disruptive, delinquent, and violent behavior, and to encourage accountability, achievement, integrity, and duty to others through adult/youth interaction, emphasizing trusting, caring, and respectful relationships and the use of effective, expert instruction (Chapter 8). These outcomes are facilitated when students experience successful learning environments.

Successful learning environments are created by:

- facilitating the success of all students, regardless of ability level or previous accomplishments (Chapters 9 & 13),
- encouraging intrinsic motivation by developing meaningful learning experiences and by eliminating extrinsic and coercive incentives (Chapters 10 &14), and
- providing opportunities for the development of pro-social self-esteem through respectful relationships, the growth of competence, opportunities to help others, and recognizing that an individual's outcomes in life are dependent upon the choices one makes (Chapters 11 & 15).

When students are not experiencing a successful learning environment, evidenced by academic failure and/or by disruptive behavior, adherents to the Self-Control Classroom model attempt to:

- reestablish a successful learning environment (Chapters 18 & 19),
- protect the learning environment for all students (Chapters 20–25), and
- teach appropriate behavior (Chapter 26).

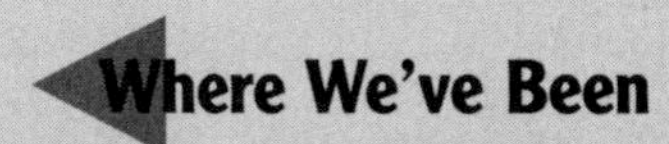

Where We've Been

Ms. Mellot's class has all the makings of a disciplinary nightmare: students who appear noncompliant, question authority, think independently, disrespect the status quo, quarrel, and appear hyperactive. Whether or not these students develop accountability for their behavior, which would diminish the potential for a disciplinary nightmare, depends upon Ms. Mellot's goals. If her goal is for her students to become compliant and obedient, unquestioning followers of authority and unfailing supporters of the status quo, ever fearful of punishment, then the likelihood of students developing accountability will decrease, and the likelihood of disruptive behavior will increase. If Ms. Mellot's goal is for her students to become independent thinkers questioning authority, courageous enough to stand up for injustices and for what they believe, and willing to accept the consequences for their behavior, then the likelihood of students developing accountability will increase and the likelihood of disruptive behavior will decrease.

The vision of the Self-Control Classroom model is that to prevent disruptive and delinquent behavior and to encourage accountability, achievement, integrity, and duty to others, a particular model of adult/student interaction must be employed. This model emphasizes trusting, caring, and respectful relationships and the use of effective, expert instruction, in order to facilitate successful learning environments for students.

Where We're Headed

The importance of the professional teacher is discussed in Chapter 2. In addition, the significant differences between the Self-Control Classroom model of teacher/student interaction and traditional models of classroom management are highlighted.

CHAPTER 1 CONCEPT MAP

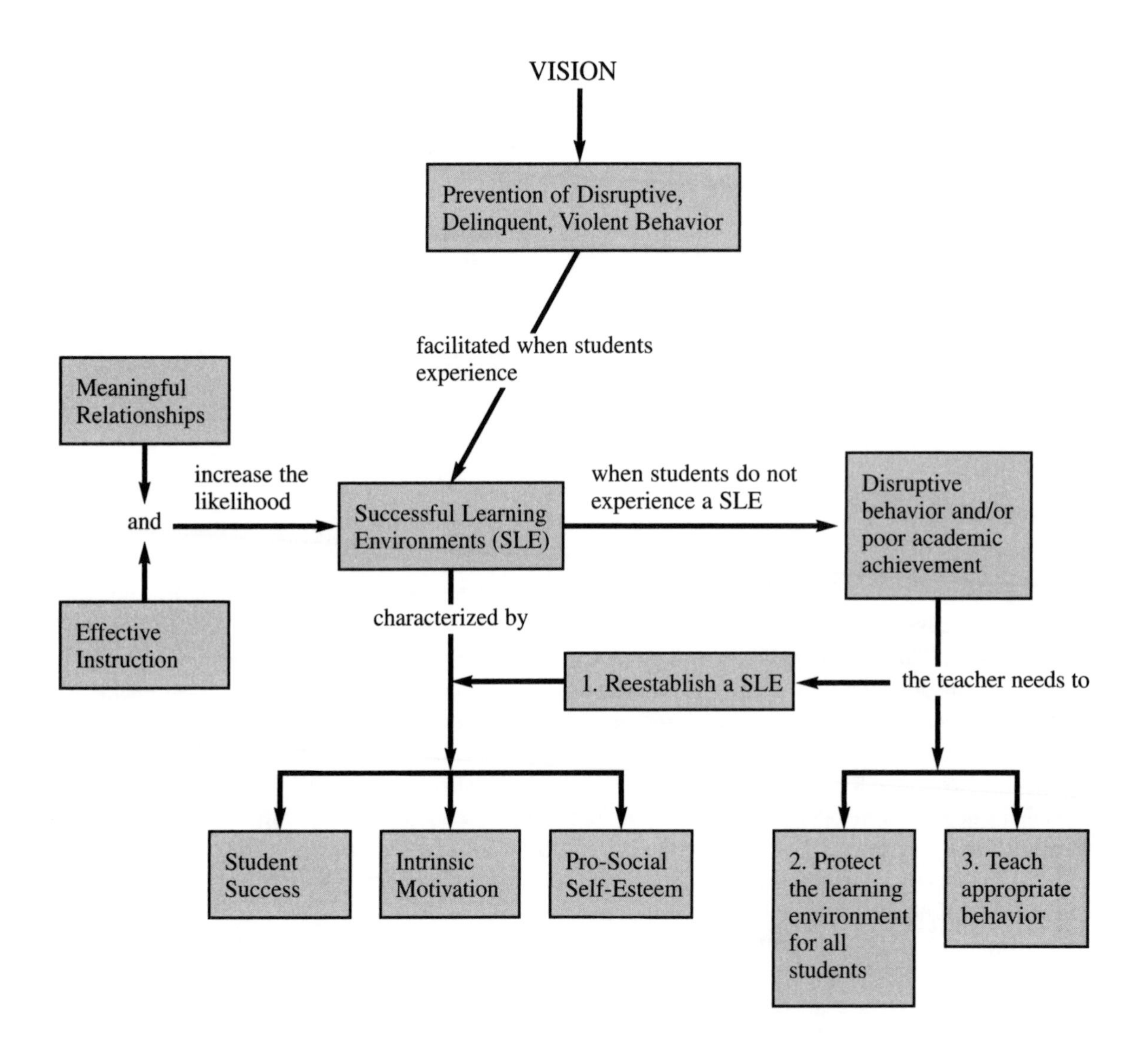

? QUESTIONS FOR THE STUDY TEAM

1. How can a teacher control and manage a class like Ms. Mellot's?

2. How do you allow students to engage in independent thought, to question authority, and to develop the courage to stand up for injustices and for what they believe, without having major discipline problems?

3. Allowing students to engage in independent thought, to question authority, and to develop the courage to stand up for injustices and for what they believe are appropriate objectives for secondary students in social studies, but how can such objectives be taught to elementary and middle school students or in other subject areas?

4. If students have a history of disruptive behavior and poor academic achievement, how can you teach them to engage in independent thought, to question authority, and to develop the courage to stand up for injustices and for what they believe if they haven't even learned the required curriculum?

5. Engaging in independent thought, questioning authority, and developing the courage to stand up for injustices and for what one believes are very abstract concepts. How can you teach these to students who are still at the concrete operational stage of cognitive development?

6. Why would you want to encourage a student to question authority when this is one of the major reasons students already get into trouble in school?

CHAPTER 2

A New Paradigm

> "Many schools have been totally turned around, ... Because they are staffed by 'star teachers.' These are teachers: who believe they can make a difference in the learning of any child in their classroom, whose gentle approach to students builds options for kids' behavior, whose expectations embrace problems and disruptions as normal aspects of their daily life, and who seize upon effort and not ability." (Haberman, 1995)

Why Do We Need Teachers?

Imagine a world where no one ever got ill and there were no accidents requiring treatment. Why would we need doctors? Imagine a world where no one violated laws, where civil suits were unheard of, and litigation of any type was nonexistent. Why would we need lawyers? Imagine a world where no one needed to file taxes (wouldn't that be nice?), and where keeping financial records was unnecessary. Why would we need accountants? Now imagine a world where all students were highly intelligent, had no learning disabilities, were highly motivated to learn, behaved appropriately, and came from families that supported education. Why would we need professional teachers?

Instead of hiring math, science, history, English, and elementary education teachers, schools could be staffed with individuals possessing math, science, English, history, and liberal arts degrees—in short, those with knowledge in the appropriate content areas only. There would be no need for professional teachers also educated in areas such as human development, motivation theory, and instructional pedagogy. The elimination of the professionally trained teacher is not so far-fetched.

Legislators throughout the country have proposed and supported various educational alternatives, the net effect of which is to undermine the professional teacher and public education. Such alternatives include charter schools (most of which have selective admission policies and are not staffed by professional teachers), home schooling, and voucher systems that support private schools (again which are selective and generally do not require certified teachers).

We need professional teachers because not every student is highly intelligent, is free of learning disabilities, is highly motivated toward learning, behaves appropriately, or comes from a family that supports education. Students come to school with complex individual characteristics representing a variety of abilities, motivations, behavioral challenges, and family backgrounds.

Just as a doctor expects his patients to have health problems, an attorney expects his clients to have legal problems, and an accountant expects his clients to have financial problems, professional teachers have to expect students to have all sorts of learning, motivation, and behavioral problems (Haberman, 1995). Only the professional teacher possesses the requisite training to effectively educate all students.

Most models of teacher/student interaction treat student problems as issues that interfere with the normal process of teaching and learning. The Self-Control Classroom model recognizes that these problems are part of a normal classroom; therefore we need professional teachers who expect the presence of these problems and who possess the knowledge base and skills to work effectively with all types of students. This is one of the differences between the Self-Control Classroom and traditional management models of teacher/student interaction. These differences are discussed in the next section.

The Self-Control Classroom model helps teachers and all other professional and non-professional staff understand that teaching appropriate behavior to students is as legitimate a function for the classroom teacher as is teaching math, English, history, or any other subject.

Differences between the Self-Control Classroom Model and Traditional Management Models of Teacher/Student Interaction

THE AMELIORATION OF LEARNING AND BEHAVIOR PROBLEMS IS THE APPROPRIATE ROLE OF THE PROFESSIONAL TEACHER

As we stated in the preceding section, the professional teacher is uniquely prepared, through his specialized training, to deal with the myriad difficulties students bring to the classroom. Rather than view these student difficulties as an interruption to teaching, as most traditional models do (Cantor, 1992; Dobson, 1996; Valentine, 1999), the Self-Control Classroom model views the amelioration of these difficulties as an integral part of the teaching process. The model helps teachers understand why students might be experiencing difficulties and empowers teachers to design interventions that help students learn more effectively and behave more appropriately.

STUDENT BEHAVIOR IS TAUGHT

We teach mathematics to students because we assume that students come to school lacking an understanding of some aspects of math. We teach English to students because we assume that students come to school lacking an understanding of some aspects of the language. We teach history to students because we assume that students come to school lacking an understanding of historical events. All subjects are taught under similar assumptions—that is, the student is lacking some degree of knowledge in that area. However, when the subject is student behavior, we "manage" it. The assumption seems to be that students come to school possessing all the requisite information about how to behave appropriately in the classroom and other school settings, as well as an understanding of why it is important to behave appropriately. Why is this assumption made? Where are students presumed to have obtained this knowledge? Teachers often say, "It's not our job," asserting that the knowledge of appropriate school behavior should be learned at home. This is analogous to a doctor refusing to treat a child for measles because their parents should have had them immunized. The reality is that many of our students are not learning appropriate behavior in the home, or these students are not exhibiting the appropriate behavior they learned in the home in the classroom. In either case, teachers need to make reality their friend. Just as doctors treat all patients, regardless of how their illness occurred, so do teachers need to teach all students appropriate behavior, regardless of why they behave the way they do. The Self-Control Classroom model helps teachers and all other professional and nonprofessional staff understand that teaching appropriate behavior to students is as legitimate a function for the classroom teacher as is teaching math, English, history, or any other subject. (Raywid and Oshiyama, 2000).

Accountable students accept responsibility for both the positive and negative consequences of their behavior.

FOCUS IS ON STUDENT ACCOUNTABILITY

When students are accountable, the excuses are over. Accountable students accept responsibility for both the positive and negative consequences of their behavior. They develop an internal compass that reduces their dependence upon others to tell them what is right and what is wrong. They have learned that life presents a series of choices.

Notwithstanding that students come from a wide variety of backgrounds, the choices all students make have an enormous impact upon the positive and negative consequences that they experience. Even students whose lives contain abuse, neglect, or other negative conditions can still choose how to behave and potentially modify the conditions of their lives. Obviously, not all students have equal opportunities to learn accountability, nor do they all have equal degrees of choice. However, the fact remains that they alone are responsible for the consequences of their choices, however limited those choices may be. Viktor Frankl (1999) reported that even prisoners in Nazi concentration camps experienced significantly different outcomes from the most horrible of conditions, based upon the personal choices they made.

The Self-Control Classroom model results in increased student accountability.

When students are required to be compliant, the excuses never end. They blame others and avoid responsibility for both the positive and negative consequences of their behavior. Positive or negative consequences are often attributed to the decisions of others, the workings of fate, or forces outside the student's control. Students develop an external moral compass that increases their dependence upon others to tell them what is right and what is wrong. They have learned that life's choices and the outcomes of those choices are predetermined or controlled by others. In contrast, accountable students learn that life's choices and the outcomes of those choices are determined and controlled by themselves.

The Self-Control Classroom model results in increased student accountability. This requires different approaches than those traditional models that emphasize student compliance.

FOCUS IS ALSO ON TEACHER ACCOUNTABILITY

When teachers are accountable, the excuses are over. If students are to learn accountability, then "Do as I say and not as I do" is no longer an acceptable demand from teachers. The most effective way to teach accountability is to model it. Teachers often work in substandard schools with students who come from deprived or disadvantaged environments and who do not seem interested in learning or behaving appropriately. Other teachers work in above average schools with students who come from enriched environments, who nevertheless do not seem interested in learning or behaving appropriately. Neither of these situations provides the teacher with an excuse for the lack of professional conduct in the classroom.

The Self-Control Classroom model increases both student and teacher accountability by focusing on the choices that both make, not just the students.

The Self-Control Classroom model increases both student and teacher accountability by focusing on the choices that both make, not just the students.

Presents a Professional Decision Making Model

Many traditional models of teacher/student interaction are presented as a series of predetermined steps to be followed by teachers in the event of inappropriate student behavior. These models incorporate a number of assumptions about teaching and learning. Among these assumptions are that all schools are the same, all classrooms are the same, all teachers are the same, and all students are the same.

- Is this your experience?
- Is your school like every other school?
- Is your classroom the same as every other classroom?
- Do you teach exactly like every other teacher?
- Are there no differences among your students?

Models that do not account for the wide diversity of educational environments, teaching personnel, and students' backgrounds, abilities, and learning styles do not help teachers utilize this diversity to effectively influence their students.

Another assumption is that teachers are "educational technicians" who require a cookbook approach to prevent or remediate inappropriate student behavior. Often these cookbook approaches are advertised to administrators as "teacher proof." Our model acknowledges that teachers are professionals who can and should utilize their specialized body of knowledge to understand inappropriate student behavior and to design and implement educational strategies to influence appropriate student behavior.

The Self-Control Classroom model focuses on the prevention of inappropriate student behavior through the establishment of successful learning environments.

The Self-Control Classroom model is a professional decision making model of teacher/student interaction that respects the wide diversity of educational environments, teachers, and students. The model provides teachers with a knowledge base that:

- increases their understanding of student behavior,
- helps them devise educational strategies to encourage appropriate behavior, and
- enables them to prevent and remediate inappropriate behavior.

Focus Is on the Prevention of Inappropriate Student Behavior by Establishing and Reestablishing Successful Learning Environments

Traditional models treat the prevention and management of inappropriate student behavior very similarly, typically through the establishment of teacher "control" (the issue of control is detailed in Chapter 3) and the maintenance of control through bribery and intimidation, better known as rewards and punishments. The Self-Control Classroom model, however, focuses on the prevention of inappropriate student behavior through the establishment of successful learning environments. These environments are characterized by encouraging student success, intrinsic motivation and pro-social self-esteem (See Chapters 13, 14 & 15). When students are not experiencing a successful learning environment, as evidenced by their academic failure and/or by disruptive behavior, adherents to the Self-Control Classroom model attempt to reestablish successful learning environments for these students, simultaneously protect the learning environment for all other students, and teach, not manage, appropriate student behavior.

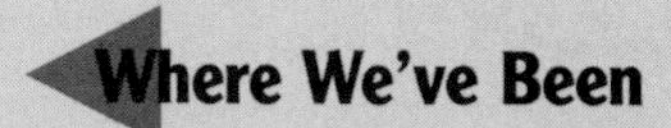

Where We've Been

We need professional teachers because not all students are highly intelligent, are free of learning disabilities, are motivated to learn, behave appropriately, or come from families that support education. Only professional teachers have the knowledge base needed to effectively teach the diverse student population present in schools today. Traditional models of classroom management respect neither the diversity of students nor the professionalism of teachers. The model also breaks with tradition by stressing that the amelioration of learning and behavior problems is the appropriate role of the professional teacher and that appropriate student behavior is taught. Additionally, both teachers and students need to be accountable for the choices that they make. The Self-Control Classroom is a professional decision making model that encourages appropriate student behavior and prevents and remediates inappropriate behavior by helping teachers to design successful learning environments and teach appropriate behavior.

Where We're Headed

Every educational model has certain philosophies or beliefs that serve as the foundation of its practices and strategies. In Chapter 3, these philosophies underlying the Self-Control Classroom model are set forth.

CHAPTER 2 CONCEPT MAP

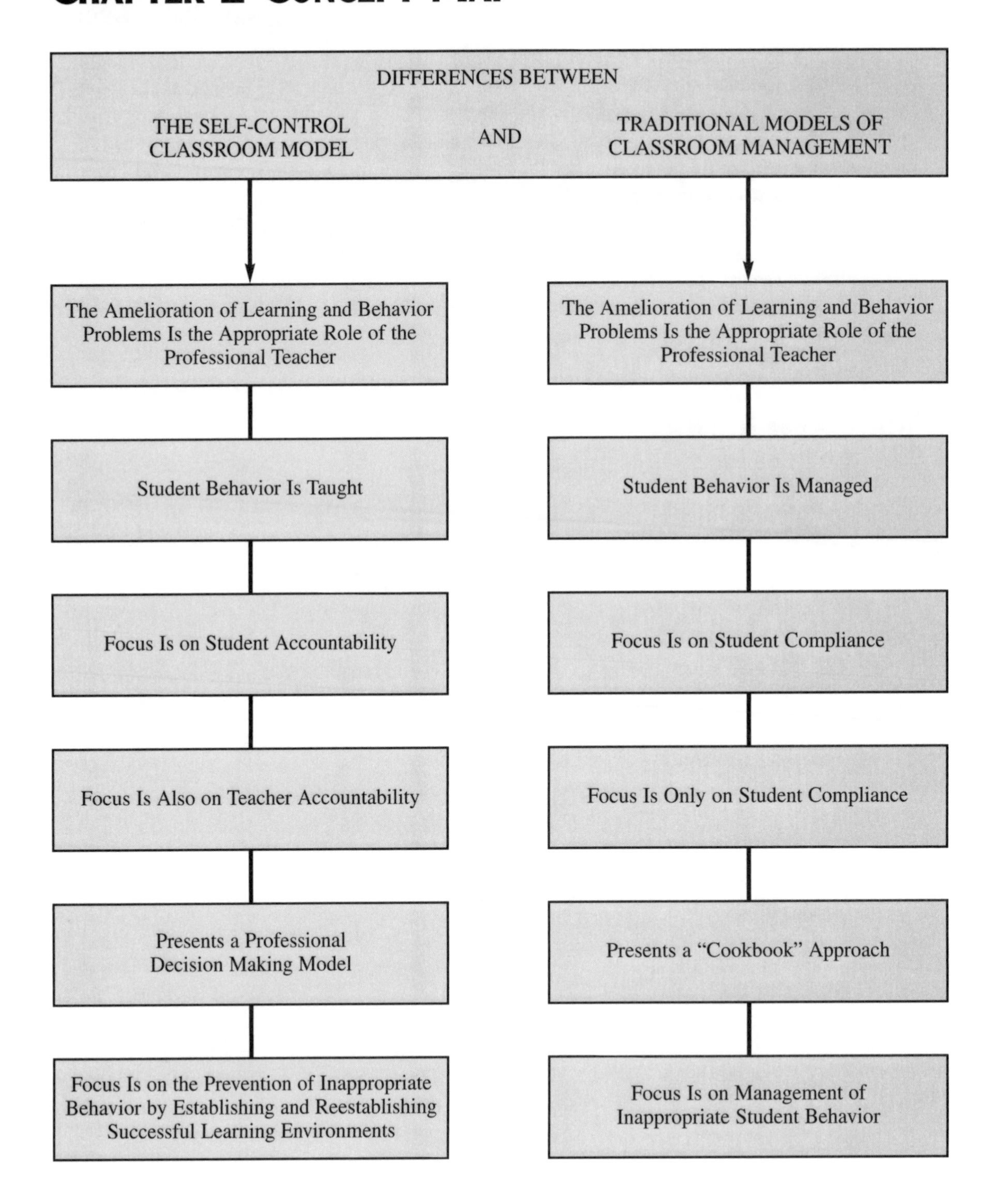

? QUESTIONS FOR THE STUDY TEAM

1. This chapter presented a number of ways the Self-Control Classroom model differs from traditional models of classroom management. The following list includes some of these. What are the implications for teachers' classroom behavior as a result of the differences?

   a. Student behavior is taught rather than managed.

   b. The focus is on facilitating student accountability rather than student compliance.

   c. The focus is on both student and teacher accountability rather than student compliance.

   d. Teachers need to make professional decisions when learning/behavioral problems arise, rather than follow a predetermined list of strategies ("cookbook").

   e. Focus is on the prevention of disruptive behavior by establishing and reestablishing successful learning environments, rather than on managing disruptive behavior.

SECTION 2

Foundations

This section describes the foundational precepts that teachers need to embrace in order to increase the likelihood that they will create successful learning environments.

As stated in the first section, the Self-Control Classroom model is a professional decision making model. Professionals make decisions based upon their knowledge base and previous experience. This section begins with the philosophies (Chapter 3), which underlie the Self-Control Classroom model. These philosophies are congruent with the vision statement (Chapter 1), and stress the individual accountability of adults and students for their own behavior.

Chapter 4 encourages you, the reader, to evaluate your own behavior by providing three questions to ask yourself each day. Answering the questions requires you to analyze your behavior in the class each day on a very personal level.

In any text dealing with the topic of classroom management, the terms "teaching," "learning" and "discipline problem" are used with great frequency. However, they are rarely ever operationally defined. In Chapter 5, we explicitly define these terms in ways that illustrate that teaching appropriate behavior is just as much a responsibility of the classroom teacher as teaching academic content.

Teachers and administrators at the beginning of the twenty-first century are called upon to find solutions to problems that were scarcely imagined by school personnel in the middle of the twentieth century. In Chapter 6 some of the significant societal changes that impact all communities are explored. These changes in our culture require very different behaviors on the part of adults, if they desire to have a positive influence upon today's youth.

The section concludes in Chapter 7, with an analysis of the parallel process, which is how teachers and students have similar thoughts and reactions to each others' behavior in the classroom, and how this affects their future behavior. It stresses the responsibility of teachers to ensure that this is a positive process through their development and use of accurate empathy.

CHAPTER 3

Philosophies of the Self-Control Classroom Model

"In effect, we are all heroes immersed in a quest to help our schools and school systems respond to the increasingly complex demands of the world of the Information Age. Old answers are no longer viable for the new questions we are confronting, just as old paradigms and old solutions are insufficient to respond to the new and unanticipated problems in contemporary education. We are all both individual and collaborative "questors," searching for viable ways to transform our schools into communities of academic integrity, lifelong learning, and extraordinary caring for the children we serve. The object of our quest is the capacity to initiate, support, and sustain meaningful educational change." (Brown and Moffett, 1999)

Importance

Every model of classroom management has at its core a set of beliefs or philosophies. Often the model's philosophy can be inferred by just reading the title of the book. For example, what do the titles *The New Dare to Discipline* (Dobson, 1996), *Don't Smile Till Christmas* (Ryan, 1970), and *Assertive Discipline* (Canter, 1992) imply? These titles imply that effective classroom management is all about courage and stoicism. It certainly is not for the faint of heart. These titles give the impression that appropriate student behavior is a function of teachers' strict and humorless behavior.

Now consider the titles *Teaching Children to Care* (Charney, 1992), *On Their Side* (Strachota, 1996), and *The Self-Esteem Teacher* (Brooks, 1991). From these titles, one is likely to infer that effective classroom management is a function of allying with students and teaching students appropriate behavior. These titles give the impression that appropriate student behavior requires an empathetic professional teacher.

It is important for teachers to understand and accept the philosophies underlying the educational model they wish to effectively employ in their classrooms. When teachers do not understand the philosophies of a specific model, the model becomes a set of isolated techniques devoid of context. When teachers understand the philosophies but do not accept them, the teacher is unlikely to wholeheartedly implement the model.

Philosophies

THE ONLY PERSON YOU CAN CONTROL IS YOURSELF

Think about all the individuals in your life over whom you have control. For many of you, this list includes your children, spouse or partner, students, and classroom aides.

- How many of these people do precisely as you desire all of the time?
- Are their actions inescapably tied to your demands and have they no other choice but to follow your instructions?

As you rethink the issue of whom you control, it becomes obvious that you have control over no one's behavior but your own. This is not to say that you are powerless in affecting people's behavior, but you do not have control. What you do or do not have is influence. If you had control, your immediate surroundings would be perfect, because you would be surrounded by students, children, spouses, partners, and co-workers all doing exactly as you wanted, all the time. All you would have to do is make a request and they would comply (wouldn't that be great?).

Depending upon how you choose to behave, you influence how the people around you, including your students, choose to behave.

The distinction between control and influence is not merely one of semantics. The misperception of how much control we have over other people's behavior contributes to the stress and frustration many of us feel in our personal and professional lives. If we believe that we can or ought to be able to control the behavior of another individual, then when they behave in a contrary manner, we feel incompetent, angry, and frustrated.

So you say, "OK, fine. I don't have control. What I have is influence. But when I tell a kid to be quiet, that kid better be quiet, if she knows what's good for her." However, most teachers we come in contact with are quick to point out that demanding a student to stop talking does not insure compliance, and, in some cases, the student's talking may actually increase.

If you are honest with yourself, you realize that there is not much you can do that guarantees compliance. So what happens when the student doesn't comply? You may make additional demands, use time out, call parents, remove privileges, and/or refer the student to the office. These techniques may be effective in gaining the desired result in the short term, but they rarely result in long-term success. In addition, when teachers rely upon these short-term strategies, they decrease the likelihood that students will accept accountability for their behavior. So, do you have control over student behavior? We would argue, not really.

You now may be thinking about that teacher down the hall from you, who doesn't scream or give detentions. Yet the students in her classroom are consistently well behaved. Surely that teacher has control. We agree that she does have extraordinary control. However, it is not control over her students; it is control over her own behavior. By controlling her own behavior, this teacher has achieved the desired result of appropriate student behavior. Teacher self-control is a long-term strategy that teaches student self-control and increases the likelihood that students will accept accountability for their behavior.

It is our belief that the only person you can control is yourself. Depending upon how you choose to behave, you influence how the people around you, including your students, choose to behave. This powerful idea of teacher self-control is paramount to the Self-Control Classroom model and is stressed throughout this book.

It is reasonable for you to ask, "Since I can only control my own behavior, how should I behave? How can I influence students to choose to act appropriately?" First, let's discuss what is not appropriate action, because inappropriate action will lessen the likelihood that your students will behave appropriately.

If You Continue to Do What You've Done, You'll Continue to Get What You've Got

This philosophy was made apparent by one of the author's first teaching experiences more than thirty years ago.

He taught secondary mathematics in a large inner city junior high school, where he was assigned five classes and was supervised by the assistant principal. Four of the classes were fine, but the fifth was plagued by extensive behavioral problems. This class was never without disruptive behavior. Lateness to class, calling out, walking around the room, put-downs, and fighting were common. In addition, there were some unforgettable behaviors, such as when a young lady displayed her displeasure with a young man's "put-down" by standing on her desk, pulling her pants down, and telling the young man to "kiss her ass."

The assistant principal supervised the author and was well aware of the difficulties he was experiencing, but she did not intervene and waited for the teachable moment. Because the author was too embarrassed to seek the help of this experienced supervisor, he continued to endure this class along with feelings of inadequacy, stress, and the accompanying headaches and stomachaches it engendered.

As Thanksgiving rapidly approached, the author finally requested a meeting with the assistant principal. He admitted to her that he was unable to control the students in this class and was seriously considering leaving the profession of teaching at the end of the year. The assistant principal calmly replied, "I've been waiting months for you to ask me about this problem. Rather than telling me about how you've tried to control your student's behavior, tell me how you've tried so far to influence your students' behavior." Almost ready to explode, the author replied, "I fail them, and they don't care. I call their parents, but they are rarely home, and they never return my calls. I change their seats, but they refuse to move. I scream at them, but they ignore me. I give them detentions, but they don't come. Whatever it takes, I don't have it."

In a supportive tone, the assistant principal replied, "You cannot control someone else. You can control only yourself." She went on to say, "If you continue to do what you've done, you'll continue to get what you've got." Thus, this author learned what not to do. He could not continue to do what he was doing.

The same applies to you. If you are dissatisfied with what you've "got" (student behavior), you must change what you are doing (teacher behavior).

When a teacher believes that she should be able to control students in her classroom and students behave inappropriately, she is likely to use strategies with the intention of forcing a change in student behavior. In other words, "she continues to do what she's done." However, teachers are shown daily that behavior intended to force a change in student behavior are ineffective; students continue to be disruptive. "We continue to get what we've got."

When a teacher understands that the only person she can control is herself, and her students behave inappropriately, she changes what she's been doing. She does this to influence a change in student behavior. The first step in this process is to challenge the belief held by many educators that students can and should be controlled. The Self-Control Classroom model provides a framework to help teachers understand how best to change their behavior to influence positive student behavior by establishing and reestablishing a successful learning environment.

IF YOU CAN'T CHANGE YOUR MIND, THEN YOU CAN'T CHANGE ANYTHING

So let's assume that you accept the philosophies that the only person you can control is yourself, and if you continue to do what you've done, you'll continue to get what you've got. Now if you are facing any persistent educational problem, you have to change your behavior to increase the probability that the outcome will change in a positive manner.

One of the reasons why teachers continue to use failed strategies and find it so difficult to change their behavior is because of erroneous beliefs about the role of teachers and students and the causes of students' academic failure and inappropriate behavior.

This is illustrated by a hypothetical, though familiar, conversation that takes place in a faculty lounge. One teacher is heard saying to another teacher, "This year has been great. I really feel that I was successful in reaching my students. But I can't tell you how much I am dreading September. I just learned that in my new class I have one boy with ADHD, a girl whose temper tantrums are legendary, and two students with significant learning disabilities. They're going to mess up all my teaching plans. I don't have the training to deal with these kids. What am I going to do?"

Feelings of inadequacy about teaching certain students are so strong for some teachers that for many, like the teacher in our example, just the anticipation of having one of these students placed in their classroom is enough to cause anxiety and dread. Certainly students with behavioral and academic problems do pose serious challenges for teachers. However, both teachers' preconceived notions, such as those held by the teacher in the faculty lounge, along with increased stress and anxiety, which that teacher was feeling, are formidable barriers to teachers' effectiveness. The reason these preconceived notions are barriers to change is because our thoughts dictate our feelings and behaviors (Ellis, 1997) (See Chapter 7).

The first step in eliminating these barriers is for you to change the way you think about students with educational problems and about the role you play in their education. This process is called cognitive restructuring, that is, challenging or reframing the way you think. An example of how a select group of teachers apply cognitive restructuring is found in Martin Haberman's *Star Teachers of Children in Poverty* (1995), his seminal study of very successful teachers in the most difficult schools in the United States. One of Haberman's findings is that these successful teachers, rather than dreading students with difficulties, expect students to come to class with all sorts of problems.

From Disrupter to Achiever will help you restructure your cognition, that is change your mind about the role of the teacher in creating and maintaining successful learning environments for all students. When you change your mind, you will feel less stressed and anxious, and you will be ready to make significant changes in how you teach students with academic and/or behavioral problems.

Having a broad professional knowledge base concerning why students behave the way they do both academically and behaviorally helps teachers change their minds (thinking) in a manner that leads to changes in teachers' behavior, in order to more effectively influence positive student behavior.

When you change your mind, you will feel less stressed and anxious, and you will be ready to make significant changes in how you teach students with academic and/or behavioral problems.

If You Know the Whys, You Can Develop the Hows

Teachers are professionals whose expertise is derived from a detailed and rich knowledge base. Teachers are decision makers. One of the primary difficulties with texts that are written in the *How To . . .* format, as in*, How to Manage the Behavior of Disruptive Children*, is that they treat the classroom teacher as a technician, not as a professional.

Technicians follow procedures and routines designed by others; professionals develop and implement procedures and routines from their knowledge base, as well as use their knowledge base to critically evaluate and choose techniques developed by others. Technicians, once they have applied all the procedures and routines, are frequently at a loss to determine what to do next if they have not accomplished their goals. Professionals are expected to draw upon their knowledge base, in order to continually adapt and change procedures and routines to best meet the demands of new and unique situations.

When interaction with students is viewed as a series of techniques, as it often is by writers of management texts, the classroom teacher is viewed as a technician. Once the teacher subscribes to this view, she is frequently at a loss to determine what to do when she has used all of the techniques prescribed in the *"How to . . ."* models.

The philosopher Nietzsche (2000), said, "If a man knows the *why*, he can bear any *how*." We believe that if you know the *whys* (why students behave the way they do both academically and behaviorally), you can develop the *hows* (how to create a successful learning environment for all students).

What this book advocates is that you, the regular classroom teacher, know the *whys;* in other words, you have an enriched knowledge base. Secondly, that you effectively develop the confidence to reference and use this knowledge to design and carry out the *hows*, changing your behavior to create and maintain successful learning environments.

There Is Nothing Vastly Different That You Need to Do for Students with Academic and/or Behavioral Difficulties, But You Need to Do It Consistently and Continuously

One of the reasons why teachers feel anxiety and dread when confronted with difficult students is because they believe that they must have a specialized body of knowledge regarding pedagogy and behavioral science beyond that required to effectively teach the so called "average" student. They believe that their training has prepared them to deal only with students without significant behavioral or academic problems. As was discussed in Chapter 2, this is analogous to doctors treating only healthy patients, lawyers having only clients with no legal difficulties, or accountants whose clients do not have any questions regarding their finances.

What if all teachers like Haberman's Star Teachers expected students to come to school with all sorts of academic and behavioral problems, rather than expecting students to have no serious academic or behavioral problems in the classroom? What might a visitor to a "Star Teacher's" classroom observe? Visitors would probably observe a stimulating and active classroom environment where students are engaged in a variety of meaningful learning activities at different levels. The teacher is frequently interacting with all students in a supportive and respectful manner. The visitors observe frequent changes in activities, the use of different learning modalities in both instruction and assessment, and the many opportunities for students to display competency. Many teachers may not believe that a classroom like this is possible, unless students are homogeneous with respect to average to above average academic ability and appropriate behavior. However, Haberman has shown in his research, ". . . that literally thousands of star teachers do "it" every day." (Haberman, 1995, p. 2). In our opinion, Haberman's Star Teachers do not have an understanding of pedagogy that is vastly different than that possessed by most teachers; however, these Star Teachers understand that they must use this pedagogy more consistently and continually, to create successful learning environments for all students, regardless of the difficulties they bring to the classroom. Students with academic and/or behavioral challenges require teachers to use their highest degree of effectiveness and professionalism. By doing this, you will become a more effective teacher for all students in your classroom.

YOU DO NOT HAVE RESPONSIBILITY FOR STUDENTS, YOU HAVE RESPONSIBILITY TO STUDENTS

One implication of adhering to the philosophy that "the only person you can control is yourself," is that it is irrational to take responsibility for the behavior of another individual. In the addiction literature, this assumption of responsibility for the behavior of another individual is termed "codependency." Codependent relationships lock individuals into never ending cycles of guilt, shame, and recrimination (Beattie, 2001). If a teacher accepts responsibility for the behavior of a student, she frequently feels disappointed, angry, resentful, frustrated, and perhaps incompetent. Such feelings detract from a teacher's ability to effectively create successful learning environments.

If a teacher accepts responsibility for the behavior of a student, she frequently feels disappointed, angry, resentful, frustrated, and perhaps incompetent.

Since teachers can rationally accept responsibility only for their own classroom behavior and not that of their students (Goulet, 1997), students alone are responsible for their own academic performance and behavior in the classroom. The acceptance of responsibility for students' own behavior by teachers, as well as students, is a prerequisite for the development of accountability.

Teachers who take responsibility *for* their professional behavior increase the likelihood that they will fulfill their responsibility *to* their students. The Self-Control Classroom model advocates professional behavior that increases the probability that every student, regard-

Teachers who take responsibility for *their professional behavior increase the likelihood that they will fulfill their responsibility* to *their students.*

less of past or present academic or behavioral performance, will experience a successful learning environment. A teacher's responsibility to students is further explained in Chapter 5 when teaching is defined.

As Important As Whether Students Behave Appropriately, Is Why They Behave Appropriately

Thea, a student in your 9th grade class, is frequently disruptive. She calls out, talks to her neighbors, refuses to follow directions, and is often argumentative. In cooperation with Thea's parents, you have developed a contingency based behavioral plan which allows Thea to go to a rock concert if she behaves appropriately in your class until the end of the marking period. Thea behaves appropriately and is allowed to go to the concert. After the concert, Thea's disruptive behavior reappears. When the teacher asks Thea why she has gone back to behaving inappropriately, Thea replies, "There aren't any good groups coming to town this report period."

Thea's return to inappropriate behavior is logically consistent and predictable, based upon the reasons she changed her behavior in the first place. Thea began to behave appropriately because she wanted to attend a rock concert. Is going to a rock concert or the promise of any other reward the reason to behave appropriately in the classroom? Secondly, is going to a rock concert or the promise of any other reward effective in maintaining long-term appropriate behavior change?

Cathy, a 12th grade student, has had her privilege to drive the family car removed until she raises her grade point average to at least 2.5 for a marking period. Cathy's grades improve for one term. After reports are issued, Cathy stops doing her schoolwork. When asked why, Cathy replies, "My boyfriend just got a car, and he takes me anywhere I want to go." Is being allowed to drive a car the reason to do school work? Is being allowed to drive a car or the promise of any other reward effective in maintaining long-term behavioral change?

Rewards and punishments are simplistic, short-term solutions to deal with difficult and complex academic and behavioral problems. Even when rewards or punishments appear to work, students' attribution that they changed their behavior because of the rewards or punishment is inconsistent with teaching accountability and the goal of long-term changes in academics and/or behavior. The long-term solutions to complex academic and behavioral difficulties must involve teaching students that there are other reasons to achieve academically and behave appropriately than bribery and extortion. The limitations of rewards and punishments and alternatives to their use are discussed in great detail in Chapters 16 and 17.

Some Alternative Reasons Why Students Should Behave Appropriately

There are reasons why students should work hard in school and behave appropriately that lead to accountability and long-term change, including the development of competence, integrity, honor, duty to others, and pride in oneself.

The most basic reason for the existence of schools is the development of student academic competence. Teachers need to help students understand that the development of their academic competence is dependent upon hard work and appropriate behavior.

0335854

Integrity is "walking the talk," doing what you say you are going to do. Teachers facilitate the development of integrity by encouraging students to set personal goals for learning and behavior, to develop personal action plans to achieve these goals, to make and follow through on their commitments to themselves and others, and to accept responsibility for their behavior.

Integrity is "walking the talk," doing what you say you are going to do.

If integrity is "walking the talk," then honor is the "talk you walk," the adherence in daily life to a set of values. Teachers need to encourage values that are congruent with academic success and appropriate behavior. These values include the importance of goals, purposeful effort, self respect, respect for other people and property, and honesty in both words and deeds.

Schools are comprised of interdependent learning communities. Students who are successful members of these communities recognize and fulfill their duty to others. These students understand that each individual's behavior impacts all other members of the community. Therefore, their duty to other students is to behave honorably and in a manner that does not interfere with the rights of others to learn. Of course it is a prerequisite that students feel that they are important and respected members of the learning community. Unfortunately this is not often the case. Our most difficult and challenging students often feel alienated from their learning community, and many traditional interventions reinforce this alienation.

If integrity is "walking the talk," then honor is the "talk you walk," the adherence in daily life to a set of values.

Pride in oneself is accomplished in many ways. Among these are the development of competency, the display of integrity, honor, and duty to others. In short, it is the feeling of having done the right thing.

One of the most effective ways to teach competency, integrity, honor, duty to others, and pride in oneself is for teachers to model these characteristic in their daily interactions with students.

It may occur to the reader that a delinquent youth may feel as though she behaves competently, with integrity and honor, fulfills her duties to others, and is in fact proud of herself. This seeming contradiction is in fact the difference between pro-social and distorted means of achieving these goals (See Chapter 11).

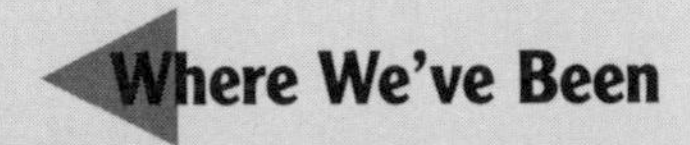

Where We've Been

Every model of classroom management has at its core a set of beliefs or philosophies. It is important for teachers to understand and accept the philosophies of any particular educational model if they wish to effectively employ the model in their classrooms.

The Self-Control Classroom model has seven explicit philosophies. Two of these are key philosophies. The first key philosophy states that **The only person you can control is yourself.** Teachers only have control over their behavior. By controlling their behavior, teachers influence student behavior.

The second key philosophy is that **As important as whether students behave appropriately, is why they behave appropriately.** Rather than bribery and extortion, students need to be taught that the reasons to behave appropriately are the development of competence, integrity, honor, duty to others, and pride in oneself.

There are five other philosophies. **If you continue to do what you've done, you'll continue to get what you got.** Teachers should not continue to use failed strategies.

If you can't change your mind, then you can't change anything. Teachers need to understand the many reasons behind students' academic and behavioral difficulties.

If you know the whys, you can develop the hows. Teachers need to continually develop and use a professional knowledge base to make professional decisions.

There is nothing vastly different that you need to do for students with academic and/or behavioral difficulties, but you need to do it consistently and continuously. The principles underlying effective pedagogy and influence upon student behavior are the same, regardless of the presenting problems. Students with academic and/or behavioral challenges require teachers to use their highest degree of effectiveness and professionalism.

You do not have responsibility for students, you have responsibility to students. Teachers need to understand that their responsibility is for their professional and personal conduct and that students are responsible for their academic and personal behavior.

Where We're Headed

In Chapter 4, three questions are presented. When teachers ask themselves these questions daily, it helps them to reflect upon their behavior in a manner that is congruent with the philosophies of the Self-Control Classroom model.

CHAPTER 3 CONCEPT MAP

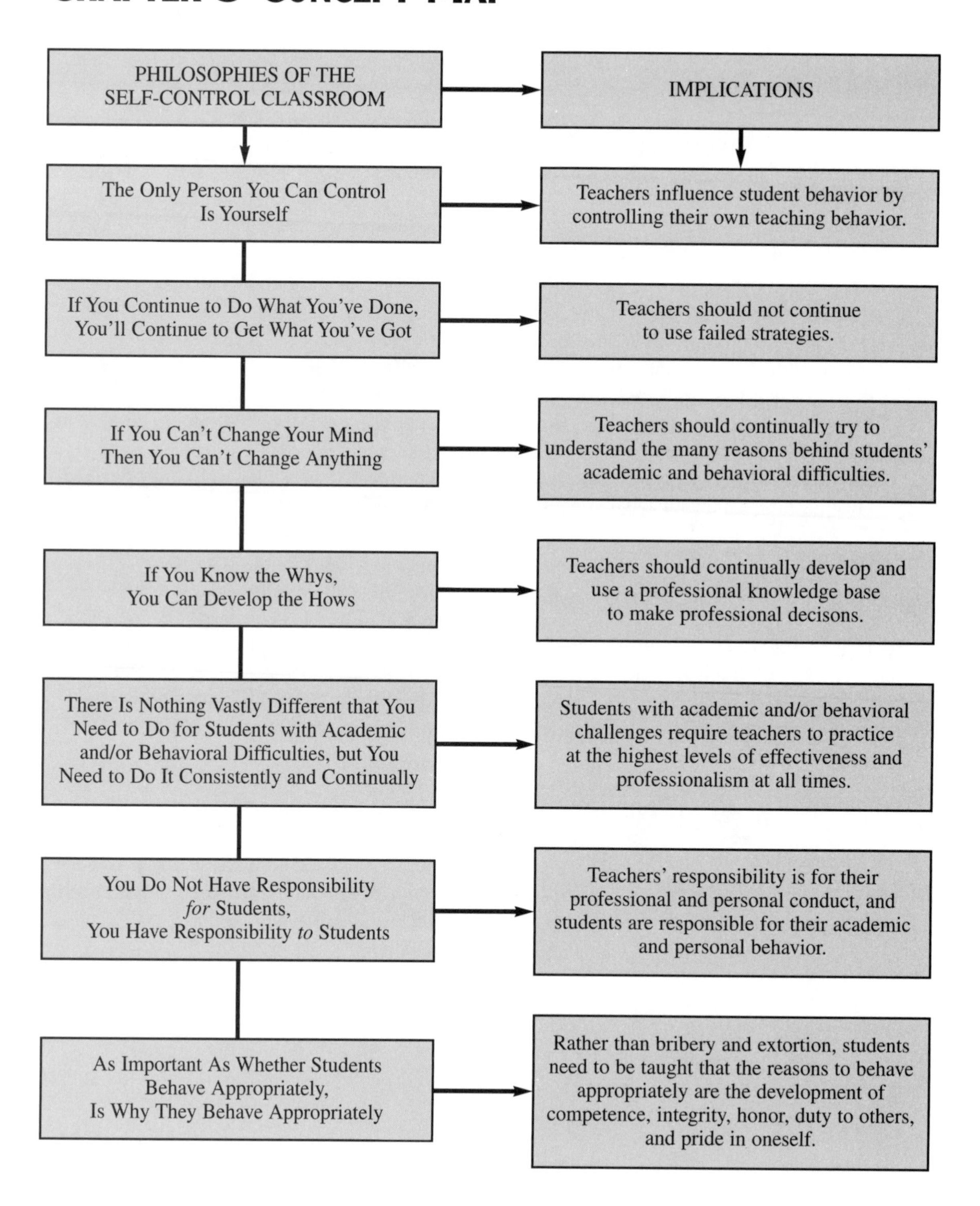

? Questions for the Study Team

1. Is it really possible for teachers to control their behavior in the classroom all the time?

2. What should teachers do when their philosophies are congruent with the Self-Control Classroom model, but not congruent with the philosophies of school administrators?

3. One philosophy states, "If you can't change your mind then you can't change anything." Why is it so important that teachers change their minds before changing their behavior? Why can't teachers change their behavior before they change their minds?

4. Why is cognitive restructuring (changing one's mind) so important for working effectively with students with discipline problems?

5. One philosophy states, "You do not have responsibility *for* students, you have responsibility *to* students." What responsibilities do teachers have to students?

6. If the philosophy in question #5 is valid, why are politicians, administrators, and parents holding teachers responsible for students' learning and performance on standardized assessments?

7. One philosophy states, "If you understand the whys, you can develop the hows." What are the whys that teachers need to understand?

8. How can teachers teach students that they are the only ones responsible for their behavior?

9. It is stated that the reasons that students should behave appropriately should not be because of the promise of rewards or the threat of punishments, but because of integrity, honor, duty to others, pride in oneself, and competence. How can you teach these concepts to students—especially young students?

10. Many disruptive and delinquent students have feelings of integrity, honor, duty to others, pride in oneself, and competence already, so if these are the reasons to behave appropriately, why are they disruptive?

CHAPTER 4

A Time to Reflect

"I've come to the frightening conclusion that I am the decisive element in the classroom. It is my personal approach that creates the climate. It is my daily mood that makes the weather. As a teacher, I have a tremendous power to make a child's life miserable or joyous. I can be a tool of torture or an instrument of inspiration. I can humiliate or humor, hurt or heal. In all situations, it is my response that decides whether a crisis will be escalated or deescalated and a child humanized or dehumanized." (Ginott, 1972)

The authors have spent many years conducting workshops on the Self-Control Classroom model. It was our practice to end these workshops by posing three questions that teachers were encouraged to ask themselves daily. The effect of the questions upon teachers was so powerful, that participants suggested that these questions should be presented early in the workshop, because this would provide them with a way to immediately understand the applicability of the philosophies and concepts to their daily practice. Respecting this feedback, we moved the questions to the beginning of the workshops.

We believe by posing these questions early in the book, readers similarly will quickly understand the applicability of the philosophies and concepts to their daily practice.

Questions to Ask Yourself

"AM I PROUD OF THE WAY I INTERACTED WITH MY STUDENTS TODAY?"

Being proud of yourself, depends upon whose behavior? Referring back to the philosophy "The only person you can control is yourself," it follows that to be proud of yourself, you focus solely upon your behavior, not your students' behavior.

It is therefore possible to have a day that is so unpleasant due to disruptive student behavior that you take notice of the "hiring now" sign as you pass the mall, seriously considering retail sales as a viable vocational alternative. Yet, you still feel proud of your teaching behavior. Everyday, in classrooms across the country, students fail to achieve at levels commensurate with their abilities, behave in disrespectful ways towards teachers and their peers, and create disruptions in their classes. Yet thousands of teachers leave these classes at the end of the day feeling they have met each of these challenges by adhering to high levels of professional conduct and accepting full accountability for their instructional and interpersonal behavior. These teachers understand that they have fulfilled their responsibility to their students by being responsible for their professional and personal classroom behavior. These are proud teachers who have confidence in their professional knowledge base and competence, and who view each day as a professional challenge requiring professional decision making and plans.

These teachers understand that they have fulfilled their responsibility to their students by being responsible for their professional and personal classroom behavior.

Being proud does not imply that you are happy, relaxed, and content. Teachers who work with difficult, challenging students often leave school displeased, frustrated, and discontented. However, because they understand over whom they have control and to whom they have responsibility, these teachers come to school the next day prepared to meet the professional challenges that await them.

Haberman (1995) describes teaching challenging students as "... a volatile, highly charged, emotionally draining, physically exhausting experience ..." (p.1), but he describes competent, effective teachers as those that accept "... their responsibility to find ways of engaging their students in learning ... [and their responsibility for] ... the continuous generation and maintenance of student interests and involvement" (p. 22).

"Would I Want My Own Child to Be in a Classroom Taught by a Teacher Like Me?"

Many readers might reply, "My child would not behave like the difficult children in my class." It is our experience that professionals, including teachers, are not immune to raising children who possess all of the myriad academic and behavioral problems that we see in our classrooms. However, whether or not your child has academic or behavioral difficulties is not the relevant issue. The question is if your child exhibited these types of problems, would you want him to be treated the same way that you treat these students in your classroom?

Several years ago, at the conclusion of a workshop, a veteran teacher approached us and told us that he had come to a realization during the workshop. He told us he was seriously considering leaving teaching at the end of the year. He said he realized he would not want his own child in a classroom taught by a teacher like him. He felt guilty about the way that he had treated his difficult students over the years and questioned his ability to change. We do not know what this teacher eventually did, but we hope that he either gained the knowledge base and insight to change his behavior or else he did, indeed, leave the profession.

We make the assumption that teachers, as parents, desire the best for their children. If their child experiences problems, either academic or behavioral, parents want teachers to treat their child with respect and care, while attempting to help their child solve the problem. Unfortunately, what teachers expect for their own children in school and how they treat students in their classrooms are not always congruent.

Unfortunately, what teachers expect for their own children in school and how they treat students in their classrooms are not always congruent.

Would I Be Offended If Someone Interacted with Me As I Interacted with My Students Today?

Imagine you're in a faculty meeting. The meeting is boring and you have assignments that need to be graded. You sit in the back of the room and begin to grade the papers. The principal asks for your opinion. You are startled and have no idea as to what topic is being discussed. The principal begins to publicly berate you, "Mr. Shotz, last year when you came to faculty meetings and consistently showed your lack of interest in the affairs of this school, I just ignored it. But it's not going to happen this year. I find your conduct rude and offensive, to say nothing of being unprofessional. Put those papers away immediately, get up front, and at the very least, have the courtesy to pretend that you care what happens in this school. If you can't, you can leave this meeting immediately."

Did the principal's behavior offend you? We suggest that, in addition to feeling humiliated, embarrassed, angry, and resentful, this interaction might lead you to file a grievance with your professional organization or union against the principal.

Now imagine a student in a class that he finds boring. He decides to catch up on some extracurricular reading. The teacher calls on the student to answer a question. The student is startled and unable to answer. The teacher says, "Jerry, last week when you came to class and read, I just ignored it. I refuse to ignore your rude behavior any more. Of all the students in this class, you are the last one that should be reading. Put those papers away immediately, get up front, and at the very least, pretend that you are learning something. If you can't, you can leave this room immediately."

Would the teacher's behavior offend the student? We believe it would. In addition, the student probably would have all of the other feelings experienced by Mr. Shotz in the faculty meeting. With whom does the student file a grievance? Having no professional organization, students are left to find alternative means to express their displeasure. Any veteran teacher is well aware of what these alternatives look like.

Many teachers, in an attempt to avoid the kind of emotional responses that Jerry experienced, have embraced methodologies that they believe will lead to appropriate student behavior without causing offense. Therefore they choose a nonverbal, and what they believe to be a non-confrontational strategy. Let's go back to the faculty meeting and have the principal use one of these methods with Mr. Shotz. When the principal sees Mr. Shotz grading papers, rather than saying anything to him, the principal goes and writes **"MR. SHOTZ"** on the board. Hearing his colleagues giggle, Mr. Shotz looks up, shakes his head and returns to his grading. After a few minutes, the principal returns to the board and places a check mark next to Mr. Shotz's name **(✔ MR. SHOTZ).** Mr. Shotz finds this offensive, wouldn't you?

Techniques that produce negative emotional responses do not increase the likelihood that a student will behave appropriately or learn accountability. They are likely to produce a desire for revenge and a feeling that the teacher is to blame for any consequences experienced by the student due to his own behavior. These outcomes are often a result of peer pressure to answer in kind and a concrete cognitive orientation that greatly reduces the student's ability to ameliorate the emotional wound.

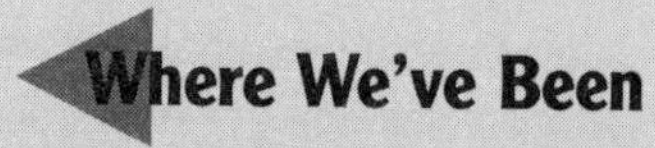

Where We've Been

If you had been paying attention to this chapter, you would not have to read this section. Oops! We slipped.

Now back to our usual summary. Three questions were asked to help you quickly understand the applicability of the Self-Control Classroom philosophies and concepts to your daily practice. Answering these questions requires teachers to:

1) reflect upon their behavior, not their students' behavior, in regard to whether or not they should feel proud,
2) imagine their own child in a classroom run by a teacher like them, and
3) consider whether their behavior would be offensive if directed to them by another person.

Where We're Headed

In Chapter 5 we operationally define learning, teaching, and discipline problems. In addition, the implications of these definitions for teachers are explored.

Chapter 4 Concept Map

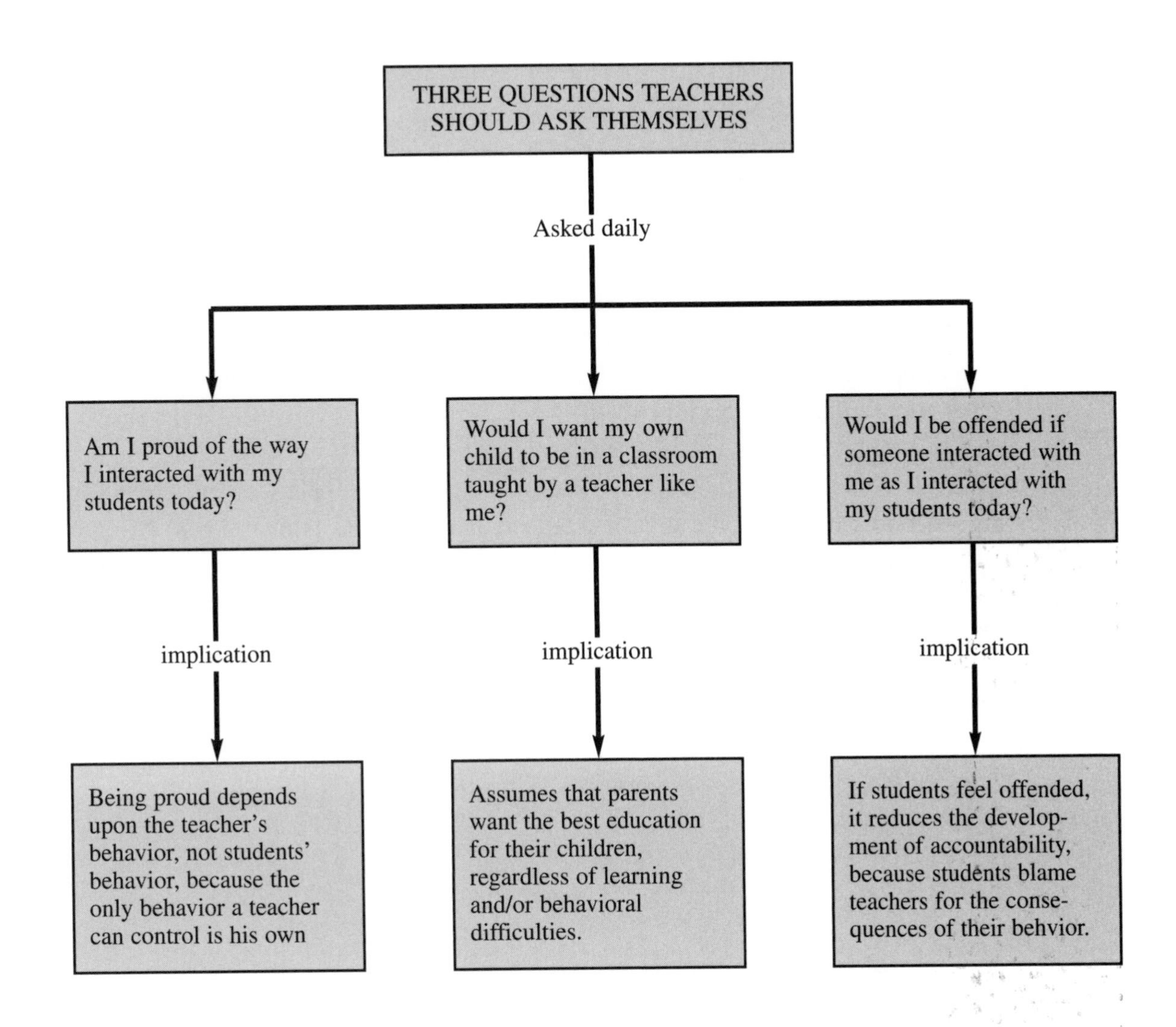

? QUESTIONS FOR THE STUDY TEAM

1. What types of behavior should make a teacher proud?

2. There are certain teachers who run their classrooms in ways that are very offensive to students. However, some of these same teachers seem very proud of their behavior and brag that students are not disruptive and they don't get away with anything in their classes. How can this paradox of being proud and offensive be resolved?

3. Sometimes teachers just lose their tempers with students and act towards a student in a manner that, upon reflection, they would find offensive if someone treated them similarly. What should they do after this occurs?

4. Many students come from families who react to inappropriate behavior by screaming, hollering, name calling, and the use of frequent and illogical punishments. In other words, their parents behave in offensive ways. Will such students understand when their behaviors are inappropriate, and will their behaviors be influenced by teachers' interventions that are not offensive?

CHAPTER 5

Definitions of Teaching, Learning, and Discipline Problems

"It [teaching] is not for the timid, the faint of heart, the aloof, or the uncommitted. It is down and dirty, five live shows a day. There is no more honorable or ennobling way to make a living." (Wesley, 1998)

Teachers understand that their job is to teach and the students' job is to learn. A frequent complaint of teachers is that discipline problems interfere with their teaching and their students' learning. It has been the authors' experience that there is considerable disagreement among teachers as to the definitions of learning, teaching, and what behaviors constitute discipline problems. How these terms are defined has significant impact upon classroom practice.

Learning

In athletics or drama, learning is readily evident. When coaches and directors are asked how they know if their students have learned the athletic plays or the drama parts, they usually respond, "The students run the plays or act out their parts." In other words, the students are able to exhibit a behavior they were unable to display before, and the coach or director observes the change in behavior. Therefore, coaches and directors define learning as an observable change in behavior.

What about the classroom teacher? When teachers want to know whether students have learned to write an introductory paragraph, solve an equation, analyze a historical event, balance a chemical equation, conjugate a verb, or any other of the myriad learning outcomes, they also must observe a change in student behavior. While a lack of observable change in student behavior does not, in itself, indicate a lack of learning, there is no way for a teacher to determine that learning has occurred unless she observes a change in behavior.

Obviously the desired change in behavior must not be a random change. It must be congruent with the learning objective. Although the predominant method of assessing students' learning continues to be paper and pencil exams, there is a growing appreciation that this type of assessment puts many students at a disadvantage in demonstrating their learning. This understanding has led teachers to use a wider array of assessments, including portfolios, rubrics, and authentic assessments.

Most teachers limit the definition of learning to the academic domain. However, this definition is also applicable when discussing any behavior. For example, when a student incorrectly solves a long division problem, the teacher infers that the student has not learned a prerequisite skill of long division. Similarly, when a student continually displays uncooperative behavior in group situations or the student is disrespectful, the teacher should infer that the student has not learned a prerequisite skill needed to successfully engage in group work, or she has not learned what respectful behavior is and how to display respect.

Teaching

When teachers desire students to learn new material or they determine that previously taught material has not been learned adequately, they have to teach or reteach. Returning to the example of long division, let's examine the teacher's behavior. Recognizing that there is a problem in the student's understanding of long division, the teacher continually changes her instructional strategies to increase the likelihood that the student will master long division. For example, the teacher might assess the student's understanding of prerequisite skills. The teacher also tries a variety of instructional methodologies, including careful observation of the student's problem-solving process, modeling, peer tutoring, the use of manipulatives, and/or the use of technology. Throughout this process the teacher is alert to a change in the student's behavior that indicates that learning has taken place. Until the teacher is assured learning has taken place, she continues to change her instructional behavior. This is what teachers do, and this is how teaching is defined: Teaching is changing teacher behavior to increase the likelihood that students will learn.

Teaching is changing teacher behavior to increase the likelihood that students will learn.

Let's apply the definition of teaching, changing teacher behavior to increase the likelihood that students will learn.

- What is the question that the teacher, Ms. Ramirez, needs to ask herself concerning her student, Terri's, difficulty with long division? Regardless of the nature of Terri's difficulties with long division or the strategies that Ms. Ramirez eventually employs, the question Ms. Ramirez must ask herself is, "How do I change my behavior to increase the likelihood that Terri will learn how to do long division?"
- Suppose another student, Haley, is not learning how to develop a bibliography for her term paper. The question Haley's teacher must ask herself is, "How do I change my behavior to increase the likelihood that Haley will learn how to develop a bibliography?"
- If Rebecca is not learning how to properly set up a serve in volleyball, the question her physical education teacher must ask herself is, "How do I change my behavior to increase the likelihood that Rebecca will learn how to serve a volleyball?"

A reasonable question that a reader may have at this point is how many changes should Terri's, Haley's, and Rebecca's teachers make to increase the likelihood that these students will learn? The answer for any professional teacher is as many changes as it takes. This answer relates to the responsibility professional teachers have to their students, as was discussed in Chapter 3.

Now let's apply the definition of teaching to non-academic behaviors.

- Lakesha is continually talking to her neighbor.
- Dara is continually making fun of other students' answers.
- Jamie often sleeps in class.

What is the question that Lakesha's, Dara's, and Jamie's teachers need to ask themselves? The answer is the same for these non-academic problems as for the academic problems above. "How do I change my behavior to increase the likelihood that Lakesha stops talking to her neighbor, that Dara stops making fun of other students, and that Jamie stays awake in class?" Again, readers may ask how many changes should be made to help students learn appropriate behavior? Again, the answer for any professional teacher is "as many changes as it takes." Just as there are many potential changes that teachers can make to increase the probability that students will learn, for example, long division, there are just as many changes that teachers can make to increase the likelihood that students will learn appropriate behavior. Examples of changes include:

- increasing the relevance of the lesson,
- changing instructional modalities,
- ignoring the behavior, and
- excluding the student from the learning environment.

The important question for teachers in all learning situations is, "How do I change my behavior to increase the likelihood that students will learn?"

Some readers may be perplexed by the fact that we are focusing solely on the teacher changing her behavior and saying nothing about the student changing her behavior. Obviously, the student needs to change her behavior in order for learning to occur. However, when analyzing the teaching/learning process, there is only one variable over which teachers have control, and that is their own behavior. This is because the only person you can control is yourself, as explained in Chapter 3. In addition, students are unable to observe a teacher's thoughts or feelings; they can only observe a teacher's behavior. If this book were being written for students or parents, we would focus solely upon the need to change either student or parent behavior.

The important question for teachers in all learning situations is, "How do I change my behavior to increase the likelihood that students will learn?"

Since teachers can change only their own behavior, they can only influence students, thus increasing the likelihood that students will learn. The probability of choosing the most effective teaching behavior increases when the teacher's behavior is not random or haphazard, but instead is based upon a professional knowledge base including learning, motivation, child development, and pedagogical theory, as well as experience (Brophy, 1988). The most effective teachers are those that are lifelong learners themselves, keeping abreast of current advances, not only in their disciplinary content area, but also in pedagogy, learning, and child development theory.

On the basis of the previous discussion, a formal definition of teaching is, "The use of preplanned behaviors, founded in learning principles and child development theory and directed toward both instructional delivery and classroom management, which increases the probability of affecting a positive change in student behavior" (Levin and Nolan, 2000, p. 4).

The five major points of this definition of teaching are:

1. You cannot force a student to behave; you can only influence the change;
2. To influence a change in student behavior, you must change your behavior, because this is the only behavior over which you have control;
3. The behavior you choose will have a much higher probability of influencing positive student behavior if you examine and use your professional knowledge base in making the choice;
4. The process of teaching is the same, regardless of whether the type of learning

difficulty the student is experiencing is cognitive, affective, social, or psychomotor; and

5. The change in your behavior increases only the likelihood of the desirable change in student behavior, but it does not cause the desired change.

While all five points of the definition are important, the heart of the definition is number 2. To influence a change in student behavior, you must change your behavior, because this is the only behavior over which you have control. It clearly stresses that the only mechanism you have as a teacher to influence a change in student behavior, is your own behavior.

To influence a change in student behavior, you must change your behavior, because this is the only behavior over which you have control.

Discipline Problems

The difficulty teachers have when they attempt to categorize behaviors that are discipline problems is similar to the difficulty many teachers have with defining learning and teaching. Teachers often describe students whom they believe have discipline problems as being lazy, unmotivated, angry, argumentative, and aggressive. These descriptions are imprecise and judgmental. These words communicate little, if anything, about the actual behavior that is considered to be the discipline problem. These descriptions are also problematic, because we all know students who are lazy or unmotivated, yet their classroom behaviors do not constitute discipline problems. In addition, these words personalize the misbehavior by focusing on the characteristics of the individual student. This violates a general guideline offered by Ginott (1972), "Speak to the situation not to the person." Because of these attributions, teachers develop negative feelings towards the student as a person, which greatly reduces a teacher's effectiveness in working with the student to modify the student's behavior (Brendtro, et al., 1990) (see Chapter 7).

An operational definition needs to provide a teacher with behavioral criteria in order that an instantaneous decision may be made as to whether or not any given behavior is a discipline problem. If it is, the teacher then needs to make a professional decision concerning which strategies to employ to increase the likelihood that the student will change her behavior to be more appropriate. In other words, once a behavior is identified as a discipline problem, the teacher needs to change her behavior, which is teaching.

So what is the definition of a discipline problem? Let's analyze five common classroom scenarios to develop an operational definition. To aid in this analysis, ask yourself three questions after you read each scenario. Fill in Table 5.1 with your answers.

1. Do you think there is a discipline problem?
2. If so, who is exhibiting the discipline problem?
3. What is the disruptive behavior?

Scenario 1: Students enter the classroom and take their seats. The teacher asks them to take out their homework. The teacher notices that Sommer has not taken out her homework, but instead is playing with the rubber bands and erasers that she managed to accumulate in her desk. *The teacher ignores Sommer and begins to involve the class in answering the homework problems.*

Scenario 2: Students enter the classroom and take their seats. The teacher asks them to take out their homework. The teacher notices that Sommer has not taken out her homework, but instead is playing with the rubber bands and erasers that she managed to accumulate in her desk. *The teacher stops the review, continues to stand in the front of the class, and publicly says "Sommer, put the rubber bands away and*

TABLE 5.1 ▶ Who Is the Discipline Problem?

Question	Scenario 1	Scenario 2	Scenario 3	Scenario 4	Scenario 5
Do you think there is a discipline problem?					
If so, who is exhibiting the discipline problem?					
What, if any, is the disruptive behavior?					

get out your assignment for this class! We will not continue until you do so!"

Scenario 3: Students enter the classroom and take their seats. The teacher asks them to take out their homework. The teacher notices that Sommer has not taken out her homework, but instead is playing with the rubber bands and erasers that she managed to accumulate in her desk. *The teacher begins to involve the class in answering the homework problems. As the homework is being reviewed, the teacher stands next to Sommer and continues to involve the class in the homework review.*

Scenario 4: Students enter the classroom and take their seats. The teacher asks them to take out their homework. Instead Sommer begins to shoot little bits of paper at her neighbors with the rubber bands that she has accumulated in her desk. *The teacher ignores this behavior and continues to review the homework. Sommer continues shooting the wads of paper at the other students.*

Scenario 5: Students enter the classroom and take their seats. The teacher asks them to take out their homework. Instead Sommer begins to shoot little bits of paper at her neighbors with the rubber bands that she has accumulated in her desk. *The teacher, while reviewing the homework, makes eye contact with Sommer, but Sommer continues to shoot the paper. Then the teacher walks up to Sommer and takes the rubber band and paper. As privately as possible, she assertively tells Sommer to please take out her homework, standing next to her until she does.*

▲

Now compare your answers in Table 5.1 with our viewpoint. In **Scenario #1,** there is no discipline problem. Sommer's behavior is not disrupting the right to learn of any other student, so the teacher has decided to ignore it for the time being, so that she does not disrupt the flow of the lesson and interfere with the learning of the other students in her class. The teacher thinks that if she ignores Sommer's behavior, Sommer eventually will catch up with what the rest of the class is doing. The teacher also knows that if the ignoring does not work, she has many other strategies to use that likely will bring Sommer back on-task, while at the same time not disrupting the other students. At this time some of you may be thinking, "I couldn't ignore Sommer's behavior. Soon all the students would be playing with rubber bands." We suggest that since Sommer's behavior is not disrupting the rights of others to learn, the teacher, for the time being, continue to ignore it. Sommer's behavior may be addressed at a later time, but not at the expense of the rest of the students' learning. The fear of others joining in is a legitimate one, but it has been our experience that this rarely occurs on a large scale. Also, the probability of others joining the behavior is significantly reduced if the teacher uses techniques that do not draw attention to Sommer's behavior.

Scenario #2 describes a discipline problem, but you may be surprised to learn that the person who is exhibiting the disruptive behavior is the teacher, not Sommer. As in the first scenario, Sommer's behavior is not interfering with the rights of other students to learn. However, in this case, the teacher chooses to immediately confront Sommer with a technique that both draws attention to Sommer and disrupts the entire class. Because the teacher chooses a technique that interrupts the lesson and reduces the learning time of the other students, the teacher is the discipline problem. In addition, by publicly calling attention to Sommer and challenging her saying, "we will not continue until you do so . . . ," she has increased the likelihood that Sommer will become confrontational, in order to show off or "save face" in front of her peers, thus preserving her self-esteem (See Chapter 11).

You now may be having thoughts similar to those of many of the teachers who attend our workshops. For example, you may be thinking, "Sommer isn't disrupting other students, but she is surely interfering with her own learning. I just can't sit idly by and let that happen. She isn't doing what the rest of the class is doing; therefore, she is a discipline problem." We believe that every student, including Sommer, has the right to choose how to behave, even if the chosen behavior may result in academic failure. What students do not have the right to do is to choose a behavior that interferes with another student's right to learn. Since Sommer's behavior is not interfering with anyone's learning but her own, her behavior is not a discipline problem.

Sommer's behavior is, however, a problem. Her behavior raises a valid issue. What is the difference between a discipline problem and all the other problems that occur in classrooms? Urgency! Discipline problems, because of their effect on other students, need immediate teacher attention. When a problem is identified as a non-discipline problem, the teacher has much wider latitude as to when and where to intervene. In Scenario #2, the teacher must concern herself with the rest of the class' right to learn, before addressing Sommer's behavior. As you will learn throughout this book, often times teachers' behaviors can simultaneously engage the class in learning activities and also bring the Sommers of the world back on-task. Such a behavior is illustrated in Scenario #3. The teacher involves the class in the homework review while moving next to Sommer, influencing her to resume on-task behavior.

There are no discipline problems in **Scenario #3.** Sommer's behavior is interfering only with her learning and not the learning of the other students in the class. Unlike Scenario #2, where the teacher stops the lesson and challenges Sommer, here the teacher chooses a strategy that does not disturb the other students and at the same time increases the likelihood that Sommer will stop playing with the rubber bands and begin to display more on-task behavior. Therefore, the teacher avoids becoming a discipline problem.

Scenario #4 presents two persons exhibiting discipline problems. Sommer is shooting wads of paper at other students. Her behavior is directly interfering with some of her classmates' learning and is potentially dangerous. The teacher is inappropriately ignoring the rubber band shooting. Because the teacher has ignored Sommer's interference with the other students' learning, the teacher has indirectly interfered with the learning of others. Therefore, the teacher is also a discipline problem.

Scenario #5 illustrates Sommer displaying the same behavior that is a discipline problem as in Scenario #4, but the teacher is not a discipline problem. The teacher chooses behaviors such as eye contact, moving close to Sommer, and finally talking privately to her, which draw as little attention as possible. At the same time, the teacher's behaviors increase the likelihood that Sommer will stop shooting paper around the room.

We are all very good at describing student behaviors that are discipline problems, but many common teacher behaviors are also discipline problems because of their interference with students' right to learn.

So far our definition of a discipline problem includes any behavior that interferes with the rights of others to learn or is physically and, we would add, psychologically injurious to another person. Furthermore, we showed why it is important for teachers themselves not to become a discipline problem. If a student's behavior is a discipline problem, and the teacher does not intervene in an appropriate manner, then the teacher's behavior is a discipline problem, as illustrated in Scenario # 4. Also, the teacher's behavior is a discipline problem, whether or not the student's behavior is a discipline problem, if the teacher intervenes in a manner that disrupts the learning of the other students, as in Scenario #2. Table 5.2 illustrates situations in which a teacher's behavior may or may not become a discipline problem.

In the previous analyses, discipline problems were attributed to students and/or teachers. We are all very good at describing student behaviors that are discipline problems, but many common teacher behaviors are also discipline problems because of their interference with students' right to learn. For example, teacher behaviors such as coming late to class, ending class early, being unprepared for class, or neglecting to consider motivational concerns in lesson planning all may cause interference with students' right to learn. Parents', classroom aides', or administrators' behavior may be discipline problems, if their behavior interferes with the learning rights of students. It is not too difficult for teachers to generate a long list of administrative and parental behavior that may be considered discipline problems.

Finally, two additional behaviors need to be added to arrive at our definition of a discipline problem. The first is any behavior that interferes with the teacher's ability to teach. When a behavior hinders a teacher's effectiveness, it is also interfering with the rights of students to learn. We are not referring here to idiosyncratic annoyances, such as the failure of students to

TABLE 5.2 ▶ When Is the Teacher a Discipline Problem?

TEACHER'S BEHAVIOR	STUDENT'S BEHAVIOR: Discipline Problem	STUDENT'S BEHAVIOR: Non-Discipline Problem
Does Not Intervene Immediately	Teacher's behavior is a discipline problem.	Teacher's behavior is not a discipline problem.
Does Intervene Immediately	Teacher's behavior is not a discipline problem (unless the intervention disrupts other students' learing).	Teacher's behavior is a discipline problem

sit correctly in their seats or having all desks in straight rows, but rather to serious student misbehavior which objectively interferes with any reasonable teacher's concentration and focus. Examples are threats to the teacher or comments about the teacher's appearance or ethnic or racial origin.

Secondly, any behavior that destroys property belonging to the school or another student is also considered a discipline problem. Students are members of a learning community and have a duty to other members to protect and preserve individual and community property. The destruction of property belonging to either the community or to individuals seriously threatens the emotional safety of the community members and therefore interferes with the learning process.

Thus the complete definition of a discipline problem is any behavior that:

- interferes with the rights of other students to learn,
- interferes with the ability of the teacher to teach,
- is physically or psychologically unsafe, and/or
- destroys property (Levin and Nolan, 2000).

The importance of this definition is twofold. First, it enables a teacher to quickly identify a discipline problem and differentiate it from other problems that commonly exist in a classroom. By doing so, the teacher can more effectively decide when and how to modify her behavior to influence a change in student behavior (See Section 5, Chapters 18–26, for a more detailed discussion). Secondly, it provides teachers with a set of behavioral criteria to ensure that they never become the discipline problem.

Where We've Been

In this chapter the definitions of learning, teaching, and a discipline problem were explored.

1. **Learning is an observable change in any behavior, whether academic, affective, social, or psychomotor.**
2. **Teaching is defined as changing teacher behavior to increase the likelihood that students will learn.**
3. **A discipline problem is any behavior that interferes with the rights of others to learn, interferes with the ability of the teacher to teach, is physically or psychologically unsafe, or destroys property.**

Where We're Headed

In the next chapter, we explore a few of the myriad changes that have occurred in American society during the last fifty years and the impact these changes have had upon the behavior of all individuals, especially students, in today's classrooms.

Chapter 5 Concept Map

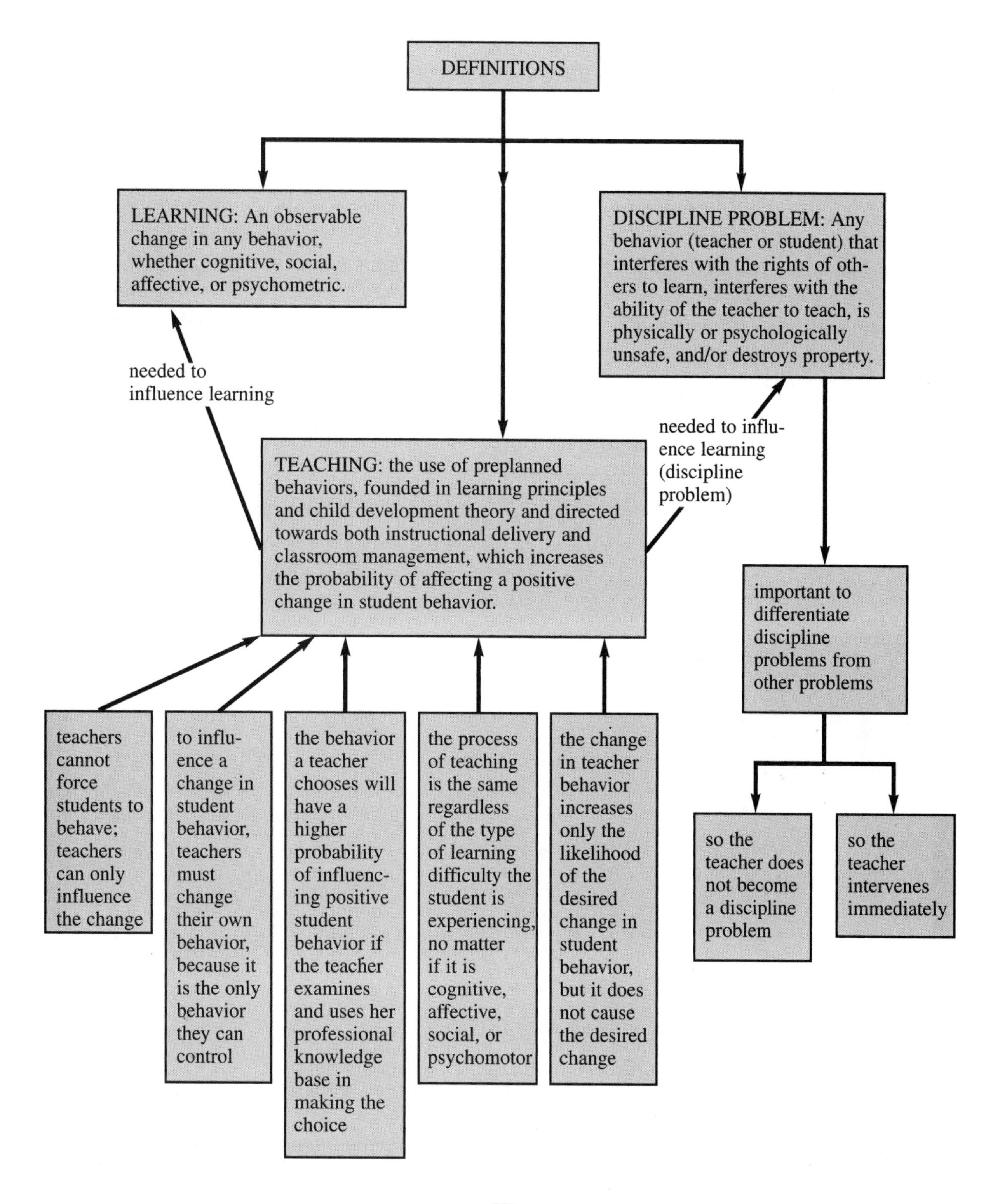

? QUESTIONS FOR THE STUDY TEAM

1. Which part of a lesson plan or unit plan reflects learning as defined in this chapter?

2. Most assessment of learning in schools continues to be through paper and pencil objective formats. Explain why the following statement might be true, "If a teacher uses only paper and pencil tests to assess learning, she increases the likelihood that some students will become discipline problems."

3. What question does a teacher need to ask herself when a student isn't learning academically? What question does a teacher need to ask herself when a student isn't behaving appropriately?

4. How does a teacher select the behavioral change she should employ to increase the likelihood that students will learn?

5. A student publicly disrespects a teacher by telling her to "drop dead" when asked to pay attention to the lesson. The teacher then changes her behavior towards the student by publicly yelling at the student, "You are rude and disrespectful! Leave this room immediately and go to the office!" Is the teacher's behavior congruent with the definition of teaching?

6. What does a teacher do when she continually has changed her behavior and the student still has not changed her behavior?

7. According to the definition of a discipline problem, a student refusing to work is not a discipline problem. However, suppose the student continues to refuse to work and other students start to say, "She's not doing anything. Why do I have to?" Does the student's refusal to work then become a discipline problem?

8. What types of teacher, administrator, and parent behavior have you observed that are discipline problems?

9. According to the definition, which of the following behaviors are discipline problems? Explain why or why not.

   — a teacher who is late for class

   — a teacher who is unprepared for class

   — a teacher who is disrespectful to a student

   — a student who is disrespectful to a teacher

   — a student who is late for class

   — a student who does not turn in homework

   — a student who refuses to participate

   — a student who calls another student a slut

   — a student who daydreams

10. What common student behaviors are not discipline problems, but because of the manner in which the teacher intervenes, the teacher's behavior is a discipline problem?

11. Why is it important that a teacher be able to distinguish student classroom behavior as either discipline or non-discipline problems?

CHAPTER 6

Cultural Factors Influencing Student Behavior in the Twenty-First Century

"Children's behavior . . . , cannot be understood without some consideration of the world into which they have been born—a world that we adults have created." (Lindquist and Molnar, 1995)

"Because something is happening here but you don't know what it is, do you Mr. Jones?" (Dylan, 1965)[1]

Children Should Be Seen but Not Heard

When the authors present the concepts of the Self-Control Classroom model to teachers, one of the most difficult tasks veteran teachers have is to resolve the discrepancy between the world in which they grew up and the present one. Often teachers ask questions such as, "How come when I was a kid we didn't have these problems?" and "When I was a kid, if I spoke to a teacher the way I've heard students speak, I would not only have been suspended, but when I got home there would have been hell to pay." The teachers who ask these questions feel life was so much easier and calmer back when they were kids. Things didn't seem so crazy. People seemed to be content. Schools taught the basics and there was respect for authority.

The authors are of an age to remember the mid twentieth century well. However, we question whether those really were the good old days in education or in society as a whole. It may be society seemed more ordered in the years after World War II. Perhaps one explanation is that most people "knew their place," which was a common comment heard then. It was used both positively and negatively to indicate that individuals were aware of and adhered to a fairly rigid social structure. Unfortunately, the concept was related to the institutional racism and sexism ingrained in American society of that era.

[1] Ballad of a Thin Man, written by Bob Dylan, recorded by Bob Dylan, issued in the Album "Highway 61 Revisited, 1965, Columbia Records.

Because everyone knew his or her place, society appeared to be safer and more predictable. Children witnessed how their parents conformed to the rigid status quo and were less inclined to behave in a manner that was out of place. Anyone raised to adulthood in the mid twentieth century knows that the place of children was "to be seen and not heard." The authors, both parents, attest to the fact that this expression is no longer operative.

The 1950s, 1960s and 1970s saw a major upheaval in our society, culminating in a cultural revolution. In addition, the 1980s and 1990s witnessed a major influx of Hispanic and Asian immigrants. As a result of the civil rights movement to guarantee equality for African Americans, Hispanics, and other minority groups, and the subsequent women's rights movement, our society was forced to change.

The authors do not mean to suggest that we now live in a race and gender-neutral society; far from it. Our society still struggles with our legacy of racism, sexism, and other forms of discrimination, including classism, ageism, ableism (discrimination against those with disabilities), and homophobia. Nevertheless, many people would assert that we are a more just and egalitarian society than we were in 1955, 1965, or 1975. The problem is that because no one has a set place anymore, understanding how to act in our society is more difficult.

The problem is that because no one has a set place anymore, understanding how to act in our society is more difficult.

One difficulty that ensues when "people don't know their place," is that old forms of authority are less effective (See Chapter 8). Adults are not as inclined to blindly listen to and obey elected officials or police. Children are not as inclined to blindly listen to and obey teachers and parents. Not only do children see that their parents are not particularly respectful to authority (as compared to previous generations of parents), they understand that the (adult) leaders have let us down. It was an assumption in post-war America, if not in every western country, that the "authorities" could be relied upon to make decisions that were, if not always found to be wise, at least intended for the greater good. This belief helped to reinforce the hierarchy of authority and place. Due in part to the extraordinary increase in the rapid dissemination of news and information (discussed in a later section), a clearer picture of world affairs, including the conduct of leaders, is freely available.

The awareness of famine, terrorism, political corruption, corporate fraud, genocide and other mass murder increases the probability that young people view adults as being relatively ineffective in managing their own world. It also increases the probability that young people will not rely upon adults for solutions to problems needed in managing the childrens' world. This lack of confidence in the capability of adults tends to cause insecurity and an increase in the questioning of authority by young people.

The old social contract of knowing one's place and the concomitant blind adherence to authority may have broken down, but we have yet to develop a new social contract that incorporates all of the hard fought and won freedoms and the changes that have occurred in our society since the 1950s. In the classroom, this is readily apparent. When teachers are faced with a lack of civil conduct and respect among students, their response is to react as if it were 1955, using outmoded forms of authority and discipline that do not recognize the changes made to our society in the last fifty years. It is no wonder that some students refuse to obey the strict hierarchically based management policies that are largely a relic of the last century.

Our children are not the creators of this "Brave New World." They are its recipients. They have been born into a world that is more in flux than at any time in history. They don't know their exact place. In order to teach them, we, their teachers, must accept the duty to embrace a new paradigm of relationships between adults and youth. This is the world we created, and, as was stated by a famous cartoon character of the mid 20th century, POGO; "We have met the enemy and he is US" (Kelly, 1970).

Despite a few highly publicized and tragic violent incidents, and contrary to the beliefs of many teachers and administrators, schools remain one of the safest places for children.

Cultural Factors Influencing Students' Behavior

The Effect of Crime, Neglect, and Abuse on Student Behavior

Despite a few highly publicized and tragic violent incidents, and contrary to the beliefs of many teachers and administrators, schools remain one of the safest places for children. The Children's Defense Fund (2002) reports that, despite a growth in the juvenile population in the last decade, there has been a 23% decrease in juvenile violent crime during this period. Children are much more likely to be a victim of crime than a perpetrator.

In the US in 2001, 81% of married couples with children have both parents working outside of the home. Additionally 70% of single mothers are in the labor force (US Department of Labor, 2002). Although not all parents work full time, seven million children are on their own after school, and a child's risk of being a victim of crime triples once school is out (US Census Bureau, 2000). Although quality after-school programs can help students structure their free time in pro-social ways and reduce the chances of victimization, they are not always available in the communities that need them most (Newman et al, 2000).

There were an estimated 826,000 victims of child abuse in 1998. The majority of these children suffered from neglect (58.4%), but many were physically (21.3%) and/or sexually (11.3%) abused (US Department of Health and Human Services, 2002).

The impact of crime, neglect, and abuse upon student behavior in schools may be significant. Lack of finished homework, lateness, truancy, sleeping in class, and surly, disrespectful behavior may be symptoms of the child's problems in the home or community, rather than direct responses to what is happening in the classroom. It is important that teachers keep in mind the tremendous pressures facing many students outside of school, to avoid personalizing students' behavior and/or labeling students as "bad kids." (The negative effects of labeling are discussed in Chapter 7.)

The Effect of the Mass Media on Student Behavior

It is commonplace in America to condemn violence in the media as a contributing factor in violent behavior by youth. According to the Center for Media Education (2002), by the time a child completes elementary school, he is likely to have witnessed over 100,000 acts of violence on TV, including over 8000 murders. The average American child spends more time watching television—on average thirty-eight hours per week—than he does in the classroom. As a result, television has become the primary source of information for young people. Along with issues about the frequency of sex and portrayal of racial/gender stereotypes on television, researchers are concerned most with the amount of violence depicted.

Television has become the primary source of information for young people.

Content analysis of TV shows indicates notable increases in television violence during the last forty years. In 2002, there were approximately twenty-six acts of violence per hour in shows watched by children, as compared to only eleven acts of violence per hour in 1950 (Center for

Media Education, 2002). Violence is not seen solely on fictional television programs, but real-life violence often consumes the majority of the nightly news and prime time news shows.

For decades, research has been conducted on the influence of television violence upon children's behaviors. A 1982 National Institute of Mental Health Report, "Television and Behavior: Ten Years of Scientific Progress and Implications for the Eighties," concluded that research findings support a causal relationship between television violence and aggressive behavior (Bouthilet and Lazar, 1982). A definitive statement was made by the American Psychological Association, "There is absolutely no doubt that higher levels of viewing violence on television are correlated with increased acceptance of aggressive attitudes and increased aggressive behavior" (American Psychological Association, 1993). It has been hypothesized that television violence influences behavior, not only through role modeling aggressive solutions to conflicts (Pearl, 1984), but also by creating the "bystander effect," which is the desensitization or callousness toward violence directed at others (Congressional Quarterly, 1993). According to the Center for Media Education (2002), the "more violence children watch on TV, the more likely they may act in aggressive ways, become less sensitive to others' pain and suffering, and be more fearful of the world around them."

Teachers can use their professional expertise to incorporate non-aggressive means of conflict resolution into their school and classroom policies.

In a recently published study, Dr. Jeffery Johnson, a Professor of Psychology at Columbia University, and his colleagues at the New York State Psychiatric Institute published a study of the long-term effects of television violence. Looking at the violent behavior of over 700 adolescents over a seventeen-year period, the researchers found that ". . . even at age 22, individuals watching more than two hours of TV per day (as children), were substantially more likely to commit an aggressive act over the next eight years" (National Public Radio, 2002). The propensity toward increased aggression found in Dr. Johnson's study held true, even when factors including prior aggression, family background, neighborhood environment, parental neglect, and psychiatric diagnosis were controlled.

Teachers probably cannot, in any significant way, influence the content or quantity of the media that their students watch. Teachers can, however, use their professional expertise to incorporate non-aggressive means of conflict resolution into their school and classroom policies. Teachers are in an ideal position to use their knowledge of popular culture to help students reframe what they are watching and listening to, as well as to help students recognize and understand how the media attempt to manipulate feelings and behavior.

THE KNOWLEDGE EXPLOSION

Have you surfed the World Wide Web lately? If you have, then you have some idea of what is meant by the term "knowledge explosion." The knowledge explosion or information age is considered to have begun in the mid 1950s after the Russians launched Sputnik, the first satellite. The catalyst for this explosion of knowledge was the national fear that the Russians were surpassing us in scientific knowledge and technological advancements.

In the early 1970s, it was estimated that in a fifty-year span from 1980 to 2030, the world's knowledge would increase thirty-two times, representing 97 percent of the world's collective body of knowledge (Toffler, 1970). In the more than thirty years since this prediction was made, the enormous advances in information technology indicate that this figure might be too low. Some of the technological advances that contributed to this knowledge explosion were extremely powerful personal computers, which enable individuals to access data instantaneously; world-wide TV; Global Positioning Satellites (GPS), which enable individuals to instantaneously plot their position anywhere on earth to within a few feet; web-enabled cellular phones, which facilitate instantaneous global connections; DVDs; FAX machines; and "intelligent agents," software that automatically searches other computers and data bases for updated information.

The knowledge explosion influences students' behavior in three ways. First, for some students, it serves as a mechanism for the erosion of respect for authority. There has always been a generation gap, but now this rapid explosion of knowledge is producing what has been called "generation discontinuities." By the end of elementary school and definitely by the end of high school, most students possess knowledge that their parents only vaguely comprehend. This is especially true for personal computing, telecommunications, environmental science, astronomy, and bio-technology. As an example, how many of us have asked a student for assistance with our computers or in accessing some aspect of the Web? Younger students, raised in a culture of computers and instant data retrieval are, in general, far more competent than their teachers in utilizing this technology. Thus respect that was historically almost automatically given to adults because of their superior knowledge and expertise has begun to erode.

When we were growing up, young people may have thought that some adults were ignorant; however, it never has been the case, in all of recorded history up until the present, that entire generations of young people have had more expertise in a technology crucial to the success of their culture, than had many fairly competent and well-educated adults. Again this serves to confound old notions as to the place of young people in the scheme of education.

The second reason that the knowledge explosion affects students' behavior is because it affects teachers' behavior. Teachers are being called upon more than ever before to restructure their instruction, while at the same time keeping abreast of the latest developments in their respective content areas. These expectations often are made without administrators providing adequate release time or training. Concentrating only on pedagogy, teachers are expected to understand and use, for example, cooperative education strategies, performance based assessments, student portfolios, authentic instruction, instructional technologies, strategies that account for multiple intelligences, multicultural curricula, and interdisciplinary units. All of this is to be accomplished in the inclusive classroom. In addition, the national push for "standards" in education increasingly forces teachers to teach to standardized tests, regardless of student interest or individual need.

Sounds overwhelming, doesn't it? Teachers constantly tell us that they are indeed overwhelmed and burned out. Teachers who are stressed are less likely to have the time and patience to accommodate all the needs of students in their classrooms. Students who themselves feel overwhelmed, find themselves confronted by harried teachers. These teachers are less likely to be able to change their behavior to increase the probability that students will change their behavior in appropriate ways.

The third reason is the direct influence that the knowledge explosion has on the curricula. In many school districts, the curricula is more packed now than ever before. Students are expected to learn more now, in the same amount of time, than any previous generation. Many curricula merely add the new material to the older material. This requirement of more material causes students to experience higher levels of stress. This stress often is relieved by disruptive behavior or just tuning out. In other districts, the curricula has not caught up with the information explosion or the technologies used to deliver the information. In these schools, many students feel that the curricula does not reflect or relate to what is happening in the real world. Unless important decisions are made about what content is most essential and how it most effectively can be delivered, many students will be bored and find their schooling lacking relevancy. What teachers often label as a lack of motivation may actually be their students' inability to feel any direct connection with what is occurring in the classroom (Gaby, 1991). It may be only a very small step between perceiving a lack of relevancy and feeling bored to exhibiting disruptive behavior. An understanding of this issue by educators is what supports the restructuring efforts in many schools.

Where We've Been

In this chapter, some cultural reasons were explored as potential influences for disruptive behavior in the classroom. In particular, the concept of a student's "place" in the scheme of society and in relation to adults was explored with the finding that, due to various reasons, many students today do not "know their place." Indeed as contrasted with the rigid hierarchical structure of the 1950s, there is no set place for students.

Other cultural influences affecting student behavior include crime, neglect, abuse, violence in the mass media, and the knowledge explosion.

Where We're Headed

In Chapter 7, the concept of the parallel process, or how interactions between students and teachers tend to result in duplicate emotions, will be covered. In addition, readers will understand how the negative labeling of students may lead to power struggles between teachers and students, and how negative labels influence teacher behavior toward students.

CHAPTER 6 CONCEPT MAP

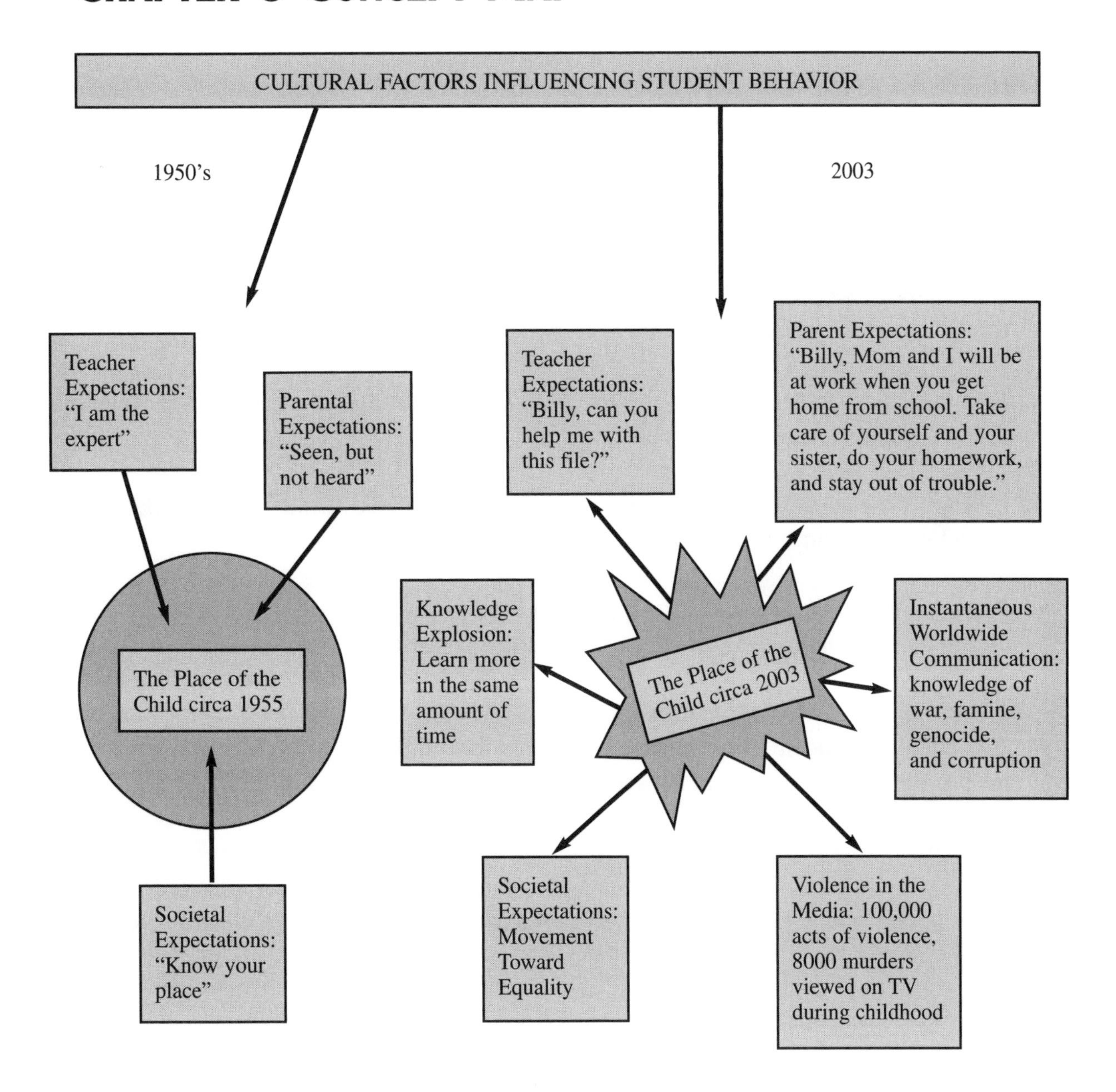

? QUESTIONS FOR THE STUDY TEAM

1. Maybe the phrase "children should be seen but not heard" is outdated, but shouldn't children respect their elders?

2. Why should teachers have to earn the respect of students? Shouldn't teachers be respected just because they are teachers?

3. If teachers aren't tough with students, won't students take advantage of that fact and ultimately lose respect for the teacher?

4. Isn't the lack of respect and self-control of students the result of the permissiveness and moral decline of American society?

5. If schools are so safe, then why are we spending hundreds of millions of dollars on school security and surveillance?

6. Why is it that other countries like Japan that have just as pervasive and violent media, do not have the high levels of aggressive student behavior and discipline problems as the US?

7. You state that students from different cultures have differing views on what respect means. Since they're living in America, shouldn't they have to adopt an American definition of respect?

8. The gap between students and teachers in regard to certain types of knowledge just keeps getting wider. If this erodes respect for teacher authority, how can teachers regain student respect?

CHAPTER 7

The Parallel Process

"Successful teachers are those who are capable of restructuring their cognitions to foster positive feelings essential for positive actions." (Brentro et al, 1990)

How do you feel when you are confronted with a student who chronically exhibits disruptive behavior? Think about the fiftieth time you've intervened for the same type of behavior in the last three months. Take a moment to write down some of the emotions you might feel.

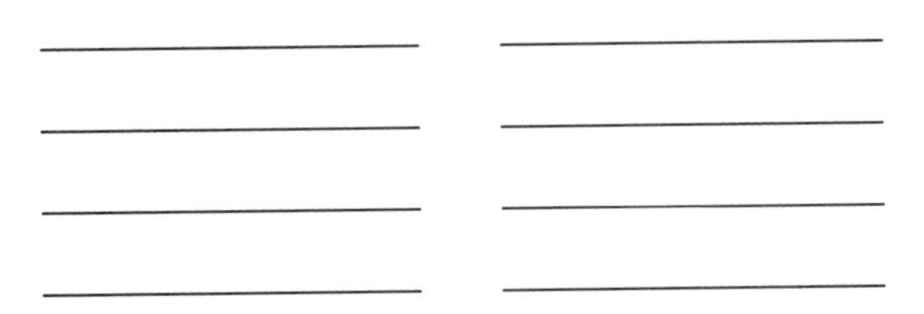

We have asked hundreds of students how they felt when being corrected by a teacher for the umpteenth time for the same behavior. Some examples of their responses include being frustrated, angry, resentful, hopeless, depressed, upset (especially in the stomach), incompetent, insignificant, powerless, vengeful, and generally aggravated.

Do you notice anything the two lists have in common? If you are like the thousands of teachers with whom we have worked, the comparison indicates marked similarities between how you and the student feel.

If you are caught up in these unpleasant emotions, are you likely to use well-thought-out professional approaches, which maximize the probability of the student regaining self-control? Probably not. How about the student who is experiencing similar feelings? Will she likely respond to the teacher's intervention in a manner that decreases the likelihood for further unpleasant interactions? Again, probably not.

This phenomenon of shared affective experience is called a parallel process. Many times when teachers and students interact, what the teacher experiences on an affective level is the same or similar to what the student experiences. This shared experience may either interfere with successful interventions by creating a spiral of hostility and suspicion between the teacher and the student, or it may create a shared expectation of positive growth. In order for positive growth to occur, one of the parties in this process must become aware of the cycle and decide to act to interfere in a positive manner. This person is unlikely to be the student. Therefore, it needs to be the teacher.

Because as an adult, the teacher is at a higher level of cognitive and moral development than her students, she has a greater understanding of causes, a greater ability to see future possibilities, and a deeper understanding of individual rights and democratic principles. In addition, the teacher is a professional who has the responsibility to use her greater capabilities to change her behavior to increase the likelihood of a positive outcome.

Many times when teachers and students interact, what the teacher experiences on an affective level is the same or similar to what the student experiences.

The following scenario demonstrates the problem when the teacher does not act in a manner that is congruent with her cognitive and moral development, but instead acts at the level of the student's cognitive and moral development.

> Dr. Klein, the vice-principal of a large middle school, is discussing why her teacher, Ms. Brown, sent Sarah to the office. Ms. Brown stated in her referral that Sarah was continually off-task and defiant and disrespectful. When Dr. Klein asks Sarah about her behavior, Sarah says, "I'll respect Ms. Brown when Ms. Brown respects me." After school, Dr. Klein speaks with Ms. Brown about her referral and shares Sarah's comment. Ms. Brown replies, "I'll respect Sarah when Sarah respects me."

This is another example of a parallel process. In this scenario, Sarah is behaving in a manner which is congruent with her cognitive and moral development. She is probably operating at the concrete stage of cognitive development and is more concerned with what's happening in the present than what may happen in the future (Piaget, 1970). Morally, Sarah has rigid boundaries regarding fairness, believing that fairness is treating others the way they treat you. On the other hand, the professional expectation for Ms. Brown is that she operates at the formal stage of cognitive development (Piaget, 1970). Therefore, she should be concerned not only with Sarah's present behavior but also should recognize the need to teach in a manner that increases the likelihood that Sarah will learn how to be respectful in the future. Morally, the expectation for Ms. Brown is that she is not concerned with treating others the way they treat her, but is concerned with modeling respect for individuals and democratic principles.

In the above example, if Ms. Brown was behaving in a manner that is congruent with her moral and cognitive development, not Sarah's, we would expect Ms. Brown to model for Sarah respect in the face of disrespect, thus ending the parallel process.

Breaking the Parallel Process

The next time that you feel angry, hostile, aggressive, disrespected, or similar negative emotions, ask yourself how the student may be feeling. According to the parallel process, there is a high probability that the student is feeling the same way. You very well may recognize the same emotions played out on her face. Then ask yourself, "What behavior on the part of this student would have to change to increase the likelihood of my feelings improving?" When you have the answer, behave that way towards your student. You may find yourself pleasantly surprised at the results.

Accurately identifying and understanding your student's feelings is what psychologist's term accurate empathy. Understanding the concept of the parallel process and using accurate empathy greatly increases the efficacy of any interactions you have with your students.

Negative Labeling

Think of the most disruptive, challenging, or difficult students either in your classroom or your school. What are the labels or names teachers often call these students, particularly in the faculty room? When you come home from school after a particularly difficult day, and your significant other asks you how your day was, do you say "That _______ was at it again!"? Fill in the blank with the names or labels you use. Having asked this question to thousands of teachers, we have gathered hundreds of names, many of which are unprintable in a professional text. Among the less objectionable terms are deviant, stupid, scumbag, pain in the ass, asshole, lunatic, brat, spoiled, and wasted. In short, teachers believe these are "bad kids."

If you are dealing with a "lazy, stupid scumbag," how are you feeling toward the student? Teachers tell us that they feel at best apathetic and avoidant and at the worst angry and hostile. When these students misbehave, teachers use highly coercive, disrespectful, and aggressive interventions (Brendtro, 1990). Students are given little, if any, opportunity to control their own behavior.

Suppose we asked these students who have been treated in a coercive, disrespectful, and aggressive manner to generate names for teachers. What names would they provide? We have done this activity and in our experience students provide even more prolific and colorful names. The vast majority of these names are unprintable, but usually describe anatomy and physical functions of the body. When students have these beliefs about teachers, they feel at best apathetic and avoidant and at the worst angry and hostile. They behave disrespectfully and aggressive.

Figure 7.1 illustrates that what is happening for the teacher is the same process that is happening for the student. It is another example of a parallel process.

Think of the well-behaved, achievement-oriented, and hard working students in your class or school. What are the names that teachers call these students? All of these names are printable and include terms such as "star," "model," "leader," "angel," and "super." In short, teachers believe these are "good kids." Teachers feel

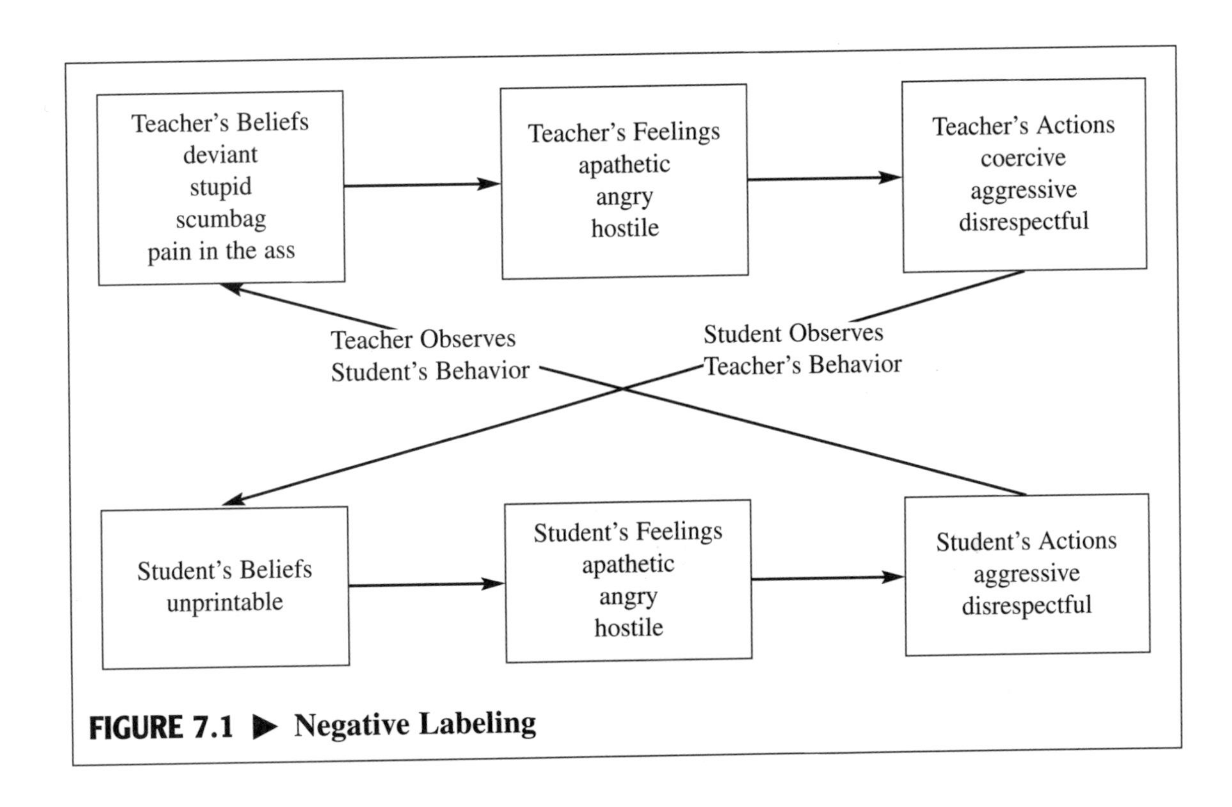

FIGURE 7.1 ▶ Negative Labeling

attracted to these students and want to nurture and empower them. When these students' behavior is disruptive, as it may be on occasion, teachers are patient and understanding, and they provide these students with many opportunities to control their own behavior.

These students have positive affiliative names for teachers, and their feelings and classroom behavior are congruently positive. Figure 7.2 illustrates this positive parallel process.

Because the only person you can control is yourself, if the teacher desires to influence a change in student behavior, she must change her beliefs.

As illustrated in Figures 7.1 and 7.2, the starting point for both parallel processes is the beliefs held by the individual. Because the only person you can control is yourself, if the teacher desires to influence a change in student behavior, she must change her beliefs. This is why we say, "If you can't change your mind, then you can't change anything" (See Chapter 3).

In the case of negative labeling, it is necessary for teachers to change the labels that they use to describe and think about difficult students. Obviously it is irrational to call these students "stars," "models," or "leaders"; they are not. In searching for names that will encourage professional teacher behavior, we suggest names such as professional challenges or struggling students. When faced with a professional challenge or a struggling student, teachers are more likely to feel motivated and hopeful and behave in more encouraging and positive ways toward the student. This is not a minor issue of semantics. The discipline of cognitive psychology is founded upon the understanding that a change in belief (as here described by names and labels) has profound effects upon feelings and behavior (Beck, 1995; Ellis, 1997).

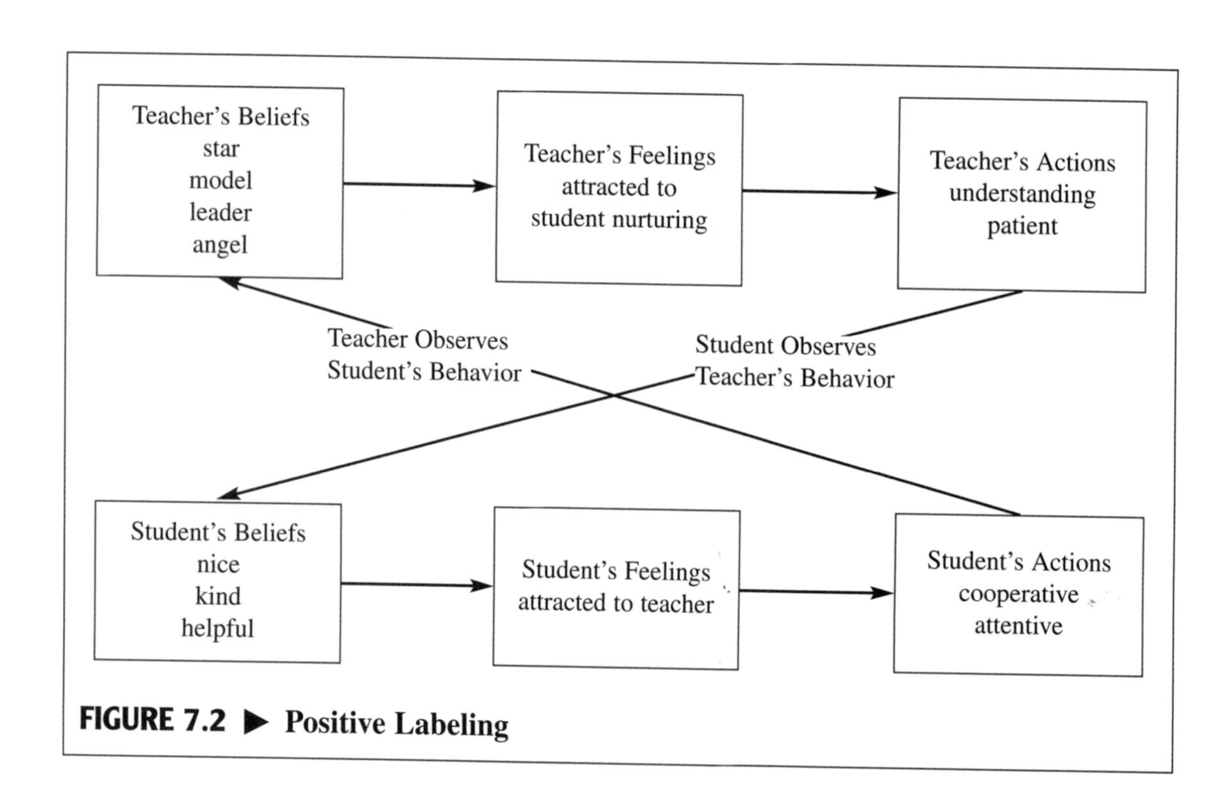

FIGURE 7.2 ▶ Positive Labeling

The authors had an experience that illustrates the importance of changing your mind (beliefs) to change your behavior.

While conducting a voluntary workshop for teachers, the authors were confronted repeatedly by a participant who mocked them, continually called out sarcastic answers, and generally behaved in an inappropriate, disruptive manner. Over lunch, one of the authors remarked to the other, "Boy, was that woman a pain in the ass or what!" His colleague did not answer, and gave him a puzzled look. Where upon the first author realized he, himself, was using negative labels and then said "Boy, was that woman a challenge." Had the initial comment been encouraged, the authors may have spent a very different lunch hour making up other negative labels for the participant, hypothesizing about the quality of life for her significant other, and about what her mother and father must have been like. Upon returning to the workshop, the authors might have requested that she leave the workshop if she continued her disruptive behavior, or they may have behaved in a manner which would have encouraged her to leave on her own accord.

By calling the teacher a challenge, the authors had to spend their lunch hour meeting their profession responsibility, to devise strategies to increase the likelihood that the teacher would cease her disruptive behavior and become more positively engaged in the workshop. The authors returned to the workshop motivated and hopeful. They requested that she volunteer in workshop activities, frequently asked for her opinion, and used her concerns for group discussions. Her behavior changed dramatically from being disruptive to being engaged in the workshop. The authors are uncertain whether she agreed with the Self-Control Classroom model, but they are certain that she ceased to be disruptive and was more on-task.

Where We've Been

In this chapter, the parallel process was described as occurring in a situation where the thoughts, feelings, and behaviors of one individual, the teacher, are highly similar to the thoughts, feelings, and behavior of another individual, the student. The parallel process is either a negative or positive cycle. A negative cycle can only be impacted by one of the participants changing her beliefs. Because the teacher is at higher levels of cognitive and moral development, the responsibility for change rests with her. The effects of negative and positive labels were explored as examples of parallel processes.

Where We're Headed

The next chapter explores the nature of authority. In addition, the differential use of authority by teachers is examined.

CHAPTER 7 CONCEPT MAP

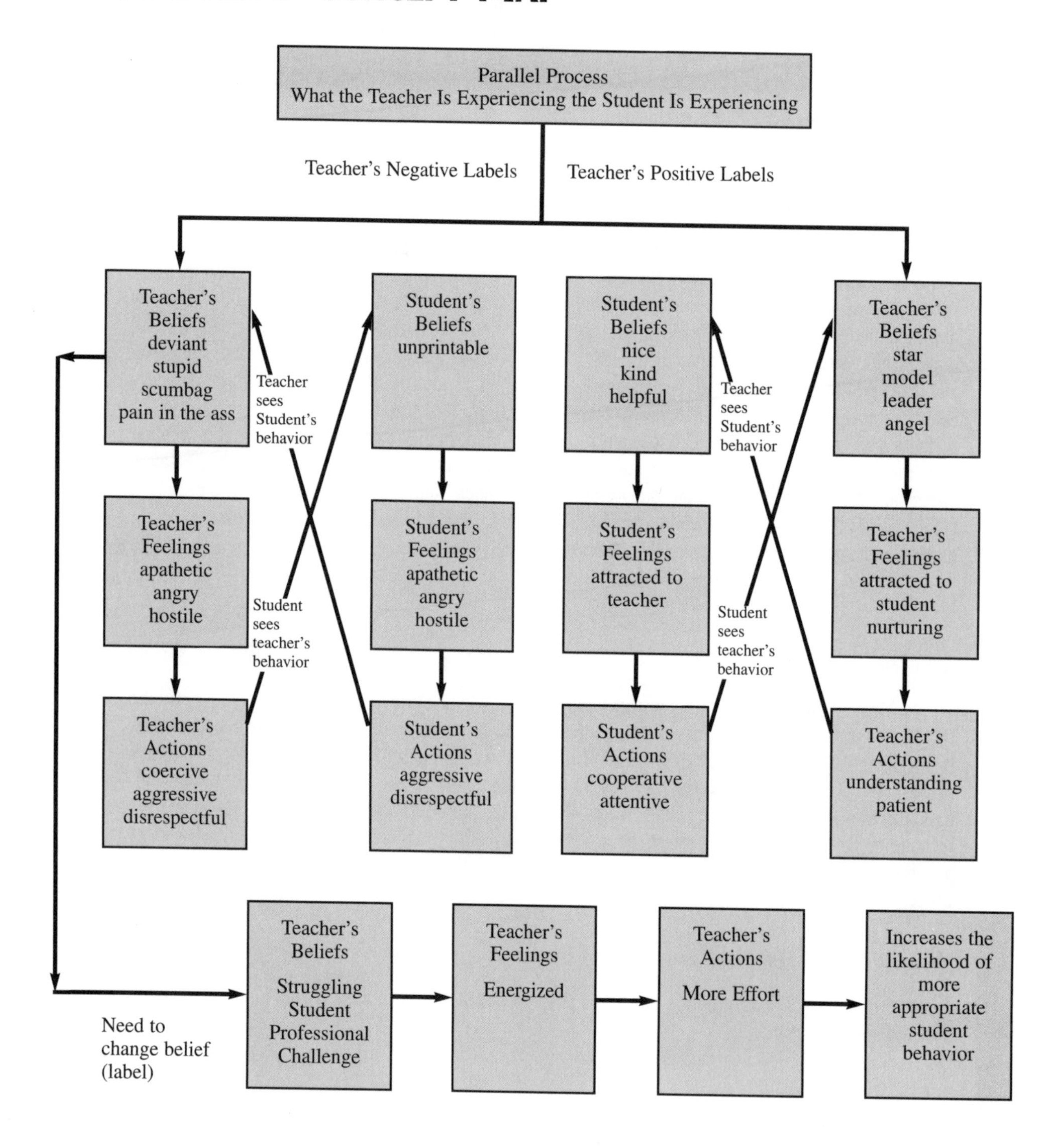

QUESTIONS FOR THE STUDY TEAM

1. The parallel process assumes that a student is experiencing the same affective response as the teacher. How can a teacher tell if this is really occurring or if the student is just pretending?

2. Explain how a teacher can use the concept of "accurate empathy" to break a negative parallel process.

3. Recall the quote used in the beginning of this chapter by Brendtro (1990): "Successful teachers are those who are capable of restructuring their cognitions to foster positive feelings essential for positive actions." Explain Brendtro's quote in reference to working with difficult children, using the philosophies in Chapter 3 and the labeling students discussion in this chapter.

4. The idea of "reframing the reasons for behavior" is helpful in reducing the likelihood that teachers will negatively label students. A teacher positively reframes the reasons for a student's disruptive behavior when, instead of assuming negative reasons for the behavior, assumes positive or action oriented reasons. Complete the following with some negative reasons for the disruptive behaviors listed. Then add some reframed reasons for the behaviors.

Disruptive Behavior	Negative Reasons	Reframed Reasons for Behavior
Example: a student getting out of her seat and visiting other students	student is oppositional, refuses to follow rules	student likes to interact with others
a student always calling out answers		
a student always calling out jokes during class		
a student always talking to her neighbors		

5. How can teachers use the reframed reasons for students' disruptive behavior to increase the likelihood that a student will behave appropriately?

6. Why is it the teacher's responsibility to break a negative parallel process?

7. Can a teacher facilitate a positive parallel process? How?

8. How can a teacher (especially new teachers) avoid negatively labeling students, when they continually hear other teachers doing so?

9. How do you influence other teachers not to negatively label students?

10. Many teachers say that calling disruptive students "professional challenges" is just a matter of semantics. Is this a valid argument? Are semantics important in influencing how a teacher behaves towards students who exhibit disruptive behavior?

11. In addition to the authors' suggestion of using "struggling student" and "professional challenge" as more positive names for students who exhibit disruptive behavior, what other names can you use?

SECTION 3

Establishing Successful Learning Environments

In this section, the components of the Self-Control Classroom model are presented and explained.

The Vision statement indicates that this is a model of prevention based upon the development of successful learning environments, the underlying belief is that when students are successful, motivated, and have a sense of self worth, they are not disposed toward disruptive behavior. The development of these successful learning environments is dependent upon teacher/student interactions which are based on mutual accountability for behavior, on authentic, supportive relationships, and on the delivery of expert instruction.

In Chapter 8, we explore the four ways that teachers can gain and exercise authority in the classroom. It will be apparent to the reader that only certain philosophies and methods of gaining authority are congruent with the goal of fostering successful learning environments through the development of supportive relationships and expert instruction.

The next three chapters define and explore the components of a successful learning environment. These components are student success (Chapter 9), intrinsic motivation (Chapter 10), and pro-social self-esteem (Chapter 11). At the conclusion of each chapter, the different authority bases are revisited to determine which are congruent with the establishment of successful learning environments.

The section concludes with the introduction of the Professional Decision Making Matrix (PDMM), a tool for the diagnosis and remediation of challenging student behavior. The PDMM will be revisited in Chapter 18, when it is demonstrated how to use the matrix and to problem solve common and chronic classroom behavioral and motivational challenges.

CHAPTER 8

The Nature and Use of Teacher Authority

"Research findings converge on the conclusion that teachers who approach classroom management as a process of establishing and maintaining effective learning environments tend to be more successful than teachers who place more emphasis on their roles as authority figures or disciplinarians." (Brophy, 1988)

When teachers are asked what word comes to mind when thinking about authority, invariably they answer, "control," referring to control of the classroom and/or control of individual students. The Self-Control Classroom philosophy states that the only person you can control is yourself. Therefore, rather than having control over students, teachers either have or do not have influence upon their students. The belief that a teacher holds about how students are best influenced is that teacher's philosophy of authority. These philosophies are classified into four broad categories or authority bases. The importance of understanding the differences among these authority bases is that the beliefs that a teacher holds about the nature and use of authority determines what behavior teachers choose when attempting to influence student behavior. Regardless of title or position, if you have no influence upon the behavior of students, you have no authority.

Authority figures typically fall into four categories, depending upon how they influence other individuals.

The Nature of Authority

In your life, whom do you consider an authority? To answer this, ask yourself the following questions.

- Who has or had influence in your life?
- To whom do you voluntarily go for advice?
- Whose advice do you seriously consider prior to making a decision?

List each of these people in the first column in Table 8.1. Next ask yourself why you listen to these people and write your answers in the second column. We have asked many teachers these same questions. Table 8.1 first lists a few of their responses to help you get started. Fill in the rest of the table.

Authority figures typically fall into four categories, depending upon how they influence other individuals. We have placed the first entry into each category in Table 8.2, to reflect how many

TABLE 8.1 ▶ Authorities in Our Lives

Person Having Authority (Influence)	Reason These People Have Authority (Influence)
1. parents	they care, trust, and respect me
2. police officer	they have formal responsibilities backed by the legal system
3. auto mechanic	they have a specialized body of knowledge
4. boss	they can write me a positive or negative evaluation
5.	
6.	
7.	
8	
9.	
10.	
11.	
12.	
13.	
14.	
15.	

TABLE 8.2 ▶ Categories of Authority

Category 1	Category 2	Category 3	Category 4
parents	auto mechanic	police officer	boss

teachers in our workshops have categorized the influence of these authority figures. Parents are placed into Category 1. Teachers tell us that they view their parents as authority figures, because their parents have influenced them through the communication of love, trust, and respect, and they have their best interests in mind. Using your entries in Table 8.1, identify individuals whom you invest with authority because their influence upon you is the result of their care, trust, and respect, and their evident concern for your best interests. Place them in Category 1 of Table 8.2.

Auto mechanics are placed in Category 2. They have authority because people are influenced by their specialized body of knowledge of how to repair and maintain cars. Identify those on your list who you invest with authority because you are influenced by their specialized knowledge. Add them to Category 2.

Police officers are placed into Category 3. Their authority results from formal legal responsibilities to uphold the law, which exerts a strong influence upon law-abiding members of our society. Are there any people on your list who influence you because of their legally or socially supported formal title or position in society or an organization? If so, enter them in Category 3.

People on your list who have the capability to influence you through the use of rewards and punishment and do so (such as a boss) are placed in Category 4.

French and Raven (1960) studied how people influence others and therefore are invested with authority. They identified four authority bases: referent, expert, legitimate, and coercive (sometimes called reward/punishment). The categories in Table 8.2 reflect these authority bases.

People who influence us through their trust, respect, and concern about us are invested with referent authority. Such people often are parents, spouses, best friends, siblings, and personal mentors. A person does not have to have a title or degree to be perceived as possessing referent authority. These individuals are respected, and their advice is sought or seriously considered, because they have positive regard and concern for us. Category 1 should include only those people whom you consider to have influence in your life due to their referent authority.

Category 2 deals with expert authority. People who have expert authority influence us because they possess a specialized body of knowledge or experience that we need and we do not have ourselves. Examples of those individuals with expert authority are auto mechanics, lawyers, doctors, plumbers, and psychologists. These people usually obtain their expertise through long years of schooling and/or on the job training. Their influence comes from the knowledge that they possess.

Category 3 contains individuals with legitimate authority. People whose influence results from their formal responsibilities and actions either sanctioned by our society or by an organization are termed as having legitimate authority. Examples of people with legitimate authority are lifeguards, traffic directors at highway construction sites, police officers, judges, and Internal Revenue Service agents. These people have influence upon us because they carry out duties that are formally assigned them by governmental agencies, Boards of Directors, or other hierarchically ordered organizations.

Category 4 contains individuals whose influence is derived from coercive authority. Coercive authority figures influence others through the use of rewards and punishments. Examples of people with coercive authority include a boss or supervisor whose predominant influence is that they can fire, demote or promote you, and/or give you a raise; an abusive spouse; a gang leader; or a bully. Table 8.3 summarizes our analyses of authority bases thus far.

Teacher Authority

Mr. Miller is a new teacher who is very concerned about student behavior. He asks his principal how best to influence students in his classroom to behave appropriately. The principal suggests four teachers, each of whom influence students in a different manner. Mr. Dowling believes in referent authority. Mr. Chang believes in expert authority. Mr. Patel believes in legitimate authority. Mr. Aronow believes in coercive authority.

Mr. Dowling advises Mr. Miller that the best way to influence students to behave appropriately is through the development of meaningful relationships characterized by trust, respect, care, and support. Mr. Chang's advice on how to best influence students to behave appropriately is to engage students in their learning through exciting, meaningful, and enthusiastic instruction. Mr. Patel's advice to Mr. Miller is to firmly establish who is in charge of the classroom and present the students with a predetermined list of rules the first day of class. Mr. Aronow's advice is to design behavioral contingency plans for the entire class and for individual students as needed, entailing rewards for appropriate behavior and punishments for inappropriate behavior.

After a few months of teaching, Mr. Miller seeks the advice of the four veteran teachers regarding Danny, a student whose behavior is particularly disruptive in his class. Mr. Dowling suggests that Danny's behavior is disruptive because Danny does not believe that he is a cared for, respected member of the classroom community. Therefore Danny does not feel the duty to others that would encourage him to behave

TABLE 8.3 ▶ Summary of Authority Bases

Authority Bases	Referent	Expert	Legitimate	Coercive
ATTRIBUTES	cares, trusts, respects you	has specialized body of knowledge	is sanctioned by society or an organization	gives rewards and punishment
MEMBERSHIP	parents spouses best friends	doctors plumbers attorneys	life guards police officers judges	bosses abusive spouses bullies

more appropriately. Mr. Chang says that Mr. Miller may not be addressing Danny's interests, abilities, or learning style. Mr. Patel advises Mr. Miller that Danny obviously does not understand that Mr. Miller is in charge of the class and that Danny does not have a choice but must follow the classroom guidelines. Mr. Aronow points out that Mr. Miller's rewards and punishments are not powerful enough reinforcers to affect a change in Danny's behavior. He also questions Mr. Miller's consistency in the application of behavioral contingencies.

Each of these veteran teachers has advised Mr. Miller in accordance with their own belief or philosophy of teacher authority about how to best influence students to behave appropriately. It is important that the reader not confuse the overriding philosophy of authority with individual classroom strategies. It is probably evident to the reader that every teacher, regardless of philosophy, uses strategies from each authority base. Even though teachers might occasionally step outside their philosophy, the overriding number of strategies used to influence student behavior is determined by the authority base in which teachers believe. The teachers' authority base also determines how they conceptualize both appropriate and inappropriate student behavior. These conceptualizations have a direct influence on how teachers label students, feel about students, and ultimately behave toward students (See Chapter 7).

Even though teachers might occasionally step outside their philosophy, the overriding number of strategies used to influence student behavior is determined by the authority base in which teachers believe.

Teacher Authority in Practice

A teacher with referent authority believes that students have the ability and responsibility to behave appropriately in the classroom. He believes that students use their ability and accept responsibility for self-control when they are in environments in which the teacher shows sincere interest in students and shows respect for students' competence and opinions.

A teacher utilizing referent authority will likely display the following behaviors in order to prevent discipline problems. The teacher demonstrates a sincere interest in the student as a unique and valuable person, shows respect for the student's opinions, and trusts the student to make appropriate choices. Differences among students are recognized and respected in all student/teacher interactions. To intervene when disruptive behavior occurs, the teacher likely uses techniques which do not embarrass or draw undue attention to the student. The teacher speaks to the student privately, uses empathy to understand the student's frame of mind, and encourages the student to problem solve in order to reassert self-control.

In the expert authority base, the teacher believes that students have the ability and responsibility to behave appropriately in the classroom. Further, the teacher believes that students use their ability and accept responsibility for self-control when they are in classrooms in which the teacher designs successful learning environments (See Chapters 13–15).

A teacher utilizing expert authority prevents discipline problems by using instructional techniques and planning instructional activities which increase the likelihood of students' success and by making on-task behavior more interesting than disruptive behavior. Differences among students are considered and respected, because this is inherent in effective instruction. In intervening when disruptive behavior occurs, a teacher operating from the expert base may use any effective technique; however, due to his emphasis on effective instruction, he most likely uses techniques which redirect the student's interest to the lesson.

In the legitimate authority base, as in the referent and expert bases, the teacher believes that students have the ability and responsibility to behave appropriately in the classroom. However, he believes that students use their ability and accept responsibility for self-control when they are in environments in which they clearly understand the legal authority of the teacher; in other words, the teacher is always the person in charge and therefore the person who makes all the classroom decisions.

A teacher utilizing legitimate authority may display the following behaviors intended to prevent discipline problems. The teacher clearly communicates to the students what his role as teacher is and what their role as students is. Unlike teachers using referent and expert authority, teachers using legitimate authority are less likely to take individual student differences into account when formulating expectations for student behavior, because individual differences are not mitigating circumstances when there is a violation of expectations for appropriate classroom behavior. When disruptive behavior occurs, the teacher likely uses techniques that remind the student that he, the teacher, is in charge and shows what exact behavior is required in the classroom. The message this teacher is most likely to send to a student is, "It's my way or the highway."

There are some caveats to each of the authority bases.

In the coercive authority base, as in the three other authority bases, the teacher believes that students have the ability and responsibility to behave appropriately in the classroom. In addition, the teacher believes that students use their ability and accept responsibility for self-control, primarily when they are in environments in which the teacher uses reward and punishment to influence students' behavior.

A teacher utilizing coercive authority may attempt to prevent disruptive behavior by designing a system of rewards and incentives for appropriate behavior and a system of increasingly unpleasant punishments for inappropriate behavior. Similar to teachers using legitimate authority, teachers using coercive authority are less likely to take individual student differences into account when attempting to understand student behavior. When disruptive behavior occurs, he may communicate to the student that a punishment is imminent if the behavior continues. If the student does not comply in a timely manner, the teacher administers the punishment.

Caveats

There are some caveats to each of the authority bases. Often new teachers confuse referent authority with being a student's friend. Although a teacher can be friendly, there are developmental reasons why teachers and students of any age cannot and should not be friends. This is due to the mutually exclusive friendship expectations of adults and young people. For instance, while young people do not expect their friends to hold them accountable, adults expect their friends to be accountable. Furthermore, teachers have a professional responsibility to hold their students accountable for their behavior.

Referent authority is believed by some to be a permissive philosophical base and one that excludes the use of consequences. In practice, referent authority holds students to high expectations and standards, and the use of consequences is recognized as a powerful means to teach students about accountability.

Some teachers believe that referent authority means that there are no classroom guidelines—that students pretty much do as they please. Teachers believing in referent authority recognize that rules and procedures are necessary for students to have an orderly classroom in which learning is facilitated. A teacher believing in referent authority is likely to develop classroom guidelines consensually with his students.

Teachers using referent authority trust that students have the will and ability to meet high expectations and are always supportive of students' efforts to do so. In addition, referent authorities understand that it would be disrespectful to stand in the way of students experiencing the positive and negative consequences of the choices they make.

Expert authority requires that teachers are competent and up-to-date with advances in their content area and pedagogy. This makes lifelong learning a specific requirement of the expert teacher. A teacher from 1955 should be totally bewildered upon entering a classroom of an expert teacher in the new millenium. The advances in knowledge and technology are staggering, yet many teachers view these advances as burdens to be avoided, rather than opportunities to be embraced. Expert teachers, like experts in all professions, recognize these advancements and put forward the time and effort necessary to master them to improve their practice, in this case, teaching.

Because of the reasons associated with changes in our society (See Chapter 6), legitimate authority has been eroded. Merely having the title of teacher or principal is no longer sufficient in influencing students to behave appropriately.

If coercive authority worked in the long term, you would not be reading this text. All teachers know how to develop contingency based management plans. Indeed, all parents know how to reward and punish. Coercive authority has been the dominant disciplinary paradigm in the United States for over fifty years, yet the most recent data available indicated that juvenile courts in the United States handled more than 1,700,000 delinquency cases in 1995 and incarcerated more than 84,000 juveniles on a single day snapshot during the same year. The number detained or committed during the course of the year far exceeds the one-day count (Amnesty International, 1998). When coercive authority is effective, it is so only in the short term, because rewards and punishments must become more powerful as students get older. In addition, rewards and punishments frequently do not generalize to other situations (Kohn, 1999) (See Chapters 16, 17).

Positive and Negative Influences: A Personal Reflection on Authority

- Of all the people who have influenced you, who has been your most positive role model?
- Who has had the most positive impact on your life?
- If someone were to compare you favorably to this person, would you be justifiably proud?
- What behaviors did this person most consistently display towards you that made he or she your most positive role model?
- Were they behaviors that demonstrated care, respect, and trust—that is, referent authority?
- Were they behaviors that turned you on to learning or opened up new opportunities, in other words expert authority?
- Were they behaviors that demonstrated who was in charge and continually reinforced their rules—that is, legitimate authority?
- Were they behaviors that provided you with rewards and/or punishments—that is, coercive authority?

Consistently, in hundreds of workshops with teachers, administrators, parents, psychologists, students, probation officers, and other professionals, participants have said that their most positive role models exhibited behavior that was congruent with the referent and/or expert authority bases. Sometimes participants said that their most positive role models were those that exhibited behavior congruent with the legitimate and coercive authority bases and gave as examples hard-nosed coaches or drill sergeants. However upon reflection, these participants realized that the reason these individuals had positive influence was not due to their legitimate or coercive behavior, but rather to the participants' beliefs that these coaches and drill sergeants truly cared about them, trusted them, and respected them (referent authority). In addition, in many circumstances, these people also really knew what they were doing and communicated it effectively (expert authority).

- Of all the people who have influenced you, who has been your most negative role model?
- Who has had the most negative impact on your life?
- If someone were to compare you favorably to this person, would you be disturbed?
- What behaviors did this person most consistently display towards you that made he or she your most negative role model?
- Were they behaviors that demonstrated care, respect, and trust—that is, referent authority?
- Were they behaviors that turned you on to learning or opened up new opportunities—that is, expert authority?
- Were they behaviors that demonstrated who was in charge and continually reinforced his or her rules—as in legitimate authority?
- Were they behaviors that provided you with rewards and/or punishments, as in coercive authority?

In hundreds of workshops, participants consistently have said that their most negative role models came from the legitimate and/or coercive authority bases.

- If your students were asked how they perceive your influence, into which authority base would they place you?
- Would it be in the authority base from which your most positive influence came or that of your most negative influence?
- Which management model do you practice in your classroom or school?
- Is the model congruent with the authority base of your most positive role model or that of your most negative role model?

If you are not satisfied with the answers to the above questions, remember that if you continue to do what you've done, you'll continue to get what you've got. Since the only person you can control is yourself, perhaps it may be time to consider changing your behavior.

Which Authority Base Should Teachers Use?

Readers might now infer that authority bases are positive or negative, effective or ineffective. Readers might further infer that the authors believe that referent and expert authority are positive and effective, while legitimate and coercive authority are negative. While these inferences have some basis in this chapter, the reader needs to be provided with sufficient information concerning their use in learning environments to draw any meaningful, definitive conclusions concerning their use in the classroom.

To illustrate the need for additional information, suppose you were provided with four tools: a screwdriver, a hammer, a saw, and a pair of pliers. Which is the most effective tool? In order to answer this question, you need more information concerning the use for which the tool is intended. Does a screw need tightening? Does a nail need to be driven? Does a piece of lumber need to be cut? Does a nut need to be threaded onto a bolt? Obviously, the task determines which tool will be selected in order to be most effective to complete the job.

Another illustration is the determination of the most positive and effective teaching strategy among direct instruction, guided discovery, and inquiry. Again, in order to to make this determination, you need additional information concerning what is the learning objective. Do students need to recall discrete facts? Do students need to use previous knowledge in new contexts? Do students need to formulate a new approach to solve a complex problem? Obviously the learning objective determines which teaching strategy is positive and effective under the circumstances.

Therefore, in order to answer the question *Which authority base is positive and effective?*, the reader must know the objectives for the use of authority. In Chapter 1, the vision statement for the Self-Control Classroom model states that the goal is the development of successful learning environments. The answer to *Which authority base is positive and effective?* must wait until the components of a successful learning environment are defined.

If your students were asked how they perceive your influence, into which authority base would they place you?

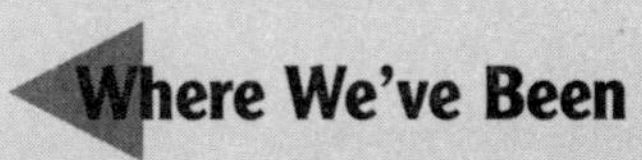

Where We've Been

The nature and use of teacher authority or influence was explicated by describing four types of authority: referent, expert, legitimate, and coercive.

- Referent authority is characterized by teacher behavior that communicates trust, care, respect, and support.
- Expert authority is characterized by teacher behavior that focuses upon effective pedagogy.
- The legitimate authority base is characterized by teacher behavior that emphasizes the legal position of the teacher and strict adherence to rules and procedures that are developed solely by the teacher.
- Coercive authority is characterized by teacher behavior that attempts to influence students through the use of rewards and punishments.

Each authority base was analyzed as to its effect on teachers' beliefs and behavior. Cautions regarding each authority base were explored. Readers were then asked to reflect upon from which base their most positive and most negative influences derived their authority. Finally the question was asked: *Which authority base should teachers use, because it is positive and effective?* It was determined that to answer this question, additional information on the components of a successful learning environment was needed.

Where We're Headed

In the next three chapters, the components of a successful learning environment are defined. In addition, the impact of teacher authority on these components is discussed. The next chapter looks at the first component of a successful learning environment, the success/failure ratio. The internal impediments to student success, as well as how teacher authority impacts student success, are also explored.

Chapter 8 Concept Map

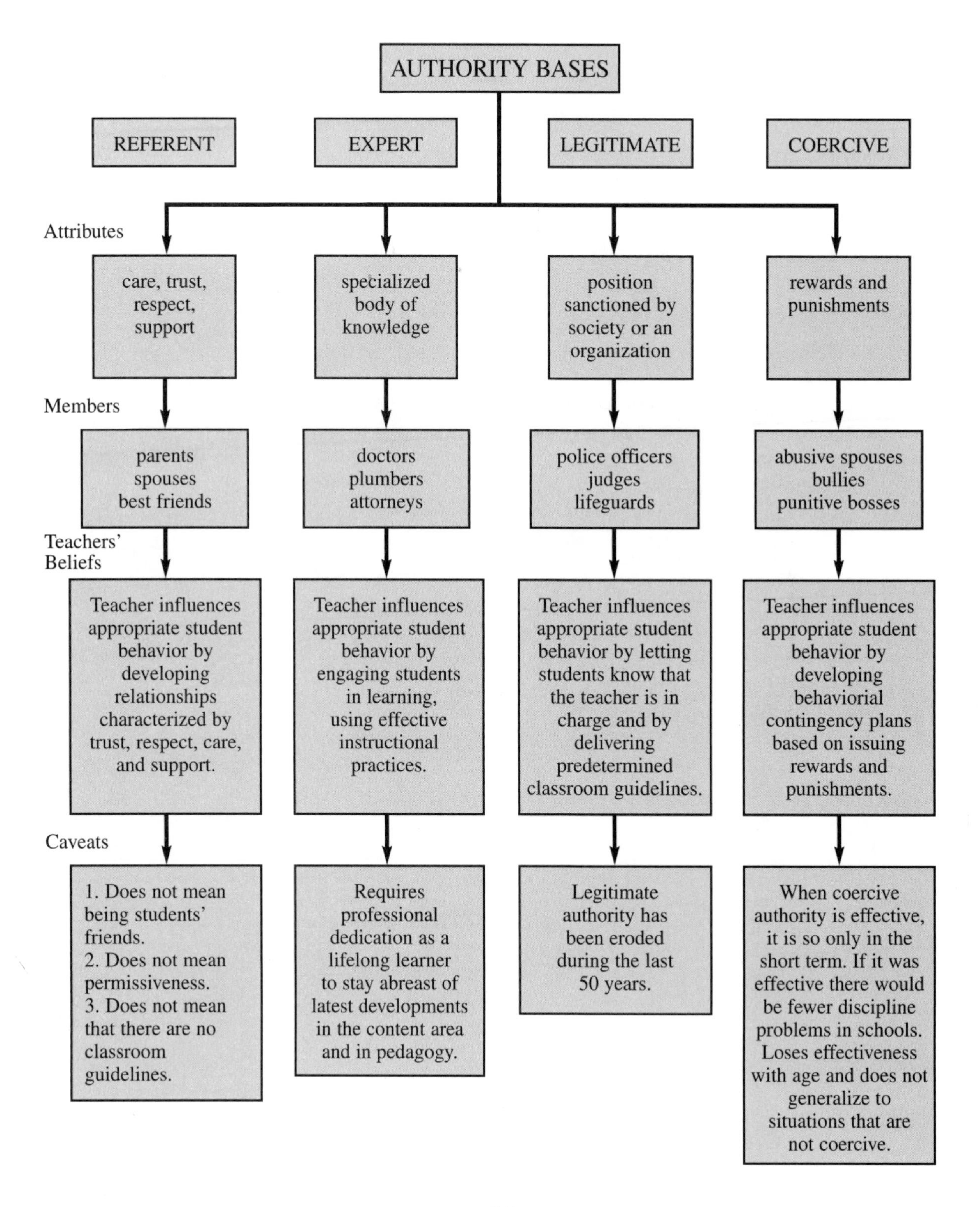

? QUESTIONS FOR THE STUDY TEAM

1. Why is the word "influence" rather than "control" used to describe the concept of authority in the Self-Control Classroom model?

2. Explain why a person's authority is determined by the individual he is trying to influence?

3. Why is it important to distinguish the philosophies or beliefs about authority from the strategies that relate to each authority base?

4. For each authority base, determine the belief regarding how to best influence another person, how discipline problems are prevented, and how a teacher would intervene when discipline problems occur. Complete the following.

Authority	Beliefs about how to best influence another person	Prevention of discipline problems	Interventions for discipline problems
Referent			
Expert			
Legitimate			
Coercive			

5. Most teachers say that they have a preferred authority base, which they believe is most effective in influencing students to behave appropriately. However, teachers also say that because they use strategies from all the authority bases, they must not have a preferred authority base. How might these statements be reconciled?

6. Teachers have said that the use of referent and expert authority to influence students to behave appropriately does not reflect how the "real world" operates. Does the "real world" operate with legitimate and coercive authority? Is the use of referent and expert authority in schools putting students at risk for later in life?

7. If a student comes from a family that uses legitimate and coercive authority, will a teacher's use of referent and expert authority be effective?

8. Many teachers say that young students do not understand the use of referent and expert authority, and they must use legitimate and coercive authority. Do you agree or disagree? Explain your answer.

9. Many teachers confuse referent authority with being a student's friend. Why can't teachers be friends with students?

10. How do the following two quotes relate to the authority bases?

    "What every student needs and what only teachers can provide is equality of dignity and quality of instruction" (Ginott, 1972).

    "A teacher is respected not for how tall he stands, but for how often he bends to help, comfort, and teach" (Anonymous).

11. Is it possible for a new teacher to be perceived by students as having referent authority, or does it take a long time?

12. How would you react to the advice, "Teachers should start off the year tough by using legitimate and coercive authority, and then after students know who's in charge, lighten up and use referent and expert authority."

13. Doesn't strong discipline like the coercive authority base build moral character? Explain your answer.

14. Aren't there some students who understand that a teacher really means business only when they use coercive authority?

15. How would a teacher believing in a particular authority base address these classroom issues listed in the following chart?

	Referent	Expert	Legitimate	Coercive
What is emphasized on the first day of school?				
How are classroom rules/guidelines developed?				
How is the importance of homework explained?				
What happens when students do not turn in homework?				
What happens when a student is late to class or cuts class?				
What happens if a student refuses to participate in class?				
What is the teacher's approach to disruptive student behavior?				

16. What are the implications of the following statement? If legitimate and coercive authority were effective, discipline problems in schools would be a footnote in educational history.

17. How can a teacher use referent and expert authority in his classroom if the administrators use legitimate and coercive authority when dealing with both with the students and the teachers in the school?

18. Case Study: Jason, a 10th grade student was standing in the hall, quietly talking to friends as classes changed. Mr. Smith, a teacher Jason had in 9th grade, called from across the hall, "Jason, get to class now!" Jason walked over to Mr. Smith and told him that he was standing outside his next class, had already been in the classroom, had his materials out, and was all ready to start class as soon as classes changed. Before Jason could finish, Mr. Smith said in a stern and loud voice, "A student like you shouldn't be standing around wasting time." Jason again tried to explain, but was interrupted by Mr. Smith who told him, "You are a rude and disrespectful kid." Jason looked at Mr. Smith and said, "Why don't you just go f*** yourself." The vice principal was summoned and Jason was immediately suspended.

    Role Play (requires two people): You are a very respected teacher in the school and you also witnessed the interaction between Mr. Smith and Jason. Therefore, the principal asks for a meeting to discuss the incident, including the appropriateness of Mr. Smith's and the vice principal's response and whether further follow-up is necessary on the part of the administration. In the chart below, the authority bases have been paired by referent/expert and legitimate/coercive. The answers to the questions depend upon the interaction of the authority bases of you the observing teacher (role played by one person) and the authority bases of the principal (role played by another person).

Authority Bases of the Observing Teacher	Authority Bases of the Principal	Appropriateness of Mr. Smith's and the Vice Principal's Actions	Is There any Other Type of Further Follow-up needed?
Referent/Expert	Referent/Expert		
Referent/Expert	Legitimate/Coercive		
Legitimate/Coercive	Legitimate/Coercive		
Legitimate/Coercive	Referent/Expert		

CHAPTER 9

Successful Learning Environment: The Success/Failure Ratio

"When students are off task, our first responsibility should be to ask, 'what is the task?'" (Kohn, 1996).

The Success/Failure Ratio

An individual's self-worth is, in large part, determined by the ratio of her successes (S) to her failures (F) or: **S/F** (Gever, 1991; James 1890). In order for an individual to have a reasonably good opinion of herself, this ratio must be greater than 1. In other words, she must experience more success experiences than failure experiences in life. We denote this as:

In large part positive Self-worth = More Successes/Less Failures

$$\mathbf{S/F > 1.}$$

This is not to say that a person who experiences 200 successes and 199 failures, or

$$\mathbf{S/F = 200/199 = 1.005,}$$

feels as positive about herself as an individual who experiences 400 successes and 199 failures or

$$\mathbf{S/F = 400/199 = 2.01.}$$

What we mean when we use the inequality notation $S/F > 1$ is that the person has many more successes than failure experiences in life. While this concept was first proposed over one hundred years ago, it only recently has been applied to understanding students' disruptive behavior.

Human beings are social animals who have an innate desire to belong, be recognized, and be accepted (Adler, 1963). When we speak of success, we are not speaking only of winning the contest or earning the highest grade in the exam. We mean that the student receives feedback from her environment, which meets her needs to belong, be recognized, and be accepted. Examples of success outside of school include each time a parent expresses positive regard toward her; each time her friends include her in activities, or each time she accepts and successfully accomplishes her responsibilities. In school, success may include receiving high or even passing grades, contributing to classroom activities, having fun during recess, or enjoying lunchtime with her friends. Throughout many students' lives, their successes greatly outnumber their failures. Of course all students have bad days and experiences. Sometimes the difficulty of an exam takes them by surprise and they fail. Sometimes the conversation that the student had in the schoolyard just has to be continued in class, leading to a negative interaction with the teacher. Sometimes friends are fickle and suddenly may exclude the student. Occasionally mom or dad is in bad humor and takes it out on the student. Each of these may be perceived as a failure experience for the individual student. However, for the average student, the total number of successes still greatly outnumber the failures, leaving S/F ratio > 1.

Students with a S/F > 1 are not necessarily model students. However, we believe they tend to present fewer behaviorial and academic challenges to the classroom teacher. When problems do occur, they tend to be transient and well within the capabilities of the average teacher to handle.

However, there are students who do not feel the same sense of belonging, acceptance, and recognition as the students described above. Frequently these students have negative interactions with parents and teachers. Many times they are excluded by their peers. More often than not, they exhibit academic difficulties. Of course these students also have their good days. They sometimes have positive interactions with parents and teachers. They are occasionally selected for games by their peers, and at times they display some academic competency. However, for these students, the total number of failures still substantially outnumbers the successes, leaving S/F ratio less than 1 (S/F < 1).

The first component of a successful learning environment is a success/failure ratio greater than one (S/F > 1).

It is not the case that students with a S/F < 1 are always disruptive or always have academic failures. However, it has been our experience that these are the students who tend to present more frequent behavior and academic challenges to the classroom teacher. The problems that do occur tend to be entrenched. They may overwhelm the capabilities of the average teacher who has not restructured her thinking about how to influence and instruct children with behavioral problems.

Take a moment to think of how you intervene with students who present frequent disruptive behavior. In the spaces below, write some of your interventions.

When asked this question, most teachers in our workshops volunteer interventions such as time out, being sent to the rear of the class, detentions, being sent to the principal, losing privileges like recess, public reprimands, calling parents, and assigning lower grades. All of these are similar in that they signal failure to the student. Once again the student has been shown to be inadequate and has not met her need to belong, be accepted, or be recognized. These types of interventions further decrease her S/F ratio, thus increasing the likelihood of future disruptive behavior.

Table 9.1 illustrates hypothesized success/failure ratios for average students and compares them to success/failure ratios for students who exhibit chronic disruptive behavior problems across a variety of settings.

It is apparent that teachers must interact with students in a manner that increases student success. The first component of a successful learning environment is a success/failure ratio greater than one (S/F > 1).

Expectations and Inoculations

There are several obstacles teachers face when attempting to alter a student's S/F < 1 to a S/F > 1. This scenario explores these obstacles.

TABLE 9.1 ▶ A Comparison of Hypothesized S/F Ratios of Average Students to Students Who Exhibit Chronic Disruptive Behavior

	Average Students		Students with Chronic Disruptive Behavior	
Parents	Mostly positive responses to daughter's or son's behavior **(success)**	Occasional negative responses to daughter's or son's behavior (failure)	Occasional positive responses to daughter's or son's behavior (success)	Mostly negative responses to daughter's or son's behavior **(failure)**
Peers	Generally positive relationships **(success)**	Brief periods of negative interactions (failure)	Brief periods of positive interactions (success)	Generally negative relationships **(failure)**
Teachers	Mostly positive responses to student's behavior **(success)**	Occasional negative responses to student's behavior (failure)	Occasional positive responses to student's behavior (success)	Mostly negative responses to student's behavior **(failure)**
Community	Frequent feelings of belonging and acceptance **(success)**	Occasional feelings of alienation and rejection (failure)	Occasional feelings of belonging and acceptance (success)	Mostly feelings of alienation and rejection **(failure)**
Academic Tasks	Frequent achievement **(success)**	Infrequent failure (failure)	Infrequent achievement (success)	Frequent failure **(failure)**
Non-academic Tasks	Frequent achievement **(success)**	Infrequent failure (failure)	Infrequent achievement (success)	Frequent failure **(failure)**
Cumulative S/F Ratio	**Success/Failure > 1**		**Success/Failure < 1**	

Kristin is a sixteen-year-old tenth grader with a S/F < 1. Her relationships with others are strained. She has frequent arguments with her parents and feels alienated and rejected by her community. Her parents and teachers view Kristin's peer group negatively. Academically, Kristin consistently receives D's and F's. On a recent day in class, Ms. Reardon, her math teacher, handed back the graded math test. Kristin earned a 45 percent. How do you think Kristin reacted on receiving her grade? Do you think it likely that she exclaimed, "What, another F! I've had it with these lousy grades. From now on, no partying for me after school. I'm studying." As welcome as that response might be, Kristin's actual response was to shrug her shoulders, crumble the paper, and toss it into the trashcan. When Kristin is asked why she got an F, she responds, "I always get F's. What's the big deal? At least I have a life. I'm not like those other kids who study all the time." It is obvious that Kristin expected to fail. Failure does not alter Kristin's perception of herself or her approach to academic tasks.

Even Kristin, with a $S/F < 1$, sometimes receives a grade higher than a D or F. One day Ms. Reardon returns a paper in which Kristin receives a C-. Surely Kristin now exclaims, "A C-, this feels so good! Now I understand what my teachers and parents have been trying to tell me about the joys of success. From now on, no partying for me after school; I'm studying." As welcome as that response might be, Kristin's actual response was to shrug her shoulders, crumble the paper, and toss it into the trashcan. When asked why she got a C-, she responds, "I don't know, I musta got lucky." It is obvious that this one minor success does not alter Kristin's perception of herself or her approach to academic tasks. This is because Kristin is inoculated against success.

What we mean by inoculation is that Kristin's history of failure acts as a "vaccination" against success. Because of her expectation of failure, successes are viewed as anomalous events. When the rare success does occur, it is attributed to luck. Since Kristin understands that she has no control over luck, she believes that her academic success is not influenced by whether or not she studies. Kristin's experience illustrates that students with a $S/F < 1$ expect to fail and are inoculated against success.

Sarah is a sixteen-year-old tenth grader with a $S/F > 1$. Her relationships with others are congenial. She has positive interactions with her parents and feels accepted by her community. Her parents and teachers view Sarah's peer group positively. Academically, Sarah consistently receives B's and A's.

On a recent day in class, Ms. Reardon handed back the graded math tests. Sarah earned an 89 percent. How do you think Sarah reacted on receiving her grade? Do you think she acted surprised? In fact, Sarah smiled, looked over her test and placed it in her notebook. When Sarah is asked why she got a B+, she responds, "I always get good grades. I pay attention in class, I take notes, and I study." It is obvious that Sarah expected to succeed. Success does not alter Sarah's perception of herself or her approach to academic tasks.

Even Sarah with a $S/F > 1$ sometimes receives a poor grade. Now suppose Ms. Reardon returns a paper on which Sarah receives a D. Surely, Sarah now exclaims, "A D, that's it! I'm not studying anymore. Kristin, can I hang out with you? At least you have a life." In fact, rather than a response that indicates that she wants to give up, Sarah is concerned and somewhat upset. When asked why she got a D, she responds, "I must have not studied enough, or I really misjudged what was going to be on this test." She stays after class to talk to Ms. Reardon about coming in for extra help or doing extra work to make up for the poor grade. This one failure does not alter Sarah's perception of herself or her approach to academic tasks. This is because Sarah is inoculated against failure.

Inoculation in this case means Sarah's history of success acts as a "vaccination" against failure. Because of her expectation of success, failures are viewed as anomalous events. When the rare failure does occur, it is attributed to lack of effort or misunderstanding on Sarah's part. Since Sarah understands that she has control over effort and understanding, Sarah reasons that her failure can be remediated through more effort and closer attention to the details of the task. Sarah's experience illustrates that students with a $S/F > 1$ expect to succeed and are inoculated against failure.

Impediments to Success

FEAR OF FAILURE

It may seem puzzling that Kristin, who expects to fail, refuses to put forth effort to succeed because she actually fears failure. The following scenario illustrates why she fears failure.

Suppose Ms. Reardon believes that Kristin has the ability to do better work and receive higher grades. She communicates this through showing personal interest in Kristin and by always offering extra help and assistance when and if Kristin requests it. Kristin believes Ms. Reardon and decides to take advantage of Ms. Reardon's assistance for the upcoming exam. She meets with Ms. Reardon a few times, and with Ms. Reardon's help, lays out a plan of study. Kristin takes the exam and receives an F. What does Ms. Reardon now say to Kristin? "Kristin I thought you were smarter. However, it seems that you're not. Please move to the back of the room and I won't bother you anymore."

While it is very unlikely that Ms. Reardon would act in this manner, this is actually what Kristin fears. As long as Kristin puts no effort into academic tasks, teachers and parents are convinced she has greater academic potential than her present achievement shows. Also Kristin can maintain a belief that she has greater capabilities than she demonstrates. Young people like Kristin actually have no idea of their abilities until they put forth effort. They do, however, enjoy that the adults in their lives believe that they are more capable and intelligent than their grades indicate. The positive beliefs of other people enables students to rationalize, in the absence of any evidence to the contrary, that indeed if they put forth effort, they would succeed. Therefore Kristin takes a tremendous risk if she puts forth effort and then fails. If that were to happen, she would lose a small degree of positive expectations of her teachers and parents and learn that she is not capable.

It is often the case that upon reflection, adults can identify many situations in which a fear of failure has altered their own behavior. For instance, these situations include not enrolling in a particularly difficult course or major, not applying for a new or higher position at work, not participating in an athletic endeavor, or not asking out a certain person for a date. In all of the above examples, the underlying motivation appears to be that if an individual cannot look smart or do well (being successful) then the next best thing is to avoid looking dumb or not doing well (being a failure). The easiest way not to be a failure is not to try. This, in part, explains why many students become apathetic and disengaged in school, particularly as they get older (Raffini, 1993; Collopy and Green, 1995).

FEAR OF SUCCESS

It is certainly possible that a student like Kristin with a long history of failure may initially fail, even with Ms. Reardon's high expectations and assistance. If this occurs, rather than giving up on Kristin, Ms. Reardon writes notes of encouragement regarding Kristin's effort and points out all instances where Kristin showed understanding of the material. Additionally, Ms. Reardon makes arrangements to meet with Kristin to review the test, reteach the areas of misunderstanding, and review how Kristin could improve her study skills for the next unit. She communicates that she still believes that Kristin is smart and competent. Kristin decides to continue to prepare and study. On the next test Kristin earns a C.

While Kristin is pleased that her efforts have resulted in a better grade, she is more anxious than before she started to try. This anxiety stems from Kristin's concern that she may not be able to continue to succeed, therefore setting herself and her teacher up for disappointment. This is understandable, due to her low success/failure ratio. Kristin fears that if she fails, Ms. Reardon may say something like, "I know you are capable of doing the work, you proved that last week. The issue is not one of capability, you just don't care. I refuse to work harder than you only to watch you go back to your old ways." As long as Kristin continues to fail, there is a minimal amount of disappointment displayed by her teacher. It is only after she succeeds, that she runs the risk of disappointing herself and others in the future. One part of fear of success is that the expectations will be higher and the student will be unable to consistently meet the higher standards. In Kristin's case, grades that once were viewed as modest successes, D's and low C's might now be viewed as failures. To ameliorate this aspect of a fear of success, teachers must expect variability in performance as students move toward achieving more successes. Also, they must communicate to the student that becoming successful is not always a straight path, but one with some ups and downs. In addition, the teacher should relentlessly communicate high expectations, trust in the students' capabilities, and continually support students in their efforts.

One part of fear of success is that the expectations will be higher and the student will be unable to consistently meet the higher standards.

Kristin is now beginning to put forth more effort in class, and her grades are beginning to improve. Ms. Reardon is making decisions regarding how to divide her class into cooperative teams to begin work on a research paper that is a substantially large portion of each student's grade for the marking period. Previously, Kristin was grouped with Carla, Maria, and Dawn, all students with long histories of failure (S/F < 1). Ms. Reardon rationalized that these students would not choose to do the work, but at least they would not negatively impact other students' grades. However, since Kristin is showing more interest and earning higher grades, Ms. Reardon decides to group her with Andrea, Gail Anne, and Janice. These students have a long history of being successful (S/F > 1). What do you think the responses of these two groups might be upon learning the makeup of each group? Is it likely that Kristin's old group of Carla, Maria, and Dawn will be pleased? Are they likely to say, "You go Kristin. We may not be able to do it, but at least you can be successful. We're proud of you." Positive responses like these are highly unlikely. Carla, Maria, and Dawn probably view Kristin as a traitor to the group and a threat to their own complacent acceptance of academic failure. They are angry at her for showing them up and because she now has less time to hang out. They are likely to say, "What the hell are you up to? What are you a schoolgirl now? Why don't you get your head out of Ms. Reardon's butt."

Luckily for Kristin, her new group of Andrea, Gail Anne, and Janice are very accepting. We are sure that they will welcome her with comments such as, "Hi Kristin. We are really happy that you will be working with us. We are looking forward to you coming over our houses to work on the project." Such positive comments from her new group are just as unlikely as the positive comments from her old group. In fact, Andrea, Gail Anne, and Janice are likely to complain to the teacher that Kristin will not work, will lower their grades, and they do not want to associate with a girl who has a reputation like Kristin's.

Kristin has a very understandable fear of changes in her relationship with her peers if she continues to alter her behavior to be more successful. Her old friends will not accept her, because she doesn't have the time to hang out and is starting to lose interest in drugs, alcohol, and partying. Her new group is not interested in accepting her, because of her past history and associations with students with problems both in and out of school.

As a result of Kristin's success, she has lost an extremely valuable component of adolescent life, the sense of belonging to a peer group. It is understandable that if Kristin begins to change her approach to school, she fears she will have no friends and will be isolated. This fear is not irrational, because this feared outcome does indeed happen to thousands of students every year as they attempt to move from a S/F < 1 to a S/F >1. This isolation can be so intense that students often will take the first opportunity to lesson the isolation by returning to their previous behaviors. In Kristin's case, all she needs to do is stop studying and begin to fail in order to once again be accepted by Carla, Maria, and Dawn. If Andrea, Gail Anne, and Janice ever accept Kristin, it will be only after she has tolerated their distrust, succeeded over a long period of time, and stopped associating with her old friends.

To ameliorate this aspect of a fear of success, teachers must expect that the student will have feelings of isolation and develop a strong desire to be accepted again by her old reference group. This may result in frequent variability in the student's behavior and her attempts to be successful. During this transitional period, it is essential that teachers relentlessly communicate high expectations, trust in students' capabilities, continually support students in their efforts, and be empathetic to students' emotional concerns.

Because of the endemic nature of the fear of success and the fear of failure of students with a S/F <1, teachers need to view their involvement with these students as a marathon, not a sprint.

Because of the endemic nature of the fear of success and the fear of failure of students with a S/F <1, teachers need to view their involvement with these students as a marathon, not a sprint. It is a marathon because working with challenging, difficult students is an endurance event that often continues after the school day and even when the student has been promoted to a higher grade. The probability of a student with a S/F < 1 becoming a student with a S/F > 1 is directly proportional to the number of teachers and other adults willing to participate in the endurance event.

The Impact of Teacher Authority on the Success/Failure Ratio

REFERENT AND EXPERT AUTHORITY

In Chapter 8, the question was asked, *Which authority base is effective?* and the answer given was that it depends upon the desired objective. The first objective of a successful learning environment is to create an environment where students are most likely to achieve a S/F > 1. Which authority base(s) best facilitates student academic success?

The expert teacher, whose focus is on influencing behavior through effective instruction, is in the best position to increase the probability of student academic success. The teacher accomplishes this primarily by diagnosing learning difficulties, designing meaningful, interesting lessons, delivering clearly structured content, and accommodating the various learning styles and multiple intelligences of her students.

Expert teachers are most effective when their students trust and respect them. In order to achieve this, teachers must display patience, care, trust, respect, and support towards their students. These are the characteristics of referent teachers who believe that behavior is best influenced by meaningful relationships. In fact, there is a popular saying in education that illustrates the relationship between referent and expert authority, "I don't care how much you know, till I know how much you care" (Anonymous).

Expert teachers are most effective when their students trust and respect them.

WHAT ABOUT LEGITIMATE AND COERCIVE AUTHORITY?

Teachers who embrace legitimate authority believe that behavior is best influenced by letting students know that the teacher is in charge and that their guidelines will determine appropriate classroom decorum. This authority base is unlikely to have a positive effect on students' success/failure ratio. Students with a S/F < 1 have repeatedly been reminded of who is in charge and to do their work and behave appropriately. If the message were effective, these students would not have a S/F < 1.

While the promise of a reward and/or the threat of a punishment does result in the occasional academic success, these successes are typically short-term and do not generalize (Kohn, 1999).

Coercive authority, the use of rewards and punishments, is the most widely used authority base in schools today (Butchart and McEwan, 1998; Hyman and Snook, 1999; Kohn, 1999). While the promise of a reward and/or the threat of a punishment does result in the occasional academic success, these successes are typically short-term and do not generalize (Kohn, 1999). In addition, students do not attribute their success to their own efforts and competency, but rather to the reward or punishment. Also, as students get older, schools cannot offer rewards that are meaningful enough or punishments that are aversive enough to maintain student success (See Chapters 16–17).

Table 9.2 presents the authority bases again, with the addition of which bases most positively impact the S/F > 1, the first component of a successful learning environment. Examples of strategies which impact the success/failure ratio are discussed in Chapter 13.

TABLE 9.2 ▶ The Impact of Teacher Authority on the Success/Failure Ratio Greater Than One (S/F > 1)

AUTHORITY BASES	Referent	Expert	Legitimate	Coercive
ATTRIBUTES	cares, trusts, respects students	has specialized body of knowledge	is sanctioned by society	gives rewards and punishments
MEMBERSHIP	parents spouses best friends	doctors plumbers attorneys	life guards police officers judges	bosses abusive spouses bullies
S/F >1	builds relationships based upon trust, respect, care, and support, which are catalysts for positive outcomes of effective instruction	effective instruction facilitates academic success and also teaches students appropriate behavior	focuses upon teachers' legal authority and title and does not focus upon student success	rewards and punishments have short-term impact, if any, upon student success, does not generalize, loses effectiveness with age

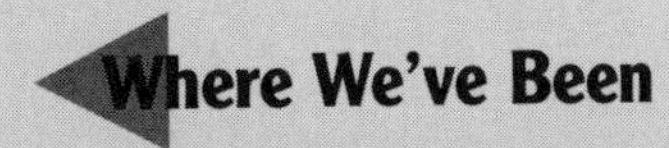

Where We've Been

The first component of a successful learning environment is the success/failure ratio greater than 1 (S/F > 1). S/F > 1 means the student has many more successes than failures. Students with a S/F > 1 expect to succeed and are inoculated against failure. Students with a S/F < 1 expect to fail and are inoculated against success. Teachers' efforts towards encouraging student success for students with a S/F < 1 are hampered by these students' fears of failure and success. The authority bases of referent and expert were shown to be those most effective in positively impacting student success.

Where We're Headed

In the next chapter, the second component of a successful learning environment, motivation, is discussed. The types of motivation, the components of motivation, its impact on student behavior, and the authority base(s) that most positively impact motivation are delineated.

Chapter 9 Concept Map

SUCCESS/FAILURE RATIO

TYPES	STUDENT OUTCOMES	IMPLICATIONS	CHALLENGE
SUCCESS/failure > 1 The student experiences many more successes than failures.	Expectation to Succeed Inoculated Against Failure	Students expect to succeed, and when they fail, they attribute it to lack of effort and next time try harder.	
success/FAILURE < 1 The student experiences many more failures than successes.	Expectation to Fail Inoculated Against Success	Students expect to fail, and when they succeed, they attribute it to luck and next time do not try harder.	How can schools overcome the resistance of students to exert more effort needed for success?

Referent	Expert
Referent authority builds relationships that are characterized by trust, respect, care, and support. Such relationships are prerequisites to helping students become successful in meeting high expectations for both academics and behavior.	Expert authority utilizes effective instructional practices to facilitate academic achievement, and teaches students appropriate behavior.

QUESTIONS FOR THE STUDY TEAM

1. Using the concept of the success/failure ratio, why do traditional interventions used for students who behave disruptively typically increase the likelihood of future disruptive behavior?

2. Many students who display disruptive behavior perceive being asked to leave the room, being sent to the office, and detentions as successes. Doesn't this raise these students' success/failure ratio?

3. When students with a S/F < 1 meet with academic success, how does this success influence their future academic behavior? Explain.

4. When students with a S/F > 1 meet with academic failure, how does this failure influence their future academic behavior? Explain.

5. What are some student behaviors that indicate to a teacher that the student may be resisting changing her behavior because of a fear of failure?

6. What are some student behaviors that indicate to a teacher that a student may be resisting changing her behavior because of a fear of success?

7. Why are the referent and expert authority bases congruent with the goal of increasing students' S/F ratios?

8. Why are the legitimate and coercive authority bases incongruent with the goal of increasing students' S/F ratios?

CHAPTER 10

Successful Learning Environment: Motivation

"School apathy is not caused by genetic deficiency, nor do students choose ignorance over competence when they have equal choice. Many students reject school because they find the academic practices in their classrooms threatening to their sense of self-worth. They have learned that withdrawing from academic effort is less painful than experiencing the feelings of failure and hopelessness created by the systematic exclusion of forced academic competition." (Raffini, 1993)

Motivation

How many times have you heard comments such as, "I know Antoine could do the work if he tried. What is it going to take to get Antoine started?" Most teachers would interpret this to mean Antoine is not motivated.

Motivation is a measure of an individual's will to initiate, direct, and sustain effort in activities from which some gain is sought. People may be more or less motivated in many different areas of their lives. For instance, there is achievement motivation, learning motivation, social motivation, athletic motivation, and economic motivation.

Motivation is a measure of an individual's will to initiate, direct, and sustain effort in activities from which some gain is sought.

When teachers think about motivating students like Antoine to learn, they have generally been taught to use behavioral contingency plans. Teachers concentrate upon what incentives or disincentives they have at their disposal to increase or decrease the likelihood and frequency of certain student behaviors. This theory of shaping human behavior is called operant conditioning and was developed by B. F. Skinner (1974).

Many theorists, including the authors, have difficulty with operant conditioning, because operant conditioning does not adequately address the internal dialogue or cognition of the individual (Atkinson, 1964; Deci et al.,

2001; Kohn, 1999; Rotter, 1966, 1975). Motivation theories that do consider an individual's cognition are termed Social Cognitive Theory. Atkinson (1964) conceptualized motivation as a product of an individual's expectation of success multiplied by the value of the outcome to the individual.

$$\mathbf{M = E \times V}$$

The expectation of success variable is defined as an individual's belief that he can attain a desired goal. The value variable is defined as the extent that this goal is important to the individual.

By examining the product of an individual's expectation and value in regard to any given endeavor, predictions may be made as to the degree of motivation that the individual brings to the task.

For example, consider the experiences of Bruce and Andy, two juniors at a large university who belong to a fraternity that sponsors a traditional Valentine's Day formal. Neither Bruce nor Andy has dates. Andy attended this formal both as a freshman and a sophomore. He had a wonderful time. He likes to dance, and he likes to socialize. When Andy thinks back over his past dating history, he realizes that he has been a very successful dater. The last ten women he has asked out on dates have accepted his invitation. What degree of motivation does Andy have to put forth effort to find a date for this year's formal? Going back to Atkinson's formulation of motivation (expectation of success × value), Andy has a high expectation of success, based upon his past dating history, and also places a high value on obtaining a date, based upon the fun that he experienced at previous formals. Therefore, Andy is highly motivated to find a date for the dance.

Bruce took a blind date to the freshman dance. He did not have a particularly enjoyable time. He does not particularly like to dance, and he often feels out of place at social gatherings. When Bruce looks back on his dating history, he is chagrined to note that only one woman out of the last ten he has invited on a date has accepted his invitation. Furthermore, she requested to be taken home early. What degree of motivation does Bruce have to put forth effort to find a date for this year's formal? Going back to Atkinson's formulation of motivation (expectation of success × value), Bruce has a low expectation of success, based upon his past dating history, and also places a low value on obtaining a date, based upon the lack of fun that he experienced at previous social events. Therefore, Bruce has a low degree of motivation to find a date for the dance. It is unlikely that Bruce would put forth any effort to find a date for this year's dance, were it not for the tremendous pressure being placed upon Bruce to attend by his fraternity brothers. The small degree of motivation that Bruce has to find a date is a result of the impact upon value of the pressure exerted by his peers.

Table 10.1 illustrates the interactions of expectation of success and value in determining motivation, using dating as an example. Andy's experience places him in cell I, while Bruce's experience places him in cell IV.

As can be seen in Table 10.1, motivation to put forth the effort to obtain a date is highest with a product of high expectation of success and high value (I). Motivation is moderate when one variable is high and the other is low (II, III). Motivation is lowest when both expectation of success and value are low (IV).

It is assumed that all students have a reasonably high expectation of success when they first start school. It is also assumed that all students initially place a reasonable amount of value upon doing well academically. Therefore, students begin school with a reasonably high degree of motivation.

As students progress through school, they experience both successes and failures. The

TABLE 10.1 ▶ Motivation = Expectation of Success × Value

		Expectation of Success: High	Expectation of Success: Low
VALUE	High	I (ANDY) $M = E \times V$ $M = E_{high} \times V_{high}$ M = (previous dating efforts were successful) × (it is important to go to the dance) M = HIGH	II $M = E \times V$ $M = E_{low} \times V_{high}$ M = (previous dating efforts were unsuccessful) × (it is important to go to the dance) M = MODERATE
	Low	III $M = E \times V$ $M = E_{high} \times V_{low}$ M = (previous dating efforts were successful) × (it is not important to go to the dance) M = MODERATE	IV (BRUCE) $M = E \times V$ $M = E_{low} \times V_{low}$ M = (previous dating efforts were unsuccessful) × (it is not important to go to the dance M = LOW

average student (see Table 9.1) has far more success experiences than failures, and so his S/F ratio > 1. Therefore, he maintains at least a moderate expectation of success. Various activities in school may be of high, moderate, or low value to this student. However, given his at least moderate expectation of success, he maintains a moderate to high level of motivation, dependent upon the relative value of the activity. His motivation generally falls in I, II, or III in Table 10.1.

What about the student who is a chronic discipline problem? He has far more failures than successes (see Table 9.1). His S/F ratio < 1. Therefore, he maintains a low expectation of success. Various activities in school may be of high, moderate, or low value to this student, as well. However, given his low expectation of success, he maintains a low, to at best, moderate level of motivation, depending upon the relative value of the activity. His motivation generally falls in II, III, or IV in Table 10.1.

Let's assume that two students have the same degree of value for a particular academic task. The first student has a history of substantially more successes than failures (S/F > 1) in similar academic tasks and thus has a high expectation for success. The second student has a history of substantially more failures than successes (S/F < 1) in similar academic tasks and therefore has

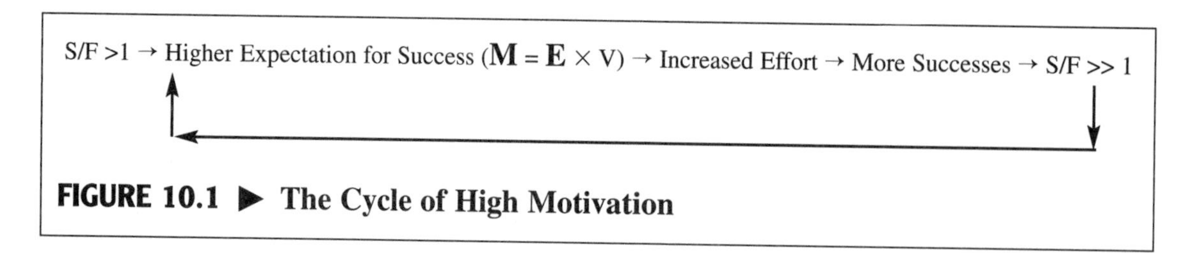

FIGURE 10.1 ▶ The Cycle of High Motivation

a lower expectation of success. Because of a higher expectation of success, the first student is more motivated and puts more effort into the task. Increased effort usually leads to additional success, which increases his S/F ratio even further. Therefore, the student's expectation for future success again increases, resulting in additional effort, which leads to more successes and a greater S/F ratio. This success cycle of continual more effort, more success, more effort, more success builds into what we term a cycle of high motivation. This student is unlikely to become a chronic disciplinary problem. This cycle is illustrated in Figure 10.1.

On the other hand, because of a lower expectation of success, the second student is less motivated and puts less effort into the task. Less effort usually leads to additional failures and a lowering of his S/F ratio even further. Therefore, the student's expectation for future success again decreases, resulting in less effort, which leads to more failure and a lower S/F ratio. This failure cycle of continual less effort, more failure, less effort, more failure, we term a cycle of low motivation and is illustrated in Figure 10.2.

While a teacher cannot directly increase students' motivation by altering a student's biology, sociology, or psychology, he can alter his own behavior to increase the likelihood that the behavior of his students change.

This formulation of motivational difficulties is applicable to all students, no matter why they have low motivation (biological, sociological, or psychological). While a teacher cannot directly increase students' motivation by altering a student's biology, sociology, or psychology, he can alter his own behavior to increase the likelihood that the behavior of his students change. To the extent that the teacher understands the S/F ratio and its role in motivation, he will choose behaviors which increase the likelihood that all of his students will be more successful and thus more motivated.

Intrinsic and Extrinsic Motivation

In the last section it was stated that expectation of success multiplied by value equals motivation. How do students explain success and failure, and how do they determine value? Students attribute their successes and failures to causes that either originate within themselves

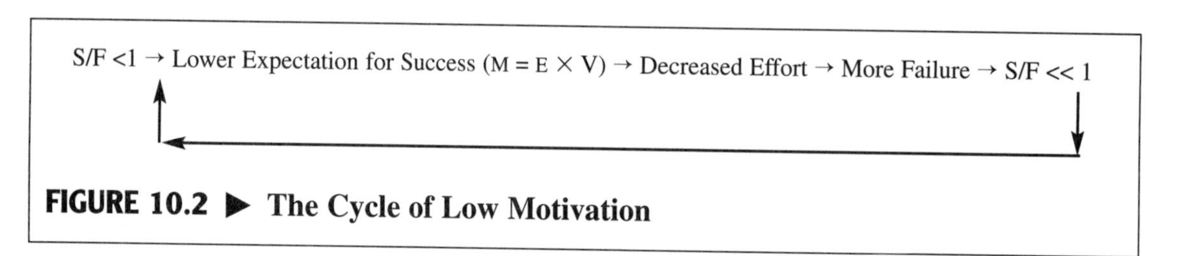

FIGURE 10.2 ▶ The Cycle of Low Motivation

or that originate from outside themselves (Rotter, 1966, 1975).

In the previous dating example, Andy was shown to have a high degree of motivation. How would Andy use this motivation to obtain a date? Andy understands that his prior success in dating was a result of his efforts in meeting, getting to know, and eventually dating young women. He understands in the current situation he is likely to be successful if he similarly puts forth effort in meeting, getting to know, and eventually asking a young lady to the dance. Andy understands that the degree of effort and the display of social competence are variables within his control. Therefore, we say that Andy's expectation of success is based upon an internal locus of control. A student with an internal locus of control attributes successes and failures to factors such as amount of effort, study habits, and/or choices he makes.

What is the other reason besides expectation of success that Andy was willing to make the effort needed to find a date? He valued the outcome of going to the dance. His value is based upon the fun he had at previous dances, because he likes to dance and socialize. Andy has an internal value structure in regard to the dance. Students who value activities which provide them with opportunities to develop new competencies, to satisfy a personal interest, or to meet personal goals, are said to have an internal value structure because these outcomes are generally independent of others (Levin and Shanken-Kaye, 1996).

When a student has an internal locus of control and an internal value structure, he is intrinsically motivated, that is, the motivation comes from within the individual. Atkinson's formula can be expressed as the following to indicate intrinsic motivation:

$$\mathbf{M}_{\text{(Intrinsic)}} = \textbf{Expectation of Success}_{\text{(internal locus of control)}} \times \textbf{Value}_{\text{(internal value structure)}}$$

What would you predict might happen if Andy asked a young lady to the dance and she refuses? Because of the high internal value that Andy places upon going to the dance, and because Andy believes that his success at dating is a result of his efforts, he is likely to continue to make an effort to find a date, until he is successful.

In our dating example, Bruce was shown to have a low degree of motivation. What effect does Bruce's low motivation have on his effort to obtain a date? Because of Bruce's previous failures at dating, he sees little connection between his efforts and dating success. If Bruce is successful in obtaining a date, he is likely to attribute it to luck, desperation on the part of the woman, or other forces outside his control. Therefore, we say that Bruce's expectation of success is based upon an external locus of control. A student with an external locus of control attributes successes or failures to such factors as luck, teachers, parents, or coincidence.

What is the source of Bruce's value? The only reason Bruce may attempt to find a date for the dance is because of the pressure his fraternity brothers are exerting on him. Bruce has an external value structure in regard to the dance. Students who value activities which provide them with opportunities to show their superiority to others, and/or to gain rewards or favors from others, have an external value structure, because these outcomes are generally dependent upon others (Levin and Shanken-Kaye, 1996).

When a student has an external locus of control and an external value structure, he is extrinsically motivated—that is, the motivation comes from outside the individual. Atkinson's formula can be expressed as the following to indicate extrinsic motivation:

$$\mathbf{M}_{\text{(Extrinsic)}} = \textbf{Expectation of Success}_{\text{(external locus of control)}} \times \textbf{Value}_{\text{(external value structure)}}$$

What would you predict might happen if Bruce asked a young lady to the dance and she refuses? Because of the low value that Bruce places upon going to the dance, and because Bruce believes that his meager success at dating is a result of luck or forces outside his control, Bruce is likely to cease making any effort to find a date and will not attend the dance.

Students' locus of control and value structure are greatly influenced by teacher behavior.

Students' locus of control and value structure are greatly influenced by teacher behavior. When teachers communicate to students that success is the result of students' effort or lack of effort, they help students develop an internal locus of control. When teachers communicate to students that the value of any activity is the opportunity it provides for developing new competencies, pursuing one's interests, increasing maturity, and experiencing general personal growth, they are facilitating students' internal value structure. Therefore, these teacher behaviors increase the likelihood that students will develop intrinsic motivation.

When teachers communicate that success is the result of luck, tricks, or other people's behavior, they help students develop an external locus of control. When teachers communicate to students that the value of any activity is the opportunity that it provides for showing superiority or gaining material rewards or praise, they are facilitating students' external value structure. Therefore, these teacher behaviors increase the likelihood that students will develop extrinsic motivation.

The second component of a successful learning environment is intrinsic motivation, which is the product of an internal locus of control and an internal value structure.

The second component of a successful learning environment is intrinsic motivation, which is the product of an internal locus of control and an internal value structure. When students are intrinsically motivated, they are less likely to be disruptive, and they exhibit effort, whether or not the teacher is monitoring them or offering any rewards. The students are less angry or frustrated with the teacher, no matter what the teacher's actions, because they attribute successes and failures to themselves and not to the teacher. In addition, when the intrinsically motivated students meet with outcomes which disappoint them, they probably will try harder to succeed.

Extrinsically motivated students tend to put forth more effort only if the teacher is monitoring them, or they are gaining a specific reward. They may be angry or frustrated with the teacher, because they attribute successes and failures to teacher behavior and not to themselves. Therefore, they are more likely to be disruptive. In addition, when the extrinsically motivated students meet with outcomes which disappoint them, they probably will give up, feign disinterest, or pretend to be successful. The students may do this by making up excuses, saying that the work is stupid, copying homework, or lying about grades.

The Impact of Teacher Authority on Intrinsic Motivation

In Chapter 8, the question was asked *"Which authority base is effective?"* The answer given was, "It depends upon the desired objective." The second objective of a successful learning environment is to create an environment where students are intrinsically motivated, having an internal locus of control and an internal value structure. Which authority base(s) best facilitates student intrinsic motivation?

EXPECTATION OF SUCCESS: INTERNAL LOCUS OF CONTROL

Referent and Expert Authority

A student's expectation of success, which is attributed to an internal locus of control, is best facilitated by the use of teacher behaviors reflecting an expert authority base. A teacher who teaches students study skills, time management, and how to structure material is facilitating student's internal locus of control. In addition, expert teachers facilitate students' internal locus of control when they diagnose learning difficulties, teach to multiple intelligences, provide many opportunities for students to demonstrate their competence, and use other effective instructional techniques.

A student's expectation of success, which is attributed to an internal locus of control, is best facilitated by the use of teacher behaviors reflecting an expert authority base.

A teacher embracing a referent authority base also impacts students' internal locus of control when he communicates confidence in students' capabilities and stresses that success is a function and outcome of student effort.

VALUE: INTERNAL VALUE STRUCTURE

To facilitate students' internal value structure, a teacher needs to design lessons that are relevant, meaningful, and interesting to students, as well as lessons that enable students to pursue personal goals. A referent teacher most likely knows what is relevant and interesting to his students, as well as what personal goals his students wish to attain, because he has developed a relationship with his students previously. Once a teacher knows what is relevant and interesting to students, an expert teacher is in the best position to design and deliver lessons that integrate students' interests, in a manner that enables students to reach their goals.

To facilitate students' internal value structure, a teacher needs to design lessons that are relevant, meaningful, and interesting to students, as well as lessons that enable students to pursue personal goals.

WHAT ABOUT LEGITIMATE AND COERCIVE AUTHORITY?

Teachers embracing a legitimate authority base are unlikely to facilitate their students' internal locus of control or internal value structure, because success and value are typically determined by students meeting certain academic and behavioral criteria that are predetermined by the teacher. Thus by definition, legitimate authority is an external force which facilitates extrinsic motivation.

Teachers who subscribe to coercive authority offer rewards or threaten punishments to students who do or do not meet predetermined criteria. Because the nature and delivery of the rewards or punishments are at the discretion of the teacher, this authority base encourages an external locus of control. Because the student attributes his effort to obtaining the reward or avoiding the punishment, the student is likely to develop an external value structure. For these reasons, teachers embracing coercive authority facilitate extrinsic motivation.

Table 10.2 presents the authority bases as in Table 9.2, including not only the impact on the first component of a successful learning environment, a success/failure ratio greater than one (S/F > 1), but now adding their impact on the second component, intrinsic motivation. Examples of strategies to impact intrinsic motivation are presented in Chapter 14.

TABLE 10.2 ▶ The Impact of Teacher Authority on the Success/Failure Ratio Greater Than One (S/F > 1) and on Intrinsic Motivation

AUTHORITY BASES	**Referent**	**Expert**	**Legitimate**	**Coercive**
ATTRIBUTES	cares, trusts, respects students	has specialized body of knowledge	is sanctioned by society	gives rewards and punishment
MEMBERSHIP	parents spouses best friends	doctors plumbers attorneys	life guards police officers judges	bosses abusive spouses bullies
S/F >1	builds relationships based upon trust, respect, care, and support, which are catalysts for positive outcomes of effective instruction	effective instruction facilitates academic success and also teaches students appropriate behavior	focuses upon teachers' legal authority and title and does not focus upon student success	rewards and punishments have short-term impact, if any, upon student success, does not generalize, loses effectiveness with age
INTRINSIC MOTIVATION **Expectation of Success** (Internal locus of control)	communicates confidence in students' capabilities and that outcomes are the result of students' effort	teaches study skills, time management, and how to structure material, diagnoses learning problems, teaches to multiple intelligences, varies assessment, and takes advantage of current pedagogical advances	by definition, legitimate authority is external, success is students meeting teacher-determined academic and behavioral criteria	by definition coercive authority is external, determined by obtaining rewards, or avoiding punishments
Intrinsic Motivation **Value** (Internal value structure)	knows what interests students and knows their personal goals	captures students' interest through meaningful, relevant instruction	by definition, legitimate authority is external, value is determined by whether or not students value what the teacher values	by definition, coercive authority is external, and value is determined by how much a student desires a particular reward or fears a particular punishment

Where We've Been

We introduced the second component of a successful learning environment, intrinsic motivation. Intrinsic motivation was defined as the product of an expectation of success that is attributed to an internal locus of control and an internal value structure. Students with intrinsic motivation understand that they are largely in control of the factors that determine success. They value the outcomes of their efforts, because they are achieving personal goals, pursuing interests, or developing competence. Referent and expert authority bases were shown to be most effective in positively impacting students' intrinsic motivation.

Where We're Headed

In the next chapter, the third component of a successful learning environment, self-esteem, is explored. The types of self-esteem, the components of self-esteem, the impact on student behavior, and the authority base(s) that most positively impact self-esteem are described.

CHAPTER 10 CONCEPT MAP

MOTIVATION

Types	Student Outcomes	Implications	Challenge
INTRINSIC	Expectation of success is attributed to factors within students' control, such as effort, time management, and study skills. (Internal Locus of Control) Effort is a result of the personalvalue of the outcomes, such as the development of competence and the pursuit of interest. (Internal Value Structure)	Students learn that success is a result of effort and that the value of learning is to develop competence. Therefore, intrinsic motivation generalizes to other situations and is a long-term strategy.	
EXTRINSIC	Expectation of success is attributed to factors outside the students' control, such as luck or an easy test. (External Locus of Control) Effort is a result of the value others place on the outcomes or competition, due to the participation of others, such as rewards or showing superiority. (External Value Structure)	Students learn that success is a result of luck or other factors outside their control. Others determine the value of learning. Therefore, motivation is not dependent on personal effort, does not generalize to other situations, and is not a long-term strategy.	How can schools replace the rewards and punishments now typically used to motivate students, by instilling in students that success is dependent upon their efforts, and the value of learning is to develop personal competence?

	Referent	Expert
Expectation of Success **Internal Locus of Control** (successes are a result of students' efforts, time, and discipline)	maintains high expectations, trust, respect, and support	teaches self-control and study skills
Value **Internal Value Structure** (the outcomes are important to students)	knows students' interests	designs and delivers relevant, meaningful, interesting, clear instruction

? QUESTIONS FOR THE STUDY TEAM

1. What are the major differences between operant conditioning and social cognitive theories of motivation concerning what motivates students and who controls the motivation?

2. How does a S/F > 1 impact the components of intrinsic motivation?

3. Why does a S/F > 1 influence a cycle of high motivation?

4. Why does a S/F < 1 influence a cycle of low motivation?

5. Why does a student with a S/F > 1 usually have a more stable degree of motivation than a student with a S/F < 1?

6. How can teachers impact students' attributions for success through students' internal loci of control?

7. How can teachers impact students' value through students' internal value structures?

8. What traditional classroom practices encourage students' extrinsic motivation (external locus of control, external value structure)?

9. One rationale for students' academic effort is to learn. Learning is also an internal value structure and thus intrinsic motivation is being facilitated. However, schools are now placing so much emphasis on standards and assessment, which are extrinsic motivators. How can teachers reconcile this conflict?

10. Are students with special needs, who have limited cognitive abilities, capable of being intrinsically motivated?

11. How does a teacher begin to facilitate students' intrinsic motivation when their parents always use extrinsic incentives at home?

12. Since our society is so extrinsically motivated, aren't teachers doing students a disservice when they attempt to facilitate their intrinsic motivation?

13. Why are the referent and expert authority bases congruent with the goal of increasing students' intrinsic motivation?

14. Why are the legitimate and coercive authority bases incongruent with the goal of increasing students' intrinsic motivation?

CHAPTER 11

Successful Learning Environment: Self-Esteem

"When young people see no hope to rise within mainstream society, they may create their own hierarchical gang cultures that provide them with opportunities to succeed within their counter-culture's mores. Those among successful people in mainstream society who decry gang symbols and exclusionary turf areas should look to the high-status symbols they use to flaunt their success and to their exclusionary golf courses and walled communities. People in both mainstream cultures and countercultures have the same biological need to succeed; they all need a positive self-concept and self-esteem." (Sylwester, 1997)

A Day in the Life of a Juvenile Disrupter

Charlene is a seventeen-year-old student in eleventh grade. Her friends generally are students who do not like school. Charlene and her friends do not participate in school or community activities. Charlene has been arrested and charged with breaking and entering, receiving stolen goods, and possession with intent to distribute. She and a friend were accused of breaking into a neighbor's house, stealing property, and selling the property in order to buy drugs. Charlene is appearing in juvenile court for the first time. As is the case in most juvenile proceedings, Charlene's hearing is non-adversarial, because Charlene had admitted to committing the offenses.

The juvenile court judge is a well respected but stern jurist. Before sentencing Charlene, the judge asked her, "Young woman, why did you do this?" Charlene answers honestly. "It was a Friday night and my friends and I were sitting around with nothing to do. Everyone wanted to get high but no one had any money. I knew my neighbor was away for the weekend. I also knew where his stereo and laptop computer were. I broke into the house, stole the stuff, drove downtown, and sold it on the street. I then bought some "E" and we all got high."

Do you think Charlene's self-esteem is high or low? What grades do you think Charlene earns in school?

A Day in the Life of a Juvenile Achiever

Margo is a seventeen-year-old eleventh grader. Her friends typically enjoy school. Margo is a member of the track team, and she volunteers a few hours a week at the Humane Society. On the same Friday night that Charlene and her friends were breaking into a neighbor's house, Margo and her friends were also bored and looking for something to do. Being a competent skater, Margo suggested that they all go to the skate park to use the ramps. Her friends liked the idea, but some of them said they couldn't go because they did not have any money. Margo had some extra money from her part-time job and agreed to lend it to her friends.

Do you think Margo's self-esteem is high or low? What grades do you think that Margo earns in school?

The Nature of Self-Esteem

In order to accurately answer the questions concerning Charlene and Margo's self-esteem and grades, it is necessary to define self-esteem. Self-esteem (SE) may be conceptualized as a sum of four factors:

- Significance (S)
- Competence (C)
- Virtue (V)
- Power (P)

Expressing self-esteem as an equation, we arrive at

SE = S + C + V + P (Coopersmith 1967).

- Significance (S) is a person's belief that she is respected, liked, and trusted by people who are important to her. This does not mean merely that some people like her, rather that people she wants to like her, do in fact like her.
- Competence (C) is a person's sense of mastery of tasks that she values. This does not mean she is good at any tasks, but that she is good at tasks which matter to her. For instance, she may be a great cello player, which her teachers and parents value. However, if that is not important to her, she will not feel an increased sense of competence.
- Virtue (V) is a person's perceived feeling of worthiness as a result of her ability and willingness to help others.
- Power (P) is a person's perception that she exerts control over important aspects of her environment. She believes that she can plan and take actions that result in predictable and desirable outcomes.

Let us assume for a moment that self-esteem (SE = S + C + V + P) is a constant. Remembering your elementary algebra, if one of the variables, (S, C, V, or P) is reduced, another variable must be raised in order to maintain the constant value of self-esteem. For the average student, this presents little difficulty. The average student, with a success/failure ratio > 1, has many opportunities in her life for successful experiences (See Table 9.1). If her social life temporarily suffers (significance), she takes solace in her skills in athletics (competence). If she has a bad day on the playing field, she might be in a faith-based organization and doing a collection of clothing for needy children (virtue). If she is not satisfied with some aspect of her life, she knows that she can go to her parents or teachers and make arrangements or get advice in order to change some condition or get additional help (power, significance). The average student, in short, has resources which can help her to maintain a healthy and positive feeling about herself. Teachers describe this student as having high self-esteem.

But what about the student who exhibits chronically disruptive behavior, the one with a S/F < 1? Is this the student whom the majority of other students, those with a S/F > 1, seek out to be with? No, not usually. Is this the student most often invited to friends' houses and parties? Does she receive lots of Valentine Day cards? Again, not usually. We have found repeatedly that these students are not, in general, very popular with the majority of their classmates. Thus these students' sense of significance probably will be low.

Most students who pose difficult behavioral problems struggle with academics, the very area that the majority of adults consider the most important thing in students' lives, and which students themselves value highly, especially early in their schooling. For these students, feelings of competency also suffer along with significance.

Keep in mind the summative nature of self-esteem. Therefore, the remaining variables, virtue and power, need to be higher to offset the deficits of significance and competence. As to virtue, unfortunately students with chronic behavioral difficulties are seldom requested to help others. In addition, many of these students are perceived by others to be self-absorbed. They often appear to have little knowledge or interest in the larger community, whether that is the family, the classroom, or society. Therefore, students with chronic behavioral difficulties have fewer opportunities to increase their virtue.

Power is the last variable. The student with chronic behavioral difficulties, due to repeated negative interactions with adults, may not feel that she can go to her parents, other caregivers, or teachers and make arrangements or seek advice to change some condition or get additional help. Therefore, students with chronic behavioral difficulties have fewer opportunities to increase their power.

The student who exhibits chronic behavioral difficulties has reduced levels of significance, competence, virtue, and power. Using the self-esteem equation, $SE = S + C + V + P$, it is assumed that this student has lower self-esteem. However, for students who exhibit chronic behavioral difficulties, this assumption may not be correct.

Pro-Social and Distorted Self-Esteem

Research indicates that children who exhibit disruptive and delinquent behavior often have similar levels of self-esteem as children who do not exhibit these behaviors, as measured by standardized instruments (Kaplan 1976, 1980). Anecdotal reports from the classroom support these findings. Is it your experience that your students who exhibit the most disruptive and challenging behaviors are withdrawn, ashamed, and powerless?

Now we are able to answer the first question about Charlene and Margo. Do they have high or low self-esteem? It is apparent that Charlene has a group of friends that like her and trust her; therefore Charlene has a high degree of significance. Charlene knows how to break into houses, fence stolen goods, and where to buy drugs. Isn't this competence? Charlene's friends were all bored. Charlene wanted to help them out. Charlene felt virtuous. Finally, Charlene made a plan, carried it out, and until she got busted, changed the evening from being a drag to having some fun. Charlene was powerful. Therefore, Charlene had feelings of significance, competence, virtue, and power. Charlene had high self-esteem.

Margo's friends also liked her and trusted her. Margo had a high degree of significance. Margo gained a sense of competence by being on the track team and also being a talented skater. Her volunteer work at the Humane Society and her willingness to lend her money to her friends contributed to her sense of virtue. Margo's suggestion to spend the night at the skate park and her ability to lend her friends money as a result of a part-time job, made her feel powerful. Margo also has high self-esteem.

Self-esteem typically is measured as a dichotomous variable, either high or low. However, the authors believe that there are at least two types of self-esteem, pro-social and distorted (Brendtro et al, 1990). Each type of self-esteem and its terms exist along a continuum from high to low. For instance, we have stated that the student who exhibits chronic disruptive behavior lacks power. Many teachers point out, however, that these kids have too much power. They disrupt the class, interrupt learning, and sometimes even make the teacher ill. Isn't that power? Indeed it is. This is an example of distorted power.

If students cannot achieve self-esteem in ways that are pro-social or acceptable to society, they achieve self-esteem in anti-social ways or ways that are unacceptable to society.

Self-esteem is a basic human need (Maslow, 1968). If students cannot achieve self-esteem in ways that are pro-social or acceptable to society, they achieve self-esteem in anti-social ways or ways that are unacceptable to society. This type of self-esteem is called distorted self-esteem.

If we as parents and teachers do not like, respect, and trust students, so that there is an increased probability that students might like, respect, and trust us, then we make it more likely that they will turn to whoever gives them positive regard. A sense of significance may be achieved, not only by being a class officer or everyone's favorite confidant, but also by membership in gangs or cults, sexual promiscuity, or embracing the drug culture.

If students are not encouraged to value and master pro-social competencies, they are likely to value and master distorted competencies.

If students are not encouraged to value and master pro-social competencies, they are likely to value and master distorted competencies. For instance, a sense of competence may be achieved not only in the classroom or athletic field, but it may also develop from being the best joint roller in the group, having the most sexual encounters in a day, or knowing how to pick locks or steal cars.

If pro-social expressions of virtue are denied to students, they seek out opportunities to feel worthy in less desirable ways. While pro-social virtue may be achieved by volunteering at the hospital, shoveling a neighbor's walk of snow, or helping another student with homework, distorted virtue may be achieved by lying to protect others, supplying your buddies with drugs, or being a "lookout." Pro-social power may be exerted by additional study to improve grades or by developing healthy eating and exercise routines to improve fitness and appearance. Distorted power may be exercised by cheating to improve grades or bullying and coercing classmates.

Therefore, the third component of a successful learning environment is not merely self-esteem, but pro-social self-esteem. Pro-social self-esteem is the sum of pro-social significance, pro-social competence, pro-social virtue, and pro-social power. When students possess pro-social self-esteem, like Margo, they feel significant, competent, virtuous, and powerful in ways that are congruent with the values held by the majority of people in a democratic society. Students with pro-social self-esteem are well on their way to becoming productive, accountable members of the school community. They seek out opportunities to interact positively with students and teachers. They strive to achieve. They willingly help other classmates and teachers, and they understand that they have the ability to set and meet personal goals.

When students possess distorted self-esteem, like Charlene, they feel significant, competent, virtuous, and powerful in ways that are not congruent with the values held by the majority of people in a democratic society. Students with distorted self-esteem are well on their way to behavioral and academic problems.

- Rather than seeking out opportunities to interact positively with other students and teachers, they often use intimidation to demean other students and teachers.
- Rather than striving to achieve academically or extracurricularly, they are likely to strive to achieve in ways that violate classroom, school, and community norms.
- Rather than willingly help classmates and teachers, they often hold themselves aloof.

Students with distorted self-esteem may understand that they have the ability to set and meet personal goals. However these goals are likely to involve anti-social and perhaps criminal behavior.

The third component of a successful learning environment is not merely self-esteem, but pro-social self-esteem. Pro-social self-esteem is the sum of pro-social significance, pro-social competence, pro-social virtue and pro-social power.

The Impact of Teacher Authority on Pro-Social Self-Esteem

The third objective of a successful learning environment is to facilitate the development of pro-social self-esteem in students, that is self-esteem based upon pro-social significance, competence, virtue, and power. Which authority base(s) best facilitates the development of pro-social self-esteem?

Students with distorted self-esteem are well on their way to behavioral and academic problems.

SIGNIFICANCE

Referent and Expert Authority

The development of pro-social significance in students is fostered by teacher behavior that communicates to students that they are trusted, respected, cared about, and supported. This is behavior associated with referent authority. Expert authority impacts pro-social significance, because teachers view each student as an individual with unique needs and talents. Teachers practicing expert authority consider individual student needs when designing and delivering instruction. They also consider individual student needs and challenges when attempting to understand disruptive behavior and intervene effectively.

What about Legitimate and Coercive Authority?

Teachers who embrace the legitimate authority base are less likely to facilitate pro-social significance. Individual student academic and behavioral needs and challenges are less likely to be important considerations to these teachers when they design and deliver instruction or intervene when a discipline problem occurs. One reason this is so is because legitimate authority often is a "one size fits all approach," where the teacher has predetermined academic and behavioral expectations and is unlikely to deviate from them in order to accommodate individual student needs, differences, or challenges. The usual message to students given by teachers whose philosophy is one of legitimate authority is the following: "This is my classroom, I'm the person in charge. This is how you will behave, and this is what and how you will learn." It is often a zero tolerance approach to both learning and behavior. Therefore, students in a classroom of a teacher who relies upon legitimate authority are less likely to feel trusted, respected, cared about, and supported.

Teachers who subscribe to coercive authority use rewards and punishments in an attempt to increase academic success and to decrease discipline problems. Because of the mechanistic nature of applying rewards and punishments, ignoring individual needs, differences, and challenges, as well as other limitations of rewards and punishments (See Chapters 16 and 17), students are less likely to feel a sense of pro-social significance in classrooms run by teachers who practice coercive authority.

COMPETENCE

Referent and Expert Authority

Students in classrooms with expert professionals are more likely to experience academic success that leads to the development of pro-social competence.

Teachers who believe in referent authority promote pro-social competence, as students are more likely to take personal risks to achieve academically or change their behaviors when they can rely on the trust and respect of their teachers, regardless of the outcomes of their efforts. There is a saying which we mentioned before with which many teachers are familiar that sums up the impact of referent authority on students' pro-social competence: "I don't care how much you know, till I know how much you care."

The essence of expert authority is the use of the best professional practices with respect to effective pedagogy. Therefore, students in classrooms with expert professionals are more likely to experience academic success that leads to the development of pro-social competence. In addition, when instruction is interesting, relevant, and considers the learning styles of individual students, there is a much greater likelihood that students will be engaged in learning and not engaged in disruptive behavior. All of the strategies these teachers use to enhance students' intrinsic motivation also increase the likelihood that students will gain a sense of pro-social competence. When students are intrinsically motivated, they put more effort towards a task, which increases the probability that they will be successful. These repeated successes increase the sense of pro-social competence.

What about Legitimate and Coercive Authority?

Teachers who embrace legitimate authority typically have very structured classrooms where there are strict routines and schedules. Admittedly, structure is important for students' learning to occur. However, there is a difference between the manner in which teachers embracing referent and expert authority provide structure and the manner in which teachers embracing legitimate authority provide structure. Teachers embracing referent and expert authority are more likely to consider both the cognitive and affective needs of their individual students with resultant flexibility in their approaches. While teachers adhering to legitimate authority are more likely to embrace an external, rigid, and idealized notion of achievement and behavior that is more reflective of group norms than the individual. These teachers are frequently at a loss when confronted with either groups of students or individual students who exhibit challenging academic or behavioral problems. This increases the possibility that only those students who "fit the mold" are likely to experience success and a feeling of competence. When the well-developed plans of teachers adhering to legitimate authority are frustrated by unique learning and behavioral challenges, they often resort to coercive authority.

Teachers who rely upon coercive authority primarily shape academics and behavior using rewards and punishments. If students achieve at certain levels and behave appropriately, they are rewarded. If students do not, then they are punished (the denial of a reward is in itself a form of punishment). Students who consistently are rewarded may feel successful and develop a sense of pro-social competence. This, however, is not the case for the majority of students, because of the major limitations of the use of coercive authority in the classroom. These limitations include the erosion of intrinsic motivation and the dependency upon extrinsic motivation (See Chapter 10), the general lack of focus upon the individual's efforts and improvements, ineffectiveness as students get older, the lack of generalization to other situations, a decrease in cooperation, and an increase in competition among students. In addition, it is obvious that punishment does not lead to success or feelings of competence. In general, punishment causes students to avoid interacting with punitive teachers, thus reducing opportunities that the teacher has to assist students in developing competence and significance. Punishment also tends to focus students' attention on the punisher, rather than on what students can do to develop competence. Students become angry when punished, which also interferes with the development of competence and significance. A detailed exploration of the difficulties and alternatives to rewards and punishments is found in Chapters 16 and 17.

VIRTUE

Referent and Expert Authority

Student virtue is influenced positively by teachers practicing referent authority. These teachers continually model voluntary efforts that are intended to help individual students, other teachers, the school, and the community at large. Teachers who continually support, respect, and trust their students, as students struggle to overcome academic and behavior challenges, exemplify virtuous behavior. These teachers facilitate the development of pro-social virtue in students by "living it" or "walking the talk."

Teachers embracing expert authority design real and meaningful opportunities for all students to engage in virtuous behaviors. Examples include peer tutoring, meaningful jobs in the classroom and school, authentic opportunities to assist the teacher in instruction, opportunities to tutor younger students, and voluntary planning and participation in community service projects. Teachers practicing expert authority recognize that giving students these opportunities develops strong and inclusive communities of learners, a prerequisite to maximizing learning and to the development of students' pro-social virtue.

What about Legitimate and Coercive Authority?

Because teachers believing primarily in legitimate authority make it clear that it is their classroom, with their objectives and rules, it is less likely that students feel that they are a meaningful part of an inclusive cooperative community. In addition, for reasons stated above, these teachers are less likely to foster students' sense of significance. In classrooms where students do not feel that they belong to an inclusive, cooperative community, and where students do not feel a sense of pro-social significance, they are less likely to develop pro-social virtuous behavior. Because teachers embracing legitimate authority are likely to adhere to more rigid instructional methodology, opportunities for virtuous behavior from students are less likely to be integrated into instructional activities.

In a classroom where coercive authority is employed, the attributions that students most often give for their behavior is to obtain rewards or to avoid punishment. There are three major reasons why such attributions do not facilitate students' pro-social virtue.

- First, if students are offered a reward for helping others, they attribute their behavior to a desire for the reward, not to feeling good for helping. Therefore, the likelihood of future displays of pro-social virtue depends upon what future external rewards are offered.
- Second, the use of rewards for grades or behavior fosters competition and reduces cooperation (Kohn, 1999), which is a prerequisite for pro-social virtue.
- Third, due to the emotional effects of punishment, when students are either punished or threatened with punishment, they are unlikely to want to help anyone.

POWER

Referent and Expert Authority

Teachers adopting referent authority impact students' pro-social power by communicating to students that they will be trusted and indeed expected to make appropriate choices concerning classroom procedures and guidelines, as well as academics and behavior. When students understand that they have meaningful choices, they experience a sense of pro-social power.

These teachers design opportunities for students to use their power in pro-social ways. These opportunities include the consensual design of classroom guidelines, allowing students choices of assignments and learning activities, provision for student feedback to the teacher on how to improve learning and teaching, and the development by each student of a set of personal learning goals. Teachers adopting expert authority are in an excellent position to positively impact students' pro-social competence. Whenever competence is increased, so is power, because the more competent the individual, the more she can plan and take actions that result in predictable and desirable outcomes.

What about Legitimate and Coercive Authority?

Legitimate and coercive authority essentially places all meaningful opportunities for power in the hands of the teacher. Because self-esteem is a sum of four factors and a basic human need, if one factor, power, is decreased, then the other factors must be raised to compensate for this decrease. For all the reasons stated above, teachers using primarily legitimate and coercive authority are not in the best position to help students develop pro-social significance, competence, or virtue. Students who are in classrooms run by these teachers are therefore more likely to obtain their self-esteem through distorted, rather than pro-social means. This phenomenon helps explain our experience that teachers primarily using legitimate and coercive authority are more often confronted with serious discipline problems and lower levels of academic achievement and cooperation in the classroom, especially in the upper grades.

Table 11.1 presents the impact of the authority bases upon all three components of a successful learning environment: success/failure >1, intrinsic motivation, and finally pro-social self-esteem.

TABLE 11.1 ▶ The Impact of Teacher Authority on S/F > 1, Intrinsic Motivation, and Pro-Social Self-Esteem

AUTHORITY BASES	Referent	Expert	Legitimate	Coercive
ATTRIBUTES	cares, trusts, respects students	has specialized body of knowledge	is sanctioned by society	gives rewards and punishment
MEMBERSHIP	parents spouses best friends	doctors plumbers attorneys	life guards police officers judges	bosses abusive spouses bullies
S/F >1	builds relationships based upon trust, respect, care, and support, which are catalysts for positive outcomes of effective instruction	effective instruction facilitates academic success and also teaches students appropriate behavior	focuses upon teachers' legal authority and title and does not focus upon student success	rewards and punishments have short-term impact, if any, upon student success, does not generalize, loses effectiveness with age
INTRINSIC MOTIVATION **Expectation of Success** (Internal locus of control)	communicates confidence in students' capabilities and that outcomes are the result of students' effort.	teaches study skills, time management, and how to structure material, diagnoses learning problems, teaches to multiple intelligences, varies assessment, and takes advantage of current pedagogical advances	by definition, legitimate authority is external, success is students meeting teacher-determined academic and behavioral criteria	by definition, coercive authority is external, determined by obtaining rewards, or avoiding punishments
Intrinsic Motivation **Value** (Internal value structure)	knows what interests students and knows their personal goals	captures students' interest through meaningful, relevant instruction	by definition, legitimate authority is external, value is determined by whether or not students value what the teacher values	by definition, coercive authority is external, and value is determined by how much a student desires a particular reward or fears a particular punishment

(continued)

TABLE 11.1 ▶ The Impact of Teacher Authority on S/F > 1, Intrinsic Motivation and Pro-Social Self-Esteem, *continued*

AUTHORITY BASES	Referent	Expert	Legitimate	Coercive
Pro-Social Self-Esteem **Significance**	communicates to students trust, respect, care, and support	considers students' needs and challenges concerning both academic and behavioral expectations	a "one size fits all" approach, does not consider students' needs, differences or challenges	because of the mechanistic nature of rewards and punishments, students' needs, differences, or challenges are not considered
Competence	relationship encourages students to take academic risks.	uses effective instructional methodology (see success/failure ratio and motivation)	more likely to embrace an external, rigid, and idealized notion of achievement and behavior that is more reflective of group norms than the individual	only those rewarded are likely to feel competent, while those that are punished are more likely to feel anger than competence
Virtue	teacher models voluntary assistance to students, other teachers, and community at large	builds communities of learners and provides meaningful opportunity for students to engage in helpful behaviors	students are less likely to feel that they are a meaningful part of an inclusive learning community, therefore they are less likely to want to help others	rewards and punishments provide reasons other than virtue as to why students should help each other, in addition to fostering competition and reducing cooperation
Power	students are trusted and encouraged to make appropriate choices regarding academics, classroom guidelines, and procedures	provides the opportunity for students to participate in the consensual development of classroom guidelines and other meaningful student choices	all meaningful opportunity for power is in the hands of the teacher	all meaningful opportunity for power is in the hands of the teacher

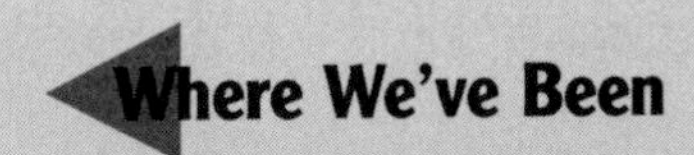

Where We've Been

The second component of a successful learning environment is pro-social self-esteem. Pro-social self-esteem was defined as the sum of pro-social significance, pro-social competence, pro-social virtue, and pro-social power. Students with pro-social significance feel trusted, respected, cared about, and supported by their peers, who are active members of the school community, teachers, and other meaningful adults. Students who have a sense of pro-social competence are successful in academics and/or extracurricular activities. Students who display pro-social virtue obtain satisfaction by helping others in the classroom, school, and community. Students exhibit pro-social power when they recognize that they have control over many aspects of their academic and social life, and in fact make appropriate choices that increase their likelihood of success. The referent and expert authority bases were shown to be those most effective in positively impacting students' pro-social self-esteem.

Where We're Headed

In Chapter 12 we present The Professional Decision Making Matrix. The matrix is a graphic illustration of the Self-Control Classroom model that depicts the interaction of the authority bases with the components of a successful learning environment.

CHAPTER 11 CONCEPT MAP

SELF-ESTEEM

TYPES	STUDENT OUTCOMES	IMPLICATIONS	CHALLENGE
PRO-SOCIAL	Pro-Social Significance	Students feel good about being trusted and respected by teachers, parents, and other students who achieve and behave appropriately.	
	Pro-Social Competence	being successful at socially acceptable pursuits, such as academics, athletics, hobbies	
	Pro-Social Virtue	volunteering to assist other students and/ or participating in community service	
	Pro-Social Power	setting socially acceptable personal goals and developing plans of action to meet the goals	
DISTORTED	Distorted Significance	Students feel good about being trusted and respected by other students who do not achieve or behave appropriately.	How can schools respect and trust students who have a history of academic failure, behavior problems, and delinquency?
	Distorted Competence	being successful at socially unacceptable pursuits, such as disrupting class or other delinquent activities	How can schools create interest and increase the likelihood of success in socially acceptable activities for those students who have a history of academic failure, behavior problems, and delinquency?
	Distorted Virtue	assisting other students in socially unacceptable pursuits, such as disruptive or delinquent activities	How can schools instill a willingness and desire to assist other students and participate in community service for those students who have a history of academic failure, behavior problems, and delinquency?
	Distorted Power	creating fear in other students, resisting the teacher, or getting away with illegal activities	How can schools encourage the setting of socially acceptable goals and the development of plans of action to meet the goals for those students who have a history of academic failure, behavior problems, and delinquency?

	Significance (students are liked, trusted, respected, and supported by people important to them)	**Competence** (students feel competent in areas that are important to them)	**Virtue** (students feel good as a result of and willingness to help others)	**Power** (students feel that they exert some degree of control over important aspects of their environment)
Referent	communicates to students trust, respect, care, support	relationship encourages students to take academic risks	teacher models virtuous behavior	students are trusted and respected to make appropriate choices regarding the classroom logistics and activities
Expert	individualized instruction	effective instructional methodology	builds community of learners and uses cooperative education practices	designs parallel assessments and activities to provide choices to students, and involves students in consensually designing classroom guidelines

? Questions for the Study Team

1. Why is it that many disruptive, delinquent students have similar levels of high self-esteem to non-disruptive, non-delinquent students?

2. Do students who come to class, refuse to work, interact with no other students, but are not disruptive, have distorted or pro-social self-esteem?

3. Do students with distorted self-esteem really feel good about themselves, or are they just pretending to feel good?

4. What are some ways that students obtain:

   Distorted significance

   Distorted competence

   Distorted virtue

   Distorted power

5. How does a success/failure ratio greater than one (S/F > 1) impact the components of pro-social self-esteem?

6. How does an internal locus of control impact the components of pro-social self-esteem?

7. How does an internal value structure impact the components of pro-social self-esteem?

8. Why do students begin to develop distorted self-esteem?

9. Why does the use of legitimate and coercive authority increase the possibility that students will use distorted means to obtain their self-esteem?

10. Why are the referent and expert authority bases congruent with the goal of facilitating students' pro-social self-esteem?

11. Why are the legitimate and coercive authority bases incongruent with the goal of facilitating pro-social self-esteem?

CHAPTER 12

The Professional Decision Making Matrix

"Research shows that parents lodge responsibility first with the school, second with the child, and third with themselves. In contrast, school personnel blame problems first on the home, then on the child, and last on the school. Such contests about problem ownership only intensifies the alienation of families and children at risk." (Brendtro et al, 1990)

Which Authority Base(s) Is Appropriate and Effective?

In Chapters 8–11, the nature of authority and the components of a successful learning environment were defined and analyzed. We are now ready to answer the question posed at the end of Chapter 8, "Which authority base(s) should teachers use?" Which authority bases prevent disruptive and delinquent behavior by positively impacting students' success failure ratio > 1 and encouraging intrinsic motivation and pro-social self-esteem, in order to ensure a successful learning environment? Chapters 9, 10, and 11 demonstrate how each of the four authority bases impacts the three components of a successful learning environment. Table 11.1 illustrates that referent and expert authority most positively impact the components of a successful learning environment.

The teacher's approach to understanding and intervening with challenging academic and behavioral problems is governed by his underlying philosophy of authority with regard to how one best influences students.

It is important to reiterate that every teacher, regardless of which primary authority base he embraces, usually uses strategies from all four bases. However, the teacher's approach to understanding and intervening with challenging academic and behavioral problems is governed by his underlying philosophy of authority with regard to how one best influences students. The teacher who believes in referent authority approaches academic and behavioral challenges by examining the relationships that students have with teachers and peers. The teacher who believes in expert authority examines the learning and teaching environment that students experience. The teacher who believes in legitimate authority focuses upon rules, guidelines, and the appropriate roles of the students and the teacher. Believers of coercive authority emphasize the adjustments of behavioral contingencies—that is, rewards and punishments for students.

The Matrix

The Professional Decision Making Matrix integrates the authority bases with the three components of a successful learning environment in a format that has practical value for classroom practice. This is illustrated in Figure 12.1.

EXPLANATION OF THE PROFESSIONAL DECISION MAKING MATRIX

Referring to Figure 12.1, the four authority bases are listed along the left column. Across the top are three learner objectives: success/failure ratio, motivation, and self-esteem. Under each learning objective are the possible outcomes for students.

Success/failure ratio is either greater than one, >1, or less than one, <1.

Motivation is the expectation of success multiplied by value. The expectation of success involves either an internal locus of control (I.L.C) or an external locus of control (E.L.C.). Value is either due to an internal value structure (I.V.S.) or an external value structure (E.V.S.).

Self-esteem is comprised of significance, competence, virtue, and power. These outcomes can be either pro-social (PS) or distorted (D).

The reader will note that only certain cells are shaded. The cells that are shaded are all on the two rows of referent and expert authority. These are:

1. success/failure ratio greater than one (S/F > 1),
2. an internal locus of control (I.L.C) and internal value structure (I.V.S.), which is intrinsic motivation, and
3. pro-social significance (S_{PS}), competence (C_{PS}), virtue (V_{PS}), and power (P_{PS}), which is pro-social self-esteem.

The shaded cells together are a graphic representation of the vision of the Self-Control Classroom model: the prevention of disruptive behavior through the creation of successful learning environments.

Where We've Been

In this chapter, the question "Which authority base(s) should teachers use?" was answered. Referent and expert authority are the most appropriate if teachers desire to prevent disruptive behavior by impacting student success/failure ratio > 1, intrinsic motivation, and pro-social self-esteem. The shaded cells of the Professional Decision Making Matrix, is a graphic representation of the answer to the question "Which authority base(s) should teachers use?", if they strive to create successful learning environments for all students. This chapter completes the section Establishing Successful Learning Environments.

Where We're Headed

Chapter 13 starts a new section, Maintaining Successful Learning Environments. Readers will learn how to maintain successful learning environments. This will include designing strategies to impact students' success/failure ratio, intrinsic motivation, and pro-social self-esteem. In addition, the Professional Decision Making Matrix will be used to diagnose behavioral problems and to analyze and design interventions that are congruent with the Self-Control Classroom model. The section concludes with an exploration of the limitations of rewards and punishments and their alternatives, encouragement and consequences.

CHAPTER 12 CONCEPT MAP

Figure 12.1 serves as the concept map for this chapter.

PROFESSIONAL DECISION MAKING MATRIX

		Components of a Successful Learning Environment														
		Success/Failure Ratio		Motivation				Self-Esteem								
		>1	**<1**	**I.L.C**	**E.L.C**	**I.V.S**	**E.V.S**	**S_{PS}**	**S_D**	**C_{PS}**	**C_D**	**V_{PS}**	**V_D**	**P_{PS}**	**P_D**
Authority Base	**Referent**															
	Expert															
	Legitimate															
	Coercive															

Key:

Motivation:
I.L.C. = internal locus of control
E.L.C. = external locus of control
I.V.S. = internal value structure
E.V.S. = external value structure

Self-Esteem:
S_{PS} = significance pro-social
S_D = significance distorted
C_{PS} = competence pro-social
C_D = competence distorted
V_{PS} = virtue pro-social
V_D = virtue distorted
P_{PS} = power pro-social
P_D = power distorted

FIGURE 12.1 ▶ The Professional Decision Making Matrix

QUESTIONS FOR THE STUDY TEAM

1. For each authority base what would be the belief of the teacher regarding how they influence students?

   a. Referent

   b. Expert

   c. Legitimate

   d. Coercive

2. In order to effectively communicate the vision of the Self-Control Classroom model to parents and other non-educational stakeholders, what are common terms that teachers can use to describe the variables included in the Professional Decision Making Matrix?

   a. Referent Authority

   b. Expert Authority

   c. Legitimate Authority

   d. Coercive Authority

   e. $S/F < 1$

   f. $E_{(I.L.C)}$: Expectation of Success due to an Internal Locus of Control

   g. $E_{(E.L.C)}$: Expectation of Success due to an External Locus of Control

   h. $V_{(I.V.S)}$: Value due to an Internal Value Structure

   i. $V_{(E.V.S)}$: Value due to an External Value Structure

   j. $S_{(P.S)}$: Significant Pro-Social

k. $S_{(D)}$: Significant Distorted

l. $C_{(P.S)}$: Competence Pro-Social

m. $C_{(D)}$: Competence Distorted

n. $V_{(P.S)}$: Virtue Pro-Social

o. $V_{(D)}$: Virtue Distorted

p. $P_{(P.S)}$: Power Pro-Social

q. $P_{(D)}$: Power Distorted

SECTION 4

Maintaining Successful Learning Environments

This section focuses on the behavior of classroom teachers and how their behavior can positively impact a student's success/failure ratio, intrinsic motivation, and pro-social self-esteem.

In Chapter 1, the vision statement for the Self-Control Classroom model was presented. Emphasized within the statement was that the model "helps to prevent disruptive, delinquent, and violent behavior . . ." and that prevention is facilitated "when students experience successful learning environments." In Chapter 3, the philosophy "If you know the whys, you can develop the hows" was introduced. It was further explained that the whys refer to a working understanding of a professional knowledge base regarding child development, cognitive psychology, and pedagogy. The hows refer to teachers using their professional knowledge base (the whys) as a basis for changing their behavior, in order to establish and maintain successful learning environments.

Section 3, "Establishing Successful Learning Environments," thoroughly explained the nature and use of teacher authority and the three components of a successful learning environment: a success/failure ratio > 1 (S/F > 1), intrinsic motivation, and pro-social self-esteem. In addition, each authority base was examined for its impact on the components of a successful learning environment.

Up until this section, we have attempted to provide the reader with the whys. Now it is time to consider the hows, in other words, the teacher behaviors in the classroom which are likely to have a positive impact on students' success/failure ratios, intrinsic motivation, and pro-social self-esteem. There is a large body of research which supports the prevention of discipline problems through focusing on the design of successful learning environments congruent with the Self-Control Classroom model. "Research findings converge on the conclusion that teachers who approach classroom management as a process of establishing and maintaining effective learning environments (referent and expert authority) tend to be more successful than teachers who place more emphasis on their roles as authority figures (legitimate authority) or disciplinarians (coercive authority)" (Brophy, 1988a, p.1).

This section presents some of the hows, the strategies which teachers can employ to impact success/failure ratio (Chapter13), intrinsic motivation (Chapter 14), and pro-social self-esteem (Chapter 15). In addition, teachers will have a greater understanding of how to design strategies to impact the components of a successful learning environment.

The section concludes in Chapters 16 and 17, with an exploration of the limitations of rewards and punishments, and how they erode successful learning environments. Encouragement and consequences are explored as alternatives which facilitate successful learning environments.

CHAPTER 13

If You Understand the Whys, You Can Design the Hows: Positively Impacting Student Success/Failure >1

"I learned long ago in my own classroom that if I treat kids like hoodlums and thugs they will rarely disappoint, but if I treat them as scholars and ethicists valued and valuable, they can just as easily stretch and grow into people of value." (Ayers, 1997)

As explained in Chapters 9 and 10, both expert and referent authority may be used to positively impact student success and therefore increase the success failure ratio. The use of referent authority impacts student success by creating an atmosphere of respect, trust, care, and support in the classroom. The use of expert authority impacts student success through the use of effective instructional methodologies. Since the primary positive impact upon student academic success is through the expert use of effective instruction, that is the emphasis of this chapter.

Effective Instruction

Although it is beyond the scope of this book to provide an exhaustive review of effective instruction, this chapter serves as an introduction. A common concern voiced by many educators is, "how can we be sure if we are using effective instruction?" Fortunately, the teaching profession has a rich body of research that delineates the best professional practices. Therefore, our teaching behaviors may be compared to and contrasted with the findings of past, present, and on-going research, to provide us with insight into the degree to which we are employing effective instructional practices.

As in any profession, our best professional practices are not static, but instead dynamically change, as researchers formulate and study new approaches and strategies. Due to recent reconceptualizations of the teaching/learning process, the practice of teaching is presently undergoing renewed scrutiny.

Historically, educational researchers focused on identifying and describing those teacher behaviors which were shown to be significantly related to improved student academic achievement. Achievement was typically concerned with lower-level cognitive skills, such as recall and comprehension, taught by direct teacher instruction and measured by the traditional paper and pencil objective test (Brophy, 1988b). This avenue of research came under attack in the mid 1980's, primarily because of its focus on only low-level cognitive processing skills. Spurred on by discoveries in cognitive psychology focusing on the active construction of knowledge by the learner and historical philosophical perceptions as to the role of the learner, educational researchers began to focus on how students learn higher-level cognitive skills, rather than on how teachers teach lower-level cognitive skills (Dewey, 1938; Piaget and Inhelder, 1971; Sigel and Cocking, 1977; Copple, et al, 1984; Von Glasersfeld, 1981; Jackson, 1986; Gardner, 1991; American Psychological Association, 1997; National Research Council, 1999). Of course teachers still play a pivotal role in the teaching/learning process. However, the emphasis has shifted away from teachers disseminating knowledge didactically, seeking correct simplistic answers to validate learning, and separating assessment of learning from the actual process of learning. The emphasis now has moved toward teachers providing opportunities for students to interactively construct knowledge, seeking students' extended explanations to assess their understanding, and integrating assessment with learning through student portfolios that contain products of their work that demonstrate the acquisition of skills and knowledge (Brooks and Brooks, 1993).

A common concern voiced by many educators is, "how can we be sure if we are using effective instruction?"

This shift to an emphasis on how students learn is known as constructivism. Our definition of teaching, changing your behavior to increase the likelihood that students change their behavior, is still applicable in the constructivist model. The difference is that the teacher is now the "guide on the side," designing appropriate learning experiences that help students actively internalize and integrate new information, thus creating new understandings for themselves, rather than the "sage on the stage," where knowledge is transmitted passively from the teacher to students (Gardner, 1991).

However, most teachers recognize that many times it is still important to be the effective "sage on the stage," because lower-level foundational knowledge is usually a prerequisite for future understanding and inquiry. Teacher-directed instruction is often quite appropriate. Therefore, we first describe effective direct instructional teacher behaviors, then various constructivist techniques are discussed.

DIRECT INSTRUCTION

For lower-level cognitive objectives, direct teacher instruction often is the most efficient and effective means of instructional delivery. Research has identified five components of lesson design that are effective in improving student achievement when teachers employ direct instructional methodologies (Hunter, 1982; Rosenshine and Stevens, 1986). These components are entry, input, checking for understanding, providing practice, and closure.

For lower-level cognitive objectives, direct teacher instruction often is the most efficient and effective means of instructional delivery.

Entry

The first component of an effective lesson is an introduction, usually called entry. Here teacher behavior is directed towards gaining students' attention and involvement, reviewing past material, and stating what the students will learn.

Attention and involvement is gained by beginning lessons with novel, discrepant, or interesting activities. The following are examples of these beginning activities.

- A sixth grade science teacher pretends to accidentally lean on a fire extinguisher. The explosive release of CO_2 gas causes many students to jump from their seats. Then the teacher states, "Today we will be starting our study of gases."
- A high school social studies class studying the legal system is shocked in the beginning of class when three prearranged students run into the room and grab the teacher's briefcase. With the students staring in utter disbelief, the teacher acts shocked and extremely nervous and requests that another student get the principal. While waiting for the principal to arrive, she asks her students to provide a description of the three students. After getting somewhat of a consensus, she invites the three students back into the room. The description of the students is usually quite dissimilar to their actual appearance. Thus, begins a lesson on the validity of eyewitness identification in the criminal justice system.
- A seventh grade class enters their English classroom. The room is filled with the aroma and sound of popping corn. Each student is provided with a small bag of freshly popped corn. The teacher has the students describe the smells, sounds, and tastes. This is an introduction to descriptive, creative writing.

Another function of entry is bringing prior content to the forefront of student awareness. This is accomplished by reviewing past material. The more students are involved in the review, the more effective is the review. One of the quickest and most effective means is by using openers. Openers are short questions or problems, written on the board or duplicated and passed out, requiring students to use previously covered material. A side benefit of openers is that students begin to arrive a little earlier to class and settle down to work more quickly.

Finally, students are made aware of the learning objectives of the lesson. The easiest way to accomplish this is by placing an outline on the board or telling the class what they will be learning. Preferably, you should relate the importance of the new learning to students' lives.

Input

Entry is followed by presenting new academic content, which is termed input. Learning is enhanced when the presentation is meaningful, organized, and clear.

Content is most meaningful to students when it is connected to prior learning or is related to the students' own experiences. Content is organized when its conceptual structure is made explicit. The use of charts, tables, diagrams, outlines, and flow charts explicitly shows how facts and concepts are related to each other. For example, students often confuse the geometric concepts of polygons, quadrilaterals, parallelograms, rectangles, squares, and rhombuses. A carefully constructed concept map that diagrams the relationships among these concepts often eliminates this confusion. If students are involved in the analysis and design of this concept map, there is an even greater likelihood that they will understand the hierarchical nature of the concepts.

Learning is enhanced when the presentation is meaningful, organized, and clear.

Content has increased clarity when instructional delivery is well paced, and teachers cue transitions, emphasize important material, provide examples of the content in many different contexts, and avoid confounding the content with extraneous information.

Checking for Understanding

During and following input, teachers need to check for student understanding. This ongoing evaluation answers the important question, "Are the students ready for me to continue?" Checking is most frequently accomplished by observing student seat work or by sampling a cross-section of the class with questions that require understanding for a correct response. This usually means asking questions that require more than one-word answers. Effective questioning techniques, including wait-time, equal response opportunities, and hierarchical ordering are used to decide if adjustments in input are needed.

Providing Practice

Once the content or academic skill has been presented and understanding has been checked, students are ready to practice their new skill. Practice starts with the teacher modeling the use of the content or skill. Often the teacher solves a problem at the board, frequently asking for student input as to the next step. The process of thinking out loud, where the teacher verbalizes each succeeding step, is particularly helpful for students because it enables the students to hear, as well as see on the blackboard, the process the teacher is using to solve the problem.

Once the content or academic skill has been presented and understanding has been checked, students are ready to practice their new skill.

Next, students are provided with coached practice. Students are given problems to practice. This practice is highly supervised, with frequent teacher feedback. Once the teacher is certain that the students are experiencing high rates of success, she provides time for the students to practice independently. One form of independent practice is homework. The probability of homework being completed is a function of the meaningfulness or relevancy of the homework and the quantity and quality of teacher feedback to the individual student regarding her effort. Retention of new learning is enhanced when opportunities are given to practice, not only immediately following the presentation of the new content, but throughout the week, month, and academic year.

Closure

Closure is the opposite of entry. As with entry, student attention and involvement are critical in this summary stage. For example, randomly questioning the class or using written exit slips during the last few minutes of class, which require all students to answer a few brief questions on the important aspects of the day's lesson, allows students to review the day's content.

A special type of exit slip ties the closure of one day's lesson to the introduction of the next day's lesson. The students write what they felt was the most important thing that they learned that day and what questions they still had about the lesson. The students' questions are then used as the openers for the next day's lesson.

Closure also provides students with a brief preview of what new material still is to be learned. The use of an ongoing outline or concept map accomplishes this.

CONSTRUCTIVISM

So far, effective instruction has focused on the delivery of lower-level cognitive skills, with the teacher being the most important variable in the teaching/learning process. Now we focus on instructional methodology that emphasizes higher order thinking skills, such as analysis, synthesis, and evaluation, emphasizing how students use these skills to develop new understanding. Therefore, the most important variable in the teaching/learning process now becomes the student.

Unlike direct instruction, with its emphasis upon specific teacher behavior, constructivism consists of theoretical models that guide, rather than prescribe, teacher behavior. The new paradigm is explained and implemented under various models, including Teaching for Understanding (Perkins and Blythe, 1994), Dimensions of Learning (Marzano, 1992), and Multiple Intelligences (Gardner, 1993). The authors believe that the shift to constructivist instruction is accomplished using instructional strategies typically categorized as authentic instruction.

Unlike direct instruction, with its emphasis upon specific teacher behavior, constructivism consists of theoretical models that guide, rather than prescribe, teacher behavior.

There are five key criteria that distinguish authentic instruction from direct instruction (Newmann and Wehlage, 1993).

- An emphasis on higher order cognitive skills.
- A deeper understanding of a fewer number of concepts.
- Connecting classroom activities to the world outside the classroom.
- Complex verbal interactions between teacher and students and between students.
- A classroom environment which encourages respect and intellectual risk taking, founded on a belief that all students are capable of learning.

In addition, many educators include a sixth criterion, authentic assessment. Authentic assessment involves the integration of the five criteria listed previously by requiring students to work through complex relevant problems using their new understanding (Brooks and Brooks, 1993; Schnitzer, 1993). Often students acquire additional skills and understanding during authentic assessment. Thus authentic assessments are viewed as ongoing instruction and not separate from instruction, as is the case with traditional paper and pencil tests.

In classroom practice, authentic instruction involves real-world types of problems, such as solving solid waste issues of the community, determining the accuracy of National Weather Service forecasts, collecting data for studies conducted by scientists, or doing historical research, rather than the typical textbook-type problem sets. As in the real world, problems are usually not well-defined and require the use of many skills and the understanding of many concepts that frequently cross traditional subject matter boundaries. Problems most often are solved by a cooperative team of students, rarely by an individual student. This reinforces that learning is enhanced when it occurs in a social context (American Psychological Association, 1997; National Research Council, 1999). This supports the old adage, "Two heads are better than one." Finally, the solution to the problem, which also serves as the assessment of student learning, is usually a complex product involving position papers, outlines of procedures or policies, or prototype models. It is never a paper and pencil test.

The cognitive justifications for authentic instruction are many. The most important is for students to achieve a deeper understanding of concepts. However, the pragmatic justification may actually be more salient—that is, the preparation of students to be competent in the technologically complex, information rich, and globally interdependent twenty-first century.

Table 13.1 outlines some strategies that can be employed for direct instruction and constructivism to positively impact the student success/failure ratio.

TABLE 13.1 ▶ Strategies for Success/Failure Ratio

Direct Instruction

Entry
- students attentive and involved
- review previous content
- state objectives

Input
- meaningful, connected to previous learning
- organized, conceptual structure made clear
- clarity of instruction, pacing, transitions, emphasize important materials, examples in many contexts

Checking for Understanding
- Is it safe to continue?
- questioning
  - vary cognitive levels
  - call on volunteers and non-volunteers
  - use wait-time after asking a question
  - have many students respond before providing feedback
  - use wait-time after a student responds
  - vary the feedback
  - ask follow-up, probing, qualifying questions

Providing Coached Practice
- teacher modeling, think out loud
- coached practice
- independent practice

Closure
- students attentive and involved
- review of what was taught
- preview

Solitary practice
- homework

Periodic Review

Constructivism

Teach to Different Learning Styles and Multiple Intelligences
- use multi-modal instruction
- integrate linguistic, logical-mathematical, spatial, kinesthetic, musical, inter and intrapersonal activities into instruction
- employ active learning strategies

Assess and Use Students' Prior Knowledge
- ask students two questions: what they already know, and what they want to know

Design Instruction for Higher Order Cognitive Skills
- plan activities that are divergent, requiring application, analysis, synthesis, and evaluation
- use real-life situations and problems that relate to students' experiences

Use Collaborative and Cooperative Groups to Accommodate the Social Aspects of Learning
- use problems and projects that require group work and different skills and abilities

Integrate Instruction and Assessment
- view assessment as formative
- design assessment which will indicate students' misunderstandings (e.g. concept maps).
- make assessment an integral part of the instruction

Utilize Multiple Types of Assessment, Emphasizing Authentic Assessment
- provide students many opportunities to demonstrate understanding
- use varied and diverse assessments
- employ criterion referenced assessments
- use real-life problems and projects
- give students choices in assessment

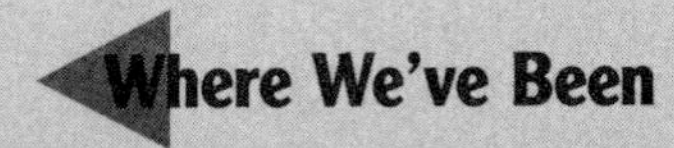

Where We've Been

This chapter explained the differences between two types of effective instruction, direct instruction and constructivism, and how each might be used to positively impact student success/failure ratio. Primarily, direct instruction is teacher centered and focuses on lower-level cognitive skills. Constructivism is more learner centered and focused on higher order cognitive abilities. There are hundreds of strategies that teachers can develop to impact student success using referent and expert authority, because if you understand the whys you can develop the hows. Some sample strategies were provided for both direct instruction and the constructivist approach.

Where We're Headed

The next chapter presents strategies that facilitate students' intrinsic motivation through the use of referent and expert authority. Both of the components of intrinsic motivation are examined; these are the expectation of success attributed to an internal locus of control and value attributed to an internal value structure.

CHAPTER 13 CONCEPT MAP

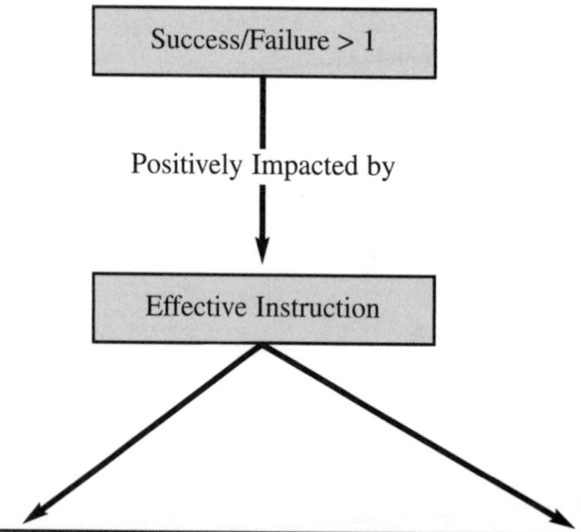

	DIRECT INSTRUCTION	CONSTRUCTIVISM
Cognitive level	lower levels, students learn facts	higher levels, students learn concepts
Students prior learning	little importance given to students' prior experiences and knowledge in their understanding of new learning	major importance given to students' prior experiences and knowledge in their understanding of new learning
Assessment	requires students to supply a set of correct answers	requires students to demonstrate their understanding by the display of academic products and the performance of behaviors that require the understanding, integration, and application of concepts
Interactions	individual student-teacher	communities of student learners
Academic tasks	primarily requiring mathematical and verbal abilities that are unrelated to the real world outside the classroom	requiring multiple intelligences, such as mathematical, linguistic, kinesthetic, and musical, reflecting and mirroring the real world outside the classroom
Teaching strategies	defined, well structured, leading to convergence of student thinking • Entry • Input • Checking for Understanding • Providing Coached Practice • Closure	less defined, less structured, leading divergence of student thinking • Multiple Intelligences • Collaborative, Cooperative, Active Learning • Integrated Instruction and Assessment • Authentic Assessment • Problem Based/Case Study Learning

? QUESTIONS FOR THE STUDY TEAM

1. What are some practical strategies that illustrate each of the components of direct instruction?

   a. Entry

   b. Input

   c. Checking for Understanding

   d. Providing Coached Practice

   e. Closure

   f. Solitary Practice

   g. Periodic Review

2. What are some practical strategies that illustrate each of the characteristics of constructivism?

   a. Teach to Different Learning Styles and Multiple Intelligences

   b. Assess and Use Students' Prior Knowledge

   c. Design Instruction for Higher Order Cognitive Skills

   d. Use Collaborative and Cooperative Groups to Accommodate the Social Aspects of Learning

   e. Integrate Instruction and Assessment

   f. Utilize Multiple Types of Assessment, Emphasizing Authentic Assessment

Chapter 14

If You Understand the Whys, You Can Design the Hows: Positively Impacting Student Intrinsic Motivation

"I have tried rewards and all I have gotten is the desire for the same reward for less action or the desire for more reward for the same action." (Hohnadel 2001)

Motivation

It has become the gospel in American education that teachers should reward appropriate student behaviors and punish inappropriate ones. This is intended to reinforce and increase the likelihood that appropriate behavior is repeated and inappropriate behavior is extinguished. The use of rewards and punishment is based on the principle of operant conditioning, which assumes that behavior is determined solely by external antecedents and consequences (Skinner, 1974). In addition to the hotly debated question as to whether or not this approach has been successful in our schools, there are philosophical and psychological misgivings concerning its' use, some of which will be discussed in Chapters 16 and 17 (Kohn, 1999).

Unlike operant conditioning, the social cognitive theory of motivation not only accounts for external antecedents and consequences of behavior, it also takes into consideration how an individual's beliefs, expectations, and emotions influence his behavior.

Like direct instruction (See Chapter 13), which places the responsibility for student learning on the teacher, operant conditioning views the teacher as the primary source of student motivation. We question this focus on the teacher as the source of student motivation, because it implicitly assumes that the role the student plays in his own motivation is unimportant. Unlike operant conditioning, the social cognitive theory of motivation (See Chapter 10) not only accounts for external antecedents and consequences of behavior, it also takes into consideration how an individual's beliefs, expectations, and emotions influence his behavior. If you recall, under this theory, motivation is the product of an individual's expectation of success multiplied by the value of the outcome to the individual,

$$M = E \times V$$

Similar to the constructivist theory of instruction (See Chapter 13), which places the student at the center of his own knowledge acquisition, the social cognitive theory of motivation places the student at the center of his own motivation. The student, rather than the teacher, is the primary source of motivation.

The teacher exhibits behavior that increases both the student's expectation of success through an internal locus of control and the intrinsic value of achievement to the student.

The teacher, rather than distributing consequences such as praise, rewards, and punishments, encourages the development of the student's intrinsic motivation. The teacher exhibits behavior that increases both the student's expectation of success through an internal locus of control and the intrinsic value of achievement to the student. Many strategies, congruent with the social cognitive motivation theory that teachers might employ, impact both the student's expectation of success and the value to the student. However, to facilitate understanding, we address each factor separately.

As teachers employing expert and referent authority are most likely to have a positive impact upon intrinsic motivation by increasing students' expectation of success and value (See Chapter 10), strategies are presented from these two authority bases.

Expectation of Success Attributed to an Internal Locus of Control

STRATEGIES EMPHASIZING REFERENT AUTHORITY

Feeling Tone

The primary impact that teachers with referent authority have upon the expectation of success of students involves setting the feeling tone of the classroom. Feeling tone has to do with the emotional feel of a classroom and is commonly referred to as the classroom climate or classroom atmosphere. Both the nonverbal and verbal behavior of the teacher establishes the feeling tone (Withall, 1969). As stated in Chapter 7, the beliefs a teacher holds about students in general (labeling) and individual students in particular greatly influences the teacher's behavior. Of particular importance for a student's expectation of success is what the teacher believes concerning the student's ability and willingness to learn. These beliefs are commonly referred to as teacher expectations for student achievement.

If a teacher has different expectations for each student, the teacher may behave differently toward each student, thus each student may perceive a different classroom climate. For example, teachers who view certain students as low achievers commonly communicate lower expectations to these students than they communicate to students whom they view as high achievers. Teachers communicate their lower expectations to certain students by:

- calling on them less often to answer questions.
- using less wait-time.
- asking a greater number of lower level questions.
- expressing less personal interest.
- standing further away from the student.
- accepting answers from low-achieving students that would be deemed unacceptable if proffered by a high-achieving student.
- expressing less personal interest in low-achieving students than in high-achieving students (Good and Brophy, 1987).

Teachers exhibiting these behaviors establish a discouraging classroom climate for these students. They indirectly are sending them a powerful message, "I don't expect you to do well in this class." This message influences students to develop low expectations of success, thus the students put less effort into academic tasks. If a student performs poorly, it reinforces the teacher's low expectations and intensifies the differential treatment of the student (Braun, 1976). Having low expectations for students sets up the following cycle. The teacher thinks, "Why should I try? He will not succeed," while the student thinks, "Why should I try? I will not succeed."

The primary impact that teachers with referent authority have upon the expectation of success of students involves setting the feeling tone of the classroom.

Some teachers believe that it is important to treat lower achievers differently, in order to not embarrass them or give them unrealistic expectations for future success. However, teachers with referent authority understand and communicate both verbally and non-verbally to students, their belief that all students can be successful. These teachers redefine student success as student effort and incremental change in student behavior over time (learning), as opposed to meeting predetermined and static performance criteria. The authors recognize that academic mastery is the goal for all students, and this goal of mastery presupposes a certain absolute level of student performance. A prerequisite for mastery, however, is student effort or motivation. In classrooms where the established feeling tone communicates the teacher's high expectation that all students can be successful, because success has been redefined, the likelihood that all students will obtain academic mastery is increased (Collopy and Green, 1995).

Teachers with referent authority understand and communicate both verbally and non-verbally to students, their belief that all students can be successful.

Figure 14.1 diagrams how a teacher's expectations influence the teacher's behavior, which in turn influences student performance. This cycle may result either in positive influences on a student's performance if the teacher has high expectations or in negative influences on a student's performance if the teacher's expectations are low.

Encouragement

Encouragement is a way for teachers to communicate to their students that success in the classroom is not solely a matter of discrete academic performance. Encouragement is teachers communicating to students the positive nature of their efforts and how their efforts relate to improved academic performance, specific feedback about what was done correctly and how to repeat it, and what was done incorrectly and how to improve upon it. Encouragement also includes teachers communicating to students their recognition of student academic risk taking, even if the risk does not lead to academic success, and how individual student interests are vital to the vibrancy of the learning community.

The following statements are examples of encouragement.

- "Marcus, your increased participation in class this week showed a real improvement in your willingness to play a positive role in the class."
- "Travis, your diagram of a food chain showed a tremendous improvement in your understanding of the interdependency of life on Earth. I believe this improvement is a direct result of your willingness to take the time to meet with me after school last week and the extra time you spent at home studying the material."
- "Chan, your introductory paragraph was clear and concise and set the stage for your paper. Your concluding paragraph ade-

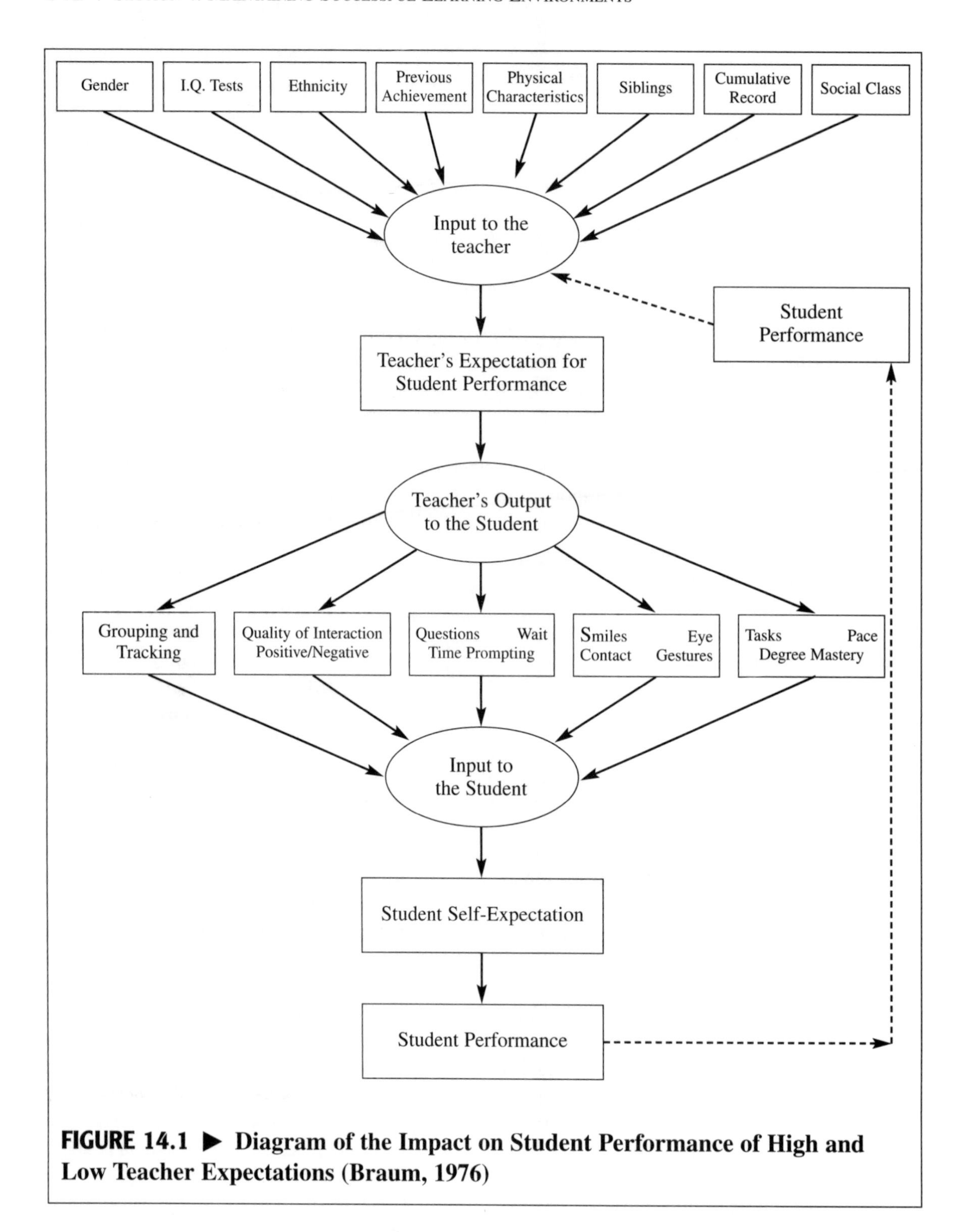

FIGURE 14.1 ▶ Diagram of the Impact on Student Performance of High and Low Teacher Expectations (Braum, 1976)

quately summarized your important points. However, the body of the text needs to focus more clearly upon the points you made in the introductory paragraph, which I've highlighted. I would be happy to provide you with examples of how to accomplish this or meet with you to further clarify what you need to do. Please get back to me."

- "Tony, you have attempted to solve this problem using a mathematical procedure that we will not learn for a few weeks. It is apparent to me that you have considerable talent in math. However, the answer you reached was incorrect. Remember that operations in parentheses must be solved from the innermost to the outermost parentheses in an equation."
- "Your willingness, Arial, to bring into class your pet snakes and your evident knowledge of reptiles and amphibians was a great kickoff to our study of cold blooded animals."

Encouragement is highly preferable to the use of rewards. The topic of encouragement as an alternative to rewards is discussed in Chapter 17.

STRATEGIES EMPHASIZING EXPERT AUTHORITY

Study Skills

It is well recognized that an important variable under the control of students is how they study. Sometimes students who dedicate adequate time to study nevertheless fail to experience academic success. The cause is often that they do not know how to make the most efficient use of time by using effective study strategies. How to study is a skill that needs to be taught. Effective study skills and how to teach them is the subject of many articles and books. Teachers often overlook the importance of teaching study skills. Teachers who believe in expert authority recognize the relationship between the acquisition of study skills and learning and thus strategically integrate study skills into their instruction.

Teachers often overlook the importance of teaching study skills.

Students who understand and use effective study skills see a clear relationship between the amount of effort they spend in study and the amount of learning they achieve. They have a higher expectation of success attributed to an internal locus of control—that is, they control the effort and time they devote to studying.

Criterion Referenced Evaluation

Criterion referenced evaluation involves the delineation of specific components, performance, or behaviors (enabling objectives), which are determined by a task analysis of terminal objectives that indicate student mastery. In short, criterion referenced evaluation clearly delineates what needs to be done to successfully complete a task. When students understand the criteria by which learning will be assessed, they also perceive the process of learning as being more directly under their control.

How many times does a student receive a paper back from a teacher with the only comment being, "Good job, but needs some additional work," and a grade of a big red C+?

- How do you think the student feels?
- Does the student have an understanding of exactly what additional work is needed?
- Does the teacher indicate that he recognizes how much effort the student put into the paper, or that the opening paragraph is a real attention getter?
- What about the paper's impressive bibliography?
- Does the teacher let the student know that the teacher notices how far back the student went to get those obscure articles?

- What effect is this type of feedback and evaluation likely to have upon the student's future expectation of success?
- How much time and effort is the student likely to dedicate to the next report?

Instead of a research paper being graded as if it involved only one academic skill, "Good job, but needs some additional work," a teacher using criterion referenced evaluation views the paper as a product of many academic skills.

Here's an example of how a teacher might use criterion referenced evaluation for an assigned research paper. First the teacher begins with an analysis of the academic components needed to be included in the research paper. These academic components include topic selection, source cards, preliminary outline, final outline, paragraph development, bibliography, rough draft, and final copy. Next, each of these components is analyzed with the intent of delineating both the subcomponents and a description of the various levels of performance for each subcomponent. For example, the teacher divides the component of paragraph development into two subcomponents, content and format, and describes various levels of performance along a continuum, as illustrated below in Figure 14.2.

This type of analysis is continued until all the main components of the research project are listed with subcomponents and performance criteria. By analyzing a final product into subcomponents, teachers are recognizing that every student is not competent in every relevant academic area, but is competent in some relevant areas. For example, a teacher using criterion referenced evaluation communicates to a specific student, "Taylor, while your grammar may need more attention, you are excellent in finding sources of information." By stating both what the student did well and what he did not do well, the teacher is increasing opportunities for Taylor's success. Criterion referenced evaluation also provides students with the opportunity to evaluate their own work, which has been shown in one study to significantly improve academic achievement (Levin and Heath, 1981).

Main Component: Paragraph Development

Subcomponent: Content

Topics from final outline were not included.	Some topics from final outline were included.	All topics from final outline were included.

Subcomponent: Format

First line is not indented. Many errors in capitalization and punctuation.	Some errors of indentation, capitalization, and punctuation.	First line is indented. Proper capitalization is used. Appropriate punctuation is followed.

FIGURE 14.2 ▶ Criterion for Paragraph Development Evaluation

Criterion referenced evaluation when designed and used to:

- eliminate the ambiguity of an academic task and thus reduce the perceived difficulty of the task (Stipek, 2001),
- have students set personal goals (Stipek, 2001),
- maximize the opportunities for success, and
- provide opportunities for self-evaluation (Bandura, 1986),

increases the probability that students will attribute their expectation of success to factors within their control (internal locus of control) and therefore will develop intrinsic motivation.

Knowledge of Results

Imagine this situation.

As a participant in a workshop demonstration, you are asked to toss a tennis ball into a trashcan while you are blindfolded. The facilitator supplies tennis balls, and you start tossing. How long will you be motivated to continue tossing the balls? If you are like the many teachers whom we have asked to volunteer for this demonstration, you'll be ready to call it quits after four or five unsuccessful tosses. The successful completion of the task—that is, getting the ball in the can—is close to impossible under these circumstances. If a participant is successful, it is a function of luck, not of effort or competence. The participant is certainly competent to toss the ball into a trashcan, but under these circumstances, his efforts are unsuccessful. Therefore, the expectation of future success, without changing the circumstances, is close to zero.

To increase the participant's motivation to continue to toss the ball, it is necessary to increase his expectation of success. Indeed, when we ask the participant what is needed to increase his motivation to continue, he replies, "I will never be successful unless you give me some feedback about my efforts."

We have a student (the participant), who is competent to achieve the assigned task (throw a ball into a trashcan), but is not achieving up to his potential. What type of feedback would be helpful? When, prior to the demonstration, we ask teachers for feedback that they give students who are competent to achieve academic mastery, but who hand in work that is far below their potential, they make the following statements. "More work is needed." "Try harder." "What happened?" "Do you understand what you are being asked to do?" and "You are working far below your potential."

Now back to the ball toss.

When the participant asks for feedback, we supply the same comments that are offered to underachieving students. "More work is needed." "Try harder." "What happened?" "Do you understand what you are being asked to do?" and "You are working far below your potential." After just a few of these comments, participants often get so frustrated and angry, the authors became the targets of a few tosses. Often the participant refuses to continue. In one instance a female participant put the balls in her blouse and said "game's over."

When we again ask the participant what it will take for them to continue and eventually be successful, they tell us they need useful feedback about what they have done correctly and what they need to do to become successful. This direct descriptive feedback is called knowledge of results. Knowledge of results is not judgmental or evaluative such as "good job" or "you're doing great." It is not a hint, as in, "You're close," or "You're warm." It is descriptive, providing the learner with the knowledge needed to increase the possibility of attaining the goal. This knowledge consists of informing the student of what is done correctly, what needs to be changed, and in some cases, how to affect the change.

Returning to the ball tossing demonstration, when the participant is given specific feedback on each toss such as "You are throwing in the right direction, but you need to toss the ball 5 feet in front of you," or "You have the right direction and length, but you need to throw the ball one foot further to the left," things change significantly. The participant now evidences more purposeful effort. The feelings of anger and frustration diminish. In many instances the participant actually is able to provide himself with corrective feedback. Under conditions of specific feedback, it is our experience that success is achieved in less than five tosses.

One of the most direct ways of impacting student expectation of success through an internal locus of control is by providing the student with meaningful opportunities to make choices about both academic tasks and the classroom environment.

Providing specific knowledge of results is not that easy. In the ball toss, when teachers are asked to provide specific knowledge of results to their frustrated colleague, they often offer feedback such as "too hard," "ooh, that was close," and "just a little to your left." While these comments are admittedly superior to the "work harder" type of comments, they are of limited use to the participant, due to their lack of specificity.

Initially when the tosses occur randomly, without the knowledge of results, the expectation of success is dependent upon luck; therefore the expectation is low, and the locus of control is external. When feedback such as "work harder" is provided, motivation ceases altogether and anger sets in. However, when the facilitators begin to provide specific feedback, the attribution for success is shifted inward, and competence and effort determine whether the participant is successful. At this point the expectation of success is high, the locus of control is internal, and therefore the motivation moves from extrinsic to intrinsic.

By definition, choice is exerting an internal locus of control.

Meaningful Choices

One of the most direct ways of impacting student expectation of success through an internal locus of control is by providing the student with meaningful opportunities to make choices about both academic tasks and the classroom environment. Students are so accustomed to being told what, how, and when to do things, that the motivational benefits of giving students choices cannot be overstated. By definition, choice is exerting an internal locus of control. Students typically will make choices that will increase their expectations of success. Only the teacher who embraces expert authority is in a position to recognize when student choice is appropriate. And when that choice involves academics, high academic standards are maintained.

Students may be given choices concerning assignments, such as, "Select five out of the ten problems for homework." They may chose a type of assessment such as, "We have just finished the unit on immigration and Ellis Island. You may demonstrate your understanding of this topic by a written report, by writing and performing a play, by building a model or diorama, by interviewing someone who immigrated through Ellis Island, by making a video or power point presentation, or you may discuss with me a project of your own design." Finally students may be given choices about their classroom environment, including consensual design of classroom guidelines, seating charts, and the order of daily activities.

Value Attributed to an Internal Value Structure

STRATEGIES EMPHASIZING REFERENT AUTHORITY

Student Interest

An internal value structure is facilitated when students are interested in what they are learning. One of the most effective ways to build student interest in the material is to integrate students' academic and nonacademic interests into instruction. A teacher who believes in referent authority is in the best position to know and understand students' interests because of the relationship he has with his students. Here are some examples of how student interest may be integrated into instruction. The teacher integrates popular music into the study of language arts; uses skateboarding, skiing, and surfing in science class; discusses current media idols in social studies to evaluate present and past cultural trends; and illustrates mathematical concepts by calculating sports team statistics, managing allowances, and if students work, calculating taxes. The number of ways that student interests may be used in instruction is limited solely by the teacher's understanding of his students and of pedagogy. Understanding students' interest is facilitated when teachers sample the music students listen to, the TV and movies students watch, the video games they play, the books and magazines they read, and the leisure activities in which they engage. Obviously it requires an expert teacher to build instruction around student interests, but the prerequisite is a teacher who believes in referent authority. Teachers with referent authority create classroom environments characterized by trust, care, and respect, and students are thereby encouraged to share their interests.

One of the most effective ways to build student interest in the material is to integrate students' academic and nonacademic interests into instruction.

Teacher Interest

Teachers who believe in referent authority work on building meaningful and supportive relationships with their students. One way teachers show students these attributes is to continually communicate to students their genuine concern for them not only as learners, but also as human beings. Teachers need to make themselves available to help students academically and to take the time to speak to students about non-academic, personal concerns when student need arises. This means setting aside scheduled times to help students, as well as unscheduled times when necessary.

An excellent example of a teacher's interest in students is illustrated by the following true story.

> Mr. Gomez is Sean's math teacher. One night, he calls Sean's home and asks Sean's father if he could please talk to his son. Sean's dad tells Mr. Gomez that Sean is out, but asks the nature of the problem. Mr. Gomez says, "I solved a problem incorrectly today, and I am calling all the students because I am concerned that they will be confused doing their homework. Please tell Sean not to solve problems 5 through 10, and I will provide the correct method to solving the problems tomorrow in class." Certainly, Mr. Gomez could have straightened out the problems in class the next day without calling each student. However, it was Mr. Gomez's respect and support for his students that motivated his calls.

When teachers consistently display the characteristics of referent authority in their classrooms by showing their genuine interest in their students, they increase the likelihood that students will value the teacher and what the teacher is attempting to help them learn.

STRATEGIES EMPHASIZING EXPERT AUTHORITY

Relevant and Meaningful Instruction

A teacher embracing expert authority strives to impact student motivation through an internal value structure, by designing meaningful and relevant lessons that accommodate student interest, are applicable to their lives, and/or result in practical useful products. Examples of lessons that integrate student interest and are applicable to their lives were illustrated and discussed previously in the section on student interest. There are many examples of instruction that lead to useful and practical products. These include some famous examples, the "Foxfire" books (Foxfire Fund, 2002), the Langley School District Music Project (National Public Radio, 2001), and Northeast High School's Project SPARC (2002). It is not necessary to have national recognition or scope in order for instruction to be relevant and meaningful to students. Everyday, literally thousands of teachers engage students in projects that result in useful and practical products for their school or surrounding community.

Everyday, literally thousands of teachers engage students in projects that result in useful and practical products for their school or surrounding community.

Teacher Enthusiasm

Most of us would agree that teacher enthusiasm is contagious. Students "catch" the teacher's internal value toward their specific subject area and also toward learning in general. Teachers who believe in expert authority are excited about learning. They seek opportunities to increase their knowledge base about their content and how to deliver that content to their students. Teachers who continue to use the same material and teach it in the same manner year after year are unlikely to feel any enthusiasm toward teaching and are unlikely to communicate any enthusiasm to their students. Dr. Uri Treisman, a nationally recognized mathematician, in an address at Penn State University in the early 1990's, communicated the importance of teacher enthusiasm by exhorting professors to approach each class as if their job depended upon students becoming interested and involved in what they were teaching.

Islands of Competence

"Islands of competence" refers to the time honored idea that everyone is good at something or as Robert Brooks, an authority on student self-esteem, states "one area that is or has the potential to be a source of pride and achievement" (1991, p. 31). Sometimes the competence is readily apparent, as when a student is very interested in animals and has knowledge concerning their habits and care. Other times competence is apparent, but the teacher believes it has no relationship to learning goals, such as the student who produces elaborate artistic doodles rather than finishing the assigned task. Still, other times it is not readily apparent and is ascertained only by careful interviewing of the student. For example, a teacher in a northern Minnesota school asks a child in his class about his hobbies and finds out that he collects and knows a lot about tropical seashells. Finally, sometimes competence is masked and needs to be extrapolated and re-framed from student behavior, such as viewing hyperactivity as high energy, a kinesthetic competency, rather than merely disruptive behavior. In addition, when high energy is channeled into appropriate classroom tasks, it may lead to other areas of student competency, which likely otherwise goes unnoticed.

When you identify a student's island of competence, you can facilitate internal value by designing tasks which directly relate to the student's island of competence or showing the student how his competency may be applied to the learning activity. The teacher allows the student interested in animals to be responsible for the care of the class' aquarium, to teach fellow students and teachers about the care and feeding of animals, or to write about animals. The teacher may intentionally integrate the subject of animals into the class' study of art, science, math, or history. The integration of a student's island of competence into instructional activities is commonplace for a teacher who believes in expert authority.

Novel and Discrepant Events

When students are interested, they have an internal value structure. One very effective way to stimulate student interest is through the use of discrepant events. Students, like all people, are naturally curious, having an innate tendency to explore (Kagan, 1972). This innate curiosity can be piqued when discrepant events are used in instruction. A discrepant event is any experience that varies from expectations or closely held beliefs.

A frequently used discrepant event in elementary science education is what's called the "floating rock" demonstration.

In this demonstration, the teacher has a water filled aquarium and an object that looks like a rock. He asks the class what will happen if he places the rock into the aquarium, and naturally all the students agree from past experience, that the rock will sink to the bottom of the aquarium. When he places the rock in the aquarium, instead of sinking, it floats. For the student, this forms a discrepancy between what they anticipated would happen and what in fact happened. The students are very interested; in other words, there is now value in exploring the reasons why this rock floats.

An example from high school social studies involves what students believe about Christopher Columbus. The teacher starts by asking students to list what they know about Christopher Columbus. The list most probably includes such "facts" as that he was a friend of the Indians, that he was a kind man, that he was the first to discover the New World, and that he brought back spices and gold to Spain. The teacher then reads the following description of how Columbus obtained gold from the Indians.

> Every man and women, every boy or girl of fourteen or older . . . had to collect gold for the Spaniards. As their measure, the Spaniards used hawks' bells. Every three months every Indian had to bring to one of the forts a hawks' bell filled with gold dust. The chiefs had to bring in about ten times that amount . . .
>
> . . . Copper tokens were manufactured, and when an Indian had brought his or her tribute to an armed post, he or she received such a token, stamped with the month, to be hung around the neck. With that they were safe for another three months while collecting more gold. Whoever was caught without a token was killed by having his or her hands cut off . . . There were no gold fields, and thus, once the Indians had handed in whatever they still had in gold ornaments, their only hope was to work all day in the streams, washing out gold dust from the pebbles. It was an impossible task, but those Indians that tried to flee into the mountains were systematically hunted down with dogs and killed . . . Thus it was at this time that the mass suicides began: the Arawaks killed themselves with cassava poison. During those two years of the administration of the brothers Columbus, an estimated one half of the entire population of Hispaniola was killed or killed themselves. The estimates run from 125,000 to one-half million." (Bigelow, 1991, p. 258).

This passage challenges students' commonly held beliefs and is, like the floating rock, a discrepant event. In both examples, the discrepancy creates what is called cognitive dissonance—that is, a disequilibrium caused by the difference between what is observed and what students believe or have experienced in the past. When this dissonance exists, students see value in obtaining information and understanding to reduce the dissonance. In the classroom, dissonance is resolved by investigating the discrepancy in more depth and thus increasing students' understanding and knowledge. Only a teacher that thoroughly understands his subject and is willing to find or develop these discrepant events—in short, a teacher embracing expert authority—can effectively use this strategy to increase student value.

In the classroom, dissonance is resolved by investigating the discrepancy in more depth and thus increasing students' understanding and knowledge.

Table 14.1 outlines some strategies that may be employed to positively influence intrinsic motivation by impacting students' expectations of success by way of an internal locus of control and value by way of an internal value structure.

TABLE 14.1 ▶ Strategies for Intrinsic Motivation (M = E × V)

Expectation of Success Internal Locus of Control		Value Internal Value Structure	
Referent Authority	**Expert Authority**	**Referent Authority**	**Expert Authority**
Feeling Tone Non-verbal or verbal behaviors of teachers that establish a respectful, trusting, caring, and supportive classroom climate **Encouragement** Any communication to students about 1) the positive nature of their effort, 2) how their effort relates to improved academic performance, 3) specific feedback about what was done correctly and how to maintain it, 4) specific feedback about what was done incorrectly and how to improve upon it, 5) recognition of academic risk taking, even if the risk does not lead to academic success, and 6) how individual student interests are vital to the vibrancy of the learning community	**Study Skills** Provide students with an important skill necessary to be successful **Criterion Referenced Evaluation** Delineation of the specific components of an academic task necessary for successful completion of the task **Knowledge of Results** Specific written and verbal feedback noting what was done correctly and what needs to be done to improve performance **Meaningful Choices** Opportunities to make meaningful choices concerning academic tasks and classroom environment	**Student Interest** The integration of students academic and non-academic interests into instruction **Teacher Interest** Teacher communication to students of their concern for them, not only as students, but also as human beings	**Relevant and Meaningful Instruction** Instruction that accommodates student interest, is applicable to their lives, and/or results in practical useful products **Teacher Enthusiasm** Students "catch" the teacher's enthusiasm toward their specific subject area and learning in general **Islands of Competence** Integrating into instruction one area that is or has the potential to be a source of pride and achievement for a student **Novel and Discrepant Events** Students see value in obtaining information and developing new understanding to reduce the cognitive dissonance caused by discrepant events

Where We've Been

This chapter detailed how teachers may positively impact students' intrinsic motivation through the use of referent and expert authority to help students develop an internal locus of control as the attribution for success and an internal value structure as the attribution for value. Because of the philosophy "if you understand the whys, you can design the hows," examples of strategies offered within the chapter are meant as starting points to guide the classroom teacher and are not meant to be a complete list of possible techniques.

Where We're Headed

The next chapter presents strategies that facilitate students' pro-social self-esteem, through the use of referent and expert authority. Strategies for each of the components of significance, competence, virtue, and power will be examined.

CHAPTER 14 CONCEPT MAP

Table 14.1 serves as the concept map for this chapter.

QUESTIONS FOR THE STUDY TEAM

1. What are some practical strategies that illustrate the use of referent and expert authority to impact the components of intrinsic motivation? Complete the chart below with these.

Expectation of Success Internal Locus of Control		Value Internal Value Structure	
Referent Authority	**Expert Authority**	**Referent Authority**	**Expert Authority**

2. What are some strategies commonly used in classrooms and schools that facilitate extrinsic motivation (external locus of control and external value structure)?

CHAPTER 15

If You Understand the Whys, You Can Design the Hows: Positively Impacting Student Pro-Social Self-Esteem

"Most positive school experiences have nothing to do with academics; they have to do with personal relationships that take less than five seconds of time." (Brooks, 1991)

Self-Esteem

As discussed in Chapter 11, self-esteem is a sum of four variables:

- Significance
- Competence
- Virtue
- Power

Self-esteem may be expressed either in distorted or pro-social ways. Teachers who believe in referent and expert authority not only understand the differences between distorted and pro-social self-esteem, but also actively strive to use teaching behaviors that facilitate student pro-social self-esteem.

In Chapter 13, when discussing how to maintain successful learning environments by positively impacting student success/failure ratio, the emphasis was upon expert authority being directed toward effective instruction. It was also noted that referent authority was necessary to create an environment of respect, trust, care, and support. In Chapter 14, concerning positively impacting student intrinsic motivation, the components of internal locus of control and internal value structure were shown to be influenced by both referent and expert authority. In this chapter, we deal with positively impacting pro-social self-esteem. The components of significance and virtue are shown to be influenced mainly through referent authority, while the components of competence and power are shown to be influenced mainly through expert authority.

Significance

As discussed in Chapter 11, significance is a person's belief that she is respected, liked, and trusted by people who are important to her.

Strategies Emphasizing Referent Authority

Accurate Empathy

A student, Marianna, comes into your classroom with a history of being demeaned, berated, and generally disliked by teachers. If you believe in referent authority, you understand that it is first necessary to show Marianna that you have respect and positive regard for her. But how can you authentically do this? To begin, you may use accurate empathy with the student (See Chapter 7). What would you want, given a history similar to this student, in order to feel cared about and to care in return? Most probably you would want a significant amount of trust, kindness, respect for your individuality and autonomy, and a clear indication that someone liked you, cared about you, and valued you. In all likelihood, this is what your student, Marianna, also needs and will respond to positively.

Islands of Significance

Much like islands of competence (See Chapter 14), we all have "islands of significance"—that is, there is something to like about every student. Sometimes to discover this island of significance, the teacher must look beyond the student's defensiveness and aggressive posturing. If teachers wish to be effective in increasing the probability that their students feel more significant, they must find something to like about every student in their class. Only if the teacher finds something to like, will the teacher be able to interact honestly with the student in a positive and authentically caring fashion. The only thing that a teacher may find to like about a student initially is the tenacity of her distorted beliefs and offensive behaviors—in other words, an expression of her distorted self-esteem. That same tenacity when focused in another direction can be an important source of pro-social self-esteem.

> "In even the most outwardly offensive student, there is something decent. It may be tiny, buried beneath monstrous behaviors. But it is worth the search, for it is the place to begin teaching. . . . When you find the grain of decency, you can reinforce it, bring it to daylight as often as possible and use it to create a base. . . ." (Goulet, 1997, p17)

> *If teachers wish to be effective in increasing the probability that their students feel more significant, they must find something to like about every student in their class.*

Treat Students As Individuals

Any time teachers talk to a student in a positive manner, especially if it is casual and not related to academics, they increase the likelihood that the student feels more significant. When we ask teachers to remember when they were students and recall experiences that made them feel good about themselves, almost without exception they relate non-academic positive interactions with teachers. They give responses such as the following. "My teacher came up to me and said I had a very nice smile." "One day, for reasons having nothing to do with school, I was feeling very down. That evening my teacher called my house and asked me how I was doing." Calling home to chat, sending postcards from trips, inquiring about out of school activities, talking to students about their special interests, remembering birthdays, and acknowledging special family events all increase a student's sense of significance.

Attend Students' Extracurricular Activities

Remember what it felt like to see one of your teachers outside of the school grounds or after the formal school day? For many, this experience caused us to view our teachers differently, because we did not have a frame of reference to accommodate the idea that our teachers were also human beings with interests that extended outside of the classroom. Imagine if the teacher had come to a school-related or community event solely to witness your participation. How would that experience have influenced you? Probably very positively.

Any time teachers talk to a student in a positive manner, especially if it is casual and not related to academics, they increase the likelihood that the student feels more significant.

Kesnya, a student in Ms. Shareef's fifth grade class, exhibited frequent outbursts of disruptive behavior. Ms. Shareef believed in the use of referent authority to influence appropriate student behavior. Upon investigation, Ms. Shareef learned that Kesnya took dance lessons after school and had a recital soon. The teacher decided to attend the recital. When Kesnya saw her there, she asked "Why are you here?" Ms. Shareef responded, "I was interested in seeing you dance." This communication of care and interest impacted Kesnya's pro-social significance and strengthened the relationship between her and Ms. Shareef, eventually leading to a reduction in her disruptive classroom behavior.

Any time a teacher takes the time and effort to communicate personal interest in a student's outside activities, the teacher is impacting pro-social significance.

Share Your Personal Interests with Students

The teacher, sharing some of her own experiences, can encourage students to reveal more of themselves to the class. Teachers might discuss a trip they've taken, music they like, experiences that have been either empowering or embarrassing to them, and their own experiences as a student. When students and teachers reveal pertinent information about themselves in class, it increases everybody's sense of connectedness. This connection is a prerequisite for the development and display of pro-social significance for students in the classroom.

Competence

Competence is a person's sense of mastery in tasks that she values.

STRATEGIES EMPHASIZING EXPERT AUTHORITY

Any strategy that positively impacts student intrinsic motivation, either through an internal locus of control or internal value structure, also impacts pro-social competence. Regardless of how intrinsic motivation is impacted, when students are motivated, they put more effort towards a task. When students put forth more effort, they increase the likelihood that they will be successful. Success impacts a student's success/failure ratio. As students experience more success, they have a concomitant rise in pro-social competence. Specific strategies to increase a student's intrinsic motivation are found in Chapter 14, and strategies to increase a student's success failure ratio are found in Chapter 13.

VIRTUE

Virtue is a person's perceived feeling of worthiness as a result of her ability and willingness to help others.

STRATEGIES EMPHASIZING REFERENT AUTHORITY

Impacting Significance

The teacher who desires to enhance a student's sense of pro-social virtue must not only provide opportunities for the student to display virtue, but also must increase the likelihood that the student cares about the teacher and the class. If the student does not care about the teacher, if the student does not feel affiliated with the class, or if she feels alienated from the school, she will not be inclined to display virtue with these groups. She will, instead, display virtue by helping another group with which she is affiliated. This may be her family, her relatives, or her community. However, this may also be a group of disruptive students; therefore, displaying virtue (distorted) may mean helping these students become more disruptive. When teachers help students feel more significant, they help these students to begin to care about themselves and the class, and so lay the foundation for future pro-social virtuous behavior.

Providing Students Many Opportunities to Help Others in the Classroom, School, and Community

Once students feel a sense of significance and so are willing to be virtuous, teachers must provide opportunities for students to display virtue, such as encouraging them to help classmates or younger students with school activities including academics, sports, and hobbies. Other examples of opportunities to display virtue in school include helping teachers prepare for back to school night, setting up their bulletin boards, cleaning closets, passing out supplies, and assisting with the myriad of other teacher activities in which students may be legitimately supportive. Some recently developed programs such as peer mediation or peer listening provide excellent opportunities for students to become engaged in virtuous behavior. Some schools have moved beyond the school building into the community to attempt to give students broader opportunities for the development of pro-social virtue by instituting service learning. Volunteering time in community organizations and services not only benefits the community as a whole, but seems to have positive effects on students' sense of virtue.

A cautionary note is that if students perceive that they are being coerced or compelled to help others by tying virtuous behavior to grades, consequences, or rewards, the positive effect of these opportunities may be lost (See Chapter 16). The positive feelings of worthiness experienced by students involved in virtuous behavior are the goals that teachers need to emphasize, not external rewards.

Collaborative and Cooperative Instructional Activities

When students feel significant and competent, they are more likely to be become fully engaged in collaborative and cooperative learning opportunities, which involves displaying virtue. Full engagement requires the desire to assist other students in the group to achieve success, achieving success themselves, and sharing of their own skills and competencies.

Teacher Modeling of Virtuous Behavior

It is difficult to expect virtuous behavior from students, if students do not see the adults in their environment display virtuous behavior in both the school and the community. Teachers display virtuous behavior to students any time they engage in unpaid, voluntary, altruistic behavior. When teachers "go the extra mile" to help students or fellow teachers with important tasks, take the lead and volunteer to chaperone student events and activities, or work in the community, they are modeling virtuous behavior which is likely to be noticed by students.

Power

Power is a person's perception that she exerts control over important aspects of her environment.

STRATEGIES EMPHASIZING EXPERT AUTHORITY

Impacting Internal Locus of Control

Any strategy that positively impacts a student's intrinsic motivation through the development of an internal locus of control also increases pro-social power. This is because the definition of power involves the display of control over aspects of one's life that are important. Students who develop an internal locus of control have learned that most of the outcomes in their life are dependent upon the choices that they make. In Chapter 14, various ways to impact students' internal locus of control are discussed.

Skills and Knowledge

Any effective instructional strategy that increases a student's affective, cognitive, or psychomotor mastery increases pro-social power. In Chapter 13, direct instruction and constructivism are discussed as means to increase student mastery.

Table 15.1 outlines some strategies that can be employed to facilitate growth in students' pro-social self-esteem.

TABLE 15.1 ▶ Strategies for Pro-Social Self-Esteem (SE = S + C + V + P)

Pro-Social Significance	Pro-Social Competence	Pro-Social Virtue	Pro-Social Power
Accurate Empathy Reflecting upon your feelings to accurately identify and empathize with your students' feelings **Islands of Significance** Finding something to like about all students **Treat Students as Individuals** Positive, casual interactions with students, not necessarily limited to academic situations **Attend Students' Extracurricular Activities** Showing personal interest in students' out of class activities **Share Your Personal Interests with Students** Teachers sharing relevant personal information with students	**Impacting Intrinsic Motivation** Any strategy that impacts intrinsic motivation by increasing either internal locus of control or internal value structure results in increased effort that leads to greater success, which leads to increased competence.	**Impacting Significance** Students need to know they are cared about and supported in order to care about and support others in the class. **Providing Opportunities to Help Others in the Classroom, School, and Community** Teachers must provide many opportunities for students to display virtue. **Collaborative and Cooperative Instructional Activities** Requires desire to assist other students achieve success, as well as sharing one's own skills and competencies **Teacher Modeling Virtuous Behavior** Virtuous behavior on the part of teachers is likely to be noticed by students.	**Impacting Internal Locus of Control** Students learn that outcomes in life are due to the choices they make. **Skills and Knowledge** Knowledge is power.

The Relationship among the Variables of Success/Failure Ratio, Intrinsic Motivation, and Pro-Social Self-Esteem

In this chapter, the components of pro-social competence and pro-social power are shown to be impacted by the same strategies used to impact the components of intrinsic motivation, which are internal locus of control and internal value structure. In addition, pro-social significance was shown to be a catalyst for pro-social virtue. In Chapter 14 the strategies shown to impact expectation of success through an internal locus of control were similar to those that impact the success/failure ratio because of an increase in intrinsic motivation.

In Chapters 12–15 it was explained that the authority bases of referent and expert clustered together to impact the variables of a successful learning environment—that is, success/failure ratio >1, intrinsic motivation, and pro-social self-esteem. The Self-Control Classroom model is one of interdependency among variables. This interdependency has significant implications for designing and implementing strategies to establish, maintain, and reestablish successful learning environments to influence appropriate student behavior. The importance of these interdependencies is illustrated in Chapter 18 where the Professional Decision Making Matrix is used to reestablish successful learning environments for students who exhibit discipline problems.

Table 15.2 graphically illustrates how referent authority impacts the components of a suc-

TABLE 15.2 ▶ The Impact of Referent Authority on the Components of a Successful Learning Environment

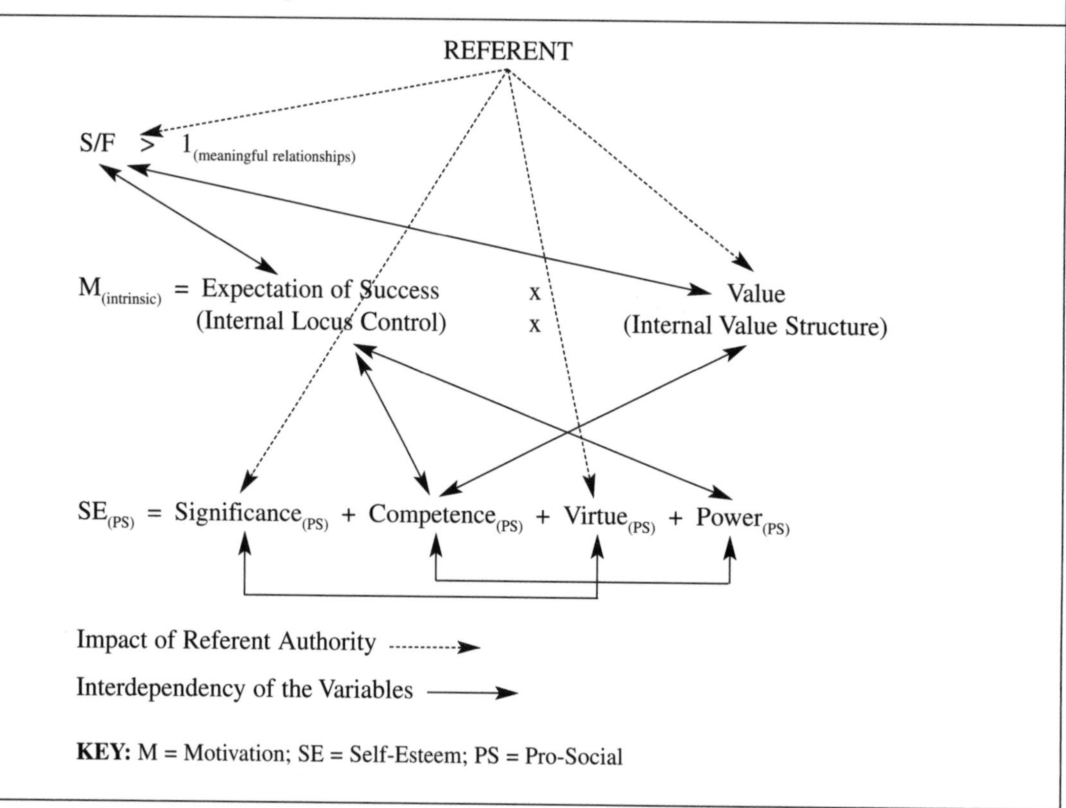

cessful learning environment. The dashed lines indicate that referent authority has a direct positive impact upon the success/failure ratio, intrinsic motivation through its impact on value (internal value structure), and pro-social self-esteem by impacting significance and virtue. The solid lines show the interdependency among all of the components of a successful learning environment that are directly impacted by referent authority.

Table 15.3 graphically illustrates how expert authority impacts the components of a successful learning environment. The dashed lines indicate that expert authority has a direct positive impact upon the success/failure ratio, intrinsic motivation through expectation of success (internal locus of control) and value (internal value structure), and pro-social self-esteem by impacting competence and power. The solid lines show the interdependency among all of the components of a successful learning environment that are directly impacted by expert authority.

TABLE 15.3 ▶ The Impact of Expert Authority on the Components of a Successful Learning Environment

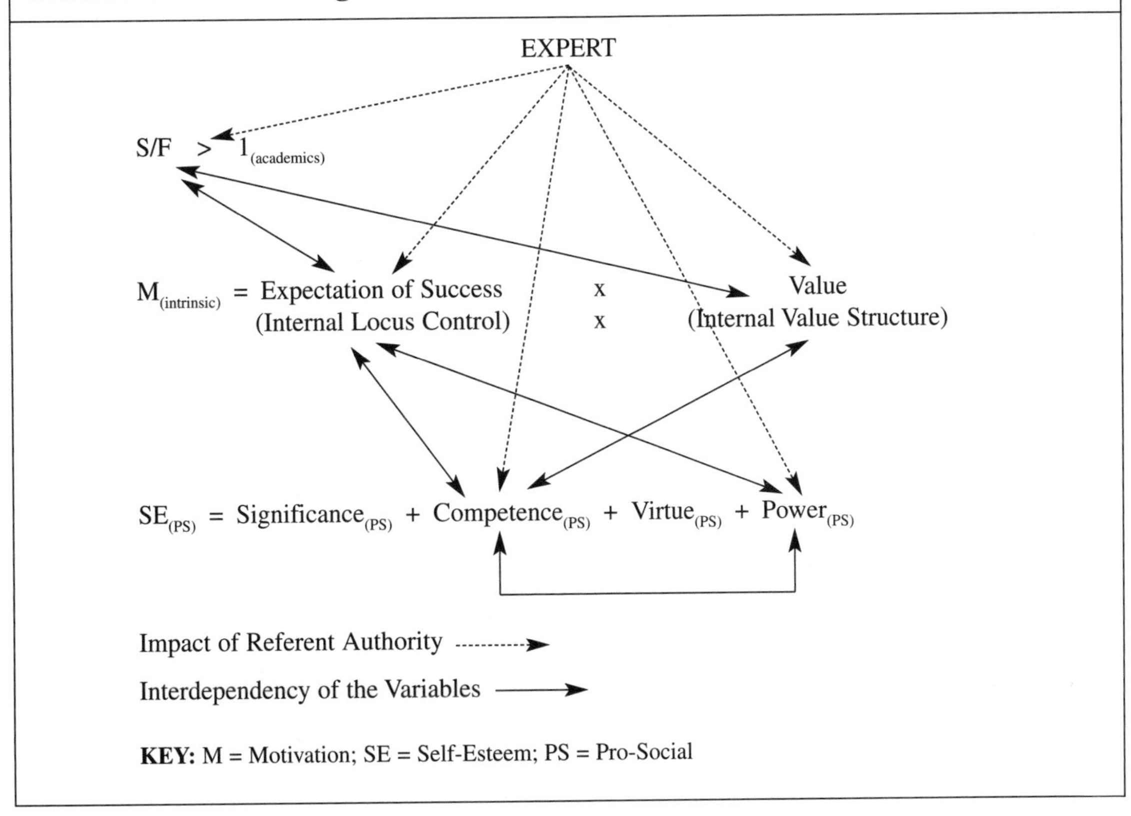

Where We've Been

This Chapter detailed ways to impact students' pro-social self-esteem through the use of referent and expert authority to influence pro-social significance, competence, virtue, and power. It was shown that impacting intrinsic motivation through either an expectation of success by increasing an internal locus of control or value by increasing an internal value structure also impacted pro-social competence. Power is also impacted by influencing intrinsic motivation, primarily through an expectation of success by increasing an internal locus of control. The strategies offered as examples are but a sample of the hundreds of possible ways to facilitate pro-social self-esteem by teachers who believe in the use of referent and expert authority and understand that if they know the whys they can design the hows.

The direct impact of referent and expert authority on the components of success/failure ratio, intrinsic motivation, and pro-social self-esteem and the interdependency of the components was graphically illustrated.

Where We're Headed

In Chapter 16, the many limitations of rewards, when used to shape appropriate student behavior, are thoroughly discussed. The alternative strategy of encouragement is compared and contrasted with rewards, both conceptually and operationally.

CHAPTER 15 CONCEPT MAP

Table 15.1 serves as the concept map for this chapter.

? QUESTIONS FOR THE STUDY TEAM

1. What are some practical strategies that illustrate the use of referent authority to impact the components of pro-social self-esteem? Complete the chart below.

Pro-Social Significance	Pro-Social Competence	Pro-Social Virtue	Pro-Social Power

2. What are some practical strategies that illustrate the use of expert authority to impact the components of pro-social self-esteem? Complete the chart below.

Pro-Social Significance	Pro-Social Competence	Pro-Social Virtue	Pro-Social Power

3. What are some strategies commonly used in classrooms and schools that lead some students to develop distorted self-esteem?

CHAPTER 16

The Limitations of and Alternative to Rewards

"Flatter me and I may not believe you. Criticize me and I may not like you. Ignore me and I may not forgive you. Encourage me and I will not forget you." (Ward, 2000)

In the Still of the Night[1]

We were singing:

"In the still of the night, darling I held you,
held you tight.
Cause I love, love you so, promise I'll never
let you go.
In the still of the night..."[2]

It's 9:00 on a warm summer night circa 1965, in a neighborhood of row houses in Philadelphia, PA. About 35 teenagers are congregated under the glow of the street light on the corner in front of the home of Mr. and Mrs. Podolnick. Every night since school ended, the authors and any interested friends gathered at the same location and time to sing doo-wop, smoke cigarettes, and pick up girls. This scene was typical of city life on the east coast, during the summer nights of the late 50's and 60's. The necessary ingredients were a group of guys who wanted to sing, a larger group of teenagers with nothing better to do, and a street corner. It was crucial to meet at the same corner, at the same time every night, so that everyone would know where to meet.

Mr. and Mrs. Podolnick had the good fortune to have the corner in front of their home be the meeting place in our neighborhood. Unfortunately, they really were not aficionados of the doo-wop genre, nor were they especially fond of anyone under the age of about 55. After many nights of enduring our renditions of such hits as "Guided Missiles,"[3] "Oh What a Night,"[4] "My True Story,"[5] and "Island of Love,"[6] not to men-

[1] Alfie Kohn (1999) has a remarkably similar story to ours in his book "Punished by Rewards"; the similarities are incredible!

[2] Written by Fred Parris, sung by The Five Satins, issued as a Standord single #200, 3/56.

[3] Written by Alfred Gaitwood, sung by The Cufflinks, issued as a Dooto single #409, 12/56.

[4] Written by Marvin Junior and Johnny Funches, sung by The Dells, issued as a Vee-Jay single #204, 8/56.

[5] Written by Eugene Pitt and Oscar Waltzer, sung by The Jive Five, with Joe Rene & Orchestra, issued as a Beltone single #1006, 5/61.

[6] Written by William Ezell and William Sheppard, sung by The Sheppards, issued as a Apex single #7750, 7/59.

tion "Maybe,"[7] and "Over the Mountain, Cross the Sea,"[8] Mr. Podolnick was fed up. He needed to come up with a plan to get rid of this adolescent crowd and do it in a manner that would not result in undue attention being paid to his property and possessions by the assembled youth. One evening, Mr. Podolnick came out of his house and said, "Guys, this is great stuff! The fact that you all come together in front of my house every night has made me more happy than I can adequately express. I love the music, and I really think you guys are good. My only fear is that you might decide not to come around with your friends and sing anymore. So, if you guys are willing to assure me that you'll come out each night at 8:00 instead of 9:00 and sing for a while, I'll pay each one of the singers $1.00. Do we have a deal?" As we pondered the deal, we thought about how much we could do with $1.00. In 1965, the price of gasoline was about 23.9¢, a cheesesteak was 35¢, as was a pack of smokes. Dinner at McDonalds was less than $1.00 for two hungry people. There was no question in our minds that this was a great deal! The next day, we were there at 8:00 sharp and so was everybody else.

For the next few nights, as promised, we arrived at 8:00, and Mr. Podolnick paid us each a buck. Each night, Mr. Podolnick thanked us profusely for coming out and singing. On the fourth night, Mr. Podolnick came out at the agreed upon time and said, "You guys know how much me and the missus love your singing. But you know, I misjudged how much this was all gonna cost me. I still want you to come out, but I can only pay you 50¢ each. Do we still have a deal?" Well, we grumbled a little bit, after all, we were fond of that $1.00 each night. But we realized that 50¢ was still a good amount of money. So the next night, there we were.

After about four nights of singing at the new rate, Mr. Podolnick came out again and addressed the group. "You know, I've been thinking about our deal. Every night you guys come out here and sing, and every night I've been paying you money. Well, me and the missus have decided that enough's enough. If you guys want to come out and sing every night, that's up to you. But I'll be darned if I'm paying you any more money." We were incensed. "The hell with you. If you ain't payin' us, we ain't singin'. Come on you guys let's go." And that was the last time we ever sang in front of that house! Looking back, the authors realized this was a prime example of the limitations of rewards.

The Limitations of Rewards

THE DISCOUNTING PRINCIPLE

A definition of a reward that is congruent with classroom use is using what people want or need by offering it on a contingent basis in order to control how they act (Kohn, 1999). "In the Still of the Night" illustrates several of the problems with rewards. The conventional wisdom is that rewards increase motivation and thus increase the likelihood that target behaviors will be achieved; yet the above story demonstrates that rewards may have the opposite effect.

In our story, why were we initially singing? We sang because we enjoyed the activity. We thought that we were good at it and we enjoyed getting together with our friends. Recall now the definition of intrinsic motivation (Chapter 10), which is a product of expectation of success that is attributed to an internal locus of control and value that is attributed to an internal value structure. Our internal values were the enjoyment of singing, a sense of competence in singing, and an enjoyment of socializing. We had an internal value structure.

Who determined when and where we would meet and sing? Initially this was wholly our

---

[7] Written by Richard Barrett and George Goldner, sung by The Chantels, issued as a End single #1005, 11/57.

[8] Written by Rex Garvin, sung by Johnnie & Joe, with Rex Garvin & His Orchestra, issued as a J&S single #1664, 2/57.

decision and under our control. In other words, our expectation of success, involving meeting and singing, was the result of our choices. Therefore, we had an internal locus of control.

When Mr. Podolnick began to pay us a dollar a piece to come and sing, our value quickly shifted from internal causes, enjoyment and competence, to an external cause, getting paid. Our value structure changed from an internal value structure to an external value structure.

Mr. Podolnick coupled the payment for singing with the requirement that we begin at 8:00 instead of 9:00, which had been our custom. This changed our locus of control from internal to external. Rather than gathering to sing being under our control, it was now under the control of Mr. Podolnick. When Mr. Podolnick stopped paying the money, our singing ended.

The reason Mr. Podolnick had such an easy time changing our motivation from intrinsic to extrinsic, and therefore our behavior from under our control to under his control, has to do with the discounting principle (Morgan, 1984). The discounting principle states that people tend to discount alternative explanations for their behavior if another explanation is more salient. For young people such as we were, a dollar is much more salient a reason for singing than enjoyment and competence. So, according to the discounting principle, we started telling ourselves that the reason to sing was to gain money, rather than our previous, more intrinsic reasons. Therefore, when the money was no longer forthcoming, we no longer had a reason to sing and we stopped.

Analogously, when a chain of pizza restaurants offers a summertime reading program, in which students are rewarded with free pizzas if they read a certain number of books, the motivation for reading any given book is linked to the possibility of getting a free pizza (external value). The student believes that the purpose of reading a book is to gain a highly evident reward, and so he does not attribute his reading behavior to pleasure, which is a far less salient explanation and an internal value. In addition, because the terms of the pizza reading program, including its duration and the number of pizzas available, are all under the control of the pizza chain, the young person experiences an external locus of control.

When the program ends, ironically at the beginning of the school year, a young student may refuse to read any more books, because he no longer can gain the sought after prize, the pizza. Other reasons to read such as enjoyment and the development of competence have been replaced. Although teachers and parents try to reinforce these internal values and provide reasons that attempt to reinforce an internal locus of control, such as the ready availability of books and the fact that reading activity can be done virtually anywhere, the attribution of being rewarded to read is so ingrained, that teachers and parents rapidly fall into step with the pizza parlor and they provide ever increasing rewards for reading. This provision of tangible rewards creates a continual downward spiraling of intrinsic motivation to read, as noted by Deci, Koestner, and Ryan (2001) in their meta analysis of the research on the negative effects of extrinsic rewards upon intrinsic motivation.

All human beings are born with the innate psychological needs for competence and self-determination (Deci, Koestner, and Ryan, 2001). In other words, all human beings are born with a need to be intrinsically motivated through an internal locus of control (self-determination) and an internal value structure (competence). When children are young, they delight in the development of new competencies such as walking, talking, tying their shoes, identifying colors, and riding bikes. No one ever has to reward or bribe a child to exert significant effort to obtain these and a myriad of other competencies. Indeed, when young children learn new things, they have an intrinsic delight in performing novel tasks over and over and in taking control of tasks like tying shoes, which previously was done by or required the help of mommy or daddy.

This intrinsic motivation to learn new skills is perfect readiness for school. The vast majority of children wait with growing excitement for the first day that they will be able to join the big kids and go to school.

This intrinsic motivation to learn new skills is perfect readiness for school.

In the the early years of school, children continue to exhibit much intrinsic motivation. In kindergarten and 1st grade, children rush home to show their families the products of their learning. "Look what I drew!" "I can spell my name!" "I know the alphabet!" "I can read this book!" The proud adults put the papers on the refrigerator and spend hours listening to recitation. When mom, dad, or grandparents ask their child what they did that day in school, the answer can take quite a while.

These happy, eager learners are unaware that significant negative changes to their intrinsic motivation are already beginning to occur. Some papers come home with more smiley faces and smelly stickers than others. As the young student progresses, prizes and awards begin to be offered only to certain children for only certain levels of performance. Eventually these prizes and awards become more formalized in honor rolls, honor assemblies, and certificates of achievement.

When schools and communities come together to develop educational programs that focus upon intrinsic motivation and eschew rewards and their drawbacks, significant positive gains are made by students in both academic achievement and behavior.

More and more, the intrinsic motivation of the young learner, his internal value of the joy of learning and his experience of competence, as well as his internal locus of control, all gained from him viewing learning as a means to develop mastery of his environment, is being replaced by extrinsic motivation. This motivation is composed of external values, such as stickers, candy, homework passes, awards, certificates, honor rolls, and an external locus of control involving doing what the teacher says. Thus when our eager young learner has been bombarded with many extrinsic motivators year after year, when he reaches middle school and is asked by his caregivers what he learned in school, he now replies "nothing." The transformation from an intrinsically motivated learner, dictating his own educational agenda and delighting in his feelings of competence and self determination, to an extrinsically motivated follower, filling in the blanks of a predetermined educational agenda, appears complete.

Disseminating performance-contingent rewards, that is, the largest rewards are given to students who perform the best, and smaller or no rewards are given to students who perform less well, constitutes the dominant classroom practice in American schools. This practice has been shown to have the largest negative impact upon intrinsic motivation of any possible reward structure (Deci, Koestner, and Ryan, 2001). One reason given for students becoming apathetic and dropping out of school, either physically or by withdrawing mentally, is related to performance-based rewards, in that it is thought that the student has resigned from the competition which these rewards engender (Raffini, 1993).

Many teachers and administrators are aware of the inherent problems with systems of rewards for performance. Unfortunately, because they are unaware or poorly educated about alternative systems, teachers and administrators acquiesce in their use of these systems, even though they know reward systems fail to create the conditions for educating intrinsically motivated, lifelong learners. However, when schools and communities come together to develop educational programs that focus upon intrinsic motivation and eschew rewards and their drawbacks, significant positive gains are made by students in both academic achievement and behavior (Collopy and Green, 1995).

OTHER LIMITATIONS OF REWARDS

Since reward giving is so ingrained in many teachers' motivational strategies, we provide additional reasons why wholesale reward giving must be rejected. For instance, what is the message when a student is given a sticker or cookie? Does the student get the message that he is a competent, able individual? Alfie Kohn (1999) states rewards are forms of control. Rewards convey little to the student, other than that he has conformed to the teacher's expectations and the teacher is pleased. The student enjoys the cookie and the positive feeling lasts as long as it takes to eat that cookie. Motivation for future projects is therefore controlled by the size and type of the cookie, the student's present desire for a cookie, and/or the student's desire to please the teacher. Each of the above is an extrinsic motivator which fosters extrinsic motivation, which is contrary to our stated goal of increasing intrinsic motivation. We seriously question whether the average teacher really wishes to send the message that the reason to study long division is to receive a snack.

Rewards convey little to the student, other than that he has conformed to the teacher's expectations and the teacher is pleased.

Some other disadvantages of rewards are listed in Table 16.1.

A particular type of reward, praise, demonstrates all of these drawbacks. Since praise feels so good to the sender and is so easy to use, it is particularly difficult to understand why praise causes problems. Many readers possibly are saying to themselves, "Now you've gone too far! My students, especially the difficult ones, need more praise not less!"

Suppose you tell a student, "You have done a good job." What are you really communicating to that student? You are pleased, and the student has met your criteria for reward. Is pleasing you really your intended goal, or is your goal that the student feels a sense of accomplishment and pride in a job well done? Also, when teachers praise students with comments like "good job, way to go, excellent work, now you're cooking," nothing is communicated to the student about what they have done correctly, what needs improvement, and how to improve in the future. Given praise, the student tends to become less intrinsically motivated for all the same reasons associated with tangible rewards.

One of the author's students wrote candidly about the limitations of rewards in her own academic experience, in the following essay.

> "At a very young age, I learned that if I did well on a test, project, or paper, I would receive an A as a grade. Over the years, I have studied and worked hard in school and have received numerous As as a result. When I do not receive As, I am very disappointed in myself, and many times mentally beat myself up about it. I do not feel as if I have accomplished anything unless I get an A. When I do assignments that are not graded, or are pass/fail, I put very little effort into them and do them simply to get them over with. If there is no possibility that I am going to get an A, I almost feel as if there is no use in trying. I admit that my sole motivation for trying is to get the A.
>
> It has been seldom that I have found myself caring about what I have learned or what I have accomplished. Most of the time, I only care about seeing the A written by the teacher on my assignment. Through the years, I have been conditioned by both my teachers and by my parents to be motivated by external agents (grades). Early

TABLE 16.1 ▶ Other Disadvantages of Rewards
▶ The distribution of rewards is mechanistic. It does not respect the individual's thoughts, feelings, expectations, or perceptions. The student is dealt with as an animal in a "Skinner Box," a device for training animals (mostly rodents), named after the late B.F. Skinner, the father of operant conditioning. As Arthur Koestller (1967) says, "For the anthropomorphic view of the rat, American Psychology substituted a rattomorphic view of man."
▶ Ascertaining appropriate rewards becomes increasingly more difficult as students get older. We begin by rewarding students with stickers and food and progress to certificates, free homework passes, and sometimes even money. What do teachers have left to reward the twelfth graders, especially those that the teacher is having a difficult time reaching, those who no longer care about school-based rewards, and whose financial requirements have outpaced the adults' ability to pay? What's left, "sex, drugs, and rock and roll?"
▶ Rewards may reduce individuals' willingness to do more than what is expected. Students have a tendency, if behavior is contingency based, to perform only as much as is needed to receive the reward. Extra effort is thereby discouraged. One teacher, reflecting upon her personal experience with rewards as motivators said, "I have tried rewards and all I have gotten is the desire for the same rewards for less action, or the desire for more rewards for the same action" (Hohnadel, 2001). The phenomenon of students lack of willingness to do more than what is expected is seen even in graduate school. When the authors have assigned a final paper to graduate students, all of whom are experienced teachers that one might assume are intrinsically motivated to learn, the first question these students usually ask is, "How long does this paper need to be?" In other words, what is the minimum quantity of product that is needed to receive a good grade?
▶ Behaviors are evidenced only under conditions of rewards. This partially explains why behaviors evidenced under conditions of rewards don't generalize to other situations. If the teacher reduces the intrinsic motives for student behavior by paying for performance, a student is apt to reason, "Why should I work for free?" This is so ingrained in students, that when a teacher provides students with something that mimics a reward, without the prior condition of performance being met, significant cognitive dissonance may ensue. One of the authors routinely provides pizza for his class at mid-semester. The objective is solely for community building and socialization. Inevitably a few students ask, "What did we do to deserve this pizza?"
▶ Rewards are available only to the winners, that is, to a few individuals. Therefore, rewards create quitters. By rewarding only certain performance, rewards guarantee that those individuals that feel they are unable or actually are unable to meet the requirements will quit (Collopy and Green, 1995; Raffini, 1993).
▶ Rewards create dependency. If student behavior is rewarded by the teacher, then the student becomes dependent upon the teacher for motivation. Indeed, sometimes teachers become annoyed by the constant demand of certain students to tell the students how they are doing. When the teacher is the source of motivation, this type of behavior is understandable and expected.
▶ Rewards discourage risk-taking behavior, stifle creativity, and decrease the opportunity for students to construct new knowledge. If the focus of the activity is to gain a reward, then any behaviors which do not move directly towards the goal tend to be discouraged. This encourages students to find the quickest, easiest way to achieve the task at hand.
▶ Rewards foster competition and thus discourage cooperative learning (Kohn, 1992). If only a few rewards are available, why would one student want to voluntarily help another student and thus increase the competition for the reward?

on, I learned that good kids got As and Bs, and bad kids got Cs, Ds, and Fs. I also learned exactly what I needed to do to get an A, and I would not do more work than needed to get that A.

Teachers have provided me with optional ungraded assignments that would enrich my learning, and I have always opted not to do them, because I did not have any desire to do something that was not going to be graded. I was conditioned to do things only for the rewards that I would receive at the end. I was a student who was dependent upon grades, therefore dependent upon my teachers as a source of motivation in school." (The authors would like to give proper credit to the student who wrote this essay. Unfortunately, the student's name has been lost over the years.)

You can provide verbal feedback to the student about the positive degree of competence and effort, not just that the student did a "good job."

Should teachers never provide rewards to students? It would be unrealistic for us to suppose that you, upon reading this book, will suddenly cease rewarding or praising students. What is more realistic is that you can learn to couple rewards with messages that are performance/content specific and intrinsically oriented. You can, in other words, provide verbal feedback to the student about the positive degree of competence and effort, not just that the student did a "good job" (Rosenfield, Folger, and Adelman, 1980). "I can see that you put a lot of effort into this project and demonstrated your understanding of the concepts. You have earned a B." Contrast this with, "Good Job! Here's what you've won!" More importantly, if you feel that you must reward a student or group, the less expected the reward is, the less problematic it may be (Deci, Koestner, and Ryan, 2001). It is when the task is performed in order to obtain the reward that most difficulties arise. Unexpected rewards may be quite exciting and pleasant. It is suggested that readers who desire to explore the issue of the limitations of rewards further, read Alfie Kohn's 1999 book, *Punished by Rewards.*

Encouragement

An obvious question may be, "If I reduce my use of rewards because of its often deleterious effects, with what should I replace it?" An alternative to rewards is encouragement. We define encouragement as any teacher behavior that focuses students' attention on their effort, capabilities, interests, self-improvement, what was done correctly or what needs to be improved, or the relevance and usefulness of any task or behavior. The purpose of encouragement, as with rewards, is to increase student motivation and thus increase the likelihood that target behaviors will be achieved. The difference is that the use of rewards influences behavior by impacting extrinsic motivation, while encouragement influences behavior by impacting intrinsic motivation, specifically by increasing an internal locus of control and internal value structure. Some benefits of encouragement are listed in Table 16.2.

As discussed in Chapter 15, the components of a successful learning environment are interdependent. Encouragement impacts intrinsic motivation, primarily through an expectation of success attributed to an internal locus of control and value attributed to an internal value structure. When expectation of success and value are positively impacted, there are concomitant increases in pro-social self-esteem through the components of competence and power. When the encouragement indicates that the teacher is aware of the unique interests and strengths of individual students, pro-social significance is also impacted.

TABLE 16.2 ▶ Benefits of Encouragement
▶ Encouragement focuses upon effort. Encouragement is available to increase the motivation of all students. Certificates of achievement, honor rolls, homework passes, gold stars, and classroom cash motivate only those students who have the capability to achieve at high levels (if at all). Encouragement is available to motivate all students, even those whose capabilities or other factors may preclude them performing at the highest levels of achievement.
▶ Encouragement creates a cycle of high motivation (See Chapter 10). Students who are encouraged try harder, because increased effort leads to increased success, which increases the expectation of future successes and thus increases future motivation. Furthermore, this increased expectation of success is attributable to an internal locus of control, because effort is within the student's control.
▶ Encouragement is congruent with the student's innate desire to develop competence (Deci, Koestner, and Ryan, 2001; White, 1959).
▶ Encouragement inspires independence. By focusing upon an internal locus of control—that is, factors within the student's capability to control—the student is less dependent upon the teacher for motivation.
▶ Encouragement increases cooperation among students because it is available to all, unlike rewards that decrease cooperation and increase competition because they are available only to a few students.
▶ Encouragement increases the likelihood that new behavior generalizes, because students' focus is upon their ability to achieve a higher level of competence, an internal value. This internal value stays with the students as they move to different learning situations, unlike rewards, which are situation specific.
▶ Encouragement increases the risk taking and creativity of learners and therefore the possibility of students constructing new knowledge, because the focus is upon student effort and the development of competence, not competition to obtain the best scores and limited rewards.
▶ Encouragement is equally effective at any age. The saliency of encouragement is consistent over the lifespan, unlike rewards, which need to be increased in saliency as students get older.

EXAMPLES OF THE USE OF ENCOURAGEMENT

Proud of an F

Duce, an eighth grade student, goes to his counselor, Mr. Davis, toward the end of the third marking period. When the counselor, who has been working all year with Duce, inquires about his progress in math class, Duce excitedly replies, "Great! I've got a 48 average!" Mr. Davis reminds Duce that a 48 average is an F. Duce says, "You remember when I first came to you? I had a 15. Mr. Davis replies, "Wow, you increased your grade over 300%." Duce says, "I know, isn't that great?" Mr. Davis says, "You should be proud of yourself." Duce truly is proud of himself.

Being proud of a 48 grade, an F, makes sense only if you understand the power and use of encouragement. When Duce first came to his counselor, Duce told him he was flunking math and that his teacher said, "No matter what you do now, you're going to fail the year because of your low average." Duce, under the circumstances as explained by the teacher, wisely decided it was useless to expend any more energy toward math and proceeded to disrupt the class (hence his referral to the counselor). Mr. Davis challenged Duce in their first meeting by asking, "Can you fail with a higher grade?" Duce said, "Why would I do that?" Mr. Davis said, "Let's put that issue aside for a minute. What I want to know is, if you tried, could you fail with a higher grade?" Duce said, "Sure." Mr. Davis continued to challenge him, "How do you know that?" "Because I'm gifted," Duce replied. "Gifted!" Mr. Davis exclaimed, "You're getting a 15 in math, that doesn't seem very gifted to me." Duce explained, "I'm getting a 15 in math because I haven't done any work. If I tried, I could get much better grades." Mr. Davis said, "Well, here's an opportunity to see how well you might do with no risk involved. Let's see if you can actually fail with a higher grade." Duce accepted the challenge, and at the end of the term, had significantly increased his average. In fact, at the end of the year, Duce had raised his average to a 59, still not a passing grade. However, he felt so proud of his quite impressive turnaround, that Duce told Mr. Davis, "Wait until you see my math grades next year!" Along with his improved grades, came a significant reduction in his disruptive behavior, since he was now in class to learn.

In the face of certain failure, only Mr. Davis' use of encouragement, increasing Duce's internal locus of control (effort) and internal value (the development of competence), could influence Duce to put forward effort in this class.

Feeling Competent, Yet Getting It Wrong

Ross comes home and announces, "My teacher thinks that I have a lot of talent in math" and hands his father his test paper. His father is confused when he sees that Ross earned a 73 on the exam. Examining the paper further, his father notices that the teacher has written extensive comments. One in particular stood out. "Ross, you have attempted to solve this equation using completing squares, a technique that we will not begin to study for a few weeks. This indicates to me that you have real insight into mathematics and an innate talent when it comes to problem solving. The proper solution, however, was ..." Next to the comment was a −10 because the problem was solved incorrectly.

Ross' teacher used encouragement to focus upon Ross' skills and willingness to take academic risks. At the same time, the teacher indicated why the problem was wrong and what needed to be corrected. Due to the use of encouragement, Ross focused on the positive message regarding his competency, rather than focusing upon the −10. In addition, because Ross was not discouraged, he was willing to learn from the specific mathematical feedback provided along with the encouragement.

Playing Quidditch Correctly

Travis wrote an essay explaining how the game of Quidditch is played in the book *Harry Potter and the Sorcerer's Stone* (Rowling, 1998). The teacher returned the essay with the following written comments. "Travis, your comparison of the game of Quidditch to the game of ice hockey really indicated your knowledge and love of ice hockey. In addition, your use of descriptive language made the essay come alive, and I felt as if I were there. All the words are spelled correctly, and your use of capitalization and paragraphs is accurate. However, it is necessary to go back and reread the section that describes the rules relating to the conduct of the Beater. You have included several interesting possibilities, but some of them, such as your idea that the Beater can throw rocks at the Seeker after knocking him off his broom, are against the rules. Please check each one of your ideas against the rules in the book to determine if they are legal. If they are, great; if not, please rewrite the paragraph."

The teacher in this case encouraged Travis, by first indicating that he recognized a personal interest of Travis' and noting everything that was done correctly. Then corrective specific feedback was given. The use of encouragement increases the likelihood that Ross will not be discouraged by the need to rework the paper.

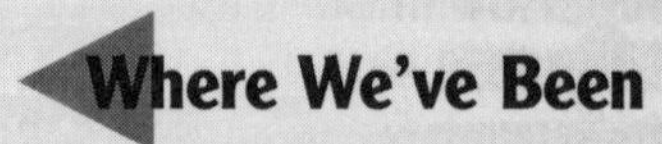

Where We've Been

This chapter explored the limitations of rewards and compared them with the advantages of using an alternative, encouragement. The outcomes of the use of rewards and the outcomes of the use of encouragement were contrasted. The major difference between the two is how rewards and encouragement impact motivation. The use of rewards influences behavior by impacting extrinsic motivation, while encouragement influences behavior by impacting intrinsic motivation, specifically by increasing an internal locus of control and an internal value structure.

The other differences between rewards and encouragement are the degree of specificity, age dependency, amount of effort, degree of generalization, dependency, risk taking and creativity, and the degree of cooperation. Specific examples of the use of encouragement were provided.

Where We're Headed

In the next chapter, there is discussion of the many limitations of punishment when used to discourage inappropriate behavior. The alternative strategy of consequences, both natural and logical, is defined conceptually and operationally. The use of consequences to impact a successful learning environment is then explored.

Chapter 16 Concept Map

REWARDS: Using what people want or need by offering it on a contingent basis in order to control how they act (Kohn, 1999)

LIMITATIONS

- Erodes intrinsic motivation and fosters extrinsic motivation because of discounting principle
- Mechanistic
- Loses effectivenss as students get older
- Reduces willingness to do more than what is expected and available only to the winners, therefore creates quitters
- Behaviors are usually evident only in reward situations, therefore behaviors do not generalize
- Creates dependency
- Discourages academic risk taking and creativity for fear of not receiving a reward
- Fosters competition and reduces cooperation among learners

ENCOURAGEMENT: Any teacher behavior that focuses students' attention on their effort, capabilities, interests, self-improvement, what was done correctly or what needs to be improved, or the relevance and usefulness of any task or behavior

BENEFITS

- Fosters intrinsic motivation because of focus upon effort and an individual's innate desire to develop competence
- Individualized
- Effective at all ages
- Available to all and focuses upon effort and competence development, therefore creates triers
- Because of the development of intrinsic motivation, behaviors usually generalize
- Creates independence
- Increases academic risk taking and creativity since these behaviors are encouraged
- Fosters cooperation and decreases competition among learners

QUESTIONS FOR THE STUDY TEAM

1. Rewards is how the real world works. After all, isn't a teacher's paycheck at the end of the week his reward for teaching?

2. If rewards have so many limitations, why do so many teachers use them?

3. If saying "good job" to a student is a form of reward, what then can teachers say to students that would be an encouragement?

4. How may the use of rewards and honor rolls make some students apathetic?

5. While teachers don't generally reward a student who is failing, what kinds of encouragement can teachers use effectively with a student who's failing?

6. School is about academic achievement, and rewards recognize the students who meet this goal. How does encouragement recognize students who meet academic goals?

7. Can't teachers overcome the limitations of rewards if they give everyone in the class a reward?

8. In reality, if students do what they are suppose to do, something nice will happen to them, whether it's a reward or an encouraging remark. Therefore, isn't the real difference between rewards and encouragement just a matter of semantics?

9. What are some practical classroom encouragement strategies?

CHAPTER 17

The Limitations of and Alternatives to Punishment

"Reform will not occur if we rely on teachers who: don't believe that all children can learn, can't create limitless ways to teach children, won't persevere, or believe that children learn best when threatened, punished, prodded, or humiliated." (Haberman, 1995).

What Is Punishment?

Punishment is typically defined by psychologists as any adverse intervention (physical or psychological discomfort) that decreases the occurrence of a targeted behavior. Educators usually believe that punishment is delivered to young people with the idea that certain objectionable behaviors will cease and will be replaced by more appropriate behaviors. Therefore, it is thought that punishment is a tool to change behavior in a positive way.

Using a not too far-fetched example from adolescence, let's see how the application of punishment fulfills this belief of educators.

Baby You Can Drive My Car

Readers, think back to that distant time when you were 16 years old and learning to drive. In particular remember clearly those weeks spent with mom or dad or the driving instructor learning the ins and outs of the rules of the road. The time came, as it does for everyone, when the licensing exam was taken and passed. Typically, upon receiving a driver's license, a young driver is permitted by their parents to begin taking short trips to gain solo experience. These include going to the supermarket, returning library books, filling the tank with gas, and ferrying little brothers or sisters to their games or lessons. Finally, though, the moment arrives that all parents fear; you are ready to have the car for the night, by yourself, to go out and enjoy.

You've been planning this night for weeks. You come home from school, eat dinner, and by 6:30 you are picking up your friends in your family's brand new Oldsmobile Cutlass and heading out to the mall. You arrive at the mall and carefully drive through the parking lot looking for a space. You find one, turn the wheel too tightly, and as you pull in to park, you hear a loud scratching noise, as the passenger side of your car impacts the fender of the pickup truck parked in the next space. On examination, there is a two foot long scratch on your car and no damage to the pickup truck.

You are panicked. You ask your friends, "What should I do?" Your friends, more interested in salvaging the evening than problem solving, encourage you to go to the mall and figure it out later. After going to the mall and back to the car, lo and behold, in spite of your fervent hopes, the scratch is still there. Now you really need some advice on how to deal with what you see as a major catastrophe in your young life.

Your friends have several suggestions. The first friend says, "Tell the truth. What's the worst that can happen?" The second friend says, "I have a better idea. When this happened to my brother, he told my parents that when he went into the mall, everything was fine, but when he came out, there was a dent in the car. All his friends backed him up." The third friend said, "That's too complicated. Just go home and park the car on the street with the side that's scratched facing outward. In the morning, when your parents see the scratch, tell them, 'It wasn't that way last night!' Somebody must have sideswiped the car while it was parked!"

Research supports that one of the major drawbacks to the use of punishment is that it motivates the individual to avoid the punishment and punisher.

Going back to when you were 16. What would you have told your parents? It's important to remember how things were for you at that time. We all know that we'd all tell the truth if it happened to us today. But what would have been your course of action then?

Reasons to Lie

When we pose this situation to participants in workshops, there are always people in the workshop who tell us they would have lied under the circumstances. The reasons typically given include:

- "My father would have killed me!"
- "I would have been grounded for months."
- "I would've never gotten the car again."
- "They would've never let me live it down."
- "They would have made me feel so guilty and incompetent."

In fact, many participants have told us that a situation like the above actually happened to them as adolescents, and their parents still don't know the truth.

All the reasons for lying given above have one thing in common: they are all in response to the anticipation of punishment, as the individuals felt there was a threat of physical or psychological discomfort. The participants who lied likely had histories of either being punished for previous inappropriate behavior or witnessing others in their families being punished.

Is the premise of some educators that punishments cause a change in behavior accurate? In the example above, the anticipation of punishment certainly effectuated a change in behavior. It caused people to lie. Research supports that one of the major drawbacks to the use of punishment is that it motivates the individual to avoid the punishment and punisher. Types of avoidance behavior are lying, cheating, and becoming better at not being caught (Kohn, 1999; Kamii, 1991).

Reasons to Tell the Truth

Many participants volunteer that they would have been honest with their parents about the incident. The reasons they give have different rationales. The first is actually a fear of punishment. People say:

- "If I was caught lying, my father would've killed me."
- "I would have been grounded for months."
- "I would never have gotten the car again."
- "They would have never let me live it down."

- "They would have made me feel so guilty and incompetent."

So these people would have told the truth for the same reasons that the people above would have lied, to avoid punishment. Some people may now reason, punishment works, because the fear of being punished caused these participants to tell the truth. The fallacy with this reasoning is that we do not want to teach young people that the reason to tell the truth is to avoid punishment. If it is, what's the reason to tell the truth when there is no punisher present, such as when students go to college or no one is there to witness the behavior?

The second reason given for telling the truth is that the participants knew that their parents would have been reasonable, supportive, and understanding, and would have worked with them to rectify the problem.

1) Their parents would have focused first upon whether anyone was injured.
2) Then the next concern would have been whether or not there was any damage to the other vehicle, and if there was, did their young son or daughter talk to the owner or leave a note on the car?
3) Their parents would have asked then how the young person was going to correct the situation, or more specifically, how would they pay for the damage.
4) Finally, these parents would discuss how to help their child avoid this situation in the future, perhaps including what type of further instruction, such as how to park, was needed.

Accountability is not fostered in an environment where young people avoid or lie to adults when there is a problem, because they fear indignation and punishment—that is, the adults make use of legitimate and coercive authority.

Of course, most parents have these concerns. When the participants anticipated punishment, their perception was not of parental concern, but of an environment of anger, blame, and retribution. In the homes of the participants who told the truth, parents were perceived as partners in solving a very real problem. Some people might say, "Aren't paying for the damage to the car and needing to relearn parking forms of punishment?" These are not punishments; they are logical consequences related to the problem. The difference in the above scenarios is that punishment is designed to cause discomfort, either psychological or physical, while a logical consequence is meant to teach appropriate behavior and problem solving. The significant differences between punishments and logical consequences are described later in this chapter.

The third reason related by participants to tell the truth is that they have learned, that "Telling the truth is the right thing to do." Telling the truth increases an individual's feelings of integrity, honor, duty to others, and pride in oneself. These individuals are intrinsically motivated to tell the truth because feelings of integrity, honor, duty to others, and pride in oneself are all internal values.

How do adults encourage young people to tell the truth because it's the right thing to do? Clearly, people who tell the truth for this reason have learned to be accountable for their behavior. In order to be accountable, young people have to trust that when a problem occurs, they can count on adults to be reasonable, understanding, and supportive—that is, to show referent authority. In addition, young people need to be assured that adults will help them solve problems—that is, to use their expert authority. Accountability is not fostered in an environment where young people avoid or lie to adults when there is a problem, because they fear indignation and punishment—that is, the adults make use of legitimate and coercive authority.

Limitations of Punishment

Educational researchers and psychologists continually have exhorted teachers and administrators about the limitations of physical punishment. Epstein (1979) stated, "There is no pedagogical justification for inflicting pain. . . . It does not merit any serious discussion of pros and cons" (pp. 229–230). Clarizio (1980) stated, ". . . there is very little in the way to suggest the benefit of physical punishment in the schools, but there is a substantial body of research to suggest that this method can have undesirable long-term side effects" (p. 141). Even the very popular teacher-centered Assertive Discipline model warns that, "Consequences should never be psychologically or physically harmful to the students . . . corporal punishment should never be administered" (Canter, 1989, p. 58).

Some types of punishment, although non-physical, nevertheless produce psychological harm.

Some types of punishment, although non-physical, nevertheless produce psychological harm. Examples include screaming at a student, public reprimands, threats, and accusations. Schoolwork itself may be punishing, as in extra assignments or writing 100 times, "I will not . . ." Additionally, examples of this type of punishment are insulting comments, sarcasm, put-downs, eye rolling, heavy sighing, or any other behavior meant to shame, berate, or humiliate a child.

It is the authors' belief that neither physical nor psychological punishment is effective, in the long-term, at reducing inappropriate student behavior or increasing the likelihood of appropriate behavior. Since punishment has always been a dominant feature of most teachers' repertoire of management techniques, if it were effective in the long run, discipline problems in the schools would be a footnote in history and this book need not be written.

When the goal of intervention is to enhance a student's ability for self-control and accountability, it is important that the student focus on her behavior and its effects on herself and on others. Punishment clouds this self-focus by concentrating the student's concern on the punisher, the teacher, and the punishment, rather than upon herself and her behaviors. The punishment is not perceived to be the result of the student's behavior (internal locus of control). It is perceived to be the result of the teacher being mean, arbitrary, and hurtful (external locus of control) (Levin and Shanken-Kaye, 1996). This leads to student rage, resentment, hostility, and a desire to get even with the teacher, "the one who did this to me" (Dreikurs, Grundwald, and Pepper, 1982).

The following scenario demonstrates how punishment clouds self-focus and decreases the likelihood of developing accountability.

While classes are in session, Carolyn, a 10th grade student, is walking to the ladies room, with the permission of her teacher. Ms. Riley, a teacher that Carolyn had in 9th grade, calls from across the hall, "Carolyn, get to class now." Carolyn walks over to Ms. Riley and tells her that she is on her way to the ladies room. Ms. Riley then asks to see her pass. Carolyn says, "I don't have one, but Ms. Recker said it was okay to go." Ms. Riley says, "You know what, Carolyn, you pulled this stuff last year with me. I don't believe you for a second. You shouldn't be leaving the class for any reason. Get back to class now." Carolyn responds, "I don't care if you believe me or not, I gotta go to the bathroom and I'm going." With that, Carolyn continues on her way to the ladies room. Ms. Riley runs after Carolyn, grabs her by the arm, and says, "Don't you dare walk away from me when I'm talking to you. Who do you think you are? Where you're going, is with me to the office." Carolyn yanks her arm back and screams at Ms. Riley, "Why don't you just go f*** yourself." Ms. Riley calls security, who escorts Carolyn to the vice principal's office.

Here we have a situation where Carolyn is in violation of the rule that students need a hall pass while classes are in session. The teacher certainly had the responsibility to enforce the school policy. However, the manner in which Ms. Riley chose to interact with Carolyn was psychological punishment. Ms. Riley displayed distorted power, as her intervention was designed to challenge Carolyn's truthfulness and to put her down. In addition, Ms. Riley attempted to reinforce her legitimate authority, in an attempt to take control of Carolyn's behavior (external locus of control). Carolyn's response was to defend herself through her own display of distorted power (a parallel process, See Chapter 7). If Ms. Riley's purpose was to teach Carolyn the reasons why a pass was required and give her the opportunity to obtain a pass, the lesson was not effective.

Ms. Ramero, the vice principal, now finds herself in a very difficult situation. No matter how she attempts to get Carolyn to understand that she needs a pass to be in the hall, even with the teacher's permission, and that it is inappropriate to curse at a teacher, Carolyn is focused on her indignation at being called a liar, a poor student, and being grabbed by Ms. Riley. Ms. Ramero gives Carolyn a two-day in-school suspension.

When Carolyn goes home, far from accepting accountability for the suspension, she tells her parents that she got suspended because, "Ms. Riley is an asshole and is out to get me," rather than "I didn't have a hall pass and I told the teacher to go f*** herself."

Punishment does not teach alternative acceptable behaviors. In fact, it models inappropriate behavior, by teaching students that when they are older and in a position of authority (or even currently) they can punish others who might be younger or with less authority (Jones and Jones, 1981).

Yinell is a 3rd grade student. Whenever she doesn't get her way with other students, she hits them. Yinell's class is taught by two teachers with very different approaches to classroom discipline. Ms. Markowitz, the math and science teacher, believes in coercive authority and insists upon punishing Yinell for any aggressive behavior. When Ms. Markowitz is teaching, and she sees Yinell become aggressive, Yinell is frequently put into a corner, sent out of the room, or kept in from recess. Yinell has learned that whether or not to be aggressive depends upon whether she thinks she will be caught and punished by Ms. Markowitz. She has developed an external locus of control for her behavior. In spite of the interventions, Yinell continues to hit other children in Ms. Markowitz's class. In addition, she has become very sneaky in her aggression.

Ms. Chang, the English and social studies teacher, recognizes that Yinell needs to be taught how her anger is harming both Yinell and other students, how to recognize her anger, and how to deal with her anger more appropriately. Ms. Chang meets with Yinell after lunch to teach her a three-step problem-solving method, which she encourages Yinell to practice in her classroom. Ms. Chang protects the learning environment for the other students, while helping Yinell gain self-control (internal locus of control) by seating her in the front of the class and providing frequent non-verbal cues during the day, to indicate to Yinell that she is watching her and is aware of her efforts. After a month, Yinell's aggression has significantly decreased, and when she is aggressive, she recognizes the fact right away and apologizes for her conduct.

Kamii (1991) delineated three other outcomes of punishment:

- the calculation of risks, where students spend time trying to figure out how they can get away with something,

- blind conformity, which fails to teach self-control and accountability, and creates a dependency upon the punisher to indicate the difference between right and wrong (facilitates an external locus of control), and
- revolt, which manifests itself in additional disruptive behavior (as with Carolyn in the hallway and Yinell hitting others), or by more covert means, such as shutting down completely (distorted power).

The irony of punishment is that the more an individual uses this distorted power to try and control others' behavior, the less real influence she has over them.

The irony of punishment is that the more an individual uses this distorted power to try and control others' behavior, the less real influence she has over them (Gordon, 1989).

When the unintended outcomes of punishment, such as lying and revolt occur, teachers reason that even stricter punishment must be needed. "After all, if I can punish this kid enough, surely she'll behave eventually." Unfortunately, this vicious cycle does not lead to appropriate student behavior, but instead to more disruption, aggression, and hostility (Kohn, 1999). Additionally, as students get older, they tend to become inured to punishment. As with rewards, the magnitude of punishment has to be increased while the probability of success decreases with age.

As with rewards, the magnitude of punishment has to be increased while the probability of success decreases with age.

A final concern is that punishment reinforces the earliest stage of moral reasoning, "punishment-obedience". In this stage of moral development, what differentiates right from wrong is determined by which behaviors are punished (wrong), and which are rewarded (right). Teachers and other adults who attempt to influence students' behavior through the application of rewards and punishments interfere with students development of more sophisticated and pro-social notions of right and wrong, such as those consistent with the "social contract" stage of moral development. In this stage, right and wrong is a function of the protection of individual rights and democratic principles (Kohlberg, 1969). The most positive, democratic, and intellectually challenging schools and classrooms set the stage for certain students to eventually achieve the highest level of moral reasoning, at which right and wrong are determined by universal ethical principles. For example, Thomas Jefferson wrote the following, "We hold these truths to be self-evident, that all men are created equal, that they are endowed by their Creator with certain unalienable Rights, that among these are Life, Liberty and the pursuit of Happiness" (Jefferson, 1776).

Creating classrooms that emphasize democratic processes to encourage the development of higher levels of moral reasoning to differentiate what is right from what is wrong is explored in Butchart and McEwan, 1998.

Consequences

So what's a teacher to do? Some readers may be thinking, "OK, I finally figured out that the authors think that kids should get away with anything. No matter what the behavior, we teachers have to be understanding, sensitive, and empathetic. After all, self-control is where it's at, and let's not do anything that will teach this kid that there are other people in this world besides her." Teachers want students to be accountable and to recognize that when they choose inappropriate behavior, there is some concrete result. Teachers believe that when students know that there are concrete results for their behavior, they will behave appropriately in the classroom.

The authors agree that students must be held accountable for their behavior, and students need to exhibit appropriate behavior in the classroom. If not, there should be consequences. When students learn the cause and effect relationship that exists between how they choose to behave and the consequences of their behavior, they may or may not develop the desired outcomes. Whether or not a student develops accountability is a function of the type of consequence that the student experiences and the attribution the student makes as to the cause of the consequence. Punishments are contrived consequences. As noted above, when students are punished, they attribute the punishment to the teacher being mean, arbitrary, and hurtful (external locus of control), rather than their own behavior (internal locus of control).

Because punishment is a distorted use of teacher power, it encourages the display of distorted power by the student due to the parallel process (See Chapter 7). A common way that students exhibit distorted power is through being disruptive and other types of inappropriate classroom behavior.

In addition to punishment, there are two other types of consequences: natural consequences and logical consequences. Starting now, contrived consequences will be referred to as punishments, while the term "consequence" will be used solely when describing natural and logical consequences.

NATURAL CONSEQUENCES

Natural consequences are probably the most powerful learning experiences that we encounter, and thus are significant modifiers of future behavior. Natural consequences have been described as the real world's classroom. Some common natural consequences include:

- locking yourself out of the house because you misplaced your key,
- waking up on Sunday morning with a hangover because you drank too much Saturday night,
- having a car accident because you drove too fast, and
- receiving a painful sunburn because you sat in the sun too long.

All of these consequences have something in common. They are the result of action or inaction of the individual and do not involve the intervention of any other person. Thus, the person responsible or the person "to blame" for the negative outcome is the individual who misplaced the key, drank too much, drove too fast, or sat in the sun too long. Because the individual controls the antecedents to the consequence, natural consequences increase the development of an internal locus of control.

Because the individual controls the antecedents to the consequence, natural consequences increase the development of an internal locus of control.

Dreikurs (1964) emphasized that by allowing students to experience the natural consequences of their behavior, they are provided with an honest and real-life learning situation. Primarily because of safety considerations, the use of natural consequences in a classroom is somewhat limited. For instance, the natural consequence of not following safety procedures in a science laboratory or a technology class may be serious bodily harm. Certainly this outcome cannot be allowed to happen. Nevertheless, whenever feasible and not dangerous, allowing students to experience the natural consequences of their behaviors is a strong learning experience. Natural consequences clearly communicate the cause and effect relationship of behavioral choices because of an internal locus of control, and natural consequences decrease the possibility of displays of distorted power between the teacher and student.

Examples of natural consequences that students may experience in the classroom are:

- losing an assignment because of disorganization,
- having less time to complete a test because the student came to class late,
- falling and scraping one's knee due to running in the hallway,
- missing class work due to cutting class,
- being cold at recess because of leaving home dressed inappropriately,
- missing announcements of an upcoming assignment or test because of talking to a neighbor, and
- being injured in physical education activities because of inattentiveness.

Some teachers cannot resist the temptation to tell the student why the natural consequence occurred.

For example, Ms. Blanco might say, "Gabriella, the reason you can't find your assignment is because you have such a sloppy notebook. It only takes a few minutes a day to keep your notebook organized. I told you before to get it organized or else this would happen." If you do this, you are in effect turning a valuable learning experience into a punishment. Gabriella obviously knows why the assignment is lost and doesn't need Ms. Blanco to tell her. By scolding Gabriella, Ms. Blanco switches the focus from Gabriella's behavior to her own behavior. Without Ms. Blanco's comments, Gabriella would think "Man, this is really a drag. I did that homework and I can't find it. Now I have to do it again." The fact that Gabriella lost her homework is the natural consequence of her lack of organization. Her decision to re-do the homework is thinking that is congruent with the development of an internal locus of control and pro-social power. However, due to Ms. Blanco's comments, Gabriella thinks, "What a moron Ms. Blanco is. What does she think, I'm stupid or somethin'? I bet she's gonna give me a lousy grade now. I'm copying the assignment from Linda at lunch and telling her I found it in my locker, the bitch." This indicates an external locus of control and distorted power.

When a natural consequence occurs, "nature" is the teacher; the classroom teacher does not have to do anything.

LOGICAL CONSEQUENCES

When natural consequences are not appropriate or do not occur, the teacher needs to intervene with a logical consequence. A logical consequence is a consequence which, although requiring the intervention of the teacher or another person, has some direct, meaningful connection to the behavior which precedes it; therefore it is not viewed as arbitrary or capricious. Unlike punishment, which is intended to cause discomfort, logical consequences are used to teach. Like natural consequences, logical consequences are powerful influences on students' behavior. Here are some examples.

- Mary must clean up the paint that she spilled on the floor during art.
- Ellen is not called upon by the teacher because she doesn't raise her hand.
- Phylicia does not receive a copy of the test until she has her books put away.
- Davida has to clean up the desk she's written on.
- Tamica has to stay after school to make up work, which she missed by being late to class.
- Francine has to work individually because she has not been cooperative with her group.
- The principal calls the police when Alicia brings a knife to school.

With the use of both logical and natural consequences, the focus is on the student's behavior and its relationship to the consequence. The student is therefore more likely to develop an internal locus of control, understanding that the outcomes in her life are largely the result of the decisions she makes. Because the student's attention is directed toward her own decision making, not the teacher's behavior, the student is more likely to learn valuable lessons about how to change her behavior to alter the outcome of future choices (pro-social power).

Because logical consequences are not given to cause discomfort, they are less likely to encourage lying, the calculation of risks, blind conformity, and the avoidance of the teacher by the student. When students understand that the outcomes in their lives are largely the result of the decisions they make, they naturally focus upon their own behavior, rather than the behavior of teachers. Self-focus facilitates the development of accountability. When students recognize their accountability, they are more likely to seek out alternative solutions to future problems in order to facilitate more positive outcomes. Thus students learn more appropriate behavior and are not dependent upon outside individuals to signal them when they are behaving inappropriately.

When students understand that the outcomes in their lives are largely the result of the decisions they make, they naturally focus upon their own behavior, rather than the behavior of teachers.

Logical, as well as natural consequences are effective at all age levels, because they are not contrived as are punishments; more importantly, they reflect the reality of the actual situation. In addition, logical consequences are consistent with the goal of moral development of students, because they do not rely upon reward and punishment as reasons why behaviors are right or wrong.

How Logical Consequences Become Punishments

Even if the outcome of an inappropriate behavior is logically related to that behavior, it may be perceived as either a logical consequence or a punishment, depending upon the delivery of the outcome. For instance, in the previous example of damaging the family car, a logically related outcome was to pay for the damage to the car and to practice parking to avoid a repetition of the problem. Let's consider two ways that this outcome can be delivered.

In the first scenario, the teenager comes home and tells her mom, "I had an accident when I was parking at the mall. Would you come outside and look at the car?" Her mother asks, with calm concern, "Was anyone hurt?" When the daughter says no, the mother asks, "Was there any damage to the other car?" When she again says no, her mother says, "If there was, do you know what you'd need to do?" The daughter answers that she'd need to leave a note on the other car with her name and phone number and write down the make, model, and license number of the other car, so she could get in touch with the owners, in case they don't get the note. "Okay," her mom says, "let's go see the damage." When they go outside to the car, the mother says, "Well, this sure is something that needs to be repaired. Even though this is going to cost several hundred dollars, I don't think we should report it to the insurance company. Tomorrow, you and your dad will go to the body shop and get an estimate of the repair cost. We'll have to figure out a way for you to pay for this. I know you probably don't have enough money, but we'll work out some kind of payment plan for you to reimburse your dad and me. In addition, you need to get more practice in parallel parking, so we'll go back to the mall this weekend and practice parking the car. Thanks for telling me the truth. Everybody has difficulty when they learn a new skill. I know you're pretty upset, but this isn't the end of the world. We'll work it out."

After this interchange, the daughter goes up to her room, and, although she's really upset about having had an accident, she's beginning to think about how to pay for the damage to the car. In addition, she feels a sense of relief that she did the right thing and that her mom was so understanding.

In the second scenario, the teenager comes home and tells her mom, "I had an accident when I was parking at the mall. Would you come outside and look at the car?" Her mother screams at the top of her lungs, "You what! You had an accident after driving the car for less than a day! Your dad and I have never had an accident and we both have been driving for over twenty-five years! I told you that you weren't ready to take the car! Didn't they teach you anything in driver's ed? Who was hurt?" The daughter says, "No one was hurt." The mother continues, "You probably didn't even leave a note on the other car! You know your careless, irresponsible behavior is killing your father! Stanley, get down here and look at what your daughter did to our car! This is not going to be reported to the insurance company! You're paying for this! I don't know how, and I don't care, but you better find a way to come up with the money! As far as your weekend plans, forget them! I'm taking you back to the mall and you'll park that car a thousand times if that's what it takes! You know, with you it's always one catastrophe after another! At least you didn't lie this time!"

The daughter goes up to her room, calls her friend and says, "Come pick me up. I'm getting out of this nut house. My parents are lunatics. If they think I'm paying for this car, they're crazy. That's the last time they get the truth from me."

In both cases, the outcomes, paying for the damage to the car and learning to park, are the same. In the first case, the outcome is perceived as a logical consequence because the teenager's mom used referent authority by demonstrating concern, support, and trust. In addition, she exhibited expert authority by offering to help her daughter figure out how she will pay for the damage and offering to take her to the mall to learn to park the car. As a result, the daughter focused upon her own behavior. She felt good about her decision to tell the truth, increasing the likelihood that the daughter will seek her parents out in the future when difficult situations arise. Finally, as a result of the logical consequence, the daughter will likely learn to be a more skilled driver.

In the second case, the outcome is perceived as a punishment. The teenager's mother yelled, was insulting, communicated distrust, didn't offer to help her daughter figure out how to pay for the damage to the car, and delivered the outcome in a manner intended to cause her discomfort and pain. As a result, the daughter focused upon her mom's behavior and felt bad about telling the truth. In addition, she planned to avoid such interactions in the future. Finally, nothing about the punishment increases the possibility that the daughter will become a more skilled driver.

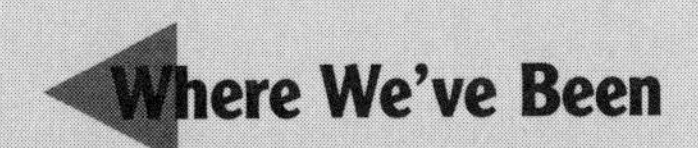

Where We've Been

This is the final chapter in the section Maintaining Successful Learning Environments. The chapter explored the different outcomes of punishment and natural and logical consequences. Punishment facilitates an external locus of control and encourages the display of distorted power, decreasing the likelihood that students develop accountability and learn to behave appropriately. In contrast, natural and logical consequences facilitate an internal locus of control and encourage the display of pro-social power, increasing the likelihood that students develop accountability and learn to behave appropriately.

Other differences we've discussed are the impact upon students' avoidant behavior, self-focus, calculation of risks, conformity, dependency, the effects of age, and the development of moral reasoning. Examples of natural and logical consequences are provided. The chapter concludes with an example of how the same behavioral outcome may be perceived either as a punishment or as a consequence, depending upon the delivery.

Where We're Headed

The next chapter is the beginning of a new section on Reestablishing a Successful Learning Environment for Students with Common and Chronic Discipline Problems. The instrument for achieving this, the Professional Decision Making Matrix, previously introduced in Chapter 12, will be discussed in more depth. Case studies will be presented to illustrate the use of the matrix to form hypotheses about student behavior and analyze and design teacher interventions that are congruent with the Self-Control Classroom model.

Chapter 17 Concept Map

PUNISHMENT: Interventions that are intended to cause physical or psychological discomfort to decrease the occurrence of a targeted behavior.

LIMITATIONS

- Fosters extrinsic motivation through an external locus of control
- Encourages avoidance behavior
- Loses effectivenss as students get older
- Facilitates students' use of distorted power
- Focus is on punisher's behavior
- Creates dependency and conformity
- Does not teach acceptable alternative behavior
- Models inappropriate behavior
- Reinforces early stages of moral development
- Outcomes are contrived
- Emotionally charged, often administered with anger

CONSEQUENCES: Natural—outcomes that are the result of action or inaction of the individual and do not involve the intervention of any other person.
Logical—interventions that have direct and meaningful connections to the behavior which precedes it.

BENEFITS

- Fosters intrinsic motivation through an internal locus of control
- Encourages accountability
- Effective at all ages
- Facilitates students' use of pro-social power
- Focus is on own behavior
- Creates independence and accountability
- Teaches acceptable alternative behavior
- Models cause and effect
- Reinforces later stages of moral development
- Outcomes are naturally occurring or logically related to the inappropriate behavior
- Emotionally neutral, administered without anger

? QUESTIONS FOR THE STUDY TEAM

1. Punishments are how the real world works. After all, if I am continually late for my job, or I perform my job incorrectly, I'll be fired. Isn't being fired a punishment?

2. If punishments have so many limitations, why do so many teachers use them?

3. What will the other students in my class say if they see that a student is disruptive and I don't punish the student?

4. Many students come from families that use punishment to attempt to control behavior. Therefore, don't teachers also need to use punishment in the classroom because punishment is the only thing these students understand?

5. If teachers don't use punishments, won't today's students take advantage of them? How can teachers expect students to take them seriously if they don't punish students when they are behaving inappropriately?

6. In reality, if students do not do what they are supposed to do, something unpleasant will happen to them, be it a punishment or a consequence. Therefore, isn't the real difference between punishments and consequences just a matter of semantics?

7. I teach very tough students. If I use consequences rather than punishments, they will perceive me as being weak. How can I preserve the students' perceptions that I have power and they have to listen to me?

8. Aren't there some disruptive behaviors that have no logical or natural consequences? If so, how should a teacher deal with these behaviors?

9. List the natural and/or logical consequences for the following common disruptive behaviors.

Disruptive Behavior	*Natural Consequences*	*Logical Consequences*
Calling out		
Walking around the room		
Talking		
Passing notes		
Showing disrespect to the teacher		
Coming to class late		
Refusing to cooperate with others		
Making noises		
Pushing others		
Cursing		
Fighting		

SECTION 5

Reestablishing Successful Learning Environments for Students Who Exhibit Common or Chronic Discipline Problems, While Protecting the Learning Environment for All Students

This section provides information on recognizing the source of a student's disruptive behavior, intervening to prevent disruptive behavior, and ways to teach appropriate behavior.

This final section is what may be described in other textbooks as the section on management. However, in keeping with the authors' belief that the Self-Control Classroom model represents a new paradigm in thinking about classroom interactions, the section is entitled "Reestablishing Successful Learning Environments." In the Self-Control Classroom model, disciplinary challenges are believed to stem from the failure of students to experience success, intrinsic motivation, and/or pro-social self-esteem, rather than the result of "bad kids" who need to be bribed or coerced into appropriate behavior. Sometimes the failure of students is the result of their internal or environmental variables. In other instances, it is the result of external classroom or school variables, often involving the use of legitimate or coercive teacher authority. Whatever the genesis of the discipline problems, recall that the Self-Control Classroom's vision statement (Chapter 1) states that teachers need to simultaneously protect the learning environment for all students as they reestablish a successful learning environment for the student who is presenting professional challenges.

To reestablish a successful learning environment, the source of the student's disruptive behavior must first be identified. In Chapter 18 we use the Professional Decision-Making Matrix (or PDMM) introduced in Chapter 12 as the tool to determine the possible source of the inappropriate behavior and how best to begin the process of remediating the student's failure to behave appropriately. Before discussing specific approaches to remediate the challenging behavior in ways that are congruent with the Self-Control Classroom model, Chapter 19 explores the concept of cognitive dissonance. It explores this as a way to explain why so many students seem immune to genuine, positive efforts on the part of teachers and administrators to influence student behavior in referent and expert ways.

Chapters 20 through 25 develop a hierarchy of teacher interventions that build upon the prevention of disruptive behavior (Chapters 8–11 and 13–15) and move from non-verbal through verbal interventions and ultimately to the referent and expert design and delivery of consequences for challenging student behavior. At all stages in the hierarchy, teachers are reminded that they have a dual task; not only are they to protect the learning environment for all students, but they should always be attempting to "make the student whole" or to reestablish a successful learning environment for the student exhibiting disruptive behavior.

The section concludes with Chapter 26, a model for teachers and administrators to use to teach appropriate behavior, the final imperative of the Self-Control Classroom vision statement in response to disruptive, challenging behavior.

CHAPTER 18

Level 1 of the Hierarchy of Interventions: Using the Professional Decision Making Matrix

"What children need and only teachers can provide is quality of instruction and equality of dignity." (Ginott, 1972)

The Self-Control Classroom model helps to create successful learning environments by:

- facilitating a success/failure ratio that is greater than 1 ($S/F > 1$),
- encouraging intrinsic motivation through the expectation of success, attributed to an internal locus of control and value, attributed to an internal value structure ($M_I = E_{I.L.C.} \times V_{I.V.S.}$), and
- developing pro-social self-esteem through significance, competence, virtue, and power ($SE_{PS} = S_{PS} + C_{PS} + V_{PS} + P_{PS}$).

These outcomes are best facilitated by the use of referent and expert authority.

In the Self-Control Classroom model, when a student is behaving inappropriately, it is assumed that he is not experiencing a successful learning environment. The first task of the teacher, according to the model's vision statement, is to reestablish a successful learning environment. This is the first of six levels in the Hierarchy of Interventions for students exhibiting disruptive behavior.

The Professional Decision Making Matrix (PDMM) (Figure 18.1), is a graphic representation of the interactions of the four authority bases upon the components of success/failure ratio, motivation, and self-esteem. It may be used to hypothesize possible reasons for inappropriate student behavior, analyze how teacher interventions impact the components of a successful learning environment, and design interventions to reestablish a successful learning environment that are congruent with the Self-Control Classroom model.

In the PDMM, the left column lists the four authority bases. Across the top are the three components of Success/Failure Ratio, Motivation, and Self-Esteem. Success/Failure Ratio is further divided into $S/F > 1$, and $S/F < 1$. Motivation is partitioned into an internal or external locus of control (expectation of success) and by an internal or external value structure (value).

Professional Decision Making Matrix

Authority Base	Success/Failure Ratio		Motivation				Self-Esteem							
	>1	<1	I.L.C	E.L.C	I.V.S	E.V.S	S_{PS}	S_D	C_{PS}	C_D	V_{PS}	V_D	P_{PS}	P_D
Referent														
Expert														
Legitimate														
Coercive														

Key:

I.L.C. = internal locus of control
S_{PS} = significance pro-social
S_D = significance distorted

E.L.C. = external locus of control
C_{PS} = competence pro-social
C_D = competence distorted

I.V.S. = internal value structure
V_{PS} = virtue pro-social
V_D = virtue distorted

E.V.S. = external value structure
P_{PS} = power pro-social
P_D = power distorted

FIGURE 18.1 ▶ The Professional Decision Making Matrix

Self-Esteem is divided into the factors of either pro-social or distorted significance, competence, virtue, and power.

The shaded cells represent the factors that make up a successful learning environment. When analyzing interventions or designing new ones, the goal is to use strategies that fall within one or more of the shaded cells of the PDMM.

Analysis of Interventions in Case Studies Using the Professional Decision Making Matrix (PDMM)

WHY DON'T YOU GET OUT OF MY FACE?

The first case study, submitted by a teacher enrolled in a graduate course on classroom management, concerns a secondary school student who exhibits very challenging behavior from the first day of class.

A 12th grade student, Ted, introduced himself the first day of class and said to me (the teacher), "Leave me alone and we'll get along just fine." Later that week, I privately went back and asked Ted to begin working on his project. He said "You better get out of my face." I answered his remark assertively but quietly, saying "I do not talk to you like that, and I do not expect to be spoken to like that," and then I continued to move around the room. I did some digging into Ted's records and discovered that he was on the wrestling team. I decided to show Ted some personal interest and attended his wrestling match. During the match, I cheered for Ted. The next day, Ted arrived at class and asked why I was at the match. I told him that I wrestled in high school and college, and I was interested in seeing him wrestle. He went to the back of the room and didn't do much work. I attended the next match also, and after the match, made it a point to talk to Ted about the match. The next day, we continued the discussion at the beginning of class. Ted again didn't do much work, but when I went back to ask him if I could help him get started, he began to work. The interest I have shown in this student's personal life has positively changed his classroom behavior. Ted is always respectful toward me and generally does his work. He earned a C+ for the marking period.

Let's begin our analysis by examining Ted's behavior in light of what we know about the impact of the three components of a successful learning environment on student behavior: success/failure ratio (S/F), motivation, and self-esteem. We know very little about Ted's behavior in general, except for his two comments to the teacher: "Leave me alone and we'll get along just fine," and "Why don't you get out of my face?" In addition, Ted sat in the back of the room and initially did not work. In forming a hypothesis as to why Ted might behave this way, do you think the comments were the result of Ted's success/failure ratio, were they about his motivation, or did Ted make the comments to impact his self-esteem? Although Ted's S/F ratio might influence his behavior, and his motivation might be problematic (as evidenced by his sitting in the back of the room and not working), his comments do not give us any information that directly bares upon these components. The only component remaining is self-esteem. It seems apparent that Ted's comments were about establishing who was in charge and what he was and wasn't going to do. Therefore, these were comments displaying Ted's sense of power. These statements to the teacher were an indication that Ted was attempting to display distorted power in his relationship with the teacher.

The Self-Control Classroom vision statement states that when a student behaves inappropriately, it is assumed that the student is not experiencing a successful learning environment. The teacher then needs to create interventions that reestablish a successful learning environment for that student. For example, if the student's behavior is the result of repeated failures, or a

S/F < 1, the teacher attempts to increase student success. If the behavior is the result of extrinsic motivation, the teacher attempts to increase the student's internal locus of control or internal value structure. In this case study, the student was displaying distorted self-esteem through distorted power. Therefore by attending the wrestling match and cheering for the student the teacher designed an intervention that addressed pro-social self-esteem.

The Self-Control Classroom vision statement states that when a student behaves inappropriately, it is assumed that the student is not experiencing a successful learning environment.

When using the PDMM to analyze a teacher's intervention, we first determine which authority base or bases the teacher is utilizing. In this case, the teacher's decision to attend the wrestling match and cheer for the student was a display of interest in and support of the student. Clearly this is a characteristic of referent authority. Therefore all entries in the PDMM would be placed in the referent authority row.

The next decision to be made is which component is being impacted by the intervention. Here the intervention was impacting self-esteem. Finally, which factor of self-esteem was involved? Clearly, attending the match and cheering for the student was intended to impact Ted's pro-social significance, because this demonstrated to Ted that the teacher was interested in him outside of the classroom. To indicate the first impact on reestablishing a successful learning environment for Ted, a 1 is placed on the PDMM (Figure 18.2) in the pro-social significance column on the referent row.

After the teacher attends two matches and talks to Ted about wrestling, Ted's classroom behavior begins to improve, because now the relationship between Ted and the teacher is based more upon pro-social significance than distorted power. Because self-esteem is a sum, if a pro-social factor is raised, then the need for a distorted factor decreases, in order to maintain the same level of self-esteem. As Ted's behavior improved, he also demonstrated a willingness to attend to the teacher's instruction and do the classwork. Effort is a sign of motivation. Because Ted now values the relationship that has developed with the teacher, he begins to value the teacher's instruction. This is an internal value structure and is the intervention's second impact on reestablishing a successful learning environment for Ted. To indicate this second impact, a 2 is placed in the internal value structure column of the referent row on the PDMM (Figure 18.2).

Effort is a sign of motivation.

Because Ted is now an active learner in the class, he earns a C+ for the marking period. This leads to the third impact of the intervention, a pro-social sense of competence, and a 3 is placed in the pro-social competence cell of referent authority (Figure 18.2). Ted's successes, which led to the C+, indicate progress toward a SF > 1, the fourth impact of the intervention. A 4 is placed in the appropriate cell on the PDMM (Figure 18.2).

In conclusion, the teacher's use of referent authority by attending the wrestling match and cheering for Ted reestablished a successful learning environment for Ted by impacting four components: pro-social significance, internal value structure, pro-social competence, and a S/F > 1. As a result, Ted's need to use distorted power to build his self-esteem was no longer necessary.

This intervention case study illustrates the interdependence of the components of a successful learning environment. When referent and/or expert authority is used to impact one of the components, other components are also impacted (See Figures 15.2 and 15.3). In Ted's case, pro-social significance impacted an internal value structure, which in turn impacted pro-social competence,

Professional Decision Making Matrix

Authority Base	Success/Failure Ratio		Motivation				Self-Esteem							
	>1	<1	I.L.C	E.L.C	I.V.S	E.V.S	S_{PS}	S_D	C_{PS}	C_D	V_{PS}	V_D	P_{PS}	P_D
Referent	4				2		1		3					
Expert														
Legitimate														
Coercive														

KEY:
1. Attending the match and cheering for the student was intended to impact Ted's pro-social significance.
2. Ted now values the relationship that has developed with the teacher, and he begins to value the teacher's instruction. This is an internal value structure.
3. Ted is now an active learner in the class. He earns a C+ for the marking period, increasing his sense of pro-social competence.
4. Ted's successes which led to the C+, indicate progress toward a S/F >1.

FIGURE 18.2 ▶ Analysis of Case Study Intervention Using PDMM, "Why Don't You Get Out Of My Face?"

which resulted in his S/F > 1. Because Ted is now experiencing a successful learning environment, he is no longer disruptive in the classroom.

I'M NOT GOING TO TELL YOU AGAIN!

One day Sean was disrupting class by making noise, talking, and making comments that caused him and other students to laugh out loud. The teacher said in front of the class, "I'm not going to tell you again, stop it!" Sean replied with a loud sarcastic, "Right!" The teacher screamed, "That's it! I don't know who you think you are! You have no manners, and no respect for anyone!" Sean said, "Yeah, yeah, yeah. We don't learn anything in here anyway. The only reason anybody does anything in this boring class is so that they can get out of here and not have to deal with you again." The teacher demanded that Sean go to the office. As Sean left the room he turned to the teacher and said, "Fine, at least I don't have to look at your crooked teeth anymore." Next he turned to the class with a big smile. The class broke up laughing and continued to laugh for a long time.

When referent and/or expert authority is used to impact one of the components, other components are also impacted

As with the first case study, we examine Sean's behavior as to the impact on S/F, motivation, and self-esteem. Sean was making noise, talking, and making comments to other students, and they were all laughing. It appears that Sean was competing with the teacher for the other students' attention by entertaining them, which was a display of distorted competence. When the teacher said, "I'm not going to tell you again, stop it!" He was attempting to get Sean to stop his behavior by using legitimate authority (I'm the teacher, and I'm telling you what to do). Sean's sarcastic response "Right!" indicates that the teacher's comment served as a catalyst for Sean's use of distorted power, (Just because you're telling me what to do doesn't mean I'm going to do it.) A 1 is placed in the distorted power column on the legitimate authority row, to show this first impact (Figure 18.3).

The teacher is now involved in a parallel process involving distorted power (see Chapter 7) and he screams, "That's it! I don't know who you think you are! You have no manners and no respect for anyone!" The teacher is now using coercive authority, making comments designed to punish Sean. Sean replies, "Yeah, yeah, yeah. We don't learn anything in here anyway. The only reason anybody does anything in this boring class is so that they can get out of here and not have to deal with you again." The teacher demands that Sean leave the class. Sean then comments about the teacher's bad teeth, and the class, in response, breaks up laughing.

Sean's comments about not learning anything in the class, the class being boring, and the only reason that students do anything is so that they can get out of the class and not have to deal with the teacher again, shows an external value structure. This is indicated by a 2 in the external value column of the coercive authority row of the PDMM (Figure 18.3). When Sean makes the comment about the teacher's teeth, and the class starts laughing, Sean is experiencing an increase in distorted competence (his ability to make others laugh), by putting down the teacher. This is indicated by a 3 in the distorted competence column of the coercive authority row of the PDMM (Figure 18.3). Finally, when Sean leaves the classroom and smiles at his

Professional Decision Making Matrix

Authority Base	Success/Failure Ratio		Motivation				Self-Esteem							
	>1	<1	I.L.C	E.L.C	I.V.S	E.V.S	S_{PS}	S_D	C_{PS}	C_D	V_{PS}	V_D	P_{PS}	P_D
Referent														
Expert														
Legitimate														1
Coercive						2		4		3				

KEY:
1. Sean's sarcastic response, "Right!" indicates that the teacher's comment served as a catalyst for Sean's use of distorted power.
2. Sean's comments about not learning anything in the class, the class being boring, and the only reason that students do anything is so that they can get out of the class and not have to deal with the teacher again is indicative of an external value structure.
3. When Sean makes the comment about the teacher's teeth, and the class starts laughing, Sean is experiencing an increase in distorted competence.
4. When Sean leaves the classroom and smiles at his classmates, he is displaying a distorted sense of significance.

FIGURE 18.3 ▶ Analysis of Case Study Intervention Using PDMM, "I'm Not Going To Tell You Again"

classmates, he is displaying a distorted sense of significance. This is indicated by placing a 4 in the distorted significance column of the coercive row of the PDMM (Figure 18.3).

The teacher's choice of interventions, using legitimate and coercive authority, did not impact any of the components of a successful learning environment. Even though the teacher did succeed in removing Sean from the class, due to the increase in Sean's distorted self-esteem, Sean likely will continue his disruptive behavior when he rejoins the class. Therefore, the teacher's intervention did not fulfill our definition of teaching: changing teacher behavior to increase the likelihood that students will change their behavior.

I'm Not Going to Tell You Again! (Revisited)

Revisiting "I'm not going to tell you again," let's devise possible strategies for intervention that are congruent with the Self-Control Classroom model, to reestablish a successful learning environment for Sean. It is unlikely that Sean has been a model student all term and has suddenly decided to become disruptive in this class. The teacher is aware of Sean's tendency to be disruptive and has noted that the inappropriate behavior usually begins at the start of class. The teacher also is aware that many of the students in the class find Sean's antics entertaining. Sean made it clear early in the term that he was not particularly interested in the subject. Using the PDMM, the teacher understands that using referent and expert authority, based upon care, trust, respect, support, and effective pedagogy will most probably impact the three components of a successful learning environment: S/F > 1, intrinsic motivation, and pro-social self-esteem.

There are thousands of interventions a teacher may choose to impact one of the seven factors of S/F > 1, internal locus of control, internal value structure, pro-social significance, competence, virtue, and power. In the present scenario, Sean's behavior was characteristic of distorted power, external value structure, distorted competence, and distorted significance. This knowledge helps us determine what types of interventions might be effective in reestablishing a successful learning environment for Sean. Table 18.1 lists some examples of interventions that the authors think may be effective. The list is by no means exhaustive.

Let's hypothesize what occurs with Sean in the classroom when the teacher changes his own behavior to be congruent with referent and expert authority.

I'm Not Going to Tell You Again!" (Revised)

Sean enters the class and the teacher hands him a paper with the day's openers, which Sean is to place on the blackboard. While Sean is putting the opener on the board, the teacher asks him if he's had a chance to play "Madden 2002" on his Playstation. As students continue to enter the classroom, Sean stops writing on the board and begins to joke around with his buddies. The teacher reminds Sean that he will have an opportunity to tell the comic "Thought for the Day" later on and to please continue writing the openers. As the students, including Sean, are working on the openers, the teacher hands out papers with the day's lesson. On Sean's paper is a comment thanking Sean for his help in putting the openers on the board and for his entertaining comments. During the lesson, the teacher makes frequent eye contact with Sean, smiling when he is on task and engaged. At the close of the lesson, the teacher turns to Sean and says, "Okay Sean, heard anything funny lately?" Sean makes some funny, but appropriate comments about the class and events in the school. The bell rings and the class leaves. On his way out, the teacher again thanks Sean and tells him to have a great day.

TABLE 18.1 ▶ Intervention Examples to Use with Sean

Distorted Power: Sean makes noises, disrupts class.	**Distorted Competence: Sean tells jokes and makes comments about the teacher that encourages others to laugh at inappropriate times.**	**External Value Structure: Sean says "We don't learn anything in here anyway. The only reason anybody does anything in this boring class is so that they can get out of here and not have to deal with you again."**	**Distorted Significance: Sean smiles at his classmates as he is leaving the room.**
▶ Pro-Social Power: Have Sean occupied with instructional readiness activities at the start of class, such as handing out papers, making certain materials are present and ready, writing opening activities on the blackboard (This will impact pro-social virtue, thereby further reducing the need to display distorted power).	▶ Pro-Social Competence: Find out what Sean's interests are outside of the subject area and attempt to bring these interests into several lessons. This builds upon Sean's islands of competence (also impacts S/F > 1). ▶ Pro-Social Competence: Allow Sean to entertain the class with a comic "thought for the day" (also builds upon pro-social power). ▶ Pro-Social Competence: Use encouragement to focus upon Sean's interest, effort, degree of improvement, and personal goals (also impacts S/F > 1 and internal locus of control).	▶ Internal Value Structure: Build upon islands of competence. ▶ Internal Value Structure: Use of encouragement. ▶ Internal Value Structure: Use novel and discrepant events for instructional purposes.	▶ Pro-Social Significance: Sean delivers a comic thought for the day. ▶ Pro-Social Significance: Build upon islands of significance. Teacher finds something likable about Sean and uses this to develop a positive relationship. ▶ Pro-Social Significance: Treat Sean as an individual. Learn about his outside interests, and have conversations with him about those interests.

Using the PDMM to analyze the teacher's referent and expert authority interventions in Figure 18.4, we indicate the impact on the PDMM of the revised interventions, using letters to contrast the initial teacher interventions, which are labeled using numerals. By having Sean put the openers on the blackboard, the teacher gets him actively involved immediately with a relevant task. This expert authority intervention impacts Sean's pro-social virtue by giving him the opportunity to help the teacher and the class. It also impacts Sean's pro-social power, because it provides Sean with the opportunity to choose to cooperate and display virtuous behavior. This intervention is indicated on the PDMM with the letter A (Figure 18.4).

While Sean is at the blackboard, the teacher enters into a conversation with him about the video game "Madden 2002." By focusing upon Sean's interests outside of class, this referent au-

Professional Decision Making Matrix

Authority Base	Success/Failure Ratio		Motivation				Self-Esteem							
	>1	<1	I.L.C	E.L.C	I.V.S	E.V.S	S_{PS}	S_D	C_{PS}	C_D	V_{PS}	V_D	P_{PS}	P_D
Referent							B,D E							
Expert					C		C		C		A		A	
Legitimate														1
Coercive						2		4		3				

KEY:

1. Sean's sarcastic response, "Right!" indicates that the teacher's comment served as a catalyst for Sean's use of distorted power.
2. Sean's comments about not learning anything in the class, the class being boring, and the only reason that students do anything is so that they can get out of the class and not have to deal with the teacher again is indicative of an external value structure.
3. When Sean makes the comment about the teacher's teeth, and the class starts laughing, Sean is experiencing an increase in distorted competence.
4. When Sean leaves the classroom and smiles at his classmates, he is displaying a distorted sense of significance.

A. By having Sean put the openers on the blackboard, the teacher gets him actively involved immediately with a relevant task. This expert authority intervention impacts Sean's pro-social virtue by giving him the opportunity to help the teacher and the class.

B. While Sean is at the blackboard, the teacher enters into a conversation with him about the video game "Madden 2002." By focusing upon Sean's interests outside of class, this referent authority intervention impacts Sean's pro-social significance.

C. The teacher reminds Sean that he will have the opportunity to tell a comic "thought of the day." By allowing Sean to display his ability for comic thinking and allowing him to entertain the class, the teacher is able to impact Sean's pro-social competence and significance. This also impacts Sean's pro-social power by permitting him to get the attention of his classmates in a manner approved by the teacher. His internal value structure is impacted because he is interested and enjoys telling jokes to entertain the class.

D. The teacher hands out today's lesson, and has written his thanks for Sean's assistance and for his entertaining comments on Sean's paper. In addition, the teacher makes frequent eye contact with Sean during the lesson. These impact pro-social significance.

E. The teacher again uses referent authority to impact Sean's pro-social significance by thanking Sean at the door when he leaves, and wishing him a good day.

FIGURE 18.4 ▶ Analysis of Case Study Intervention Using PDMM, "I'm Not Going to Tell You Again" Revised.

thority intervention impacts Sean's pro-social significance. This is indicated by the letter B on the PDMM (Figure 18.4).

When he begins to joke around with his classmates, the teacher reminds Sean that he will have the opportunity to tell a comic "thought of the day" later in the class period. By allowing Sean to display his ability for comic thinking and allowing him to entertain the class, this expert authority intervention impacts Sean's pro-social competence and significance. This intervention also impacts Sean's pro-social power by permitting him to get the attention of his classmates in a manner approved by the teacher. His internal value structure is impacted, because he is interested and enjoys telling jokes to entertain the class. These interventions are indicated by the letter C on the PDMM (Figure 18.4).

The teacher hands out today's lesson, and has written his thanks for Sean's assistance and for his entertaining comments on Sean's paper. In addition, the teacher makes frequent eye contact with Sean during the lesson. These interventions are further examples of the teacher's referent authority. By showing appreciation and positive regard for Sean, the interventions impact Sean's pro-social significance, indicated by the letter D on the PDMM (Figure 18.4). Finally, the teacher again uses referent authority to impact Sean's pro-social significance by thanking Sean at the door when he leaves and wishing him a good day. This is indicated by a letter E on the PDMM (Figure 18.4).

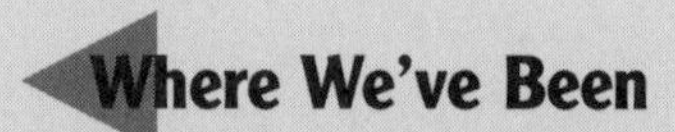

Where We've Been

The Professional Decision Making Matrix (PDMM) introduced in Chapter 12, was used to diagnose students' behavior in relation to S/F ratio, motivation, and self-esteem, in order to design effective interventions to reestablish a successful learning environment. Two case studies were presented, illustrating how the PDMM may be used to hypothesize reasons for inappropriate student behavior and to analyze teacher interventions. The PDMM was also used to demonstrate that certain teacher interventions which fall outside of the desired outcome of a successful learning environment, lead to an increase in disruptive behavior. This was contrasted with a demonstration of how the same disruptive student behavior may be ameliorated by teacher behavior that is consistent with the outcome goals of a successful learning environment.

Where We're Headed

In Chapter 19, the issue of cognitive dissonance will be discussed. Cognitive dissonance will be used to explain why certain students may increase their inappropriate behavior in response to positive changes in teacher behavior founded in referent and expert authority.

CHAPTER 18 CONCEPT MAP

The concept map in this chapter is the first level of the development of an intervention hierarchy to reestablish successful learning environments for students exhibiting disruptive behavior and to protect successful learning environments for all other students. Note that prevention precedes intervention for all students.

HIERARCHY OF INTERVENTIONS
LEVEL 1: REESTABLISHING SUCCESSFUL LEARNING ENVIRONMENTS

ALL STUDENTS

Prevention: Establishing Successful Learning Environments

S/F > 1
Intrinsic Motivation
- internal locus of control
- internal value structure

Pro-Social Self-Esteem
- significance
- competence
- virture
- power

STUDENTS EXHIBITING COMMON DISCIPLINE PROBLEMS

Prevention: Establishing Successful Learning Environments

S/F > 1
Intrinsic Motivation
- internal locus of control
- internal value structure

Pro-Social Self-Esteem
- significance
- competence
- virture
- power

Level 1: Reestablishing Successful Learning Environments

SF > 1
Intrinsic Motivation
- internal locus of control
- internal value structure

Pro-Social Self-Esteem
- significance
- competence
- virtue
- power

STUDENTS EXHIBITING CHRONIC DISCIPLINE PROBLEMS

Prevention: Establishing Successful Learning Environments

S/F > 1
Intrinsic Motivation
- internal locus of control
- internal value structure

Pro-Social Self-Esteem
- significance
- competence
- virture
- power

Level 1: Reestablishing Successful Learning Environments

SF > 1
Intrinsic Motivation
- internal locus of control
- internal value structure

Pro-Social Self-Esteem
- significance
- competence
- virtue
- power

? QUESTIONS FOR THE STUDY TEAM

For each of the case studies, use the PDMM to analyze how the teacher's interventions impact the student. It may be helpful to first form a hypothesis as to why the student is exhibiting disruptive behavior. Is the student experiencing a low S/F ratio, extrinsic motivation, or distorted self-esteem?

REESTABLISHING SUCCESSFUL LEARNING ENVIRONMENTS
PROFESSIONAL DECISION MAKING ANALYSIS MATRIX

CASE STUDY 1

Description of Intervention: Brad is a retained 6th grade student. He is disruptive and continually looks for ways to degrade other students. He continually tells me, "I don't care" or "This is stupid." I asked Brad if I could speak with him after class. I told him that he could do well, and that I was ready to help him succeed in social studies. We decided that we would spend time on his study skills and set a time for him to come in. His eyes lit up and he said "great." He came in for help, and we both learned that he often knew the correct answers, but he was afraid to answer, because he might say something stupid, and the other students would make fun of him. We role played the classroom question and answer sessions. The next day he reluctantly began to volunteer answers. Next we began preparing for the test. We decided that when he took the test, he would pretend that I was asking the question, and he would write what he would have answered in class. I also encouraged him to raise his hand during the test if he had any questions. The next day as I passed out the test, I made eye contact with Brad and gave him a big smile. Brad received a 69%. I returned his paper and wrote "your increased effort showed in your improved grade." After class, Brad told me that he was going to try harder, and that he was going to study for the next test himself. In class, Brad seemed more relaxed and participated more. On the day of the next test, Brad entered the room and said that he was going to pass this test. Brad got an 80%. I passed back the test with the comment "You should be proud of yourself. Your hard work pays off."

Professional Decision Making Matrix

Authority Base	Success/Failure Ratio		Motivation				Self-Esteem							
	>1	<1	I.L.C	E.L.C	I.V.S	E.V.S	S_{PS}	S_D	C_{PS}	C_D	V_{PS}	V_D	P_{PS}	P_D
Referent														
Expert														
Legitimate														
Coercive														

Key:
I.L.C. = internal locus of control; E.L.C. = external locus of control; I.V.S. = internal value structure; E.V.S. = external value structure
S_{PS} = significance pro-social; C_{PS} = competence pro-social; V_{PS} = virtue pro-social; P_{PS} = power pro-social
S_D = significance distorted; C_D = competence distorted; V_D = virtue distorted; P_D = power distorted

Case Study 2

Description of Intervention: Ted, who has a reputation as a behavior problem, came to class about five minutes late, without a legitimate excuse note. He knew he was late and walked in angry, upset, and ready to do battle. Since we had changed assigned seats at the beginning of that period, I directed him to his new seat and showed him where we were in the material. He actually got busy, although two other students in class wished to discuss why he was late and what was going to happen. I told them that I would talk to Ted later, and that it was a problem that we were not going to take class time to discuss. I managed to keep everyone on task and continue with the lesson. Reflecting back, had I made more of an issue of his tardiness when he entered the room, I'm sure the lesson and the rest of the period would have been totally lost.

Professional Decision Making Matrix

Authority Base	Success/Failure Ratio		Motivation				Self-Esteem							
	>1	<1	I.L.C	E.L.C	I.V.S	E.V.S	S_{PS}	S_D	C_{PS}	C_D	V_{PS}	V_D	P_{PS}	P_D
Referent														
Expert														
Legitimate														
Coercive														

Key:
I.L.C. = internal locus of control; E.L.C. = external locus of control; I.V.S. = internal value structure; E.V.S. = external value structure
S_{PS} = significance pro-social C_{PS} = competence pro-social V_{PS} = virtue pro-social P_{PS} = power pro-social
S_D = significance distorted C_D = competence distorted V_D = virtue distorted P_D = power distorted

Case Study 3

Description of Intervention: Tanya refused to go to the board when it was her turn. We were diagramming sentences, and everyone else had gone to the board. Formerly, I would have entered into a power struggle with her. Instead, I stopped the process and examined why she refused to go. I realized that perhaps she was simply afraid of looking "stupid." I decided to skip over her and asked someone else to go to the board. I waited till after class and caught her before she left. I offered to help her during my prep period which coincided with her study hall. Her face lit up, and she seemed surprised. She thanked me and said that she had never had sentence diagramming before. With some help and encouragement, she began to try. Since then, she has been a model student, and she has asked several times for help during her study hall. I noticed such a change in her behavior and her willingness to try more difficult subject matter. She has experienced some success and is eager to be more successful. Her grades have gone up, too. I'm glad I was able to recognize that what I had originally perceived as a discipline problem, was only a plea for attention and help.

Professional Decision Making Matrix

Authority Base	Success/Failure Ratio		Motivation				Self-Esteem							
	>1	<1	I.L.C	E.L.C	I.V.S	E.V.S	S_{PS}	S_D	C_{PS}	C_D	V_{PS}	V_D	P_{PS}	P_D
Referent														
Expert														
Legitimate														
Coercive														

Key:
I.L.C. = internal locus of control; E.L.C. = external locus of control; I.V.S. = internal value structure; E.V.S. = external value structure
S_{PS} = significance pro-social C_{PS} = competence pro-social V_{PS} = virtue pro-social P_{PS} = power pro-social
S_D = significance distorted C_D = competence distorted V_D = virtue distorted P_D = power distorted

Case Study 4

Description of Intervention: Ted, a senior at the high school, has been a disruptive behavior problem since elementary school. He is well known and somewhat feared by students and teachers alike. Recently he was arrested for being an accomplice to a burglary (he was the lookout) and placed on probation. I was asked to work with his probation officer to try and help Ted behave in more appropriate ways. Part of Ted's consequence is community service. Ted has so far refused to comply and has actually served a weekend in detention rather than obey the court's directive. With the consent of his probation officer, I devised a plan to have Ted do community service. I teach music and know Ted because music is the one subject he takes seriously. I asked Ted if he would serve as a DJ for a dance at the elementary school. He asked, "What's in it for me?" I replied that there would be no compensation, but that he had the largest library of current music of any student I knew, and I had heard that he loved to dance. I assured him that the students would really enjoy his doing this. Much to my delight, he accepted. The dance was fantastic! Ted was really great with the younger kids. I collaborated with the elementary music teacher to have Ted come into four different classes and teach children about the guitar, an instrument Ted plays well. Ted willingly cooperated. After the dance and the lessons, Ted began hanging out in my room even more, and I asked him to help sort music for the band and to play with the school jazz band. Well, he refused to play in the band, but he did agree to become the music librarian, helping to sort music for the orchestra and band and giving me feedback about different pieces I'm thinking about using. I logged all of Ted's hours of help, and last Friday his P.O. came in to school. Ted was apprehensive about seeing him. He was downright shocked when the officer congratulated Ted on completing his community service! Ted continues to have difficulties, but he is off probation and continuing to work with me.

Professional Decision Making Matrix

Authority Base	Success/Failure Ratio		Motivation				Self-Esteem							
	>1	<1	I.L.C	E.L.C	I.V.S	E.V.S	S_{PS}	S_D	C_{PS}	C_D	V_{PS}	V_D	P_{PS}	P_D
Referent														
Expert														
Legitimate														
Coercive														

Key:
I.L.C. = internal locus of control; E.L.C. = external locus of control; I.V.S. = internal value structure; E.V.S. = external value structure
S_{PS} = significance pro-social C_{PS} = competence pro-social V_{PS} = virtue pro-social P_{PS} = power pro-social
S_D = significance distorted C_D = competence distorted V_D = virtue distorted P_D = power distorted

Case Study 5

Description of Intervention: Joan is in my 6th grade class. From the very first day, she just has not seemed to understand the importance of modifying her behavior to conform to the norms of the class. This September I began the first day as I always do. After welcoming the students to class, I instructed them that the important factor to understand, so that learning could take place, was that they were here to learn, and I was here to teach. I instructed them in the class procedures and rules and let them know the benefits of compliance and the consequences of non-compliance. I also told them that I would be pleased to help any of them with problems during specific periods I've set aside for this purpose. I try and make myself available to the students and let them know I care about them and their welfare. Joan began her disruptive behavior the very first day! I had to send her to the back of the room before the day was out. Despite my efforts to get her to meet with me during recess or lunch (my stated times), she has thus far refused. Currently, Joan is forced to stay in the in-school suspension room during recess each day, because she refuses to pay the consequence for her disruption of class, which is to write 500 times "I will not disrupt class." Her intransigence has turned a 1 or 2 day consequence into one lasting 9 days and counting. I've about had it with Joan.

Professional Decision Making Matrix

Authority Base	Success/Failure Ratio		Motivation				Self-Esteem							
	>1	<1	I.L.C	E.L.C	I.V.S	E.V.S	S_{PS}	S_D	C_{PS}	C_D	V_{PS}	V_D	P_{PS}	P_D
Referent														
Expert														
Legitimate														
Coercive														

Key:
I.L.C. = internal locus of control; E.L.C. = external locus of control; I.V.S. = internal value structure; E.V.S. = external value structure
S_{PS} = significance pro-social; C_{PS} = competence pro-social; V_{PS} = virtue pro-social; P_{PS} = power pro-social
S_D = significance distorted; C_D = competence distorted; V_D = virtue distorted; P_D = power distorted

Case Study 6

Description of Intervention: Alice is a student in my 7th grade class. She is having a lot of difficulty adjusting to middle school. I feel that students need to understand that they are responsible for their behavior and that my job is to create a positive learning environment with interesting work, clear guidelines, and expectations. Their job is to make choices which will help them learn and to be accountable for those choices, whether positive or negative. Alice seems to believe that her job is to socialize and disrupt. She is rarely on task, rarely hands in homework, and disrupts class frequently. I have begun an anecdotal record and progressed to sharing it with her. In 2 weeks there has been no change. I had her parents in for a conference and, although they seem genuinely concerned, they seem as frustrated as I. I've devoted many hours trying to find a way "in" with Alice: exploring her interests, giving her fun jobs in the class, even attending a soccer match in which she was playing. Alice has been positive each time we interact, but her behavior, rarely changes for more than a day, if it changes at all. Alice seems as frustrated as everyone else. Alice might have to be removed from my class, at least temporarily, and this genuinely pains me. I have referred Alice to the school psychologist through the instructional support team, and I hope with testing, we might get to a solution which will help Alice.

Professional Decision Making Matrix

Authority Base	Success/Failure Ratio		Motivation				Self-Esteem							
	>1	<1	I.L.C	E.L.C	I.V.S	E.V.S	S_{PS}	S_D	C_{PS}	C_D	V_{PS}	V_D	P_{PS}	P_D
Referent														
Expert														
Legitimate														
Coercive														

Key:
I.L.C. = internal locus of control; E.L.C. = external locus of control; I.V.S. = internal value structure; E.V.S. = external value structure
S_{PS} = significance pro-social C_{PS} = competence pro-social V_{PS} = virtue pro-social P_{PS} = power pro-social
S_D = significance distorted C_D = competence distorted V_D = virtue distorted P_D = power distorted

Case Study 7

Description of Intervention: Cathy is in 3rd grade. Whenever we would line up for recess, lunch, or to change classes, she was the last to get into line. When she did get in line, she would push and touch the other students. I would usually demand that everyone return to their seats and line up again and again until Cathy could line up properly. This strategy caused the children to miss time from lunch and recess and to be late for other classes. More often than not, this caused more disruptions than it solved. I decided that I would make Cathy the door monitor and the line leader. On discussing this with her, she enthusiastically agreed. This has resulted in Cathy performing her duties quite appropriately, and more importantly, instead of being disruptive, she has become a responsible student.

Professional Decision Making Matrix

Authority Base	Success/Failure Ratio		Motivation				Self-Esteem							
	>1	<1	I.L.C	E.L.C	I.V.S	E.V.S	S_{PS}	S_D	C_{PS}	C_D	V_{PS}	V_D	P_{PS}	P_D
Referent														
Expert														
Legitimate														
Coercive														

Key:
I.L.C. = internal locus of control; E.L.C. = external locus of control; I.V.S. = internal value structure; E.V.S. = external value structure
S_{PS} = significance pro-social C_{PS} = competence pro-social V_{PS} = virtue pro-social P_{PS} = power pro-social
S_D = significance distorted C_D = competence distorted V_D = virtue distorted P_D = power distorted

CHAPTER 19

Cognitive Dissonance of Students Exhibiting Disruptive Behavior

"With adult-wary students, adult-dominated methods backfire. Coercion feeds rebellion and fosters delinquent subcultures. The antidote to aggression and hedonism is to get students hooked on helping. Schools that enlist antisocial students as partners in their own healing are creating pro-social adult and peer bonds." (Vorrath and Brendtro, 1985)

Along Came Jones

Jackie is a sixteen-year-old 11th grade student in Ms. Jones' math class. Jackie is disruptive. She frequently speaks out of turn, makes fun of other students, and passes notes. Ms. Jones has recently discovered the Self-Control Classroom model. Using the PDMM, Ms. Jones recognizes that Jackie is exhibiting distorted power and significance, and she decides to intervene using referent authority to impact Jackie's pro-social significance. At the beginning of class, Ms. Jones greets Jackie and asks her if she had a nice weekend. To Ms. Jones' chagrin, Jackie replies "What I do on my weekend is none of your business," and walks away rolling her eyes. Her behavior in the class continues to be disruptive. Ms. Jones asks Jackie to assist a new student with the class work. Jackie says, "What's in it for me?" Ms. Jones, wanting to impact intrinsic, not extrinsic motivation, responds, "Mahn can really use your help. I'm sure she would appreciate it." Jackie says, "Right, get someone else." Not to be dissuaded, Ms. Jones then investigates Jackie's interests and learns that she is on the track team. Ms. Jones decides that she will attend the next practice of the track team and show Jackie that she is interested in her non-academic pursuits. She finds a seat in the bleachers, in a location that Jackie cannot help but notice her. As Jackie runs by, Ms. Jones waves and says "Way to go, Jackie." Jackie, without slowing down or even turning to look at Ms. Jones, gives her the finger. Upon returning home that evening, Ms. Jones for a moment thinks that the text *From Disrupter to Achiever* may make excellent kindling for her fireplace.

Jackie's Experience

What explains Jackie's robust disregard and disrespect of Ms. Jones' efforts to exert a positive influence on Jackie through the use of referent authority? Jackie's behavior may be explained by the concept of cognitive dissonance. It is unlikely that Jackie exhibited disruptive behavior only in Ms. Jones' classroom. Most likely, Jackie entered 11th grade with a history of both disruptive behavior and the resulting negative interactions with teachers and administrators. These negative interactions most probably were typified by teachers and administrators using legitimate and coercive authority. After a number of years of negative interactions, Jackie probably came to expect that teachers would treat her in a punitive, disrespectful fashion. Therefore, she thinks of a teacher as an adversary.

Cognitive dissonance is created when an individual experiences situations or thoughts that contradict with the individual's previous experiences, beliefs, or understanding.

"And then along came Jones. . . . Slow walkin' Jones, slow talkin' Jones. . . ."[1]

Ms. Jones, instead of behaving as Jackie expected in a punitive, demanding manner, which she is used to and knows how to handle, behaved in a respectful, affiliative manner. This is the situation that has created Jackie's cognitive dissonance. Cognitive dissonance is created when an individual experiences situations or thoughts that contradict with the individual's previous experiences, beliefs, or understanding. It is an uncomfortable mental state that creates disequilibrium. People are motivated to relieve the cognitive dissonance and restore equilibrium. This may be accomplished in one of two ways: she can either ignore the new information and revert to the previous understanding, or she can incorporate the new information into a new understanding.

[1] Along Came Jones, written by Jerry Leiber and Mike Stoller, sung by The Coasters, Issued as an Atco Records single #6141, 5/59.

In the present case, Jackie may accept Ms. Jones' referent behavior and change her own behavior accordingly, thereby negating years of negative experience with teachers. On the other hand, she may decide that Ms. Jones is at best, misguided, or at worst, deceptive. She may think that Ms. Jones will show her true, coercive colors eventually, so Jackie will ignore Ms. Jones' efforts. Either strategy will resolve the cognitive dissonance. Jackie chooses the safer route of going with her previous experiences and disregards Ms. Jones' attempts at developing a pro-social, significant relationship. Once Jackie decides to believe that Ms. Jones will turn on her sooner or later, she does everything in her power to make that moment occur sooner to resolve her dissonant state. In practical terms, this means that Jackie's behavior gets worse as Ms. Jones behavior gets more and more referent.

In order for Jackie to accept Ms. Jones as a supportive, trusted person, Jackie needs to change her behavior in ways that leave her extremely vulnerable. Similar to the reasons for students' fear of success discussed in Chapter 9, Jackie also has fears, as she attempts to alter her behavior to become more pro-social. Jackie will be placed in a vulnerable position where she no longer knows who she is or how she ought to behave. This resistance to change is the paramount challenge for Ms. Jones, in her attempts to influence Jackie toward appropriate behavior.

Ms. Jones' Experience

Jackie's persistent inappropriate behavior in response to positive supportive teacher behavior has the potential to create cognitive dissonance in Ms. Jones. Many classroom teachers begin the school year attempting to give all students, including those with histories of disruptive behavior, the benefit of doubt, by interacting with all students in positive, supportive ways. However, when teachers are confronted with the continuing and worsening disruptive behavior of some students, they resolve their own cognitive dissonance by fulfilling the most negative teacher stereotypes held by their disruptive students. These teachers become increasingly legitimate and coercive.

Ms. Jones, however, understands the cognitive dissonance that Jackie is experiencing and further understands Jackie's objective in trying to resolve this dissonance by trying to get Ms. Jones to behave negatively towards her. Therefore, Ms. Jones continues to display supportive behaviors. Ms. Jones does not experience cognitive dissonance herself, because she had predicted this outcome before she began her attempt to positively influence Jackie's behavior.

Ms. Jones' and Jackie's Further Experiences

Ms. Jones continues her referent strategy of engaging Jackie personally, as well as her expert strategy of engaging her academically, throughout the school year. For the first several months, Jackie's display of disruptive behavior persists and escalates at times, occasionally necessitating the delivery of logical consequences (See Chapters 17 and 23). Around Thanksgiving, Ms. Jones notices a thaw in her relationship with Jackie. Gradually Jackie begins to respond positively to Ms. Jones' daily inquiries concerning her activities and well being. By the end of the school year, Jackie has greatly reduced her disruptive behavior and improved her academic performance in Ms. Jones' class. She still is not as appropriate as the average student, but her behavior in June has significantly improved from her behavior in September. When Jackie is occasionally disruptive, she usually adjusts her behavior in response to Ms. Jones' redirection. It is apparent that Jackie has resolved her cognitive dissonance, by slowly taking the risk of accepting Ms. Jones' supportive behavior as sincere and changing her own behavior in an appropriate manner.

At the close of the last day of school, as the class runs out to begin their summer vacation, Jackie stays behind. When there is no one left in the class except the two of them, Jackie says "Hey, I hope you have a really good summer. See you next year." Ms. Jones smiles and wishes her the same. A few days later, as Ms. Jones prepares to leave school for the summer, she receives a thank you note from Jackie's mother.

Dear Ms. Jones:

I don't know if Jackie ever told you how important you've become to her this year. Many evenings Jackie has told me how nice you were to her and how much she enjoyed your class. Jackie even studied for your exams—something I've rarely been able to get her to do for any class in the past several years. Thank you for your support of my daughter and all of your hard work. Have a nice summer.

Regards,
Jackie's Mom

Where We've Been

This chapter explored how cognitive dissonance might cause the disruptive behavior of a student to escalate in response to teacher interventions founded in referent and expert authority. The teacher who understands this process and predicts it, rather than being surprised by this escalation, will persist in her positive interactions in the face of what might appear to be failure to the less aware professional. With persistence, teachers often overcome the resistance of students who display disruptive behavior, and effectuate long-term, positive, behavioral change.

Where We're Headed

The next chapter begins the exploration of how teachers influence students exhibiting disruptive behavior to return to on-task behavior, while protecting the learning environment of the other students in the classroom. Specifically, intervention guidelines and pro-active intervention strategies will be presented.

CHAPTER 19 CONCEPT MAP

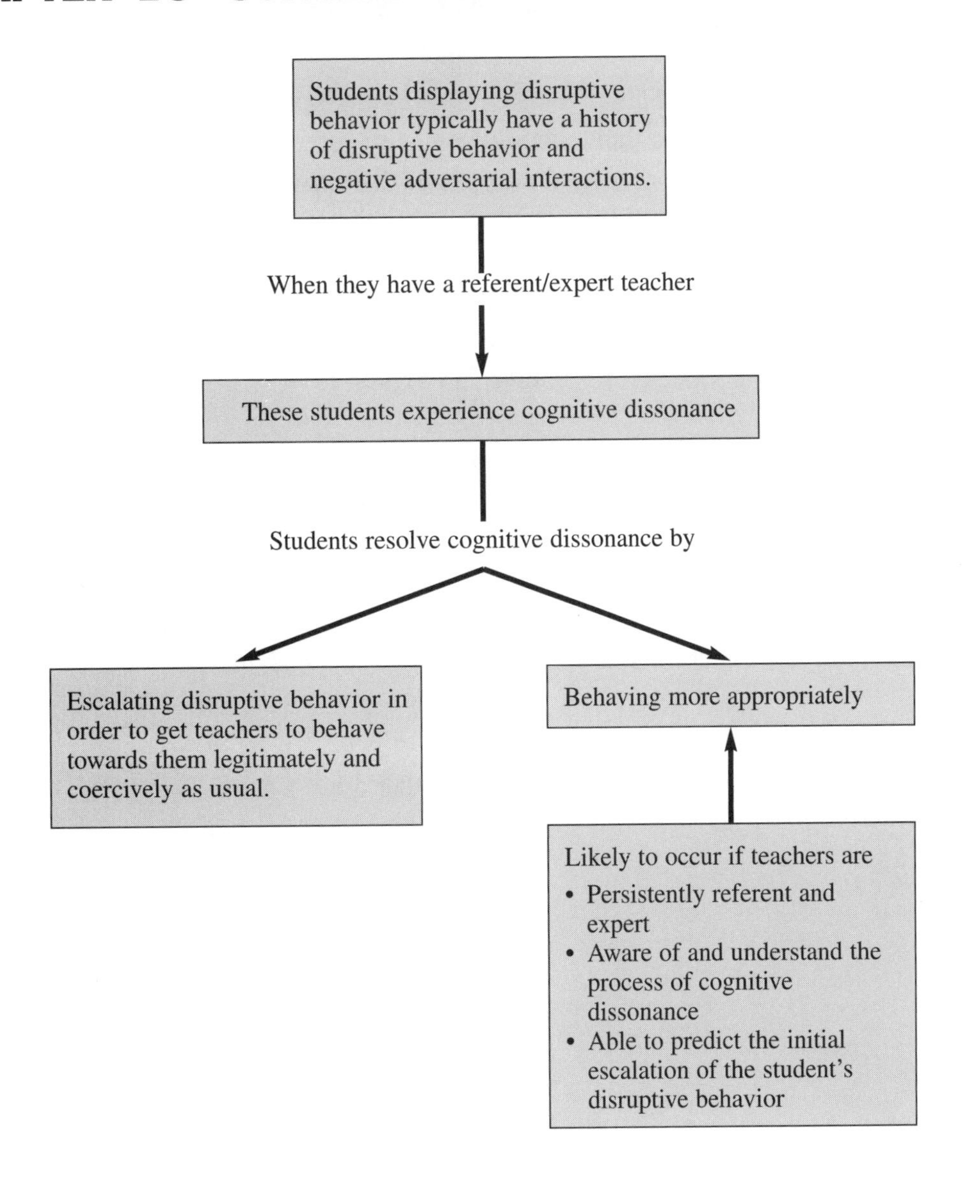

? Questions For The Study Team

1. Why is there a likelihood that students exhibiting disruptive behavior, who experience cognitive dissonance due to their interactions with referent and expert teachers, escalate their disruptive behavior? Why doesn't their disruptive behavior remain at the same level?

2. Can a teacher who normally interacts with students in referent and expert ways, but becomes legitimate and coercive in the face of continual inappropriate student behavior, ever return to treating students referently and expertly?

3. How long should a teacher try to remain referent and expert when a student is escalating her disruptive behavior because of the cognitive dissonance the student is experiencing?

4. Isn't it better to continue to interact with students exhibiting disruptive behavior in legitimate and coercive ways, if interacting with them referently and expertly will increase the likelihood that the disruptive behavior will escalate?

5. What should be done about a student's disruptive behavior while the teacher is waiting for the student to resolve her cognitive dissonance by behaving in ways that are more appropriate?

CHAPTER 20

Guidelines for Intervention with Students Exhibiting Disruptive Behavior and Level 2 of the Hierarchy of Interventions: Pro-Active Interventions

"It is imperative that a teacher uses appropriate behavior to address inappropriate behavior." (Toni Biuiano, Penn State student, 1994)

Even when teachers establish and then re-establish successful learning environments by increasing opportunities for student success, facilitating intrinsic motivation in students, and promoting students' pro-social self-esteem, some discipline problems still occur. When discipline problems occur, the challenge for the teacher is to reestablish a successful learning environment for the student who is exhibiting disruptive behavior and teach him appropriate behavior while protecting the successful learning environment of all the other students in the classroom. If the interventions are pre-planned and systematic, rather than arbitrary, the probability is increased that the interventions will be effective in ending disruptive behavior before it escalates and will ultimately teach appropriate behavior.

This chapter continues the development of a hierarchy of teacher interventions for both common and chronic disruptive behaviors which was begun in Chapter 18. First we stress the fact that teachers must always protect the safety of their students and themselves. We then present general intervention guidelines and pro-active interventions.

Safety First

Protecting the physical and psychological safety of all students and the teacher must be the highest priority at all times. If at any time the teacher feels that the physical safety of any member of the classroom is compromised, he should immediately seek assistance. It is just as important to protect the psychological safety of students. Teachers need to analyze empathetically any technique or intervention in order to determine its potential impact upon a student's sense of self-esteem. If the intervention demeans, condescends, or attacks the student, then it also decreases the student's success/failure ratio, intrinsic motivation, and pro-social self-esteem and must be scrupulously avoided.

When discipline problems occur, the challenge for the teacher is to reestablish a successful learning environment for the student who is exhibiting disruptive behavior and teach him appropriate behavior while protecting the successful learning environment of all the other students in the classroom.

Guidelines for Intervention

Level 1 of the Hierarchy of Interventions is reestablishing successful learning environments for students exhibiting disruptive behavior (Chapter 18). The next five levels of the hierarchy are specific interventions to protect the learning environment for all students and are to be used simultaneously while reestablishing a successful learning environment for the student exhibiting disruptive behavior.

Before discussing specific intervention strategies to be used when discipline problems occur, here are four intervention guidelines that should always be followed. They are designed to ensure that teachers intervene in a manner which does not increase a student's sense of failure, preserves intrinsic motivation by encouraging an internal locus of control, and maintains pro-social self-esteem.

Guideline #1: Teachers must provide the student with maximum opportunities for controlling his own behavior in appropriate ways. The philosophy underlying this guideline and stressed in the Self-Control Classroom model is that people control only their own behavior. By providing maximum opportunities for students to appropriately control their own behavior, teachers communicate respect for the student and his choices. This impacts the student's pro-social significance, competence, and power. Student success in self-management increases the student's intrinsic motivation through an internal locus of control. When a student understands that he has control over the choices he makes (internal locus of control), the development of accountability is facilitated. As teachers move through the Hierarchy of Interventions with students who exhibit more chronic disruptive behavior, those students have fewer opportunities to exhibit self-control, because of the teacher-centered nature of the interventions.

Teachers must provide the student with maximum opportunities for controlling his own behavior in appropriate ways.

Because teachers often make negative predictions about students who have a history of disruptive behavior (See Chapter 7), they are quick to make demands and use coercive interventions with these students. When compared to students who rarely exhibit disruptive behavior, these students usually are given less opportunities by teachers to make their own choices as to how to behave. While it is understandable that teachers may want to intervene quickly with students who exhibit chronic behavior problems, the message that is sent to the student is, "I do not trust your ability or desire to control your behavior in an appropriate manner. Therefore, I will take control of your behavior." This message erodes the student's pro-social significance, competence, and power and facilitates extrinsic motivation through an external locus of control. One of the outcomes of the erosion of these components of pro-social self-esteem is the likelihood that the student will compensate with ever increasing displays of distorted significance, competence, and power.

While it is understandable that teachers become wary of students who frequently exhibit disruptive behavior, it is essential that teachers treat every student everyday as if the student has the desire and competence to behave appropriately. In this manner, teachers are providing students with the opportunity to demonstrate that they have learned how to control their own behavior.

Teacher's interventions must be less disruptive to the learning environment than the student's disruptive behavior.

Guideline #2: Teachers' interventions must be less disruptive to the learning environment than the student's disruptive behavior. This guideline prevents the teacher from becoming a discipline problem (See Chapter 5). A teacher who verbally reprimands a student who is passing notes is more disruptive to the learning environment than the student. A teacher who stops a lesson to comment on a student's lateness when he enters the class and takes his seat is disrupting the learning environment more than the student. To deal with the passing of notes and lateness, the teacher can choose many interventions that are less disruptive than the student's behavior.

When teachers prematurely move through the Hierarchy of Interventions, they increase the likelihood of becoming more disruptive to the learning environment than the student exhibiting disruptive behavior.

Teachers must use interventions that decrease the likelihood of escalating the confrontation with the student.

Guideline #3: Teachers must use interventions that decrease the likelihood of escalating the confrontation with the student. Any confrontation with a student exhibiting disruptive behavior potentially provides the student with the opportunity to display distorted power. Sometimes it is necessary to assertively confront students with their behavior. This confrontation should be done in a manner that is referent (respectful) and designed not to escalate the situation.

Although the total hierarchy includes some very confrontational techniques, the purpose of a hierarchical structure is to help you manage behavior in the least confrontational manner possible. If the teacher uses strategies which are more confrontational than needed to encourage appropriate student behavior, he is likely to become the discipline problem.

Guideline #4: Teachers must leave open the greatest number of future interventions. As teachers move through the hierarchy, they reduce the number of interventions they have available for future use. When confronted with a student who exhibits disruptive behavior, often teachers will give that student a few opportunities to behave appropriately. If these few interventions fail, teachers often ignore many potentially successful interventions at the top of the hierarchy and remove the student from class, an intervention that is near the bottom of the hierarchy. Thus, the teacher can no longer teach that student; the teacher can no longer change his behavior to increase the likelihood that the student will learn.

Teachers must keep in mind that not only is it critical to end the disruptive behavior, but it is imperative to increase the likelihood that future disruptive behavior is prevented. Therefore, the Self-Control Classroom model stresses two objectives: reestablishing a successful learning environment for students who exhibit disruptive behavior, which increases the probability of appropriate behavior in the future, and immediately protecting the learning environment of the other students. Literally thousands of combinations of interventions are available to assist teachers in meeting these objectives.

Proactive Interventions

The second level of the hierarchy is proactive interventions. The purpose of proactive interventions is to prevent predictable disruptive behavior, such as when students move through instructional transitions, or to diffuse low level off-task behavior that threatens to become disruptive behavior, such as fidgeting, staring out the window, or doodling. These interventions reduce the need to move further into the hierarchy. The benefits of proactive interventions are that:

When a teacher becomes aware that students are losing attention and focus, it is time to change the instructional pace.

- they represent highly effective teaching practices,
- do not draw undue attention to the student or his off-task behavior,
- provide excellent means whereby a student can be directed toward more appropriate behavior, and
- maximize the student's ability to exert self-control.

Many teachers use these interventions in their daily practice and it is the rare early elementary teacher who has not perfected their use.

Changing the Instructional Pace

When instructional tasks require students to remain quiet too long or active too long, some students will lose interest and drift off-task. Off-task behavior is often a precursor to disruptive behavior. When a teacher becomes aware that students are losing attention and focus, it is time to change the instructional pace. For example, when an instructional objective requires long periods of concentration, the experienced teacher builds in frequent short breaks or intersperses other instructional activities requiring more active student participation. Some teachers view breaks as time lost to instruction. However, when the need for students to refresh themselves is respected, actual engagement time is increased. On the other hand, when instruction requires much movement or other active student participation, it is a good idea to slow things down periodically and give students some "down time."

It may be possible in some classrooms to give students the opportunity to self-monitor their fatigue and to stand, walk to the back of the class, or stretch in place, without gaining additional permission from the teacher, or causing a disruption. When teachers are in professional development workshops that last all day, they would consider it disrespectful if the presenters insisted upon total lack of movement except during permissible periods. It is the author's experience that nothing builds more empathy for student's need for time off-task than having the teacher sit through six hours of in-service instruction.

Boosting Interest

When students' focus on a task begins to wane for any reason, it is time to boost their interest. Changing the instructional pace is an effective means to boost interest. Others ways to increase interest include:

- changing instructional modality,
- using novel or discrepant events,
- integrating students' interests and experiences into the lesson, and
- illustrating the real-life applicability of the content.

Redirecting Behavior

Giving students a task that is incongruent with disruptive behavior illustrates the idea of redirecting behavior. For example, Trevor is annoying his neighbor. Instead of the teacher drawing attention to his disruptive behavior, the teacher asks Trevor to start the computer and locate the power point presentation for the next lesson. Other ways to redirect disruptive behavior include:

- having students run teacher errands,
- erase the board,
- put work on the board,
- pass out and collect materials, and
- organize a storage area.

These interventions not only redirect off-task or disruptive behavior, but also impact the student's pro-social significance, competence, and virtue by giving the student the opportunity to be of assistance to the teacher.

Some teachers complain that these redirecting activities are rewards for poor behavior and should be reserved for students who are behaving appropriately. Redirecting a student's behavior by allowing students to perform helpful classroom tasks does not meet the definition of a reward (Chapter 16). Furthermore, it is the authors' opinion that all students need to have the opportunity to feel they are valued and important members of the classroom community, not only those students who are the best behaved. By using these opportunities for raising students' self-esteem, the teacher is following the dual objectives of intervention: protecting the learning environment for all students and preventing future disruptive behavior by reestablishing a successful learning environment. If the teacher at this point uses interventions that are more reactive and further down the hierarchy, he is not:

- providing the student with the maximum opportunity to control his own behavior,
- maximizing the number of future interventions, or
- taking the opportunity to impact the student's successful learning environment through impacting pro-social self-esteem.

Where We've Been

This chapter stressed the need that teachers must protect the physical and psychological safety of all students all the time. Next, four teacher intervention guidelines were outlined for intervening with students exhibiting disruptive behavior. The guidelines direct teachers to choose interventions which achieve the following:

1. maximize opportunities for student self-control,
2. are least disruptive to the learning environment,
3. are least confrontational, and
4. maximize the number of teachers' interventions remaining.

These guidelines are designed to protect the successful learning environment of all students while reestablishing a successful learning environment for the student exhibiting disruptive behavior.

The chapter ended with a discussion of level 2 of the Hierarchy of Interventions, the proactive interventions of changing the instructional pace, boosting interest, and redirecting student behavior. Proactive interventions are intended to prevent predictable disruptive behavior or to diffuse low level off-task behavior that threatens to become disruptive behavior.

Where We're Headed

In the next chapter, Level 3 of the Hierarchy of Interventions, the use of nonverbal interventions to influence appropriate student behavior is discussed.

CHAPTER 20 CONCEPT MAP

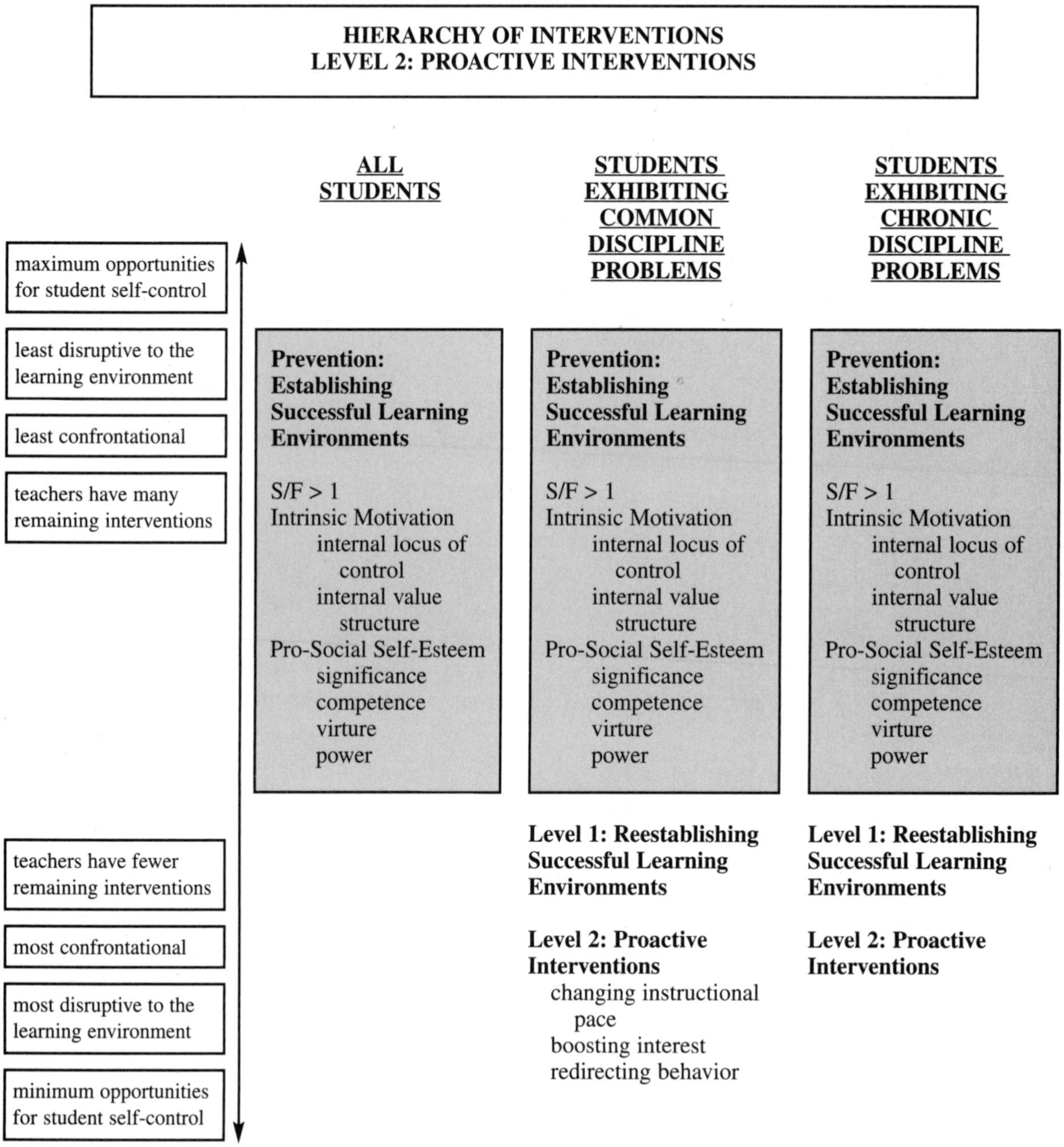

HIERARCHY OF INTERVENTIONS
LEVEL 2: PROACTIVE INTERVENTIONS

	ALL STUDENTS	STUDENTS EXHIBITING COMMON DISCIPLINE PROBLEMS	STUDENTS EXHIBITING CHRONIC DISCIPLINE PROBLEMS
maximum opportunities for student self-control least disruptive to the learning environment least confrontational teachers have many remaining interventions	**Prevention: Establishing Successful Learning Environments** S/F > 1 Intrinsic Motivation internal locus of control internal value structure Pro-Social Self-Esteem significance competence virture power	**Prevention: Establishing Successful Learning Environments** S/F > 1 Intrinsic Motivation internal locus of control internal value structure Pro-Social Self-Esteem significance competence virture power	**Prevention: Establishing Successful Learning Environments** S/F > 1 Intrinsic Motivation internal locus of control internal value structure Pro-Social Self-Esteem significance competence virture power
teachers have fewer remaining interventions most confrontational most disruptive to the learning environment minimum opportunities for student self-control		**Level 1: Reestablishing Successful Learning Environments** **Level 2: Proactive Interventions** changing instructional pace boosting interest redirecting behavior	**Level 1: Reestablishing Successful Learning Environments** **Level 2: Proactive Interventions**

? Questions For The Study Team

1. The Self-Control Classroom model stresses that it is critical to try to prevent discipline problems from occurring by establishing successful learning environments. What does a teacher do when discipline problems arise in the first few weeks of class, when there hasn't been enough time for prevention measures to be successful?

2. How may each guideline for intervention be explained to other teachers and parents who are not familiar with the Self-Control Classroom model, in order for them to understand why you do not immediately intervene assertively with students exhibiting disruptive behavior?

3. What are some specific ways that teachers can change the pace of instruction and use boosting interest and redirecting behavior to proactively prevent discipline problems?

4. How can changing the pace of instruction, boosting interest, and redirecting behavior be built into lesson plans and curriculum?

CHAPTER 21

Level 3 of the Hierarchy of Interventions: The Use of Nonverbal Interventions

"To many people, discipline means punishment. But actually, to discipline means to teach. Rather than punishment, discipline should be a positive way of helping and guiding children to achieve self-control." (Marshall, 1998)

"A teacher is respected not for how tall he stands, but for how often he bends to help, comfort, and teach." (author unknown)

It is axiomatic that nonverbal techniques afford the maximum opportunity for students to control themselves. Nonverbal techniques are less disruptive than the student behavior. These techniques are the least confrontational, and leave open to the teacher many interventions in the hierarchy that may be used in the future if necessary.

Nonverbal techniques must be consciously applied in a preplanned fashion. When a teacher is skilled in the use of nonverbal techniques, she uses them in a manner which preserves the privacy and dignity of the student exhibiting disruptive behavior. A nonverbal technique serves as a private message between the teacher and the student, that it is time for the student to use self-control to bring her disruptive behavior into appropriate limits. This use of nonverbal techniques does not interrupt the flow of the teacher's lesson. Nonverbal interventions are broadly classified as:

- planned ignoring,
- signals,
- proximity, and
- touch.

These nonverbal interventions are presented in hierarchical order to follow the intervention guidelines presented in the previous chapter.

Planned Ignoring

Planned ignoring is not looking at, recognizing, or in any other manner reacting to a student's disruptive behavior. This does not mean that the teacher is not monitoring the disruptive behavior;

it means the teacher has made a conscious decision to ignore the behavior. The rationale for the teacher's decision is that by denying the student an opportunity to display distorted power and competence through her disruptive behavior, the teacher increases the likelihood that the student will choose more appropriate behavior. When more appropriate behavior occurs, the teacher stops ignoring the student and treats the student as she treats all students who are actively involved in the lesson.

For example, a teacher handing out test papers walks by and ignores Carly and Chantelle while they are talking. She hands out papers to all the other students who are exhibiting appropriate test-taking behavior. When Carly and Chantelle stop talking, bringing their behavior back into appropriate limits, the teacher, without saying a word, hands them their test papers. Another example involves Alexis, who always calls out answers. The teacher does not respond to Alexis in any manner, turns her back on Alexis, and calls upon students who raise their hand. When Alexis raises her hand, the teacher immediately calls upon her for the answer.

When a teacher is skilled in the use of nonverbal techniques, she uses them in a manner which preserves the privacy and dignity of the student exhibiting disruptive behavior.

Several caveats must be given concerning the use of planned ignoring:

- Teachers must not ignore behavior which is either physically or psychologically dangerous to any individual, and threats to property cannot be ignored.
- This technique cannot be used when the student's behavior is attracting the undue attention of other students.
- The use of planned ignoring must be consistent. If a decision is made to ignore a behavior, and then later the same behavior is attended to, the likelihood that planned ignoring will be effective in managing that behavior in the future is greatly reduced.
- With some students, such as those with Attention Deficit Hyperactivity Disorder (ADHD), planned ignoring may be totally ineffective because oftentimes they don't notice that you are ignoring them.

When disruptive behavior is ignored, the behavior often initially intensifies, because the student concludes that she needs to increase her disruptive behavior in order to achieve her goal of distorted power. This increase in a student's disruptive behavior causes many teachers to discontinue the strategy prematurely. However, if the student's behavior does not violate any of the above cautions, continued ignoring by the teacher often results in the student positively changing her behavior. When teachers prematurely discontinue ignoring, it reinforces the student's increased level of disruptive behavior through the reinforcement of that student's display of distorted power.

Signals

When planned ignoring is either ineffective or not suitable under the circumstances, the use of signals is the next nonverbal intervention in the hierarchical scheme. Signaling is the preplanned and systematic use of body language or other signals or cues which clearly communicate to the student that her behavior is inappropriate and/or communicate what is the desired appropriate behavior. Additionally, signals may communicate teacher approval of student behavior. Typical types of signals are facial expressions, eye contact, hand gestures, musical sounds, and turning the lights off and on.

When a student is "fooling around," often a look serves as a signal to the student that it is time to get back to work. If a student is roaming around the room, a finger pointed at her chair redirects her back to her desk. Another type of hand signal is the familiar finger to the lips to signal "stop talking." Simply shaking the head up and down, or smiling indicates approval to the student. The facial expression of the teacher must be congruent with the message that the teacher intends to send to the student. Smiling while placing the finger to the lips in order to signal quiet is an example of an incongruent display that is liable to confound the message and confuse the student as to its meaning.

Signaling is the preplanned and systematic use of body language or other signals or cues which clearly communicate to the student that her behavior is inappropriate and/or communicate what is the desired appropriate behavior.

A strategy which oftentimes works well is to have the teacher and the students mutually agree upon signals for the classroom which everyone in the class recognizes. These signals may be developed at the beginning of the school year and/or as the need arises. For example, when Ms. Allen stands at the doorway of the room, all her students recognize that her position means it is time for recess, clear your desks, get your coats, and line up to go outside. When Ms. Chofnas flicks the lights, it is understood by the students to mean that it is too noisy and to talk more quietly. Ms. Aronow plays the C chord on the piano which communicates to her students to stop working at their learning centers and return to their desks.

For students who exhibit chronically disruptive behavior, mutually agreed upon private signals may not only improve on-task behavior, but may increase the student's sense of significance and therefore improve the relationship between the teacher and the student. For example, Ms. Worth tugs on her ear, which is the agreed upon private signal to Roberta that she needs to take out her book and begin work. This type of message frequently goes unnoticed by other students and is, in any case, meaningless to all but the targeted student.

A benefit of signals is that they can be utilized at a distance and therefore, as with planned ignoring, do not interfere with what the teacher and the rest of the class are doing.

A benefit of signals is that they can be utilized at a distance and therefore, as with planned ignoring, do not interfere with what the teacher and the rest of the class are doing. For example, the teacher may send a signal while continuing to work at the blackboard, from across the room, while running the overhead projector, or on the playground.

Proximity

Students frequently behave more appropriately when the teacher stands near them. Therefore, teachers who move around the classroom prevent much misbehavior from occurring. If a discipline problem does occur, the teacher is in the position to move rapidly toward the student, without everyone in the class being aware that a problem exists. However, if the teacher typically does not circulate throughout her classroom, but then moves and stands next to a specific student who is off-task, the teacher increases the confrontational nature of this intervention, because proximity is a rare event. A relaxed teaching style in which the teacher frequently walks around the room allows proximity to be both positive and encouraging for all students, as well as a signal to some students to stop their disruptive behavior. In addition, because teachers who move around the classroom tend to create more student interest than teachers who instruct from a stationary position, teacher movement is a proactive intervention.

Remember however, proximity is a nonverbal intervention. Resist the urge to say something to the student about her behavior. Instead, conduct the class as usual, but from a different location.

Proximity may be combined with a signal to create an even more effective intervention. For example, if Ms. Hrach makes eye contact with Sam and then walks purposefully toward Sam's desk, it sends a stronger message to Sam.

Touch

Touch is a highly effective but problematic intervention in today's classrooms. It used to be that teachers felt comfortable to appropriately touch students. This is no longer the case. Although touch is a human need, and most younger students seek touch, it is an intervention which must be very cautiously and very sensitively used. A touch on the shoulder or a hand on the shoulder or arm is an unmistakable signal. Whether that signal is positively or negatively perceived is a function of students' past experiences with you and others, their particular sensitivity to touch, as well as a function of culture and age. Some individuals are hypersensitive to touch, either for reasons of physiological arousal, a history of physical or sexual abuse, anxiety, or fear. Certain cultures encourage touch, while others proscribe it. It is important, therefore, to know your student well before intervening with touch.

Teachers who move around the classroom prevent much misbehavior from occurring.

If you frequently use touch to signal acceptance, approval, and affection you increase the probability that touch as an intervention for disruptive behavior will not be resented because of this positive association. If, on the other hand, you touch students only as a way to intervene with disruptive behavior, the converse is true. As a general rule, younger students are more accepting of touch than are adolescents. Adolescents may frequently perceive touch as aggressive, or worse, sexual. If you doubt this, think of how often and at what age students seek to sit in your lap. To the kindergarten student of either gender, sitting in the teacher's lap during story time may be a real treat. However, certainly for an adolescent student to do the same would be highly inappropriate and likely would lead to serious allegations and/or sanctions against the teacher.

In spite of these concerns, a slight touch to an off-task student can effectively alert the student to her inappropriate behavior and encourage her to choose more appropriate behavior. It is helpful when establishing consensually derived class guidelines also to spend a moment discussing all the ways in which you will intervene nonverbally, including the occasional use of touch. This explanation of the use of touch may serve to help avoid any negative responses.

When touch is used, it should be applied as light, non-aggressive physical contact. Touch may be used to guide a student to appropriate conduct, such as when a teacher gently directs a student back to her seat. Touch also may serve to increase the efficacy of proximity; for example, placing a hand lightly upon the shoulder of Joy, whom the teacher observes is throwing her pencil in the air and letting it hit the floor.

Although these nonverbal techniques have been presented in a hierarchical order, the sequential delivery represents an idealized classroom situation. In the real classroom, the sequence of delivery depends upon the characteristics of the individual student, the type of disruptive behavior, and the nature of the learning activity. For example, if a teacher observes Joan firing spit balls at her neighbor, the teacher likely skips planned ignoring and signal interference in favor of proximity and removal of the straw.

It has been the authors' experience that when some teachers intervene with students exhibiting chronically disruptive behavior, they are less likely to use nonverbal techniques, and are more likely to move prematurely to lower levels of the hierarchy, because these teachers have a low expectation of these students' ability to control themselves. The authors believe that all students are capable of learning self-control. Remember that the definition of learning is an observable change in behavior. If students are not given opportunities every day to display their self-control by the teacher using nonverbal interventions, the student cannot demonstrate that they have learned anything from previous experience.

In a study conducted by Shrigley (1985), more than 50 teachers reported that 40 percent of all disruptive behavior was managed effectively using nonverbal interventions. In other words, close to half of all student disruptive behavior in the classroom was managed without the teacher uttering a word or interrupting her lesson. The majority of the remaining disruptive behaviors were effectively managed by verbal interventions which will be discussed in the next chapter.

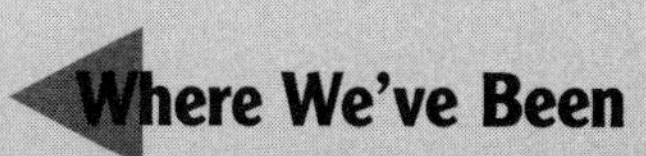

Where We've Been

This chapter discussed the nonverbal strategies of the intervention hierarchy. These strategies are ordered to be congruent with the intervention guidelines presented in the previous chapter. The strategies are:

- planned ignoring,
- signals,
- proximity, and
- touch.

Examples for each strategy were provided, as well as suggestions for their effective use.

Where We're Headed

Explanation of teacher movement through the Hierarchy of Interventions continues, with Chapter 22 covering verbal interventions and specific guidelines for their use. In addition, examples of effective and ineffective verbal interventions will be provided.

CHAPTER 21 CONCEPT MAP

HIERARCHY OF INTERVENTIONS
LEVEL 3: NONVERBAL INTERVENTIONS

- maximum opportunities for student self-control
- least disruptive to the learning environment
- least confrontational
- teachers have many remaining interventions
- teachers have fewer remaining interventions
- most confrontational
- most disruptive to the learning environment
- minimum opportunities for student self-control

ALL STUDENTS

Prevention: Establishing Successful Learning Environments

S/F > 1
Intrinsic Motivation
- internal locus of control
- internal value structure

Pro-Social Self-Esteem
- significance
- competence
- virture
- power

STUDENTS EXHIBITING COMMON DISCIPLINE PROBLEMS

Prevention: Establishing Successful Learning Environments

S/F > 1
Intrinsic Motivation
- internal locus of control
- internal value structure

Pro-Social Self-Esteem
- significance
- competence
- virture
- power

Level 1: Reestablishing Successful Learning Environments

Level 2: Pro-Active Interventions

Level 3: Nonverbal Interventions
- planned ignoring
- signals
- proximity
- touch

STUDENTS EXHIBITING CHRONIC DISCIPLINE PROBLEMS

Prevention: Establishing Successful Learning Environments

S/F > 1
Intrinsic Motivation
- internal locus of control
- internal value structure

Pro-Social Self-Esteem
- significance
- competence
- virture
- power

Level 1: Reestablishing Successful Learning Environments

Level 2: Pro-Active Interventions

Level 3: Nonverbal Interventions

? QUESTIONS FOR THE STUDY TEAM

1. How much disruptive behavior does a teacher ignore from a student before moving on to other nonverbal interventions?

2. What types of student disruptive behavior should be ignored? What types of student disruptive behavior should not be ignored?

3. Brainstorm the different types of signals that teachers may use to privately communicate to students that their behavior is inappropriate.

4. I teach very tough students. Won't these students perceive me as being weak if I use nonverbal behaviors?

5. Are there any types of student disruptive behavior for which, when exhibited, the teacher should skip nonverbal interventions entirely and move immediately to verbal interventions?

Chapter 22

Level 4 of the Hierarchy of Interventions: Using Verbal Interventions

"Treat people as if they are what they ought to be and you help them become what they are capable of being" (Göethe).

Sometimes after the application of various nonverbal techniques, the student is still disruptive. Many teachers become increasingly frustrated and begin to resort to threats, yelling, and punishment. Though these teachers' behaviors may be understandable under the circumstances, they violate the four guidelines for effective intervention established in Chapter 20. In addition, these negative interventions reduce the success/failure ratio, increase students' external locus of control, and foster students' distorted self-esteem. Contrast these effects of the negative interventions to the verbal interventions which represent the 4th tier of the hierarchy of intervention strategies. These verbal interventions continue to emphasize students' ability for self-control and are less disruptive to the class than angry teacher displays. Although these verbal interventions are more confrontational than nonverbal interventions, they are less likely to escalate students' disruptive conduct than are angry teacher displays. These verbal interventions continue to protect the physical and psychological safety of the student and preserve additional strategies for later teacher intervention.

It is important to continue signaling students, now using verbal interventions, that their behavior is inappropriate and to give them additional opportunities to choose appropriate behavior. While these verbal interventions are somewhat confrontational, if done properly the confrontation is less likely to escalate.

Guidelines for the Effective Use of Verbal Interventions

The suggestions in Table 22.1 increase the probability that students will maintain an internal locus of control and reduce the movement toward distorted self-esteem.

Ineffective Verbal Interventions

When using verbal interventions, be sure you do not encourage inappropriate behavior, focus on irrelevant behavior, provide abstract and

TABLE 22.1 ▶ Suggestions to Increase the Probability that Students Maintain an Internal Locus of Control and Reduce Distorted Self-Esteem

- ▶ Speak to the situation not the person (Ginott, 1972), or, as Albert Ellis (1997) says, "I am not a worm for behaving wormily." For example, saying, " Gian, I do not like it when you act disrespectfully to me," is vastly different than saying, "Gian, you are a very disrespectful person." Speaking to the person, as was done in the second statement, increases defensive and angry student behavior. It may very well lead to an increase in the student's display of distorted power.

- ▶ Make your verbal behavior useable. Tell the student what you want him to do rather than point out what he is doing. "Gregory, I want you to raise your hand" rather than, "Don't call out, Gregory."

- ▶ Set limits on behavior, not feelings (Ginott, 1972). "Tyler, I can see you're angry, but you must keep your hands to yourself," not "Tyler there's really no reason to be so angry."

- ▶ Use referent authority. Respect the student at all times, avoiding the use of sarcasm and condescension. Let's look at the following situation. Peter is talking to his neighbor, Dimitri. The teacher says very sarcastically, "Dimitri, isn't Peter's conversation incredibly interesting? I'll bet you haven't heard such brilliant commentary before." Compare this with, "Dimitri and Peter, what we're doing right now in class is very important, and I want both of you to learn the material. Please wait until lunch to continue your conversation." Another situation is when a teacher has a policy that he will publicly read any notes that he sees being passed between students. A more productive way to deal with note passing is for the teacher to use proximity to intercept the note, quietly pocket it, and then return it after class.

- ▶ Keep the interventions brief. This is not the time to dialog past and future events or to argue. Prolonged interventions take additional time away from instructional activities, and therefore they tend to be more disruptive. "Bruce, this is the third time today that I've had to speak to you about your behavior. Do you understand why you need to sit down? I've explained before that if I have to keep telling you to sit down, I will call your parents. Is that what you want me to do? Because I don't know any other way to get you to behave!" is less effective than, "Bruce, please sit down." In addition to being disruptive, long verbal discourses provide additional opportunities for students who behave disruptively to engage in distorted power by mocking the teacher, putting their hands over their ears, or otherwise using the teacher's words against the teacher.

- ▶ Keep the interventions as private as possible. The milder verbal interventions may generally be more public. For example, Max is wandering around the back of the room. The teacher says, "Max, please take your seat." However, as the level of confrontation rises, so does the need for privacy. Again, you need to avoid providing a potential platform for the student to display distorted power. If Max does not sit down, the teacher moves to the back of the room and conducts further verbal interventions in private.

- ▶ Intervene in a timely manner, as close to the inappropriate behavior as possible. The farther removed from the event that your intervention is, the less its impact may be. In contrast, the closer your intervention is to the event, the more impact it is likely to have. When environmental or other constraints prevent timely intervention, it might be better to allow the situation to pass without comment. The younger the student, the more critical it is that time interval between the disruptive behavior and the verbal intervention of the teacher be minimal.

meaningless directions, or use classification systems.

ENCOURAGING INAPPROPRIATE BEHAVIOR

The consequences of a statement such as, "I dare you to do that again," are easy to imagine, especially if the teacher is confronting an adolescent who tends to be oppositional and defiant. Think about the consequences of a teacher's sarcastic comments, "Let's wait and see if Doug will quiet down," or the more confrontational, "Keep that up, and you'll learn what will happen to you." These types of interventions provide irresistible invitations for a student to exhibit distorted power by maintaining or escalating the problem behavior.

Similar to nonverbal interventions, verbal interventions are also ordered to follow the intervention guidelines.

FOCUSING UPON IRRELEVANT BEHAVIOR

Statements focusing upon irrelevant behavior include, "Aren't you sorry for what you've done?" "Why can't you admit you have a problem?" "You better think twice before you do that in my class again!" and the ever popular, "If you know what's good for you, you better never let me catch you doing that in my classroom again." All of these comments are extremely confrontational, and they do not specifically provide information to the student as to what he has done inappropriately or what he needs to do to behave appropriately. Additionally, several of these comments are challenges to the student to continue with his inappropriate behavior.

The first level of verbal intervention is using a student's name.

PROVIDING ABSTRACT AND MEANINGLESS DIRECTIONS

Teacher comments such as "Grow up!" or "Act your age," do not send the student any useful information as to what needs to be done differently and the comments are disrespectful.

USING CLASSIFICATION SYSTEMS

When teachers say "You have an attitude problem," or "You are rude and immature," they are not providing students with useful information. The student feels attacked, and may either respond defensively using distorted power or may agree with a retort such as, "Yeah. So what?"

Effective Verbal Interventions

Verbal intervention is more confrontational than nonverbal intervention. If you are at this point in the hierarchy, it necessarily must be because your use of nonverbal interventions has not been effective, or the behavior is too serious to enter the hierarchy at the nonverbal level. Similar to nonverbal interventions, verbal interventions are also ordered to follow the intervention guidelines. Verbal interventions include using a student's name, inferential statements, questions, I-messages, and lastly, demands.

USING THE STUDENT'S NAME

The first level of verbal intervention is using a student's name. Often during a lesson, merely saying the student's name is effective in returning the student to on-task behavior. For example, Mr. M'fwumi says, "Netscape continually competes with Internet Explorer to be the most popular Internet browser, Joseph."

Another way to use a student's name is to call on the student to answer a question. "John, what were some of the events that led to the Berlin Wall being torn down?" When using this method, it is less confrontational to say the student's name first, and then ask the question. Compare this with asking the question first and then saying the student's name. "What were some of the events that led to the Berlin Wall being torn down, John?" This virtually ensures the student will not answer correctly, because if he is not paying attention, then he probably has not heard the question before his name was called. While this may be effective in regaining on-task behavior, it is more confrontational than needed, because it tends to embarrass the student in front of his peers.

Regardless of the antecedent behavior, if the student does not know the answer to the teacher's question, he should be treated as any other student who doesn't know the answer, with methods such as giving the student additional time, providing prompts, pointing out where the answer can be found, or asking another student. The teacher must not make an issue of the student's inattention, for instance stating, "If you were paying attention, then maybe you'd know the answer." This comment serves only to embarrass and belittle the student in front of his peers, increasing the likelihood that the student will respond with face saving displays of distorted power.

Inferential statements serve to gain the attention of the student in a good natured way.

INFERENTIAL STATEMENTS

Inferential statements serve to gain the attention of the student in a good natured way. Some examples of inferential statements are:

- "Harold, you seem to have a lot of energy today!" The teacher said this in order for Harold to focus on his inappropriate wandering around the room and to increase the probability that Harold will sit down.
- "Will, I bet you'll have a lot to talk to Art about at recess." The teacher made this statement to get Will to attend to the fact that he is talking to Art and to increase the probability that he will stop talking until recess time.
- "Jerry, recess is only five minutes away." The purpose of the teacher's comments is to increase the probability that Jerry will stay on task for another five minutes, because he knows that he will have a break in a few minutes.

It might appear to the reader that these interventions violate our guideline that verbal interventions need to tell students what we want them to do. Hints are exceptions to the rule, because at this point in the hierarchy, it is preferable to keep the level of confrontation low. A hint, especially when delivered by a referent teacher, is often all that is needed to return a student to appropriate behavior. The teacher has not yet directly told the student what is expected. The teacher still is exhibiting significant respect for the student's ability to recognize what is expected of him and to choose more appropriate behavior without more teacher assistance.

Care must be taken when using inferential statements to avoid being sarcastic or snide. In the examples, a subtle change in tone might have turned a mildly amusing comment, meant to get the student's attention, into a sarcastic comment which most likely would have been perceived as an attack on the student. Also, if you respect your students and encourage a referent relationship, then you increase the probability that your inferential statements are perceived positively.

If you respect your students and encourage a referent relationship, then you increase the probability that your inferential statements are perceived positively.

The use of adjacent reinforcers such as, "I like the way Carl and Andy are sitting quietly," to get Steven sitting nearby back on task, seems similar to inferential statements. However, it is the authors' opinion as well as Alfie Kohn's (1999), an authority on the difficulty with rewards and punishments, that adjacent reinforcers tend to potentially reduce the intrinsic motivation of Carl and Andy by praising them, as discussed in Chapter 16. It also disrespects Carl and Andy by using them to manipulate Steven. Adjacent reinforcement also does little to enhance Carl and Andy's standing with the other members of the class, because the teacher's statements sets up a competition with Carl and Andy in the lead. We therefore do not endorse the use of other students to remind or reinforce the behavior of their classmates.

The purpose of questions, therefore, is to help the student display pro-social virtue by altering his behavior so that it is no longer disruptive.

QUESTIONS

Let's assume that the student is still exhibiting disruptive behavior. According to the hierarchy, the teacher next uses questions. Questions are designed to alert the student more directly to the inappropriate nature of his behavior. A question also alerts the student to the effect that his behavior is having upon other students in the class. The purpose of questions, therefore, is to help the student display pro-social virtue by altering his behavior so that it is no longer disruptive. Again, be aware that these statements need to be delivered privately, with sincerity and without sarcasm or condescension. By delivering the questions in a respectful manner, the teacher reduces the possibility of the student displaying distorted power by, for instance, providing a sarcastic answer. Some examples of such questions are:

- "Eddy, are you aware that tapping your pencil is disturbing the class?"
- "Jesús, do you know that your humming makes it difficult for others to concentrate?"
- "Tom, could you work a bit more quietly? The noise is distracting others!"

I-STATEMENTS

I-statements (Gordon, 1974) are slightly more confrontational than using the student's name, inferential statements, or questions. They more directly communicate what behavior the teacher desires of the student and why, as well as providing feedback about the effect of the behavior upon the teacher and the rest of the class.

I-statements have three components, communicating

- what the student is doing,
- the effect the of the student's behavior on the class, and
- how the teacher feels about it.

I-statements are an example of assertive delivery discussed in more detail in Chapter 23. Some examples are:

- "Lennox, when you tap your pencil, it is difficult to concentrate on the math lesson. This disturbs me, because I want everyone to do well in math."
- "Jack, when you arrive late to class, it disrupts the lesson for everyone, and this bothers me because I want everyone to have enough time to learn the material."
- "Ethan, when you pass notes to Ibrahim, it distracts both of you from your work, and this disturbs me, because I would like you both to learn the lesson."

The use of I-statements, because it relies upon the student caring how the teacher feels about student behavior, is effective only when the teacher is perceived as a referent authority. If the student does not have this perception, disruptive behavior might actually increase after the use of I-messages, as the student now knows which behaviors are likely to increase his distorted competence and power by making the teacher angry and upset.

DEMANDS

At this point, all other methods having failed, the teacher makes a demand of the student. In general, demands are more effective when you tell students what you want them to do, rather than what you don't want them to do. Demands are the most confrontational of all verbal interventions, except for the verbal delivery of consequences (See Chapter 23). Therefore, demands are reserved for those instances when either it is essential that the behavior cease immediately (such as if it threatens physical safety or may cause property damage) or the behaviors are very disruptive and persistent. Once the teacher has issued a demand, the student either must comply immediately, or much more aversive consequences ensue.

Some teachers might think, "Great! Why don't we just cut to the chase and start with demands?" To do so violates the underlying premises of the Self-Control Classroom model. Beginning with demands is the hallmark of the old paradigm of classroom management. As mentioned several times, this old paradigm or traditional model leaves the teacher with very few options before he can no longer teach the target student. In addition, techniques congruent with the old paradigm do nothing to teach appropriate behavior in the present, prevent disruptive behavior in the future, or teach self-control.

Demands are more effective when you tell students what you want them to do, rather than what you don't want them to do.

Some examples of demands include:

- "Corey, return to your seat and continue working on problems 5 through 10," is more effective than "Corey, stop wandering around the class!"
- "Jean-Pierre, put the paper away and start working on your computer journal," rather than "Jean-Pierre, stop writing notes to Pandit."
- "Evan, put your coat in your cubby and begin answering the openers," not "Evan, don't put your coat on the floor!"

To the extent that you make the demands privately, you decrease the effect of "playing to the audience," and less of a power struggle is set up between you and the student. Any struggle for power increases the student's distorted self-esteem. Therefore, at least for some students, compliance is less of an issue when the entire class is not an audience for the demand. When making a demand, be brief and to the point. This is not the time to reflect upon students' past transgressions or to editorialize upon the future. Stating, "This is the 5th time I've had to tell you! Don't you ever learn? Now SIT DOWN!" or "How do you expect to pass this class if you can't stay in your seat? SIT DOWN!" is not effective. The fact that a student has exhibited the same behavior previously is not of immediate importance in getting him to comply with the current demand.

The effectiveness of demands like I-statements is increased when they are delivered assertively. Demands should be made with a firm but not loud voice, in close proximity to the student whenever possible, and with constant eye contact.

A Troubling Question

The use of verbal interventions, particularly demands, are more confrontational and insistent than nonverbal interventions. Therefore, the teacher runs the risk of communicating failure to the student, encouraging an external locus of control, and fostering distorted self-esteem. Because it is being made ever more explicit to the student that his behavior is inappropriate, this constitutes a failure experience. To the extent that the student believes he is being forced by the teacher to comply, the student perceives an external locus of control. To the extent that the student experiences failure and an external locus of control, he also experiences a decline in his sense of pro-social power and competence. To maintain a sense of self-esteem, the student is therefore likely to compensate for the deficits in pro-social power and competence through displays of distorted competence and power, such as continued non-compliance, and/or escalation of disruption.

The critical reader may ask, "Why would I ever use verbal interventions if I'm going to run the risk of increasing students' resistance and increasing their disruptive behavior?" The answer is that you have a responsibility to all students in your class to maintain a successful learning environment, and you need to do something to increase the likelihood that this student's disruptive behavior will stop; however, the nonverbal interventions have not worked. Therefore you must continue down the hierarchy.

You minimize possible negative consequences of using verbal interventions by continuing to prevent all disruptive behavior.

How can you minimize the negative impact of verbal interventions? You minimize possible negative consequences of using verbal interventions by continuing to prevent all disruptive behavior. At the same time, your verbal interventions must be delivered assertively and with respectful affect. Each incident must be dealt with separately.

First focus upon continuing prevention. If you utilize the strategies outlined in the Self-Control Classroom model, then the student has likely experienced an increased success/failure ratio, has moved toward an internal locus of control and internal value structure, and has experienced an increase in pro-social significance, competence, virtue, and power. Most importantly, the student has been encouraged to view you, the teacher, as a referent and expert authority. Therefore, the student should be somewhat resistant to the potential negative effects of verbal interventions, and the probability of success of verbal interventions is increased.

Secondly, focus on assertive and affective delivery. Throughout this chapter we have stressed that it is important to deliver verbal interventions assertively, but without anger, frustration, or condescension, and in as private a manner as possible. This delivery increases the probability that the student will focus upon his behavior and not your behavior. Respectful, affective delivery encourages the student's development of an internal locus of control because the student is more likely to feel that compliance is a matter of personal choice rather than adherence to a command. The issue of student choice is discussed in Chapter 23.

Lastly, it is crucial that each incident of disruptive behavior be treated as separate and discrete. When the student brings his behavior back into appropriate limits, he is welcomed back into the class community and is treated the same as every other student, as if nothing has happened. Obviously, chronic disruptive behavior may require additional interventions which are discussed in Chapter 23 and Chapter 24.

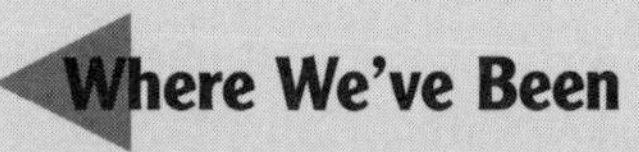

Where We've Been

This chapter discussed verbal interventions. We began with guidelines for the effective use of verbal interventions. The guidelines are:

1) speak to the situation not the person,
2) make the verbal behavior useable,
3) set limits on behavior, not feelings,
4) use referent authority, respecting the student at all times,
5) keep the interventions brief,
6) keep the interventions as private as possible, and
7) intervene in a timely manner, as close to the inappropriate behavior as possible.

Ineffective interventions were listed to aid in their avoidance. They include:

1) encouraging inappropriate behavior,
2) focusing upon irrelevant behavior,
3) providing abstract and meaningless directions, and
4) using classification systems.

Effective verbal interventions then were discussed. They include:

1) using the student's name,
2) inferential statements,
3) questions,
4) I-Statements, and
5) demands.

Where We're Headed

In the next chapter, the assertive delivery of consequences is described. The reader is taught how to phrase and deliver an assertive message that simultaneously communicates the consequence, while preserving and facilitating the pro-social self-esteem of the student.

CHAPTER 22 CONCEPT MAP

HIERARCHY OF INTERVENTIONS
LEVEL 4: VERBAL INTERVENTIONS

maximum opportunities for student self-control

least disruptive to the learning environment

least confrontational

teachers have many remaining interventions

↕

teachers have fewer remaining interventions

most confrontational

most disruptive to the learning environment

minimum opportunities for student self-control

ALL STUDENTS

Prevention: Establishing Successful Learning Environments

S/F > 1
Intrinsic Motivation
- internal locus of control
- internal value structure

Pro-Social Self-Esteem
- significance
- competence
- virture
- power

STUDENTS EXHIBITING COMMON DISCIPLINE PROBLEMS

Prevention: Establishing Successful Learning Environments

S/F > 1
Intrinsic Motivation
- internal locus of control
- internal value structure

Pro-Social Self-Esteem
- significance
- competence
- virture
- power

Level 1: Reestablishing Successful Learning Environments

Level 2: Pro-Active Interventions

Level 3: Nonverbal Interventions

Level 4: Verbal Interventions
- use students' names
- inferential statements
- questions
- I-statements
- demands

STUDENTS EXHIBITING CHRONIC DISCIPLINE PROBLEMS

Prevention: Establishing Successful Learning Environments

S/F > 1
Intrinsic Motivation
- internal locus of control
- internal value structure

Pro-Social Self-Esteem
- significance
- competence
- virture
- power

Level 1: Reestablishing Successful Learning Environments

Level 2: Pro-Active Interventions

Level 3: Nonverbal Interventions

Level 4: Verbal Interventions

QUESTIONS FOR THE STUDY TEAM

1. Is it ever appropriate to skip verbal interventions and move immediately to the delivery of consequences?

2. If a teacher knows from past experiences that a particular student responds only to demands, isn't it a waste of time to use the other verbal interventions?

3. How can a demand ever be successful in influencing a student to stop disruptive behavior if there is no consequence for noncompliance?

CHAPTER 23

Level 5 of the Hierarchy of Interventions: The Delivery of Consequences

"The goal of punishment is to force compliance with the rules by using external controls or authoritarian discipline. . . . The goal of logical consequences is to help children develop internal understanding, self-control, and a desire to follow the rules. . . . The belief underlying the use of logical consequences is that with reflection and practice children will want to do better, whereas the belief behind punishment is that children will do better only because they fear punishment and will seek to avoid it." (Northeast Foundation for Children, 1998)

A teacher needs to move to Level 5, either because she has used several less confrontational nonverbal and verbal techniques, and the student is still exhibiting disruptive behavior, or because the disruptive behavior is extreme, seriously threatens the physical or psychological safety of other students or the teacher, or the behavior threatens to destroy property. The teacher needs to make clear to the student that her disruptive behavior must stop immediately, or logical consequences will follow. There are two requirements in order to have an effective delivery of consequences. First, there must be an explicit communication to the student that the student still has a right to control her own behavior by making a choice, even at this confrontational point in the hierarchy. Therefore, it is important to carefully phrase the content of the message to state this accurately. Secondly, the teacher must remain in control of her affective expression, so that the student is likely to take the message seriously but without becoming defensive. If the student becomes defensive, the focus of attention is likely to shift from the student's own behavior, which is necessary for the development of accountability, to the teacher's behavior, which allows the student to avoid accountability.

Phrasing the Message "You Have a Choice"

Heidi is disrupting the other students in her cooperative learning group. You have moved through several nonverbal and verbal techniques without successfully influencing Heidi to change her behavior. You approach Heidi and say, "Heidi, you have a choice. Work cooperatively with your team or move to the back of the room and work by yourself. You decide." Phrasing the message as one of self-choice communicates clearly to the student that the choice is hers to make, thus impacting Heidi's sense of pro-social power. The outcome is dependent solely upon what Heidi chooses, thus impacting her internal locus of control.

Consequences determined in the heat of the moment are more likely to be harsh and less likely to be logically related to the disruptive behavior.

If Heidi chooses to behave cooperatively, the disruptive behavior will be something that happened in the past, and you will treat her as if the disruption never occurred. However, if Heidi continues to be disruptive, you again approach Heidi and say, "Heidi, you decided to move to the back of the room. Please move." Once Heidi has made her choice, the discussion is over. It is not appropriate to further penalize the student, for example, with further negative comments or facial expressions just because she has not made the choice that you wanted her to make. The discussion is over, even if Heidi throws her chair backwards or uses profanity toward you on the way to the back of the room. Even under these challenging circumstances, due to the heightened tension of the moment, unless Heidi is threatening the physical safety of her classmates or you or destroying property, there should be no further dialogue at this time. Any discussion of the manner in which Heidi complied is deferred to a later time, for instance, after class, after school, or other times when you can speak privately to Heidi.

Do not move to this level of the hierarchy until you are ready to enforce the consequence. Preplanning is important because it is difficult to arrive at a logical consequence on the spur of the moment. Consequences determined in the heat of the moment are more likely to be harsh and less likely to be logically related to the disruptive behavior. Therefore, spur of the moment consequences are more likely to be perceived as punishment—precisely what you are trying to avoid. In contrast, when consequences are logically related to the disruptive behavior (See Chapter 17), there is a greater likelihood that the teacher will feel comfortable enforcing the consequence and the student will be more likely to accept the consequence as reasonable.

Delivering the Message "You Have a Choice"

The manner in which you communicate "You have a choice" is as important as its content, in determining whether or not this technique is effective in influencing a student to change her behavior. By using an assertive response style, teachers increase the likelihood of the student choosing appropriate behavior.

Aggressiveness is often confused with assertiveness. Aggressiveness is a communication style in which the teacher, in addition to communicating the message, also communicates hostility and threat by her choice of language and/or her delivery of the message. Aggressiveness disregards the student's power and the emotional impact of the teacher's behavior upon the student. When the teacher uses aggressiveness, the student is more likely to choose confrontation. When teachers are aggressive, students often accurately interpret the proposed consequences as threats of something that the teacher is going to do to them because the teacher is angry. This style reduces a student's sense of pro-social significance and power. It may lead either to an escalation of hostility and confrontation through the defensive display of distorted power, such as arguing with the teacher, refusing to comply with the consequence, and/or engaging in further disruptive acts, or to a total shutdown and withdrawal of the student from any future classroom interaction. Such fight or flight responses are natural human reactions to perceived personal attacks.

Aggressiveness disregards the student's power and the emotional impact of the teacher's behavior upon the student.

In contrast, when the teacher uses assertiveness, the student is more likely to choose appropriate behavior. An assertive response style includes the teacher not only clearly communicating what is expected, but also communicating both firmness and respect. An assertive message respects the student's right to choose and the student's feelings. In addition, the teacher is conveying to the student that the student is solely responsible for the consequences of her behavior. When the teacher communicates respect, the student feels no loss of pro-social significance. When the teacher communicates to the student that the student is responsible for the outcome of her behavior, the student also is likely to feel an increase in her internal locus of control.

When the teacher uses assertiveness, the student is more likely to choose appropriate behavior.

The message, "You have a choice," is delivered in as privately a manner as possible, when ideally only the teacher and student are present. In the classroom, when other students are present, the teacher should be in close proximity to the student, without violating the student's personal space. The teacher maintains constant eye contact with the student while speaking in a firm, emotionally neutral tone of voice, no louder than needed to allow the student to hear the message. The teacher's hands should be at her side or on the student's desk. It is important to keep in mind the cautionary statements about touching students from Chapter 21; most importantly, older students are likely to view touch as aggressive or sexual when coupled with demands.

In the example of Heidi not cooperating with her team, the teacher has given Heidi several opportunities to choose appropriate behavior by using several nonverbal and verbal interventions. The teachers last intervention was to demand that Heidi work cooperatively with her group. Heidi continues to choose to be uncooperative. The teacher now is ready to assertively deliver "You have a choice." The teacher quietly, but purposefully, walks up to Heidi's desk. She leans down to be on the same level as Heidi, placing her hands on Heidi's desk. She does this without violating Heidi's personal space. The teacher now makes eye contact with Heidi and quietly but firmly says, "Heidi, you have a choice. Work cooperatively with your team or move to the back of the room and work by yourself. You decide." During the delivery of the message, the teacher's facial expression is congruent with the seriousness of the message. At the conclusion of the message, the teacher maintains eye contact for a few seconds. The teacher does not hover over Heidi waiting for compliance, but returns to what she was doing previous to interacting with Heidi.

Table 23.1 illustrates the differences between assertive and aggressive delivery styles.

TABLE 23.1 ▶ Comparison between Common Behaviors Associated with Assertive and Aggressive Styles of Communication of Consequences

Assertive	Aggressive
usually private with student	often public in front of peers
in close proximity to student without violating personal space	often violates student's personal space
eye contact is made, but face stays neutral	eye contact not made, however if there is eye contact, it is often accompanied by negative facial expressions, like frowning or narrowed eyes.
voice is firm, neutral, soft	voice is often tense, loud, fast
hands at side, on student's desk, or gently on student's arm or shoulder	hands on hips, folded at chest, or harshly touching the student
always uses student's name	often uses the pronoun, "you"

The Student Chooses Not to Behave Appropriately

You have delivered "You have a choice" assertively, and Heidi continues to misbehave. You approach Heidi saying, "Heidi, you decided to move to the back of the room and work by yourself, please move." Heidi responds, "This is really unfair. I don't see you asking Jackie to move, and she's been talking all period." When this occurs, it is important that you do not get sidetracked, enter into a power struggle, or move to a more aggressive style. We suggest you remain assertive and use what Canter (1989) has called the "broken record" or "that's not the point," followed by another final "You have a choice."

Let's look at an illustration of how the integration of these techniques work. Teacher (T): "Heidi, you have a choice. Begin working cooperative with your group or move to the back of the room and work by yourself. You decide." Heidi continues to be disruptive.

(T): "Heidi you have decided to move to the back of the room. Please move."

Heidi (H): "This is really unfair, I don't see you asking Jackie to move, and she's been talking all period."

(T): "Heidi, that's not the point. Please move to the back of the room."

(H): "You're always picking on me."

(T): "Heidi, that's not the point. Please move to the back of the room."

(H): "I might as well not even come to this class, I don't learn anything in here, anyway."

(T): "Heidi, that's not the point. Please move to the back of the room."

(H): "Well guess what, I'm not going!"

At this point, you should stop the broken record technique. Heidi is exhibiting a new disruptive behavior, and therefore it is time to point out to Heidi that she needs to make a different choice, or accept further consequences.

(T): "Heidi, you have a choice. Move to the back of the room now, or I will ask Ms. D'Angelo (the aide, security person, or vice-principal) to escort you to the office. You decide."

As illustrated, after two or three broken records, a final "you have a choice" is given. After this, the teacher disengages from the discussion with the student and follows through with the final consequence. Be careful not to threaten a consequence which you cannot or will not deliver. Use a consequence that you know is available and then follow through. Examples of some commonly used final consequences are:

- removing the student from the classroom,
- contacting the student's parents to inform them of what occurred,
- issuing a detention in order to discuss the matter further without taking more class time, and
- referring the student to an administrator.

Keep in mind not only that a student is likely to feel insignificant and powerless when a teacher acts aggressively and may react with hostility and distorted displays of power, but also that the teacher may have negative feelings when a student behaves aggressively toward her. This student is displaying distorted power by defying the teacher and also trying to get the teacher to lose her temper, thereby changing the focus from her behavior to the teacher's. It is therefore important that the teacher remain calm and assertive. This is not a contest with a winner and a loser. You gain much more respect not only from the disruptive student, but from the rest of the students in your class (who are probably very interested at this point), if you remain in control of yourself, regardless of the student's response when giving her a choice.

The Self-Control Classroom Model Doesn't Work

Often when the authors have conducted workshops with teachers and return after a period of time, they are informed by a few well meaning but disgruntled teachers that the model doesn't work. These teachers invariably say "I gave the students choices and they are still disruptive." This illustrates the great difficulty many teachers have in grasping that what is required is a paradigmatic shift and not merely the application of a few intervention strategies. The strategies discussed in the intervention hierarchy (Chapters 18 and 20–25) have been known and used by teachers for decades; however, they must be imbedded into a framework in which teachers seek continually to prevent disruptive behavior by establishing and reestablishing successful learning environments through the use of referent and expert authority. This is the new paradigm. Teachers and administrators embracing the paradigm understand that all of their efforts are designed to increase the possibility that students will choose to behave appropriately. Therefore instead of an end point of the teacher doing A (intervening and delivering consequences) and the student doing B (behaving appropriately), success is a continual process, facilitated by respectful interactions between students and teachers and the delivery of expert pedagogy.

Where We've Been

In this chapter we have presented the effective delivery of consequences, specifically using the message, "You have a choice," delivered assertively. Assertive versus aggressive delivery was contrasted. Then a discussion of what the teacher does when the student will not choose appropriate behavior was presented. Finally teachers were cautioned about believing the Self-Control Classroom model was dependent upon any specific strategy to lead to a change to appropriate student behavior. It was stressed that preventing disruptive behavior is not an end point, but is a continual process of establishing and reestablishing successful learning environments through the use of respectful interactions and the delivery of expert pedagogy.

Where We're Headed

Next, additional strategies are added to the Hierarchy of Interventions that have the potential to effectively influence students who continue to exhibit disruptive behavior to behave more appropriately.

In the next chapter, teachers prepare to intervene with students who exhibit chronic behavior problems by reflecting upon the student's behavior, and the teacher's response to that behavior. The teacher is shown how to keep anecdotal records and how to use these records to develop a Teacher Individual Management Action Plan (TIMAP). This TIMAP is a tool for analysis of past interventions and a planning tool for future interventions.

CHAPTER 23 CONCEPT MAP

HIERARCHY OF INTERVENTIONS
LEVEL 5: THE DELIVERY OF CONSEQUENCES

(Top of arrow)
- maximum opportunities for student self-control
- least disruptive to the learning environment
- least confrontational
- teachers have many remaining interventions

(Bottom of arrow)
- teachers have fewer remaining interventions
- most confrontational
- most disruptive to the learning environment
- minimum opportunities for student self-control

<u>ALL STUDENTS</u>	<u>STUDENTS EXHIBITING COMMON DISCIPLINE PROBLEMS</u>	<u>STUDENTS EXHIBITING CHRONIC DISCIPLINE PROBLEMS</u>
Prevention: Establishing Successful Learning Environments S/F > 1 Intrinsic Motivation internal locus of control internal value structure Pro-Social Self-Esteem significance competence virture power	**Prevention: Establishing Successful Learning Environments** S/F > 1 Intrinsic Motivation internal locus of control internal value structure Pro-Social Self-Esteem significance competence virture power	**Prevention: Establishing Successful Learning Environments** S/F > 1 Intrinsic Motivation internal locus of control internal value structure Pro-Social Self-Esteem significance competence virture power
	Level 1: Reestablishing Successful Learning Environments **Level 2: Pro-Active Interventions** **Level 3: Nonverbal Interventions** **Level 4: Verbal Interventions** **Level 5: Applying Consequences** "you have a choice"	**Level 1: Reestablishing Successful Learning Environments** **Level 2: Pro-Active Interventions** **Level 3: Nonverbal Interventions** **Level 4: Verbal Interventions** **Level 5: Applying Consequences**

? Questions for the Study Team

1. It was suggested that the delivery of consequences be phrased in the following way, "Heidi, you have a choice. Work cooperatively with your team, or move to the back of the room and work by yourself. You decide." Analyzing the phrase by parts, explain why each of the following parts is important with respect to the Self-Control Classroom model.

   a. "Heidi,

   b. you have a choice.

   c. work cooperatively with your team,

   d. or move to the back of the room and work by yourself.

   e. You decide."

2. Why is it important that consequences stated in the teacher's "You have a choice" message be logical consequences?

3. How does a teacher decide what are logical consequences for students' inappropriate behavior?

4. I have a student in my class who keeps accepting the logical consequence. What should I do now? Shouldn't the logical consequence become more severe?

5. If I use the "You have a choice" model of delivering consequences, won't I just have a classroom of students choosing to do anything they want?

6. Making eye contact is a nonverbal behavior that communicates assertiveness. What should a teacher do if the student looks away?

7. Won't teachers lose authority with the rest of the class if using "You have a choice" doesn't result in the student complying by behaving more appropriately?

8. It is usually suggested to ignore the manner in which students comply with logical consequences. If, for example, the logical consequence is to move to the back of the room and the student walks to the back of the room cursing or even after flipping her chair, and I don't do anything, won't I lose the repect of the rest of the students?

CHAPTER 24

Preparing to Work Effectively with Students Who Exhibit Chronic Discipline Problems

"So now I'm praying for the end of time, to hurry up and arrive. Cause if I gotta spend another minute with you, I don't think that I can really survive."
(Steinman, J. 1977)[1]

Kobe continues to exhibit disruptive behavior, despite your nonverbal and verbal interventions and the delivery of consequences using "You have a choice." It is at this point, that many teachers seriously consider leaving the profession. In fact, McKenna (2001) notes that feelings of frustration and incompetence, due to discipline problems in schools, are currently responsible for almost half of America's new teachers resigning within their first five years of teaching. Short of leaving the profession for a less stressful, but potentially less meaningful vocation, what can you do now to increase the likelihood that Kobe will experience a successful learning environment and choose to behave more appropriately?

Even at this point in the hierarchy, it is important that teachers and administrators continue to diagnose why Kobe isn't experiencing a successful learning environment and continue to try to provide this environment for Kobe through the use of referent and expert authority (See Chapter 18). Simultaneously, teachers protect the learning environment for the other students in the classroom, by using nonverbal and verbal interventions (See Chapters 21, 22, 23). In addition, teachers now begin to employ additional specific interventions designed to effectively influence students who exhibit chronic disruptive behavior to behave more appropriately.

This chapter prepares the teacher to intervene effectively with students who exhibit chronic disruptive behavior. The teacher, prior to using the very confrontational techniques discussed in Chapter 25, needs to set the stage by analyzing what has taken place so far, what the behaviors of both the student and the teacher have been, and to check his own responses to the student to ensure that the maximum opportunity

[1] Paradise by the Dashboard Light, Written by Jim Steinman, recorded by Meatloaf, issued in the Album "Bat Out of Hell", 1977, Columbia Records.

remains to reestablish a successful learning environment.

Abandoning the Model

Many times when working with students who exhibit chronic disruptive behavior, teachers begin to abandon the philosophies and strategies of the Self-Control Classroom model. Most commonly, teachers revert back to the old paradigm of trying to control the student, rather than controlling their own behavior. As we stated in Chapter 23, they come to the conclusion that the model just doesn't work, and feel that it's time to get tough with the student. It is clearly a time to be firm, but practitioners of the Self-Control Classroom model are always firm. What some teachers and administrators mean by getting tough is to become abrupt, hostile, and aggressive, in a misguided effort to strike back at a student who is, admittedly, exhibiting difficult behavior. It is very important that teachers and administrators at this junction, model for the student, that when faced with adversity, the answer is not aggression, but a professional posture based upon expert knowledge and an unremitting respect under fire (Goulet, 1997).

"Bad Kids"

The temptation at this point is for teachers to think that if they have not been successful so far, they must be dealing with inherently "bad kids." Recalling the discussion on avoiding labeling in Chapter 7, if teachers take this "bad kids" view, they will be more inclined to be harsh and punitive in their approach, further alienating an already distant and discouraged student. In addition, negative interactions will reduce students' success/failure ratio. By being punitive, teachers encourage students to develop an external locus of control, thereby fostering extrinsic motivation. By teachers using distorted power to protect their own self-esteem, they necessarily encourage students' similar use of distorted power to protect their self-esteem. Keep in mind that resorting to labeling students as bad, deviant, delinquent, or otherwise dysfunctional, is an attempt to absolve oneself from feelings of failure. It is believed that minimizing the student's personhood by calling him a name will preserve our own feelings of competence, which may have been severely shaken. Teachers and administrators need to recognize that success in this model is predicated upon controlling themselves and using expertise and referent authority to the best of their ability. Therefore teachers' success or failure is not dependent upon the students' behavior, but rather upon the teachers' behavior involving daily attempts to positively influence students, including those students, like Kobe, with the most disruptive behavior.

When working with students with very disruptive behavior, teachers restructure their thoughts about these students, in order to foster positive feelings which are essential for positive actions (Brendtro et al, 1990). If you continue to have positive expectations for Kobe, focusing upon his behavior and not his moral fiber, and if you continue to have confidence in your own instructional efficacy, then you send a message to Kobe that is positive and hopeful. This message very well may be, "I still believe that you have the ability to control your behavior in appropriate ways, and I am willing to give you the opportunity and support to do so."

Perhaps the most effective action you, the teacher, can take at this point is to write on a large Post-It note, "The only person I can control is myself." Place this note on your desk, in your roll book, or any other place where you frequently look. Refer to this note often. Teachers may find that this reminder helps to renew their strength and confidence to continue with the difficult task that lies ahead. The task is helping the student with chronic disruptive behavior to experience a successful learning environment and gain the self-control needed for appropriate behavior. Successfully intervening with very difficult students and building positive relations with them is an "endurance event" (Brendtro et al, 1990, p. 65); in other words, it is a marathon, not a sprint (Levin and Shanken-Kaye, unpublished manuscript).

Preparing to Intervene with Students Exhibiting Chronic, Disruptive Behavior

Before deciding upon further interventions, a teacher takes a step back and assesses what has occurred up to this point. This enables the teacher to continue to make professional, preplanned decisions and not be reactive or make spur of the moment decisions. This assessment also provides feedback which may encourage the teacher to retrace his steps and return to earlier levels of the hierarchy where appropriate. We suggest the use of two interrelated techniques: keeping anecdotal records of both the student's behavior and the teacher's behavior and then using anecdotal records to develop the Teacher Individual Management Action Plan (TIMAP).

ANECDOTAL RECORD KEEPING

Anecdotal records (Levin and Nolan, 2000) provide the needed data and justification for teachers to intervene effectively with students exhibiting chronic, disruptive behavior. The appropriate time to start an anecdotal record is sometime before the necessity arises to use the techniques for chronic behavior problems discussed in Chapter 25. We suggest that when a teacher is working with a student who repeatedly exhibits disruptive behavior and requires frequent nonverbal and verbal interventions, he start an anecdotal record. If the student brings his behavior into appropriate limits, the anecdotal record is saved in case the problem surfaces again. If the student chooses not to control his behavior in appropriate ways, the teacher makes decisions based on the data concerning what other interventions are appropriate. The anecdotal record is also valuable in helping to accurately communicate to the student's parents or guardians or other professionals what the student's behavior has been, what subsequent interventions were used, and on what basis they were chosen. Anecdotal records are also evidence of the professional practices that have been chosen and implemented, in the unfortunate event that a due process hearing is initiated by the student's parents or guardians alleging either inappropriate placement or treatment of the student.

An anecdotal record is a succinct account of observed student behavior and teacher interventions. Both appropriate and disruptive student behaviors are recorded, as well as what the teacher has done to encourage a successful learning environment and to influence appropriate behavior. Initially this record is only for the teacher's use; the student does not need to know that it is being kept. Figure 24.1 illustrates a suggested format and the type of observations that need to be recorded.

Examining the record on the next page, it becomes apparent why positive, as well as negative interactions need to be recorded. First, this allows the teacher to become aware that there are times when the challenging student behaves appropriately. Secondly, it enables the teacher to determine if he is using all possible opportunities to prevent disruptive behavior by helping to reestablish a successful learning environment. In the example above, the teacher calls on Kobe frequently when he is behaving appropriately (encouraging pro-social competence), and then, at the end of class, inquires about music (encouraging pro-social significance and competence). Finally, without notation of positive interactions, the record of a student that frequently exhibits disruptive behavior may be so negative that a parent might justifiably ask, "You mean to say my son has never done anything right?" Noting positive student behavior allows the teacher to have a more productive meeting in which he has established credibility concerning his observations of the student.

Student Name: Kobe

Phone Number:____________________

DATE	STUDENT BEHAVIOR and RESPONSE TO INTERVENTION	TEACHER ACTION
2/19	1. Kobe arrived late to class 2. Began to participate in class 3. Called out that Lee's answer was stupid 4. Passed notes to Vito and refused to work with Taylor	1. Said nothing to him, will talk with him after class 2. Called on him frequently, used his answers to continue lesson 3. Made eye contact with him 4. Used proximity control 5. Spoke with him after class about lateness, he said he will make it on time from now on 6. Asked him if he would be willing to bring in a mix of his current favorite music so that I could get a feeling for what he and other students were listening to
2/20		
2/21		

FIGURE 24.1 ▶ Sample Anecdotal Record Format

The teacher maintains the anecdotal record for a reasonable period of time. A "reasonable period of time" is a professional decision that is a function of the severity of the disruptive behavior, the amount of effort the student exhibits toward change, and the progress made. If after doing this, it becomes clear that the student has not begun to exhibit more appropriate behavior, even though the teacher has continually attempted to reestablish a successful learning environment and has intervened nonverbally, verbally, and delivered logical consequences, it is necessary to plan for additional interventions. The written Teacher Individual Management Action Plan (TIMAP) assists the teacher in planning for these future interventions. The data that has been collected in the anecdotal record is used to complete the TIMAP.

TEACHER INDIVIDUAL MANAGEMENT ACTION PLAN (TIMAP)

A TIMAP (Figure 24.2) is the teacher's analysis of how he has applied the concepts and strategies of the Self-Control Classroom model to the student who still exhibits disruptive behavior. The TIMAP is a series of eight questions which the teacher answers as a prerequisite for deciding future action. The questions help the teacher to

- objectively describe the student's behavior, and why it is a discipline problem (See Chapter 5),
- recognize any negative prejudices or labels that have been used in regard to the student (Chapter 7),
- determine the student's perception of the teacher's use of authority (Chapter 8),
- hypothesize the possible goals of the inappropriate behavior, using the Professional Decision Making Matrix (Chapter 18),
- describe how the teacher has attempted to facilitate a successful learning environment for the student (Chapters 13–15),
- examine what the teacher has done to encourage the student towards appropriate self-control, in using both nonverbal and verbal interventions, as well as logical consequences, and determine if there are any other opportunities that the teacher can provide to help the student to develop self-control (Chapters 21–23),
- plan for reestablishing and maintaining a successful learning environment for the student, and
- plan for future interventions, using the hierarchy of interventions for students exhibiting chronic disruptive behavior (Chapter 25).

Figure 24.2 is the TIMAP with a further discussion of each question.

Student's Name ________________________	
1. What is the specific behavior that the student exhibits, and why is this behavior a discipline problem warranting intervention?	Not all behavior that students exhibit are discipline problems. In order to be a discipline problem, the behavior must interfere with the rights of others to learn or the teacher to teach, be physically or psychologically unsafe, or be destructive to property (Chapter 5). An objective evaluation of the student's behavior by the teacher helps determine whether or not the teacher is reacting to observed, nondisruptive, although annoying behaviors, such as daydreaming, unpreparedness, or wearing a hat, as if they were discipline problems. If the teacher determines that the problem behavior is not a discipline problem, then when answering the questions concerning prior and future interventions, the teacher carefully analyzes the interventions for their appropriateness. Corey, a student who daydreams because he is not interested in the content of the geography lessons, will not be brought back on-task using techniques intended to manage chronic disruptive behavior. If, upon analysis, the teacher determines that, while a problem exists, it is not a discipline problem, the teacher may not need to act immediately, and the teacher needs to ensure that he, himself, is not a discipline problem. It is very important to be concrete and specific. A global statement such as "Kobe annoys the other students," is not as effective for planning future interventions as "Kobe repeatedly hits other students when he gets angry." *(continued)*

FIGURE 24.2 ▶ Teacher Individual Management Action Plan

2. What names or labels do I use when referring to the student, or how am I thinking about this student?	Upon reflection, the teacher may realize that he uses negative names or negative labels when referring to the student. Even if the teacher does not use negative labels, it may be that the teacher thinks of the student in negative ways. Both this covert thinking and overt negative labeling often lead to negative emotions and actions toward the student. It also may set up a parallel process, in which the student calls the teacher names, has negative feelings towards him, and acts out accordingly. In Chapter 7, we state that the appropriate name for the student who behaves disruptively is "professional challenge." When teachers are faced with a professional challenge and think of the student in this professional manner, they are energized to develop professional responses.
3. How does this student perceive my use of authority?	Remember authority is in the eye of the beholder (Chapter 8) and is constructed by the student through the behavior of the teacher toward the student over time. Comments about you that the student makes, either in direct interaction with you or with others, as well as the student's other behavior in the classroom, may be indicative of his perception of your use of authority. For example, if the student perceives you as a legitimate/coercive authority, it is likely that the student will respond to you in ways that express his distorted power (Chapter 11). In contrast, if a student perceives you as a referent and expert authority, he is more likely to exhibit respectful behavior toward you, even when the two of you are discussing his disruptive behavior.
4. What are the possible goals of the behavior being exhibited, using S/F ratio, motivation. and self-esteem?	The teacher now needs to form hypotheses about the goals of the student's inappropriate behavior. This is similar to the exercises in Chapter 18, where we analyzed disruptive behavior using the Professional Decision Making Matrix. Using the Professional Decision Making Matrix, the teacher must ask whether or not the behavior described in question number one is the result of a success/failure ratio less than one, extrinsic motivation stemming from an external locus of control and/or external value structure, and/or distorted self-esteem, stemming from distorted significance, competence, virtue, or power.
5. How have I attempted to increase the likelihood that this student will experience a successful learning environment?	Using the anecdotal record, the teacher indicates how, on a daily basis, he has attempted to impact one or more of the components of a successful learning environment, S/F >1, intrinsic motivation, and/or pro-social self-esteem (Chapters 13–15). *(continued)*

FIGURE 24.2 ▶ Teacher Individual Management Action Plan, *continued*

6. How have I provided this student with opportunities for self-control by using nonverbal interventions, verbal interventions, and/or logical consequences? Are there further opportunities for self-control that can be provided to this student?	It is important to remember that every day students need to be greeted as though they have both the competence and desire to behave appropriately. Every day in the classroom is a new beginning. The teacher starts at the top of the intervention hierarchy with Level 1, reestablishing successful learning environments. If, however, an individual student needs an intervention, the teacher starts at Level 3, non-verbal interventions, and proceeds from there (Chapters 21–23). Refer once again to the anecdotal record to answer these questions. Did you move too rapidly through the intervention hierarchy? Did you skip any interventions that might now be useful to try? Did you deliver the interventions in a referent manner? Did you allow adequate time for the interventions to be effective? Did you allow the natural consequences of the student's behavior to happen, or did you intervene to prevent their occurrence? If logical consequences were promised, were they delivered appropriately, using "You have a choice"? Students who frequently exhibit disruptive behavior are often subjected to the threat of consequences immediately, when their behavior has just begun to deteriorate. If students are not given the maximum opportunity to exhibit self-control, they are unlikely to demonstrate that they have learned to do so.
7. What further strategies will I use to maintain and reestablish a successful learning environment for the student?	Similar to question #5, the teacher now uses the Professional Decision Making Matrix to determine future efforts to positively impact the student's success/failure ratio, intrinsic motivation, and pro-social self-esteem (Chapter 18).
8. What interventions will I use to gain the cooperation of the student in reestablishing a successful learning environment, while protecting a successful learning environment for all students?	You will familiarize yourself with the techniques presented in Chapter 25 to complete this answer.

FIGURE 24.2 ▶ Teacher Individual Management Action Plan, *continued*

If the teacher has doubts about any of his answers to these questions, he may want to consider going back to earlier techniques before going to the final level of the hierarchy, those interventions only intended for students with chronic behavior problems. If, on the other hand, the teacher is satisfied with his interactions with the student, he is now ready to implement techniques from the last level of the hierarchy intended for chronic behavior problems.

AN EXAMPLE OF A TEACHER INDIVIDUAL MANAGEMENT ACTION PLAN (TIMAP)

Figure 24.3 is an example of a completed TIMAP for Kobe.

Student's Name ______________________	
1. What is the specific behavior that the student exhibits, and why is this behavior a discipline problem warranting intervention?	Kobe makes fun of other student's answers, and he frequently passes notes or attempts to talk to other students during class. These are discipline problems because they interfere with the rights of other students to learn. I will use this TIMAP to focus upon these particular disruptive behaviors. Kobe is also late to class and sometimes refuses to work with other students. Although these are problems warranting concern, they are not discipline problems, and therefore do not need to be addressed immediately.
2. What names or labels do I use when referring to the student, or how am I thinking about this student?	While I do not use negative labels at any time when referring to Kobe, I do have some negative thoughts about him. I sometimes think he is lazy and a troublemaker. I will try to view Kobe as a professional challenge and find reasons for his behavior that do not attack Kobe's character and that allow me to design interventions that will increase the likelihood that Kobe will behave more appropriately.
3. How does this student perceive my use of authority?	I greet Kobe by name every day and show interest in his welfare. When Kobe participates in class, I use his answers to stimulate further class discussion. I try to make my interventions as private as possible, frequently waiting until class is over to discuss his behavior. Although Kobe is disruptive in class, he is never directly disrespectful or confrontational with me. It is my belief that Kobe views me as a person who is interested in his well-being (referent authority) and who wants to help him learn (expert authority).
4. What are the possible goals of the behavior being exhibited, using S/F Ratio, Motivation. and Self-Esteem?	When Kobe makes fun of other student's answers, I believe he is building upon either a distorted sense of significance or a distorted sense of power. When he passes notes, I believe this is another attempt to build distorted significance. Kobe struggles academically and does not seem to have many friends. This reduces his pro-social competence, significance, and possibly power. His disruptive behavior may be an attempt to compensate for these reductions in pro-social self-esteem.
5. How have I attempted to increase the likelihood that this student will experience a successful learning environment?	I have attempted to increase Kobe's internal value structure by integrating Kobe's interest in NASCAR into our science lessons. When Kobe puts forward effort to complete academic tasks, I make certain that I provide encouragement in an attempt to build an internal locus of control. I talk to him about his music and asked him to make me a mix of his favorite tunes, hoping to impact his pro-social significance. *(continued)*

FIGURE 24.3 ▶ An Example of a Completed Teacher Individual Management Action Plan

6. How have I provided this student with opportunities for self-control by using nonverbal and/or verbal interventions, and/or logical consequences? Are there further opportunities for self-control that can be provided to this student?	Upon reflection, I realize that I have substantially skipped level 4, verbal interventions, and level 5, applying consequences. Therefore, I haven't really been giving Kobe every opportunity to control his behavior.
7. What further strategies will I use to maintain and reestablish a successful learning environment for the student?	As the result of answering question 4, I realize that I need to give Kobe opportunities to positively impact his pro-social self-esteem. In an effort to impact his pro-social significance, I will continue to learn more about Kobe's outside interests and have conversations with Kobe about them. I will impact his pro-social competence by offering to meet with him before or after school to go over the material from class and also to teach him study skills. I can impact his pro-social virtue by providing meaningful opportunities for Kobe to be helpful to me and to other students in the class. By helping Kobe determine his academic goals and brainstorming strategies to achieve those goals, Kobe will experience an increase in pro-social power.
8. What interventions will I use to gain the cooperation of the student in reestablishing a successful learning environment, while protecting a successful learning environment for all students?	After realizing that I have basically skipped levels 4 and 5 of the intervention strategies, I plan to use nonverbal interventions and to apply consequences with Kobe. I will continue to keep anecdotal records and see if these interventions are more successful in facilitating Kobe's self-control. If not, I will proceed to level 6.

FIGURE 24.3 ▶ An Example of a Completed Teacher Individual Management Action Plan, *continued*

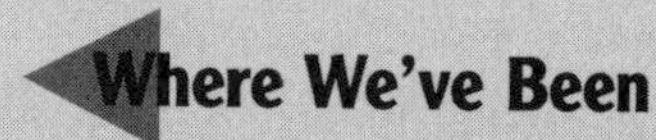

Where We've Been

In this Chapter, two procedures that teachers need to use in preparation for intervening with students who exhibit chronic disruptive behavior were detailed. The first preparation (and one that is invaluable for effective intervention) is the anecdotal record. This daily record documents both student and teacher behavior. The second is the Teacher Individual Management Action Plan (TIMAP), a self analysis of the history of the teacher's intervention with the student and a planning tool for future interventions.

Where We're Headed

Next additional strategies are added to the Hierarchy of Interventions that have the potential to effectively influence students who continue to exhibit disruptive behavior to behave more appropriately. These strategies are found in level 6, the final level of the Hierarchy.

CHAPTER 24 CONCEPT MAP

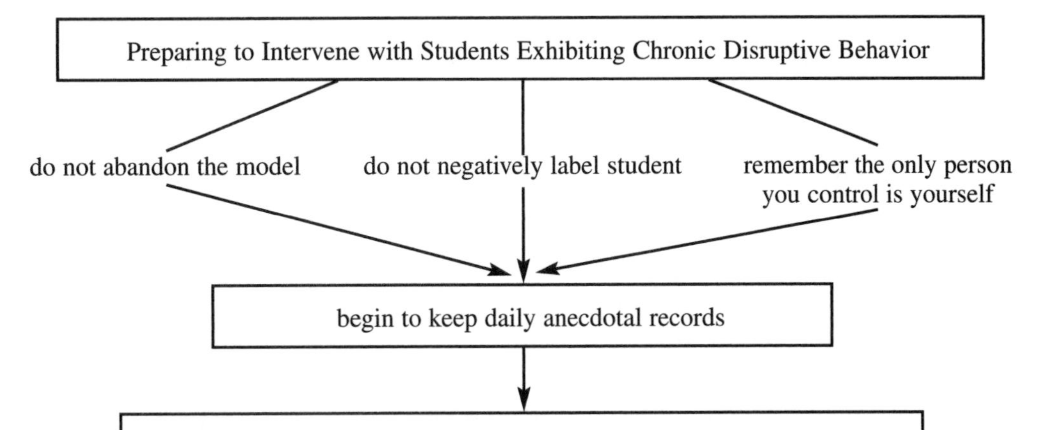

Complete a Teacher Individual Management Action Plan (TIMAP)

1. What is the specific behavior that the student exhibits, and why is this behavior a discipline problem warranting intervention?
2. What names or labels do I use when referring to the student and how am I thinking about this student?
3. How does this student perceive my use of authority?
4. What are the possible goals of the behavior being exhibited using S/F ratio, motivation, and self-esteem?
5. How have I attempted to increase the likelihood that this student will experience a successful learning environment?
6. How have I provided this student with opportunities for self-control by using nonverbal interventions, verbal interventions, and logical consequences? Are there further opportunities for self-control that can be provided to this student?
7. What further strategies will I use to maintain and reestablish a successful learning environment for the student?
8. What interventions will I use to gain the cooperation of the student in reestablishing a successful learning environment, while protecting a successful learning environment for all students?

? QUESTIONS FOR THE STUDY TEAM

1. I teach 120 students a week. How am I supposed to find the time to do anecdotal records and complete TIMAPs?

2. How am I supposed to develop all of the innovative strategies necessary to impact students' S/F ratio, intrinsic motivation, and pro-social self-esteem?

3. You say not to label kids, but I'm only human. Isn't it natural to put negative labels on people that continually frustrate and annoy you?

4. I can understand the negative impact of calling kids names, but what is the problem with thinking negative labels? After all, it's my behavior that the student sees, not my thoughts.

5. I've examined my philosophies, behaved in a referent and expert manner, tried different strategies to impact students' successful learning environment, used nonverbal and verbal interventions and natural and logical consequences, and the negative behavior continues. How long do you stay with a sinking ship? Isn't it time to abandon this model?

CHAPTER 25

Level 6 of the Hierarchy of Interventions: Interventions for Students Who Exhibit Chronic Disruptive Behavior

"Zero tolerance needs to be examined in terms of how it teaches children to behave. Would anyone want a school board or superintendent who had a zero tolerance attitude when dealing with stakeholders? Do you know anyone who was raised by a zero tolerant parent? What might that person say about how it affected his or her childhood? Could a marriage survive a zero tolerant spouse? More important, do we want children to have zero tolerance for others, particularly when they are angry?" (Curwin, R. L. and Mendler, A.N. 1999)

You already have given Kobe many opportunities to control his behavior, and he has consistently chosen not to do so. At this point, many teachers feel that their only alternative is to remove Kobe from the class. Although this might ultimately be necessary, there are still available several additional, highly effective interventions, along with many additional opportunities to reestablish a successful learning environment.

Many teachers have asked how quickly they should move through level 6 of the hierarchy, if they need to employ all of the techniques, and if not, how many of the techniques should they employ? There are no absolute answers to these questions. Teachers use their professional judgment based upon the individual student's characteristics. However, the movement through level 6 is a function of both the degree of disruptiveness of the student's behavior and the student's efforts towards self-control. If the teacher observes what appears to be a genuine effort toward appropriate self-control, then she may want to allow more time for success for the intervention she is using presently, or the teacher may be more willing to try additional interventions. On the other hand, if the student is not showing any effort to curtail her behavior, then the teacher rapidly shifts to another strategy and limits the number of interventions. When the behavior is not very disruptive, more time is allowed for success or to try additional interventions, even in the face of low effort. When the behavior is very disruptive or dangerous, the teacher may decide to go directly to the interventions at the end of the hierarchical structure. Table 25.1 summarizes these guidelines.

Similar to interventions for non-chronic behavior problems, interventions for chronic behavior problems must:

- maximize opportunities for student self-control,
- be no more disruptive to the class than the student's behavior,
- decrease the likelihood of a confrontation with the student,
- protect the physical and psychological safety of all students, and
- leave open opportunities for further intervention.

Below is a list of ten interventions for chronic behavioral problems which are ordered from the least to the most confrontational. This list is not exhaustive, but provides a guide for the type and sequence of interventions that are consistent with the Self-Control Classroom model. These interventions are:

- teacher/student conference with authentic questions,
- goal attainment behavior: Goal, Plan, Do, Check,
- student self-monitoring,
- first teacher/parent-guardian conference,
- contracting for behavioral change,
- anecdotal record keeping with student participation,
- referral to other professionals inside the school,
- conditional removal of the student from class,
- second teacher/parent-guardian conference, and
- referral to outside professionals.

With each level in the hierarchy, the teacher's work load increases, the student has fewer future choices and opportunities to demonstrate self-control, and the possibility of the teacher and student developing anger and resentment towards each other is heightened. This is especially true of Level 6. To minimize student anger and resentment, the teacher must have continually shown and continue to show respect and positive regard for the student and must endeavor

TABLE 25.1 ▶ Guidelines for Determining Speed of Movement Through and Number of Interventions to Use from Level 6 of the Hierarchy of Interventions

	NOT VERY DISRUPTIVE BEHAVIOR	VERY DISRUPTIVE BEHAVIOR
HIGH STUDENT EFFORT TOWARDS SELF-CONTROL	slow movement through hierarchy, many interventions	moderate movement through hierarchy, moderate number of interventions
LOW STUDENT EFFORT TOWARDS SELF-CONTROL	moderate movement through hierarchy, moderate number of interventions	rapid movement through hierarchy, few interventions

to gain the student's trust as a reliable, caring adult. In addition, the teacher must have continually used expert authority to help the student reestablish a successful learning environment.

Interventions for Students Who Exhibit Chronic Disruptive Behavior

TEACHER/STUDENT CONFERENCE WITH AUTHENTIC QUESTIONS

The authors have repeatedly stated our belief that effective teachers attempt to establish caring, respectful relationships with all of their students. Because we do not want students to view meeting with the teacher as an aversive condition, conferences are not limited to only those times when there is a problem. Instead, teachers meet frequently and privately with students to discuss positive events, as well as negative ones.

The meeting now taking place, however, is to discuss the student continuing to exhibit disruptive behavior. In this conference, the teacher assertively tells the student what she observed and how she feels about it. The teacher also asks authentic questions that encourage the student to work with the teacher to solve the problem. As part of the process, the teacher seeks to discover the student's perception of the problem and how the teacher can assist the student to exert the self-control necessary for appropriate behavior. The teacher does not argue with the student. The anecdotal records show what the teacher observed, so now the only question is, "How are we going to work together to solve this problem?"

At the conference, the teacher first shows the anecdotal record to the student. The record not only details the specific disruptive behaviors that have been observed, but also lets the student know that the teacher has gone to considerable effort to document the difficulties that the student is having. It also informs the student of any success that she has experienced and how the teacher has tried to help. The student is now aware of the seriousness with which the teacher views the problem. The student is also aware that the teacher cares enough about her to take the time to document her classroom behavior, both positive and negative. Whether or not this is perceived positively or negatively by the student is in large part a function of the teacher's respectful interactions with the student up to this point and the respect that the teacher shows her during the conference. Teachers should always remember not to attack the character of the student, but focus upon the student's observed behavior. During this portion of the conference, the teacher points out the positive notations in the record, not just the negative.

Teachers should always remember not to attack the character of the student, but focus upon the student's observed behavior.

The second part of the conference involves the teacher's resolve to protect the learning environment of the class, making absolutely clear that she will protect the learning environment of the class, regardless of the decisions the student may make about her own conduct.

The third part is giving the student the opportunity to make a commitment to work with the teacher on exploring more appropriate classroom behavior, which will meet both the student's and teacher's needs.

The fourth part of the conference, once the student makes the commitment, entails problem solving. The use of authentic questions is a helpful technique for gaining the student's participation in solving the problem of her disruptive behavior (Strachota, 1996). Authentic questions engage the student in active problem solving, rather than telling the student what to do. Authentic questions honor a student's pro-social competence by assuming that she can devise a viable solution to the problem at hand. Teachers posing authentic questions share power with the student in devising solutions, which increases the student's pro-social power and intrinsic motivation through an internal locus of control. Bob Strachota (1996), in his book "*On Their Side,*" states, "(I) wonder with children about what to do about a problem, to have them share in the responsibility of creating a solution instead of telling them what to do."

By posing authentic questions, teachers approach the problem as an opportunity for the student to assume responsibility, take control of her own behavior, and create solutions that meet her own needs, as well as the teacher's and classmates' needs. For instance, the teacher at a conference with Kobe says; "You have a need to be social in school and to interact with lots of students during class. I have a need to have a classroom that allows all students to learn and not have that learning disrupted by off-task behavior. How can we each get our needs met?"

In the above example, the teacher assertively stated the problem and what she wants as the outcome (student learning, lack of disruption). However, instead of presenting the solution, the teacher invites Kobe to join in solving the riddle by devising a solution to seemingly competing needs. Strachota (1996) reflects:

> "The instinct simply to be directive is very strong in me. But when I tell (students) what to do at the expense of wondering with them, their capacity to assume real responsibility for their actions is diminished. Being directive also obstructs my view of the varied dynamics that are in play in any situation. To put it another way, I have come to believe that leaping into action tends to stop thought for both teacher and learner, and without struggle and reflection to back up the doing, the learning becomes hollow." (p. 6)

Kobe now is asked to brainstorm several different strategies to decrease the occurrence of his disruptive behavior and to stop impeding the learning of others. Any suggested strategy, no matter how bizarre, or unlikely it seems to result in appropriate behavior, is written down and discussed. This serves the dual purpose of respecting Kobe's point of view and respecting his problem-solving capabilities. It may also provide some levity, if and when bizarre solutions are considered. A teacher may be tempted to predetermine what the successful strategy is and then attempt to sway or manipulate the student into accepting the teacher's solution. However, the use of authentic questioning requires the teacher to be open to solutions she may not have considered. Every proposed solution is discussed in relation to meeting the teacher's and other student's needs, as well as those of the target student in the classroom. It is our opinion that students who devise their own strategies or who feel empowered to choose among several strategies are more likely to adhere to the strategy after the meeting.

Let's see how this problem-solving portion of the conference might work. This is an example of the initial authentic questioning with Kobe, involving one of his disruptive behaviors.

Teacher (T): Kobe, I realize that you have a need to interact with other students during class time. This disturbs me, because I have a need for you, as well as all of the other students, to learn. How can we both get our needs met?

Kobe (K): This class is so boring! I get fidgety and I gotta do something!

(T): I understand that you feel bored and disconnected from the learning (accurate empathy). However, I need to have the class focused on the lesson. How can we achieve that?

(K): If we could only do half the class time that would work.

(T): I can see how that might be pleasant for you, but it doesn't meet my need to teach. What else might be successful?

(K): Well, how about another break?

(T): That might be possible; I can discuss it with the other students...

(K): They would want it! Everybody gets tired and bored!

(T): You may be right, but this is a class decision.

(K): Maybe if we could stand occasionally or move around.

(T): We could put a "stand and study" section in the back of the room, but students could not talk to each other when they were standing.

(K): That would be great! Could we have more videos and class discussions? That would be more interesting too.

(T): I will think about these possibilities, and we'll discuss them next week. In the meantime, we will talk to the class about the other changes tomorrow. Are you willing to commit to ending your disruptive behavior if I set aside a "stand and study" section in the room and discuss with the class some of the other suggestions?

(K): Yeah. I wouldn't be as bored if I could move around more and have more breaks.

(T): Okay, I'm going to write down what we've discussed. We'll meet next week to see if it's working. Thanks for helping me come up with a solution.

Most students at this point in the hierarchy will make a commitment to change.

In the above example, the teacher is displaying referent behavior, stating she cares both about Kobe's learning, as well as everyone else's. She is treating Kobe as a problem solver, increasing his pro-social power and competence, as well as his internal locus of control. Because Kobe has played an active role in solving the problem, he has made an investment in the outcome, which positively impacts his internal value structure. For these reasons, Kobe is likely to try harder not to engage in disruptive behavior in the future.

Notice that Kobe's stated reasons for his disruptive behavior were different than what the teacher had assumed, so the solutions discussed during the conference were also different than the teacher expected.

The final portion of the conference is to note the outcome on the anecdotal record. Whether or not Kobe makes a commitment for change, Kobe's behavior during the conference is recorded in front of him on the anecdotal record.

In the above example, Kobe made a commitment to change. Most students at this point in the hierarchy will make a commitment to change. There will always be a few students in a school who will refuse to make this commitment. According to the guidelines for movement through the hierarchy (Table 25.1), this lack of student effort to change requires the teacher to rapidly move to a more confrontational intervention in Level 6.

Another suggested format to assist the student in problem solving during the conference involves a pre-printed sheet of questions which the student answers in writing. The questions with Kobe's answers follows in Figure 25.1.

When a number of strategies are listed, the student and the teacher try and agree upon one or two likely solutions. During the discussion, the more bizarre or unlikely to succeed strategies are evaluated and discarded. Elementary students usually need more assistance with problem solving than older students.

When the meeting is finished, Kobe has a clear action plan which he agreed to put effort into implementing. Again, if Kobe refuses to agree to a solution, the teacher moves to other interventions in the hierarchy. The meeting with the student and the student's behavior during the conference is noted in his anecdotal record in front of the student.

A difference between authentic questions and written problem solving is that authentic questions are more likely to uncover students' motives for their behavior, while written problem solving focuses upon eliminating the behavior without taking into account the cause. In the above example, Kobe may have difficulty honoring his commitment not to make fun of Lee's answers, since the underlying cause, Kobe's boredom, has not been addressed.

1. **What is the problem?**
   I keep making fun of Lee's answers.

2. **What can I do about it?**
   I can put tape over my mouth. I cannot say anything at all in class. I can write myself a big note that says; "Don't make fun!"

3. **What is the best solution?**
   I'll write myself a note and tape it to my desk.

4. **I agree to follow the solution.**

Student signature ___________________

FIGURE 25.1 ▶ An Example of a Pre-Printed Series of Questions for Problem Solving

GOAL ATTAINMENT BEHAVIOR: GOAL, PLAN, DO, CHECK

If the commitments made during the conference with authentic questions and problem solving do not result in noticeably improved behavior, a second conference is scheduled. The teacher explains that the student has not been successful in honoring his commitment, and she again communicates the absolute need for more appropriate behavior. She offers the student another problem solving strategy. This is Meichenbaum's (2001) Goal, Plan, Do, Check. This technique is innovative, in that it can be used to eliminate disruptive behavior and to increase more appropriate behavior. In addition, once it is learned, the student can apply the goal attainment to a vast array of challenges, both in and out of school.

First the student is asked to hypothesize about the goal of her disruptive behavior. The student may provide many goals. The teacher instructs the student to select the goal that she most wants to attain. The teacher helps the student select initial goals that are within the capability of the student. In addition, the teacher guides the student to select goals that are pro-social or that advance some positive agenda. For instance, the student might initially say that her goal in making fun of another student is to get that student angry. The teacher works with the student to help her understand that accepting this particular goal will cause her to continue exhibiting disruptive behavior. Therefore, the student is encouraged to look at other goals that are being met by making fun of others, such as a desire for attention from other students. By selecting a goal to gain attention, the student may attain the goal by behaving in more appropriate ways. The teacher encourages the student to commit to a plan to attain this goal. It is important that the teacher help the student develop concrete, observable criteria for goal attainment. For example, if the student has a goal of attaining an average of 80%, it is evident to both the student and to the teacher when this goal is attained. When the goal is more subjective, such as gaining the attention of other students, the student and the teacher need to answer the question of what "more attention to the student" would look like in the classroom. For example, the student may agree that he would recognize that he was receiving more attention if he were called upon more frequently, was asked to volunteer more often to perform tasks for the teacher, or given the opportunity to tell a "joke of the day" at the end of class. Whatever is decided becomes the criteria for measuring success when the time comes to check the plan.

Next the student is asked to develop a plan to help him achieve his goal. The plan should consider the incremental steps that progress toward goal attainment and an explanation as to why these steps will result in successfully meeting the agreed upon criteria. The teacher works with the student in developing a plan to ensure that the steps are within the capability of the student and are likely to lead to success. At the conclusion of the conference, the agreement to use Goal, Plan, Do, Check, and the student's behavior during the conference is recorded on the student's anecdotal record.

The student is now given the opportunity to follow or "do" the plan. Teacher input at this stage may involve determining if the student has a clear understanding of the plan and practicing one or more steps of the plan with the student.

At a predetermined time, the student needs to check his progress toward the goal. With younger students, the check is generally frequent and done with the help of the teacher. Older students may or may not be able to perform a check on their own. If the student has made satisfactory progress toward attaining her goals, she continues with the plan until she is satisfied that the goal has been attained. When the check indicates that the student has not made progress or has made unsatisfactory progress toward attaining her goal, she needs to be taught to determine whether the problem is with the nature of the goal, or with the plan she has devised for implementation. By adjusting one or the other or both, the likelihood of the student attaining her goal is greatly increased.

The initial conference with Kobe did not result in noticeable changes in his disruptive behavior. The teacher schedules another conference with Kobe and reiterates her need for Kobe to stop disrupting other students. She suggests that Kobe needs to learn how to set appropriate goals and work toward attaining them. The teacher shows Kobe how to use Goal, Plan, Do, Check. The conference with Kobe might look like this:

(T) "Kobe, last week you said that the reason you were being disruptive was because you were bored. You made a commitment that you would behave more appropriately if we had a "stand and study" section of the classroom, and if we could have more frequent breaks. I instituted these changes, but you continue to be disruptive. Kobe, we addressed the issue of boredom, and you didn't change, so I think maybe we were focusing on the wrong goal for your behavior. What else might be causing you to disrupt the class?"

(K) "Nobody ever pays attention to me, except when I'm being funny or bothering somebody. I don't feel like I have any friends."

(T) "So you're saying that you're disruptive to get the attention of your classmates, and you think this will get you friends?"

(K) "Yeah, I guess so."

(T) "Well Kobe, you've been disruptive all term. How's it working? Do you feel that the other students like you more?"

(K) "Maybe not, but they do pay attention to me."

(T) "I think we need to figure out how to get the other students to pay attention to you and like you at the same time."

(K) "That would be great."

(T) "Well, we can certainly set as a goal that you will get attention from other students in a way that is not disruptive to the class. Once this goal is attained, I think you'll find that the other students might be more willing to be friendly towards you."

The teacher now works with Kobe to devise a plan that will include observable steps toward gaining the goal of getting attention from his classmates in a manner that will not be disruptive. Kobe's participation in devising a plan to change his behavior has impact on both his internal locus of control and his internal value structure. Some of the steps include Kobe volunteering and being called upon more often to answer questions (pro-social competence), being given meaningful jobs in the classroom (pro-social virtue), and being allowed to post a "joke of the day" on the board at the start of class with the teacher's approval (pro-social virtue, significance, and power).

Kobe now begins to Do the plan. Kobe and the teacher agreed that they will Check the plan after the first week to see if the desired goals, Kobe gaining more positive attention and not being disruptive in class, are being met. At the meeting, Kobe and the teacher have an opportunity to tweak the plan and/or revisit the goals, if necessary, to increase progress. Figure 25.2 shows Kobe's completed Goal, Plan, Do, Check worksheet.

Kobe's first week of using Goal, Plan, Do, Check has resulted in progress toward the goals of Kobe receiving more positive attention from his classmates and being less disruptive. The teacher and Kobe decide to continue with the plan and meet again the following week.

STUDENT SELF-MONITORING

Self-monitoring is initiated when the solutions arrived at in the previous student teacher conferences have not resulted in a positive

Goal, Plan, Do, Check Worksheet

Name: Kobe

Time Period: March 5–9

Goal:
To get attention from other students in a way that is not disruptive to the class.

Plan:
1. I will volunteer to answer more questions in class.
2. I will seek to do jobs in the classroom to help the teacher and other students.
3. I will submit a joke each day to the teacher for approval and write the joke on the board if it is appropriate.

Do:
I volunteered each day at least three times to answer questions. I spoke to the teacher about being allowed to pass out our readiness materials at the start of class and collect them at the end of class. I brought in a joke every day. Sometimes I brought in more than one just to be safe.

Check:
The teacher calls on me almost every time I raise my hand. I think other kids are surprised that I know the answers. The teacher said another student is handing out the materials, but that I can take the daily temperature and barometer readings and post them on our weather chart. I've gotten to post a joke every day. Some of them were really funny and got a big laugh. The teacher only had to remind me twice not to talk to Lee.

FIGURE 25.2 ▶ An Example of a Goal, Plan, Do, Check Worksheet

change in the student's behavior. Self-monitoring is a method which assists the student who has developed a solution, in cooperation with her teacher, to monitor her progress toward achieving the agreed upon goal of reducing disruptive behavior. Self-monitoring techniques are very effective for the student who wants to behave more appropriately, but seems to need frequent reminders to do so. The student takes control of her own behavior by giving reminders to herself.

Self-monitoring is explained to the student, and the student is asked whether she agrees to put forth the effort to self-monitor her behavior. If she does not, movement to another intervention in Level 6 of the hierarchy is necessary.

To make it easier for the student to learn how to self-monitor and to increase the probability of initial student success, it is important that the self-monitoring instrument focus, at the beginning, on only one or a very few behaviors.

How self-monitoring is explained to the student, significantly influences the likelihood of success or failure. If the explanation by the teacher results in the perception of the student that self-monitoring is a punishment, the technique takes on all the drawbacks associated with punishments (Chapter 17), and the likelihood of success is diminished. On the other hand, if the explanation by the teacher results in the perception of the student that self-monitoring is a way for the student to help herself with teacher support and encouragement, there is a greater likelihood of the student improving her behavior.

To be effective, the student must clearly understand how to use the instrument and how to identify the specific behaviors that are being monitored. When the student first begins using self-monitoring, she may need cues from the teacher as to when to check her behavior. The more private the cue, the better, as it will not draw attention to the student. Private cues also communicate pro-social significance to the student. As the student learns to self-monitor, the need for teacher cues diminishes.

Self-monitoring also may take place in tandem with teacher monitoring, where the mutually agreed upon target behavior is monitored by both the teacher and student. The decision to have the teacher monitor in tandem is a professional decision based upon the teacher's knowledge of the student's developmental level and/or the need for the student to receive feedback as to the student's accuracy in self-monitoring. At the end of a specified period of time, the student and teacher compare records. The goal here is not only to increase the student's appropriate behavior, but to help the student to be accurate in self-appraisals.

Self-monitoring techniques are very effective for the student who wants to behave more appropriately, but seems to need frequent reminders to do so.

When using this or any other technique designed to help change chronic disruptive behavior, the teacher must keep in mind that she is attempting to modify long-term, and possibly habitual, negative behavior. Success may come in small steps, with frequent lapses in progress. These behaviors did not develop in a day, and they will not be replaced by new appropriate behaviors in a day. The teacher must remain patient and, in the beginning, focus on the effort that the student is making to change her behavior, rather than the actual behavioral change.

A simple method of self-monitoring is having a paper on the student's desk on which the student records every occurrence of appropriate and inappropriate behavior (See Figure 25.3). The student puts a check mark in the corresponding box every time she displays an appropriate behavior and every time she displays an inappropriate behavior. If her behavior is appropriate, fine. If her behavior is inappropriate, then the check is a signal to her to change her behavior. Of course the teacher must be sure that the student clearly understands what behaviors are being

Number of other students' answers	I did NOT make fun of another student's answer	I MADE FUN of another student's answer
1		
2		
3		
4		
5		
6		
7		
8		
9		
10		

TABLE 25.3 ▶ Self-Monitoring Instrument Using an Occurrence Schedule

monitored. When self-monitoring is agreed upon, it is noted in the student's anecdotal record.

Although Kobe made progress initially, using Goal, Plan, Do, Check, his behavior again became disruptive. For Kobe's first self-monitoring task, inappropriate behavior was defined as making fun of other students' answers. Appropriate behavior was not making fun of other students' answers. If the initial self-monitoring is successful, then Kobe and his teacher design another instrument to self-monitor additional behavior.

Another type of self-monitoring instrument is one that is on a time interval schedule. For example, the student monitors her behavior every 15 minutes, as illustrated in Figure 25.4. This type of instrument is appropriate for helping students stay on-task during seat work or direct teacher instruction.

Self-monitoring, if handled effectively, increases a student's sense of pro-social competence and power, as the student sees herself making progress. This also serves to encourage an internal locus of control, because improvement of the student's behavior is the result of the student's efforts. If the student has agreed to participate and has set goals, achievement of these goals is the only positive outcome needed. Often teachers offer rewards to the student for successful completion of self-monitoring. This is unnecessary, since the student has obtained for herself a positive outcome. It is also detrimental to the student's development of an internal value structure, due to the discounting principle discussed in Chapter 16. The teacher increases the likelihood that students accurately self-monitor if the teacher ensures that the goal, the instrument, and the types of questions asked are developmentally appropriate. For instance, while the use of smiley face questions for early elementary students and yes/no questions for later elementary students may be appropriate, a Likert scaled instrument may be more appropriate for older students.

TIME	Am I ON Task?	Am I OFF Task?
8.00		
8:15		
8:30		
8:45		
9:00		
9:15		
9:30		

TABLE 25.4 ▶ Self-Monitoring Instrument Using a Time Interval Schedule

FIRST TEACHER/PARENT-GUARDIAN CONFERENCE

When it is apparent to the teacher that the interventions have not resulted in appreciable positive change in the student's behavior, parents or guardians are contacted. It may seem to be a contradiction to conventional wisdom that we include teacher /parent-guardian conferences at this point in the intervention hierarchy. Many educators would assert that parents should be contacted at the very first signs of a discipline problem; however, this violates the Self-Control Classroom model. Think for a moment about how average parents of a difficult student react when confronted with the fact that their child is disrupting your class. It is our experience that parents react with embarrassment and anger. It is the rare parent who successfully manages these feelings and avoids using coercive behavior at home in an attempt to force the student into compliance. This is exactly what the teacher has been trying to avoid, because rewards and punishments focus the student's attention away from his behavior and toward his parents' behavior. Also, think how Kobe feels when you contact his parents. Kobe is likely to feel betrayed, embarrassed, and angry. Once again, his focus is on your behavior, rather than his own behavior, where it should be.

Some parents of students who exhibit chronically disruptive behavior have negative attitudes toward their child's teachers and school in general. This is unfortunate, because parental support of school has a major impact on students' positive attitudes toward school (Jones, 1980). Negative parental attitudes result, in part, because chronic behavior problems rarely occur over night. Most likely throughout the student's school years, his parents have had many teacher contacts concerning their child's behavior. In addition, some students who chronically exhibit disruptive behavior have parents who also may have had behavior problems when they were in school. Therefore, contacting parents about their child's behavior is often the least desirable and most difficult aspect of a teacher's job. It is the professional, highly skilled teacher who remains positive and respectful when parents tell teachers, "You should be able to control him; that's why you're getting paid 45,000 dollars a year." or "I've tried everything I know to get Kobe to behave; I give up."

When a teacher does contact the parents or guardians, she must keep in mind not only to inform the parents about the problems she is having with the student's behavior, but also to encourage the parents to become cooperative partners with their child's teacher and other school staff members, to help the student learn and choose more appropriate behavior.

Research supports the finding that students who come from households in which caregiver behavior can be described as referent and expert are more likely to achieve academic, as well as social success (Perry and Weinstein, 1998). Therefore, any teacher behaviors that encourage parent support for the person of their children as well as their capabilities, are more successful in helping students learn and behave more appropriately.

As was discussed in Chapter 7, the teacher increases the probability of encouraging parent support if she safeguards herself from personalizing the parents' behavior, just as she has worked hard on not personalizing the student's behavior. The message to the parents from the teacher is "How can we work together to help Kobe?" The message is not "What can we do **to** Kobe?" or "We have done all we can. Now it's up to you, the parents."

Only when the parents do not feel threatened and blamed, will they fully participate in the cooperative school/ home team approach that is needed to help the student.

In addition, caregivers are much more supportive of the teacher's efforts if, previous to this contact, the teacher routinely involved them in positive aspects of the school and their child's education. School-wide programs, such as back-to-school night, volunteer programs, parenting workshops, parent-teacher organizations, and parent advisory boards are, therefore, very important. Teachers may supplement these programs with invitations to visit or volunteer in their classrooms, sending "good news" notes home, phoning parents to inform them of their children's progress, maintaining homeroom websites that are updated frequently, and generally making themselves available to parents when any concerns arise.

Once the conference is scheduled, the teacher and any other school staff member who will be present, work toward ensuring that the meeting will be as positive an experience for the parents as possible. First, the decision concerning who will attend the conference needs to be made. This depends upon the particular problem and the expertise needed to answer parents' questions. Since the atmosphere of the conference should be least intimidating to the parents, we suggest as few people as possible. Students are always present, unless it is determined prior to the conference that the discussion will involve serious concerns about the student's health, home, or legal problems, or if it is inappropriate due to the student's developmental level or cognitive deficits. Prior to the meeting, the school notifies the parents as to who will attend the conference.

During the entire conference, professional behavior is practiced by all staff. Parents' views are encouraged and respected, and at no time are the student or the parents attacked, blamed, or in any other manner put on the defensive. Only when the parents do not feel threatened and blamed, will they fully participate in the cooperative school/home team approach that is needed to help the student. The conference should have a serious tone, with the focus being on positive outcomes for the student.

One necessary aspect of professional behavior is the use of data in decision making. The data to be used at the conference is the anecdotal record that the teacher has been keeping. The record provides a longitudinal documentation of the student's behavior and the interventions the teacher has employed. This data:

- reduces the likelihood of the conference eroding into a debate,
- illustrates the seriousness of the problem, and
- defuses any attempts by the parents to suggest that the teacher or the school has not taken proper and necessary actions (Levin and Nolan, 2000).

During the conference, the teacher may be called upon to explain and defend her decision not to contact the parents-guardians earlier. It is at this time that the teacher needs to educate the parents about her philosophy. Early in this book, it was stressed that if you understand the whys you can design the hows. It is now time to explain to the parents the whys. It is necessary that the parents understand whom they can and cannot control. It is stressed that they do not have total control over their child and they are not bad parents because their child is disruptive in school. Our experience is that parents greet this news with a welcome sense of relief. This new understanding is not meant to communicate to the parents that they have no responsibility with respect to their child's behavior, because in fact they do. However, the responsibility is not **for** their child, but it is **to** their child. Their responsibility to their child is to decide how they can cooperate and interact with the teacher and school to encourage the student towards more appropriate behavior.

Contracting for behavioral change is designed to further impress upon the student what is expected of her and to receive from the student a written commitment of positive behavioral change.

Hopefully, the outcome of the meeting is consensus about the next appropriate intervention. With some students, the decision is that the teacher and/or the school will try more interventions with little or no additional parental involvement. This outcome usually results because the meeting uncovers information about the student that enables the teacher and/or the school to design and implement strategies not previously considered, that may help to reestablish a successful learning environment. Unfortunately, it may also be the outcome when parents show a real disinterest in their child or any additional involvement.

With other students, the decision may be additional parental involvement. For example, everyone may agree to use integrative routines involving the use of the same intervention strategies in school and in the child's home. Other interventions may include daily progress reports to the parents or even participation by the parents in effective parenting classes. Finally, it may be decided that consultation or referrals to other professionals within or outside the school are neces-sary. The outcome of the teacher/parent-guardian conference is recorded on the student's anecdotal record.

Assuming Kobe's previous interventions did not result in appropriate changes in his behavior, a teacher/parent-guardian conference would now be held concerning Kobe's continued disruptive behavior. At Kobe's parent/teacher conference, he, his parents, and the teacher agree that the teacher would send home daily progress reports of his behavior. In addition, it was decided that Kobe and his teacher would write a contract for behavioral change.

CONTRACTING FOR BEHAVIORAL CHANGE

Contracting for behavioral change is designed to further impress upon the student what is expected of her and to receive from the student a written commitment of positive behavioral change. The contract for change is a document which is mutually developed and agreed upon. Writing out your demands and insisting that the student sign with a threat of punishment or a promise of a reward is not a contract for change; it is extortion, and has all the drawbacks associated with punishment. It must be acknowledged that the student might not agree to a contract for change, or there may not be legitimate student desire to bring her behavior into appropriate limits. In these cases, the teacher may decide to forgo the contract for change and proceed to techniques further along in the hierarchy.

A conference to develop a student contract begins by the teacher outlining her observations and assessing the student's understanding of the seriousness of the situation. In addition, the need for a contract as a method to help the student make positive changes is thoroughly explained. The student is told what she needs to accomplish and is asked what she is going to do to make changes in her behavior. While the terms of the contract are negotiable, the need for the student to change to more appropriate behavior is not. If the teacher believes that the student is being vague, unrealistic, or setting up roadblocks, she does not sign off on the contract. Instead, the teacher considers either continuing the negotiation or moving to a different intervention.

Each contract's specifics necessarily are different. However, each contract generally includes:

- the behavioral goal(s),
- the strategies to reach the goal(s),
- a method for determining whether the goal(s) has been met,
- an agreed upon time to meet and discuss the student's progress, and
- a place for both teacher and student signatures.

After discussing and specifying the conditions of the contract, both the teacher and the student sign and date the agreement. The private conference and the student's behavior during the conference are recorded on the student's anecdotal record.

Sometimes contracts do not result in student behavioral change. This is usually a result of one, or more factors. First, the statement of goal(s) may be unclear to the student or to the teacher, or there may be too many goals stated. Student goals need to be few and clearly specified so that there are no student or teacher misunderstandings as to what is expected. Secondly, there is sometimes a tendency for teachers to expect the student to correct the problem immediately and once and for all. This is highly unrealistic and sets up a situation that is more likely to result in failure than success. Problems that have existed for long periods of time do not disappear merely because a contract has been written. Goals need to be written that are successive approximations of the appropriate behavior. In other words, goals can be successfully met without expecting students to undergo a total behavioral change all at once. Once the initial goals are met, the student feels some success and is now ready to set additional goals in a series of successive contracts. Thirdly, many contracts result in less than desirable outcomes, because the time period between teacher and student progress checks is too long. To be effective, in the beginning of the contract, progress checks may occur five or six times a day for elementary school students and twice a week for older students. As the student's behavior begins to change, the time between progress checks is lengthened. Figure 25.5 shows a well-designed contract for a middle school student.

Some teachers may look at the sample contract and think there is no place to specify what the rewards are for improved student behavior. For reasons that have been detailed in Chapters 16 and 17, we believe that it is inappropriate to promise the student a reward for compliance or to threaten the student with a punishment for noncompliance. The student complies with the contract because she wants to accomplish the goals she has outlined, not because of an extrinsic reward. Nevertheless, some students' teachers may decide that it is necessary to provide incentives to some students for improved behavior. Although we are, in general, opposed to this, if you decide to offer incentives, we suggest that they be directly related to learning, such as additional library time, working with educational computer games, learning more about computers, or giving the student a book or magazine related to a particular student interest, rather than the tangible rewards of candy, homework passes, or tokens to be cashed in later for special prizes or privileges. There are, of course, logical consequences for repeated refusal to cease disruptive behavior. However, it is not ap-

Name: Kobe

1. Expected Behavior

   Kobe will not make fun of other students during class.

2. Time Period

   The week of 3/19 – 3/23.

3. Evaluation

   Self-monitoring instrument and teacher monitoring.

4. Progress checks

   Each day during study hall.
   A meeting with Ms. Allen on Friday 3/23 at 2:50 PM to discuss the week's progress and talk about next week's contract.

Student Signature: ____________________ Date: ________

Teacher Signature: ____________________ Date: ________

FIGURE 25.5 ▶ Sample Contract

propriate to use these consequences as a threatened punishment (See Chapter 17), because this tends to decrease compliance and fosters an external locus of control, as well as encouraging defensive displays of distorted power.

Once the contract has begun, the teacher carefully monitors and records the student's progress toward attaining her goal(s) in her anecdotal record. This record provides accurate data to discuss at the next conference with the student.

ANECDOTAL RECORD KEEPING WITH STUDENT PARTICIPATION

When the student refuses to participate in the previous interventions or participates but the interventions are not successful, and the student continues to be a discipline problem in the classroom, the student becomes an active participant in the use of anecdotal records. The student is already aware that the teacher has been recording her daily behaviors, both appropriate and disruptive, and has seen the teacher make notations in the record after each teacher/student conference. Now the student is made aware of everything the teacher is recording daily.

Let's see how this works.

A private conference is scheduled again with Kobe. He is shown the anecdotal record and is informed that at the end and of the class (or day) he is required to read what the teacher has written and sign the record (for elementary students, the reading and the signing of the record may take place more frequently during the day). The teacher also informs Kobe that if he does not make substantial progress, defining explicitly what that means, other stated actions will be warranted. This is not a threat; it is a promise of consequences, delivered using "You have a choice" and following all the guidelines discussed in Chapter 23. The message is delivered assertively and respectfully, "Kobe, you have a choice. You raise your hand, stay in your seat, and quit making fun of Lee, or you may be removed from the class. You decide."

The details of this meeting are entered into the anecdotal record, and Kobe is asked to read and then sign the record. Most students now understand that this is an extremely serious situation, and that they are going to be strictly held accountable for their disruptive behavior. The conference ends with the student signing the record. The teacher thanks the student and says sincerely that she feels that the student's behavior will become more appropriate.

Upon being asked to sign the record, some students become very resistant and defiant and resort to a display of distorted power. They may say things like, "This sucks, I'm not signing anything," "You gotta be nuts if you think I'm signing this," or "You can do whatever you want, but forget it, I'm not signing this now and certainly not every day." If the teacher yells or berates the student, the intervention is no longer a logical consequence of the student's disruptive behavior, but a punishment which focuses the student's attention on the teacher, rather than where it belongs on the student. Instead, the teacher must remember her Post-It note, "The only person I can control is myself." The teacher calmly and respectfully records verbatim what the student said on the anecdotal record, thanks her for coming, and communicates the positive expectations which the teacher has for her improved behavior.

Each day, the student is shown the anecdotal record and requested to sign it. Either the student signs it or doesn't sign it, but the teacher is always respectful. An example of Kobe's anecdotal record, assuming either that he refused to participate in previous interventions or they were not successful, may look similar to the one in Figure 25.6.

The effectiveness of this technique depends upon the consistent recording of daily behavior and the student's signature. If, at any time, the student refuses to sign the record, like Kobe, the teacher records it. The teacher communicates that the student is solely responsible for her behavior and that the teacher is an impartial recorder of the observed behavior. The signature is not the important issue. What is important is the student's improved behavior, which usually occurs with time, especially if the teacher is conscientious in recording not only the disruptive behavior, but also the appropriate behavior of the student. If the behavior is improving and the student refuses to sign the anecdotal record, that's fine. It's probably the student's last attempts at exerting distorted power.

When presented with this technique, many teachers anticipate that it will consume way too much time; however, this is not the case. The daily recording is done during the last few minutes of class, which is often the time that students are getting ready to leave, copying their homework, or completing the class work. However, there is a concept called conservation of time. In other words, you have a choice. You can spend the time maintaining the anecdotal record or spend the time continually attempting to manage a chronically disruptive student. You decide.

There is no absolute rule concerning when to stop using the anecdotal record. When the student has displayed behaviors within acceptable limits for a number of consecutive days, it is appropriate to discuss with the student whether or not the record keeping is still necessary. If the behavior is only intermittently appropriate, or there is a slight reduction in the degree of disruptiveness, it may be worthwhile to request another private conference with the student to discuss her progress and explain that the record will be continued a little longer. However, if there is no notable change in the student's behavior within a few days, the record is contin-

Student Name: Kobe

Phone Number: ____________________

DATE	STUDENT BEHAVIOR and RESPONSE TO INTERVENTION	TEACHER ACTION	STUDENT SIGNATURE
2/19	1. Kobe arrived late to class	1. Said nothing to him, will talk with him after class	
	2. Began to participate in class	2. Called on him frequently, used his answers to continue lesson	
	3. Called out that Lee's answer was stupid	3. Made eye contact with him	
	4. Passed notes to Vito and refused to work with Taylor	4. Used proximity control	
		5. Spoke with him after class about lateness, he said he will make it on time from now on	
		6. Asked him if he would be willing to bring in a mix of his current favorite music so that I could get a feeling for what he and other students were listening to	
2/20 to 4/1	(The teacher during this period has kept detailed records of all of Kobe's behaviors in the classroom, both negative and positive. In addition, the teacher has noted all of Kobe's attempts at problem solving using authentic questions, problem solving using goal attainment, self-monitoring, and contracting. In addition, Kobe's behavior during each of the conferences has been noted.)	(The teacher during this period has kept detailed records of all of her responses to Kobe's behavior in the classroom. In addition, the teacher has noted details of each of the following conferences: problem solving using authentic questions, problem solving using goal attainment, self-monitoring, the first teacher/parent-guardian meeting, and contracting.)	

(continued)

FIGURE 25.6 ▶ Anecdotal Record

DATE	STUDENT BEHAVIOR and RESPONSE TO INTERVENTION	TEACHER ACTION	STUDENT SIGNATURE
4/2	1. Came to class on time	1. Welcomed Kobe to class and greeted him with a smile	
	2. Got out of his seat numerous times and took other student's papers	2. Delivered "you have a choice" with the consequence of doing his work by himself in the back of the room	
	3. Remained in his seat for the rest of the class	3. Walked by his desk and told him privately that I was glad he made an appropriate choice	
	4. Made fun of Lee's and Taylor's answers	4. Made eye contact and moved closer to his seat	
	5. He said "no way, I'm never signing this" and he refused to sign it	5. At the end of class asked Kobe to see me after school	
		6. When Kobe came to see me, I shared the anecdotal record with him and explained that I was going to continue the record and that he was to read it and sign it each day before he left my class.	
		7. Told him that I expected more appropriate behavior and thanked him for coming	
4/3 to ?	(The teacher continues to record all of Kobe's behaviors on a daily basis until either Kobe's behavior shows a significant improvement over time or the school year ends.)	(The teacher records her responses to Kobe's behavior on a daily basis until either Kobe's behavior improves or the school year ends.)	(The teacher on a daily basis requests that Kobe read and sign the record.)

FIGURE 25.6 ▶ Anecdotal Record, *continued*

ued and the student is referred to the Instructional Support Team (I.S.T.).

Although teachers voice concerns both about how students may react to this very confrontational intervention, and how much time it takes, anecdotal records are a technique that has been shown to be quite effective in influencing appropriate behavior of students who exhibit chronically disruptive behavior (Levin et al, 1985,). Examples of actual teachers' recorded logs detailing how they felt when using anecdotal records and the impact on their students' behavior are included in Levin et al, 1985.

REFERRAL TO OTHER PROFESSIONALS INSIDE THE SCHOOL

When the teacher has approached this point in the hierarchy, she should consult with the school counselor and/or a school administrator. It is likely that the student is referred to the counselor and/or the principal or vice-principle. These staff members may play a vital role in assisting the classroom teacher in influencing the student to behave appropriately. For example, the counselor, as an outside observer, visits the classroom and provides objective feedback to the teacher on new approaches for working with the student, while at the same time works directly with the student to develop more acceptable behavior. Additionally, the counselor may help to improve the strained teacher/student relationship that most likely exists by this time. Administrators must also be consulted if there is a possibility that the student may be placed permanently in another classroom, assigned to specialized educational settings in or outside the school, or referred to other professions such as a school or private psychologist.

CONDITIONAL REMOVAL FROM CLASS

No student can be allowed to disrupt the learning process of other students indefinitely. Let's take a look at Kobe's situation. The teacher attempted to prevent disruptive behavior by increasing Kobe's success/failure ratio, enhancing his intrinsic motivation, and facilitating his development of pro-social self-esteem. In addition, the teacher intervened nonverbally by planned ignoring, signals, and proximity, and intervened verbally by inferential statements and demands. The teacher delivered logical consequences on numerous occasions; worked individually with Kobe to solve authentic questions; and taught Kobe written problem solving, goal attainment, and self-monitoring. In addition, the teacher met with Kobe's parents, developed with Kobe, a contract for behavioral change, and had Kobe participate in anecdotal record keeping. Each intervention was delivered with respect and with the expectation of a positive outcome. However, as he has not exhibited appropriate behavior yet, Kobe may no longer be a member of the class, until he makes a written commitment to behave appropriately in the classroom.

The teacher holds a private conference with Kobe. The teacher explains, "Kobe you have continually disregarded the rights of your classmates to learn, by making fun of them, taking their papers, and hitting them. Therefore, at this time, you are no longer a member of the class. You are welcome back to our classroom, as soon as you provide me with a written promise that you will behave appropriately. Tomorrow, please report to Ms. Black's room." Because this technique removes the student from her assigned classroom, it requires both the approval and support of the administration and the cooperation of another teacher.

Whenever possible, the student is placed in a classroom with older or younger students. It is the authors' experience that placing a disruptive student with older or younger students has a tendency to diminish disruptive behavior. In addition, students tend to be less disruptive when they are in unfamiliar surroundings. Therefore, even if the student is in the highest grade, assigning her to a different class that is not learning the same material, has the tendency to reduce her disruptive behavior. While the teacher who accepts Kobe into her class may not be delighted to have him, we encourage you to form partnerships with teachers with the same philosophy, so that they too have an outlet for students displaying very disruptive behavior, when necessary. Other locations to which the student may be sent are the principal's, guidance counselor's, or departmental offices. We do not recommend the use of classrooms set aside specially for the sole purpose of housing students who are given in-school suspension or for other disciplinary purposes. These rooms tend to exhibit a climate of punishment, exactly what we are trying to avoid.

It is made clear to Kobe that he is still responsible for all work and assignments, even though he is not in his regular classroom. In whatever classroom he is placed, he continues to work individually on his own class work; he is not a member of the new classroom. Therefore, the teacher has the responsibility to provide Kobe with the class assignments each day he is out of the class. The teacher continues to respect Kobe's right to fail and to make the poor choice of remaining oppositional, even if the teacher is extremely displeased with Kobe's choices.

If Kobe writes a promise of more appropriate behavior, he rejoins the class and starts anew. It is important that Kobe, in developmentally appropriate manner, indicate both his understanding of why he was removed from the class and specifically how his behavior will change.

When Kobe returns to his classroom, the teacher demonstrates that his past behavior is not being held against him. Any disruptive behaviors that may occur are dealt with from the beginning of the intervention hierarchy, with non-verbal interventions, even though this time the teacher may move more rapidly through the interventions. This helps to mitigate the failure experience of being removed from the class, by reaffirming the teacher's positive regard and renewed expectation in Kobe's ability to use prosocial competence and power to control his own behavior in appropriate ways.

There is always the chance that Kobe will not make the written commitment for positive behavior change or he may become disruptive in his new classroom. If a commitment is not forthcoming within approximately three days, or he becomes disruptive in the other classroom, the teacher immediately arranges for a teacher/parent-guardian conference.

SECOND TEACHER/PARENT-GUARDIAN CONFERENCE

When it is apparent to the teacher that her interventions have not resulted in appreciable positive change in the student's behavior, parents again must be contacted. At this meeting, attendance is determined by the pervasiveness of the problem. If all or most of the student's teachers have similar problems with the student, then they all should attend. If the student is having difficulty only in one teacher's class, then attendance probably will be limited to the teacher, counselor, school psychologist, and administrator. Whether the student is present is a decision made taking into account the student's developmental level, ability to tolerate a meeting discussing her behavior, and her desire to change.

At this conference, the anecdotal record is reviewed again, along with any other supportive documents, such as contracts and letters of commitment to change. The student at this point, may not, depending upon the pervasiveness and severity of the problem, continue in this teacher's class, or possibly even in her current school. Therefore, the need for alternative class placement, alternative school placement, and/or referral to outside professionals is considered.

REFERRAL TO OTHER PROFESSIONALS OUTSIDE THE SCHOOL

The last intervention in the hierarchy is referral to outside professionals. It is last because it is the only intervention that doesn't take place in the school setting.

If this point in the hierarchy is reached, the teacher likely may perceive herself as having failed. However, this is not a failure, because the teacher has no control over Kobe's choice to continually be disruptive. Most probably the causes of Kobe's continual disruptive behavior have nothing to do with what the teacher has or has not done. The teacher controlled her behavior, using the best professional practice. Similar to a competent medical doctor who refers her patients to specialists, it is the competent educator who recognizes when a student's behavior is outside the teacher's expertise and initiates the referral process.

Different school districts have different referral processes. In some districts, the referral is initiated by the teacher, while in others it is made by the school counselor or school psychologist. Some schools have instructional support teams or child study teams who make the referral.

We encourage schools and teachers to familiarize themselves with the philosophies and approaches of the counseling and psychological services in the community, so that a proper referral may be made.

In many cases, the first referral is made within the school district to the district's learning specialist or psychologist. The teacher's input, particularly Kobe's anecdotal record, is valuable data for this individual as she attempts to understand Kobe's problem and works with Kobe, helping him make appropriate changes in behavior.

In cases where it is deemed necessary, the student may be referred to specialists other than district personnel. We encourage schools and teachers to familiarize themselves with the philosophies and approaches of the counseling and psychological services in the community, so that a proper referral may be made. For example, referring a student to a behavioral psychologist who designs systems of classroom rewards and punishment would be contradictory to the teacher's philosophy and techniques if she subscribes to the Self-Control Classroom model. In addition, referrals should be made to those individuals who are active in schools and knowledgeable about how classrooms operate, particularly in regard to influencing appropriate classroom behavior. A psychologist or counselor who does not have frequent contact with schools and teachers is unlikely to be able to successfully impact classroom behavior of students.

The teacher may continue to assist Kobe by remaining involved with Kobe and in contact with his parents and the outside professionals with whom he is working. This continued interest and concern for Kobe by the teacher (referent authority), increases the likelihood that Kobe will learn how to control his behavior within acceptable limits and experience a success/failure ratio > 1, develop an intrinsic motivation, and display pro-social self-esteem.

Symptoms of Serious Problems That Need Immediate Referral

Some students may display symptoms that are indicative of serious physical or emotional problems, or associated with substance abuse or home abuse. These symptoms may or may not be accompanied by disruptive behavior. All of these fall outside the expertise and responsibility of the teacher. However, it is incumbent upon, and in some states required by law, that teachers report these symptoms, as soon as they are observed, to appropriate school officials, who are knowledgeable as to the next steps that must be taken.

Some of the symptoms are noticeable changes in:

- physical appearance,
- activity level,
- personality,
- achievement status,
- health,
- socialization,
- physical abilities, or
- any appearances of unusual burns, bruises, or abrasions.

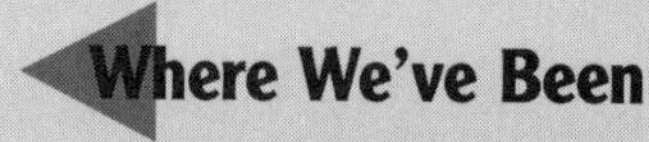

Where We've Been

This chapter presents the last level of the intervention hierarchy. It poses the most difficult challenge of how to intervene with students exhibiting chronically disruptive behavior, while at the same time protecting or facilitating their success/failure ratio, and whatever degree of intrinsic motivation and pro-social self-esteem they may have.

There are ten interventions in the last level of the hierarchy. As with the entire hierarchy and within each of the previous levels, these interventions are ordered from least confrontational to most confrontational. The movement through this level and the number of techniques to employ are functions of the degree of disruptiveness of the student's behavior and the amount of sincere student effort towards displaying appropriate behavior.

The ten interventions are:

1) teacher/student conference with authentic questions,
2) goal attainment behavior: Goal, Plan, Do, Check,
3) student self-monitoring,
4) first teacher/parent-guardian conference,
5) contracting for behavioral change,
6) anecdotal record keeping with student participation,
7) referral to other professionals inside the school,
8) conditional removal of the student from class,
9) second teacher/parent-guardian conference, and
10) referral to professionals outside the school.

By the teacher continuing to make professional decisions; communicating her belief that the student has the ability to behave appropriately; focusing on the student's behavior, not the student's character; and by respecting the student's right to choose how she will behave, the teacher increases the probability that these techniques will be effective.

Lastly, some students exhibit symptoms of serious physical or psychological problems, which may or may not be accompanied by disruptive behavior. Teachers need to recognize these symptoms and report these potential serious problems to the appropriate school official.

We have now completed the first two objectives stated in the vision statement for dealing with students who exhibit common or chronic behavior problems: 1) reestablishing the successful learning environment for the student, while 2) protecting the learning environment for all students.

Where We're Headed

The last chapter in this book completes the change in paradigm to the Self-Control Classroom model from traditional models of classroom management. While classroom management models view disruptive behavior as something to be punished, adherents to the Self-Control Classroom model view disruptive behavior as an opportunity to teach appropriate behavior. Throughout this book, teachers have been encouraged through their relationships with students (referent authority) and their expertise (expert authority) to model appropriate behavior. Chapter 26 is concerned with how teachers and administrators can develop curricula to teach specific aspects of appropriate behavior. Teaching appropriate behavior to all students completes the Vision of the Self-Control Classroom model stated in Chapter 1 and developed throughout the book.

CHAPTER 25 CONCEPT MAP

HIERARCHY OF INTERVENTIONS
LEVEL 6: INTERVENTION FOR STUDENTS EXHIBITING CHRONIC DISRUPTIVE BEHAVIOR

maximum opportunities for student self-control

least disruptive to the learning environment

least confrontational

teachers have many remaining interventions

teachers have fewer remaining interventions

most confrontational

most disruptive to the learning environment

minimum opportunities for student self-control

ALL STUDENTS

Prevention: Establishing Successful Learning Environments
S/F > 1
Intrinsic Motivation
- internal locus of control
- internal value structure

Pro-Social Self-Esteem
- significance
- competence
- virture
- power

STUDENTS EXHIBITING COMMON DISCIPLINE PROBLEMS

Prevention: Establishing Successful Learning Environments
S/F > 1
Intrinsic Motivation
- internal locus of control
- internal value structure

Pro-Social Self-Esteem
- significance
- competence
- virture
- power

Level 1: Reestablishing Successful Learning Environments
Level 2: Pro-Active Interventions
Level 3: Nonverbal Interventions
Level 4: Verbal Interventions
Level 5: Applying Consequences

STUDENTS EXHIBITING CHRONIC DISCIPLINE PROBLEMS

Prevention: Establishing Successful Learning Environments
S/F > 1
Intrinsic Motivation
- internal locus of control
- internal value structure

Pro-Social Self-Esteem
- significance
- competence
- virture
- power

Level 1: Reestablishing Successful Learning Environments
Level 2: Pro-Active Interventions
Level 3: Nonverbal Interventions
Level 4: Verbal Interventions
Level 5: Applying Consequences
Level 6: Chronic Disruptive Behavior
- teacher/student conf.: authentic questions
- goal attainment behavior: Goal, Plan, Do, Check
- student self-monitoring
- first teacher/parent-guardian conference
- contracting for behavioral change
- anecdotal record keeping: student participation
- referral to professionals inside school
- conditional removal from class
- second teacher/parent-guardian conference
- referral to professionals outside school

? QUESTIONS FOR THE STUDY TEAM

1. What should a teacher do if she asks a student to stay after class to discuss the student's behavior and the student refuses?

2. How may a teacher use the hierarchy of interventions for students who exhibit chronic disruptive behavior, if the school's administrators believe in suspending these students?

3. What should a teacher do when parents refuse to come to a teacher/parent conference?

4. What should a teacher do if after a teacher/parent conference, the parents threaten the student with punishments that are incongruent with the Self-Control Classroom model?

5. What should a teacher do if a student's private therapist recommends strategies, such as rewards and punishments, which are incongruent with the Self-Control Classroom model?

6. The strategies and interventions in the Self-Control Classroom model take a considerable amount of time. Should a teacher take so much time to influence students who exhibit disruptive behavior when they have so many appropriately behaved students to teach?

7. The interventions suggested for students who exhibit chronic disruptive behavior may be used effectively if a teacher has only one such student in a class. However, what should a teacher do if she has more than one such student in the same class?

8. What should a teacher do if none of the prevention strategies and/or interventions suggested by the Self-Control Classroom model are effective in influencing students to behave appropriately?

CHAPTER 26

Teaching Students Appropriate Behavior

"I have taught in high school for ten years. During that time I have given assignments, among others, to a murderer, an evangelist, a pugilist, a thief, and an imbecile.

The murderer was a quiet little boy who sat on the front seat and regarded me with pale blue eyes; the evangelist, easily the most popular boy in school, had the lead in the junior play; the pugilist lounged by the window and let loose at intervals a raucous laugh that startled even the geraniums; the thief was a gay hearted Lothario with a song on his lips, and the imbecile, a soft-eyed little animal seeking the shadows.

The murderer awaits death in the state penitentiary; the evangelist has lain a year now in the village churchyard; the pugilist lost an eye in a brawl in Hong Kong; the thief, by standing on tiptoe, can see the windows of my room from the county jail, and the once gentle-eyed little moron beats his head against a padded wall in the state asylum.

All of these pupils once sat in my room, sat and looked at me gravely across worn brown desks. I must have been a great help to those pupils—I taught them the rhyming scheme of the Elizabethan Sonnet and how to diagram a complex sentence." (author unknown, 1937)

As stated in Chapter 5, when a student encounters any type of difficulty in school, regardless of whether the difficulty is academic or behavioral, the question the teacher needs to ask herself remains the same, "How can I change my behavior to increase the likelihood that the student will learn (change her behavior)?" This is the definition of teaching in the Self-Control Classroom model. When a student is having difficulty with mathematics, the teacher asks, "How can I change my behavior to increase the likelihood that the student will learn math?" If the student is struggling in English, the teacher asks, "How can I change my behavior to increase the likelihood that the student will learn English?" Similarly, when the student is having difficulty behaving appropriately, the teacher asks, "How can I change my behavior to increase the likelihood that the student will learn how to behave appropriately?"

Teaching appropriate behavior to students increases the likelihood that disruptive behavior is prevented in the classroom and in the entire school.

It is important now to mention again that some teachers have strong resistance about the reasonable expectation of teaching appropriate behavior. Teachers frequently maintain that teaching appropriate behavior is a parental responsibility and should take place in the home. We agree. However, just as schools provide breakfast and lunch to students who demonstrate need or offer intensive reading instruction to students who lag behind in reading because their parents do not encourage reading in the home, so teachers need to make reality their friend and acknowledge that often parents do not, and in some cases cannot, effectively teach appropriate behavior in the classroom. Therefore, instead of complaining about "lousy," "dysfunctional," or "permissive" parents, professional teachers recognize their responsibility to teach appropriate behavior in school, in order for other, academic learning to take place.

Teachers who instruct all their students about appropriate behavior, rapidly discern that far from being a waste, this instruction saves the enormous time and energy which teachers often spend dealing with students who exhibit disruptive behavior. Teaching appropriate behavior to students increases the likelihood that disruptive behavior is prevented in the classroom and in the entire school. While the authors encourage every teacher to use some instructional time to teach all their students appropriate behavior every year, it is important to note that there are students who require more intensive one-on-one instruction in how to behave appropriately. This remedial instruction should be viewed by teachers in the same light that they view remedial instruction in subjects such as math, science, English, and social studies.

Preparing for Instruction of Appropriate Behavior

In order to prepare for classroom instruction of appropriate behavior, the authors feel it is helpful to provide a brief review of how to prepare to teach a learning objective directed toward an academic outcome. The same process then will be utilized to prepare for instruction of learning objectives directed at appropriate behavior.

Analyze the definition of teaching, which is, "How can I change my behavior to increase the likelihood that the student will learn?" The phrase "students will learn" is analogous to student learning objectives in lesson plans, and the phrase "How can I change my behavior" is analogous to the teaching strategies used to facilitate these learning objectives.

A lesson plan is the initial step in the process of preparing for instruction. Although there are many widely used and acceptable lesson plan formats, all lesson plans include student learning objectives and teaching strategies. A common, easy to use format is illustrated in Figure 26.1.

Student Learning Objectives (what students will do)	Teaching Strategies (what teachers will do)	Evaluation (did the student master the objective?)

FIGURE 26.1 ▶ Sample Lesson Plan Format

AN EXAMPLE OF AN ACADEMIC LESSON

You are a new elementary school teacher. The curriculum requires that students master the terminal objective of "Students will be able to multiply any one digit number by any other one digit number." In order to design instruction to help students meet the terminal objective, the teacher: 1) Task analyzes the terminal objective into enabling objectives (prerequisite skills), 2) Hierarchically orders the enabling objective from most complex to least complex, 3) Designs teaching strategies that are intended to increase the likelihood that the students master each objective, and 4) Designs evaluations for each objective.

Task Analyzing the Terminal Objective into Enabling Objectives (Prerequisite Skills)

For the terminal objective, "Students will be able to multiply any one digit number by any one digit number," there are five enabling objectives. These are:

1. Students will transform (write) chain addition problems, involving one whole number, into multiplication problems using two whole numbers.
2. Students will identify the ones and tens place values.
3. Students will transform (write) multiplication problems, involving two whole numbers, into chain addition problems involving one whole number.
4. Students will set up multiplication problems using proper operational notation.
5. Students will list whole numbers by ascending and descending order.

HIERARCHICALLY ORDERING THE ENABLING OBJECTIVES FROM MOST COMPLEX TO LEAST COMPLEX

After listing all the enabling objectives, the teacher orders them from the most complex to the least complex. These enabling objectives are then placed into the lesson plan as illustrated in Figure 26.2.

Student Learning Objectives (what students will do)	Teaching Strategies (what teachers will do)	Evaluation (did the student master the objective?)
Terminal Objective: Students will be able to multiply any one digit number by any other one digit number.		
5. Students will set up multiplication problems using proper operational notation.		
4. Students will identify the ones and tens place values.		
3. Students will transform (write) multiplication problems, involving two whole numbers, into chain addition problems involving one whole number.		
2. Students will transform (write) chain addition problems, involving one whole number, into multiplication problems using two whole numbers.		
1. Students will list whole numbers by ascending and descending order.		

FIGURE 26.2 ▶ Multiplication Lesson Plan with Enabling Objectives

DESIGNING TEACHING STRATEGIES FOR EACH OBJECTIVE

The next step is to design teaching strategies for each objective.

Student Learning Objectives (what students will do)	Teaching Strategies (what teachers will do)	Evaluation (did the student master the objective?)
Terminal Objective: Students will be able to multiply any one digit number by any other one digit number.	T.O.1 Have students generate 15 one digit by one digit multiplication problems and pass the problems to the student on their left. T.O.2 Assign 10 problems to be completed as homework.	
5. Students will set up multiplication problems using proper operational notation.	5.1 Introduce students to proper operational notation of multiplication problems. 5.2 Have students set up multiplication problems, using proper notation from a list of multiplication problems verbally presented to the students by the teacher.	
4. Students will identify the ones and tens place values.	4.1 Ask students to identify the ones place value for each number in a list of two digit numbers. 4.2 Ask students to identify the tens place value for each number in a list of two digit numbers.	
3. Students will transform (write) multiplication problems, involving two whole numbers, into chain addition problems involving one whole number.	3.1 Ask students to write five multiplication problems using two whole numbers. 3.2 Ask students to transform their multiplication problems into chain addition problems. 3.3 Ask students to volunteer to place their examples on the board. 3.4 Ask other students to identify those problems that have been accurately transformed.	

(continued)

FIGURE 26.3 ▶ Multiplication Lesson Plan with Enabling Objectives and Teaching Strategies

Student Learning Objectives (what students will do)	Teaching Strategies (what teachers will do)	Evaluation (did the student master the objective?)
2. Students will transform (write) chain addition problems, involving one whole number, into multiplication problems using two whole numbers.	2.1 Ask students to write five chain addition problems using one whole numbers. 2.2 Ask students to transform their addition problems into multiplication problems, using two whole numbers. 2.3 Ask students to volunteer to place their examples on the board. 2.4 Ask other students to identify those problems that have been accurately transformed.	
1. Students will list whole numbers by ascending and descending order.	1.1 Give students random lists of whole numbers (1–9) and request that students order the numbers in ascending and descending order.	

FIGURE 26.3 ▶ Multiplication Lesson Plan with Enabling Objectives and Teaching Strategies, *continued*

DESIGNING EVALUATION STRATEGIES FOR EACH OBJECTIVE

Finally evaluations to determine mastery are designed for each objective.

Student Learning Objectives (what students will do)	**Teaching Strategies (what teachers will do)**	**Evaluation (did the student master the objective?)**
Terminal Objective: Students will be able to multiply any one digit number by any other one digit number.	T.O.1 Have students generate 15 one digit by one digit multiplication problems and pass the problems to the student on their left. T.O.2 Assign 10 problems to be completed as homework.	T.O.1 Students will correctly solve 80% of the 15 problems given to them by their neighbor. T.O.2 Students will correctly solve 90% of the 10 problems given as homework.
5. Students will set up multiplication problems using proper operational notation.	5.1 Introduce students to proper operational notation of multiplication problems. 5.2 Have students set up multiplication problems, using proper notation from a list of multiplication problems verbally presented to the students by the teacher.	5.1 Students will identify the correct and incorrect examples of proper operational notation for multiplication problems from a list of 30 addition, subtraction, and multiplication problems (100%).
4. Students will identify the ones and tens place values.	4.1 Ask students to identify the ones place value for each number in a list of two digit numbers. 4.2 Ask students to identify the tens place value for each number in a list of two digit numbers.	4.1 Students will correctly identify the ones and tens place values in a list of 30 multiplication problems (100%).
3. Students will transform (write) multiplication problems, involving two whole numbers, into chain addition problems involving one whole number.	3.1 Ask students to write five multiplication problems using two whole numbers. 3.2 Ask students to transform their multiplication problems into chain addition problems. 3.3 Ask students to volunteer to place their examples on the board. 3.4 Ask other students to identify those problems that have been accurately transformed.	3.1 The majority of the class will volunteer to place problems on the board. 3.2 The majority of the class will identify the accurately transformed problems placed on the board.

(continued)

FIGURE 26.4 ▶ Multiplication Lesson Plan with Enabling Objectives, Teaching Strategies, and Evaluations

Student Learning Objectives (what students will do)	Teaching Strategies (what teachers will do)	Evaluation (did the student master the objective?)
2. Students will transform (write) chain addition problems, involving one whole number, into multiplication problems using two whole numbers.	2.1 Ask students to write five chain addition problems using one whole numbers. 2.2 Ask students to transform their addition problems into multiplication problems, using two whole numbers. 2.3 Ask students to volunteer to place their examples on the board. 2.4 Ask other students to identify those problems that have been accurately transformed.	2.1 The majority of the class will volunteer to place problems on the board. 2.2 The majority of the class will identify accurately transformed problems placed on the board.
1. Students will list whole numbers by ascending and descending order.	1.1 Give students random lists of whole numbers (1–9) and request that students order the numbers in ascending and descending order.	1.1 Students will order list of whole numbers with 100% accuracy.

FIGURE 26.4 ▶ Multiplication Lesson Plan with Enabling Objectives, Teaching Strategies, and Evaluations, *continued*

How to Design a Lesson Plan to Teach Appropriate Behavior

As we have stated, the process of teaching is the same, whether the terminal objective is academic or behavioral. In both cases, the teacher needs to ask, "How do I change my behavior to increase the likelihood that students will learn?" As in the above example, any teaching goal begins with a lesson plan stating objectives, strategies, and evaluations.

TEACHING RESPECT

The authors have conducted hundreds of workshops across the country detailing the Self-Control Classroom model. When we ask teachers at these workshops their major concerns about student behavior, the top concern is frequently that students do not respect each other or the teacher. Therefore, it seems that students need to learn respect. The terminal objective of a lesson on respect is, "All students will respect all other members of the school community." As in the academic example, in designing instruction which would allow the students to meet the terminal objective of respect, the teacher would:

- task analyze the terminal objective into enabling objectives (prerequisite skills),
- hierarchically order the enabling objective from most complex to least complex,
- design teaching strategies that are intended to increase the likelihood that the students will master each objective, and
- design evaluations for each objective.

There are hundreds of different lesson plans that may be designed to teach respect. The lesson plan will be different according to the grade and developmental level of the students, the creativity of the teacher, the culture of the school and of the community, the time allotted to the task, and whether the lesson will be taught by one teacher or will be integrated across the curriculum. For these reasons, we will not present a "model" lesson plan for teaching respect. As with other issues presented in the book, it is our belief that if you know the whys, you can design the hows. Nevertheless, here are some suggestions that the authors feel will be of importance in most lesson plans and may serve as a starting point in helping you design your own lesson to teach respect.[1]

Teachers need to be aware of how the students' different cultures define and display respect.

First, it is necessary to task analyze the terminal objective, "All students will respect all members of the school community," into enabling objectives. Some examples of enabling objectives are:

- students will define respect,
- students will define disrespect,
- students will recognize examples of respectful behavior,
- students will recognize examples of disrespectful behavior,
- students will state why respect is important, and
- students will define the components of the school community.

This list of enabling objectives is by no means exhaustive. A team of teachers will uncover many more enabling objectives that are necessary to reach the terminal objective. Once all the enabling objectives are uncovered, the next step is to place them in a hierarchical order from most to least complex.

For each enabling and terminal objective, teaching strategies need to be designed. Examples of appropriate teaching strategies include student group discussions, modeling by students and teachers, role plays, analyzing messages in popular media (eg. TV shows, movies, music, video games), analyzing literature, analyzing the school code, designing plays or videos that illustrate respect and disrespect, and sharing personal experiences. Again, the list of potential strategies is massive and limited only by the imagination of the teacher, her students, and time.

The final step is to design methods to evaluate whether the terminal objective and each enabling objective have been mastered. Because of the nature of the terminal objective involving respect, the evaluation is ongoing and formative. It involves observing students over time and across settings, to see if learning has occurred—that is, whether or not the students' behaviors have changed. In addition, because of changes in cognition from year to year, the influence of modern culture, moral development, and the different demands and expectations placed upon students as they move from grade to grade, respect needs to be re-taught in ways that are developmentally appropriate. Another important concern is that America is a country of diversity, largely consisting of immigrants from other cultures. Teachers need to be aware of how the students' different cultures define and display respect. Teachers must not assume that there is one settled and agreed upon standard, that is appropriate or acceptable to all groups.

An important caveat is that if students are expected to change their behavior and become more respectful members of the school community, a concomitant change involving increased respect must take place on the part of teachers, administrators, counselors, secretaries,

---

[1] Although we are discussing a discreet lesson plan to teach respect, teaching respect should be integrated across the curriculum, throughout the year, every year. One lesson plan can, however, serve as a starting point to gain entrance to the subject.

non-teaching assistants, cafeteria workers, bus drivers, and all other staff.

Some other terminal objectives that address concerns that teachers commonly have are:

- Students will consensually design classroom guidelines.
- Students will commit themselves to consensually derived rules and procedures.
- Students will demonstrate appropriate behavior in the cafeteria.
- Students will transition between classes in an orderly fashion.
- Students will resolve disputes and conflicts through peer mediation or other nonaggressive means.
- Students will recognize bullying and other forms of harassment as victimization and know how to avoid becoming a bully and to assertively confront bullies.
- Students will volunteer for community and school service projects without seeking extrinsic rewards.

Again, the above learning objectives are only suggestions for a few lessons that will enhance the successful learning environment for all members of the school community and increase the probability that students will be accountable for their behavior.

Where We've Been

This chapter used an example of preparing to teach an academic lesson to help teachers prepare a behavioral lesson. In both cases, the process is the same: 1) state the terminal objective, 2) task analyze the terminal objective into enabling objectives, 3) hierarchically order the enabling objective from most complex to least complex, 4) design teaching strategies for each objective, and 5) design evaluations for each objective. Some suggestions on how to develop a lesson for teaching respect were provided. The chapter concludes with examples of terminal objectives to address behavioral concerns commonly voiced by teachers.

Where You're Headed

By reading this book and embracing the philosophies of the Self-Control Classroom model, you are beginning a journey that will lead to the creation of successful learning environments for your students. The ultimate outcome is that the disrupters in your class and school will choose to become achievers. We are very interested in hearing from you about both your successes and continued challenges. Many teachers have, through the years, shared innovative strategies with us that are congruent with the model. We have adapted many of them for your use. We'd love to include your ideas in our continued refinement of the model. You can e-mail us at LSK@selfcontrolclassroom.com

CHAPTER 26 CONCEPT MAP

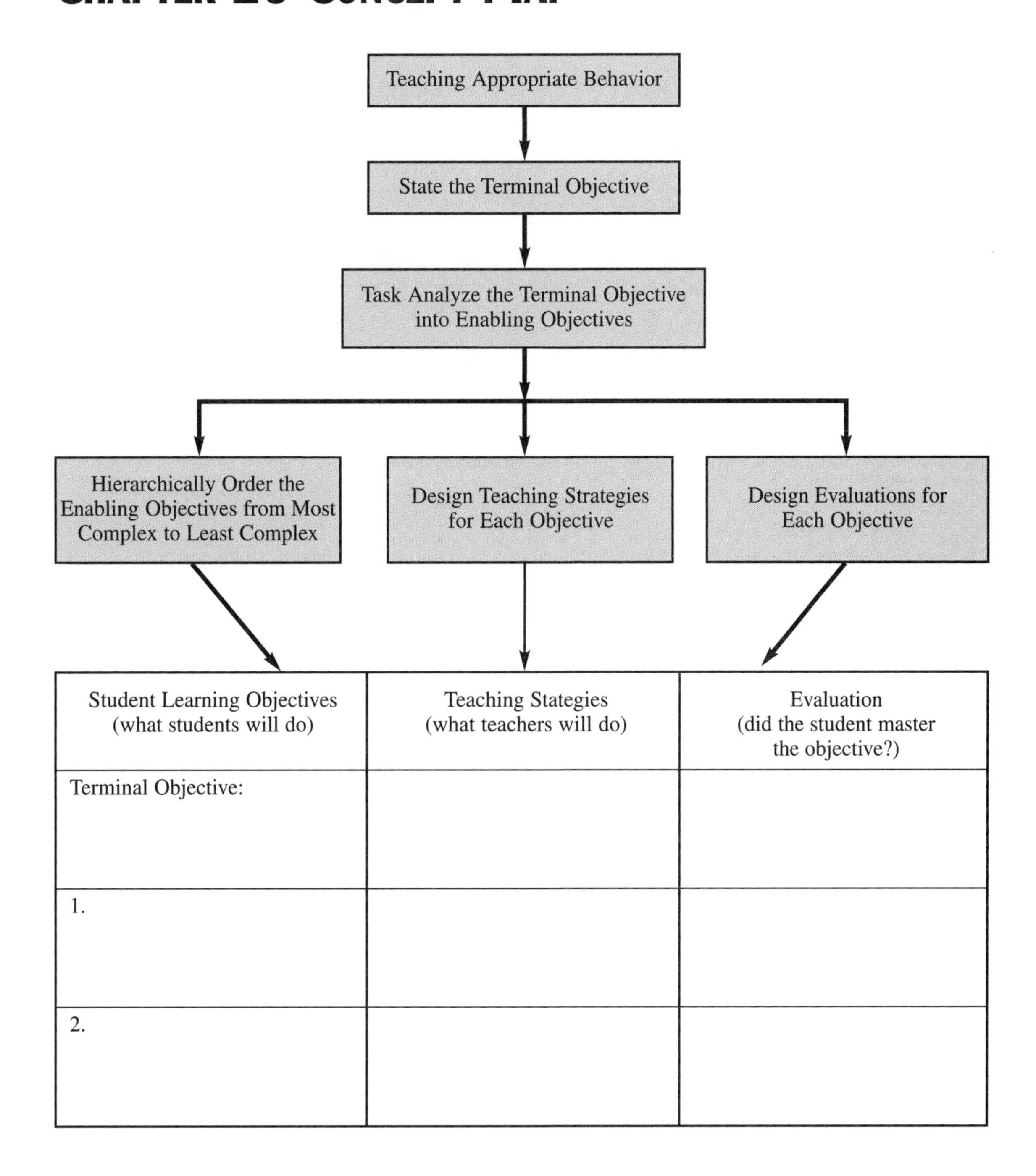

Student Learning Objectives (what students will do)	Teaching Stategies (what teachers will do)	Evaluation (did the student master the objective?)
Terminal Objective:		
1.		
2.		

? QUESTIONS FOR THE STUDY TEAM

1. a. State a terminal objective that is related to facilitating appropriate student behavior.

   b. Determine for which grade level (elementary, middle, high school) the lesson will be designed.

   c. Task analyze the terminal objective into a hierarchy of enabling objectives that are developmentally appropriate for the grade level.

   d. For each enabling objective and the terminal objective, design developmentally appropriate teaching strategies.

   e. For each enabling objective and the terminal objective, design developmentally appropriate evaluations.

2. How may the terminal objective in question 1a. be taught across the curriculum, that is, in different subject areas?

3. Should behavior as well as academic objectives be taught in school or is the teaching of appropriate behavior solely the responsibility of parents in the home environment?

4. There is not enough time to adequately teach a curriculum that is packed with academic objectives; so how can a teacher afford the time necessary to teach objectives directed towards appropriate behavior?

5. How can a teacher take the time to teach behavior without jeopardizing students' results on high stakes test brought about by the standards movement?

References

Adler, A. (1963). *The Problem Child.* New York: Capricorn.

American Psychological Association. (1997). *Learner-Centered Psychological Principles: A Framework for School Reform and Redesign.* Washington, DC:

American Psychological Association. (1993). *Violence and Youth: Psychology's Response, Vol. 1.,* Washington, DC: American Psychological Association.

Amnesty International. (1998). *Betraying the Young: Human Rights Violations Against Children in the US Justice System.* AI Index AMR 51/57/98.

Atkinson, J. (1964). *An Introduction to Motivation.* Princeton, NJ: Van Nostrand.

Ayers, W. (1997). "I Walk With Delinquents." *Educational Leadership,* 51(2), 48–51.

Bandura, A. (1986). *Social Foundations of Thought and Action: Social Cognitive Theory.* Englewood Cliffs, NJ: Prentice Hall.

Beattie, M. (2001). *Codependent No More: Beyond Codependency.* Fine Communications.

Beck, J. S. S. (1995). *Cognitive Therapy.* New York, NY: Guilford Publications.

Bigelow, B. (1991). "Columbus in the Classroom." From H. Koning, *Columbus: His Enterprise: Exploding the Myth.* New York: Monthly Review Press.

Biuiano, T. Personal Communication 1994

Bouthilet, P. D., and J. Lazar, (eds.). (1982). *Television and Behavior: Ten Years of Scientific Progress and Implications for the Eighties.* U.S. Department of Health and Human Services, National Institute of Mental Health, Washington, DC: U.S. Government Printing Office.

Braun, C. (1976). "Model of Teacher Expectations Cycle." *Review of Educational Research,* 46(2), 185–213.

Brendtro, L., M. Brokenleg, and S. V. Van Bockern. (1990). *Reclaiming Youth At Risk, Our Hope for the Future.* Bloomington, IN: National Education Service.

Brendtro, L., and N. Long. (1995). "Breaking the Cycle of Conflict." *Educational Leadership* 52(5), 52–56.

Brooks, R. (1991). *The Self-Esteem Teacher.* Circle Pines, MN: American Guidance Service.

Brophy, J. E. (1988a). "Educating Teachers about Managing Classrooms and Students." *Teaching and Teacher Education.* 4(1), 1.

Brophy, J. E. (1988b). "Research on Teacher Effects: Uses and Abuses." *The Elementary School Journal,* 89(1) 3–21.

Brown, J. L. and C. A. Moffett. (1999). *The Hero's Journey, How Educators Can Transform Schools and Improve Learning.* Alexandria VA: Association for Supervision and Curriculum Development.

Butchart, R. E. and B. McEwan, (eds.) (1998). *Classroom Discipline in American Schools: Problems and Possibilities for Democratic Education.* Albany, NY: State University of New York Press.

Canter, L. and M. Canter. (1992). *Assertive Discipline: Positive Behavior Management for Today's Classroom.* Santa Monica, CA: Lee Canter & Associates.

Canter, L. (1989). "Assertive Discipline—More Than Names on the Board and Marbles in a Jar." *Phi Delta Kappan,* 71(1), 57–61.

Center for Media Education, (2002). *TV Violence,* Retrieved from http://www.cme.org/children/kids_tv/violence.html on 4/20/02.

Charney, R. S. (1992). *Teaching Children to Care: Management in the Responsive Classroom.* Greenfield, MA: Northeast Foundation for Children.

Children's Defense Fund. (2002). *Key Facts about Education,* Retrieved from www.childrensdefense.org/key/facts_education.htm, on 3/10/2002.

Clarizio, H.F. (1980). *Toward Positive Classroom Discipline,* 3rd ed. New York, NY: Wiley.

Collopy, R. B. and T. Green. (1995). "Using Motivation Theory with At-Risk Children." *Educational Leadership,* 53(1), 37–40.

Congressional Quarterly. (1993). "TV Violence." *CQ Researcher,* 3 (12), 165–187.

Coopersmith, S. (1967). *The Antecedents of Self-Esteem.* San Francisco, CA: W. H. Freedman.

Copple, C., I. Sigel, and R. Saunders. (1984). *Educating the Young Thinker.* New York: Van Nostrand.

Curwin, R. L. and A. N. Mendler. (1999). Zero Tolerance for Zero Tolerance. *Phi Delta Kappan* 81(1), 119–120.

Deci, E. L., R. Koestner, and R. M. Ryan. (2001). "Extrinsic Rewards and Intrinsic Motivation in Education: Reconsidered Once Again." *Review of Educational Research,* 71(1) 1–27.

Dewey, J. (1938). *Experience and Education.* New York: Macmillian.

Dobson, J. C. (1996). *The New Dare to Discipline.* Carol Stream, IL: Tyndale House.

Driekurs, R. (1964). *Children the Challenge.* New York, NY: Hawthorne.

Driekurs, R., B.B. Grunwald, and F.C. Pepper. (1982). *Maintaining Sanity in the Classroom, Classroom Management Techniques,* 2nd ed. New York: NY. Harper and Row.

Ellis, A. and R.A. Harper. (1997). *A Guide to Rational Living,* 3rd ed. N. Hollywood, CA: Wilshire Book Co.

Epstein, C. (1979). *Classroom Management and Teaching: Persistent Problems and Rational Solutions.* Reston, VA: Reston Publishing.

Foxfire Fund. (2002). Retrieved from http://www.foxfire.org/ on 4/27/02.

Frankl, V. E. (1999). *Man's Search for Meaning.* Boston, MA: Beacon Press.

French, J. R. P. and B. Raven. (1960). In D. Cartwright and A. Zander (Eds.), *Group Dynamics: Research and Theory.* Evanston, IL: Row-Peterson.

Gaby, J. (1991). *ASCD Update,* Jan.

Gardner, H. (1991). *The Unschooled Mind: How Children Think and How Schools Should Teach.* New York: Basic Books.

Gardner, H. (1993). *Frames of Mind:The Theory of Multiple Intelligences.* New York: Basic Books.

Gever, B. (1991). "Psychiatric Manifestations of Learning Disorders." *Reading, Writing, and Learning Disorders,* 7, 231-242.

Ginott, H. (1972). *Between Teacher and Child.* New York, NY: Peter H. Wyden Publishing.

Good, T. and J. Brophy. (1987). *Looking in Classrooms,.* 4th ed. New York, NY: Harper & Row.

Gordon, T. (1974). *Teacher Effectiveness Training.* New York: Peter H. Wyden.

Gordon, T. (1989). *Teaching Children Self-Discipline . . . at Home and at School.* New York, NY: Times Books.

Goulet, L. (1997). Maintaining Respect Under Fire. *Reaching Today's Youth,* Summer, 17–20.

Haberman, M. (1995). *Star Teachers of Children in Poverty.* West Lafayette, IN: Kappa Delta Pi.

Haberman, M. (1995). *The Haberman Newsletter.* 1 (2)

Hohnadel, L. (2001). *Personal Communication.*

Hunter, M. (1982). *Mastery Teaching.* El Segundo, CA: TIP Publications.

Hyman, I. A. and P. A. Snook. (1999). *Dangerous Schools: What We Can Do about the Physical and Emotional Abuse of Our Children.* San Francisco, CA: Jossey-Bass Publishers.

Jackson, P. W. (1986). *The Practice of Teaching.* New York: Teachers College Press.

James, W. (1890). *Principles of Psychology* (2 vols.). New York: H. Holt and Co.

Jefferson, T. (1776). *Preamble to the United States Declaration of Independence.*

Jones, V.F. and L. S. Jones. (1980). *Adolescents with Behavior Problems.* Boston, MA: Allyn and Bacon.

Jones, V.F. and L. S. Jones. (1981). *Responsible Classroom Discipline: Creating Positive Classroom Environments and Solving Problems.* Boston, MA. Allyn and Bacon.

Kagan, J. (1972). "Motives and Development." *Journal of Personality and Social Psychology,* 22, 51–56.

Kamii, C. (1991). "Toward Autonomy: The Importance of Critical Thinking and Choice Making." *School Psychology Review,* 20(3), 382–388.

Kaplan, H. B. (1976). "Self-Attitudes and Deviant Response." *Social Forces,* 54, 788–801.

Kaplan, H. B. (1980). *Deviant Behavior in Defense of Self.* New York: Academic Press.

Kelly, W. (1970). Poster for 1970 Earth Day Celebration © 1980 The Estate of Walt Kelly.

Kohlberg, L. (1969). *Stages in the Development of Moral Thought and Action,* New York, NY: Holt, Rinehart & Winston.

Kohn, A (1992) *No Contest: The Case Against Competition.* Boston, MA: Mariner Books.

Kohn, A., (1996). *Beyond Discipline: From Compliance to Community.* Alexandria, VA: Association for Supervision and Curriculum Development.

Kohn, A. (1999). *Punished by Rewards, The Trouble with Gold Stars, Incentive Plans, A's, Praise, and Other Bribes.* Boston, MA: Houghton Mifflin.

Laurence-Lightfoot, S. (1999). *Respect.* Reading MA: Perseus Books

Levin, J. and R. Heath. (1981). *Criterion Referenced Evaluation: Its Effect on Student Achievement, On-Task Behavior, and Teacher Behavior.* Paper presented at the Annual Conference of the Pennsylvania Association for Supervision and Curriculum Development, Harrisburg, PA.

Levin, J. and J. Nolan. (2000). *Principles of Classroom Management, A Professional Decision Making Model.* 3rd ed., Needham Heights, MA: Allyn & Bacon.

Levin, J., J. Nolan, and N. Hoffman. (1985). "A Strategy for the Classroom Resolution of Chronic Discipline Problems." *National Association of Secondary School Principals Bulletin,* 69(479), 11–18.

Levin, J. and J. Shanken-Kaye. (1996). *The Self-Control Classroom: Understanding and Managing the Disruptive Behavior of All Students, Including Students with ADHD.* Dubuque, IA: Kendall/Hunt Publishing Co.

Lindquist, B. and A. Molnar. (1995). "Children Learn What They Live." *Educational Leadership,* 52(5), 50–51.

Mann, L. (1998). "Who's In Charge?" *Education Update,* 40(6), 1,4.

Marshall, M. (1998). "Empower—Rather than Overpower." *Education Week,* XVII(37), 32, 36.

Marzano, R. J. (1992). *A Different Kind of Classroom: Teaching with Dimensions of Learning.* Alexandria, VA: Association for Supervision and Curriculum Development.

Maslow, A. (1968). *Toward a Psychology of Being.* New York: Van Nostrand.

McKenna, M. A. (2001). "Who Will Prepare Tomorrow's Quality Teachers?" *Connection, New England's Journal of Higher Education.* Fall 2001, 18.

Meichenbaum, D. (2001). *Treatment of Individuals with Anger Control Problems and Aggresive Behavior: A Clinical Handbook.* Clearwarwe, FL: Institute Press.

Morgan, M. (1984). "Rewards-Induced Decrements and Increments in Intrinsic Motivation." *Review of Educational Research,* 54(1), 5–30.

National Public Radio, (2002). *Langley Music Project.* Retrieved from http://search1.npr.org/opt/collections/torched/wesa/data_wesa/seg_132233.htm on 4/27/02.

National Public Radio, (2002). *TV Violence.* Morning Edition, March 29, retrieved from http://search1.npr.org/opt/collections/torched/me/data_me/seg_140777.htm, on 7/14/02.

National Research Council, (1999). *How People Learn.* M. S. Donovan, J. D. Bransford and J. W. Pellegrino (eds.), Washington, DC: National Academy Press.

Newman, S. A., J. A. Fox, E. A. Flynn, and W. Christesson. (2000). *America's After School Choice: The Prime Time for Juvenile Crime, or Youth Enrichment and Achievement,* A Report From Fight Crime: Invest in Kids: Washington, DC.

Newmann, F. and G. Wehlage. (1993). "Five Standards of Authentic Instruction." *Educational Leadership,* 50(7), 8–12.

Nietzsche, F. W. (2000). *Basic Writings of Nietzsche.* New York, NY: Random House.

Northeast Foundation for Children. (1998). "Punishment vs. Logical Consequences: What's the Difference?" *Responsive Classroom Newsletter,* 10(3), 1–2.

Northeast High Magnet: Project SPARC (2002). Retrieved from http://home.earthlink.net/~nemagnet/sparc_history.html on 4/27/02.

Pearl, D. (1984). "Violence and Aggression." *Society,* 21(6), 15–16.

Perkins, D. and T. Blythe. (1994). "Putting Understanding up Front." *Educational Leadership,* 51(5), 4–7.

Perry, K. E. and R. S. Weinstein. (1998). "The Social Context of Early Schooling and Children's School Adjustment." *Educational Psychologist.* 33(4), 177–194.

Piaget, J. (1970). "Piaget's Theory." In P. H. Mussen (Ed.), *Carmichael's Manual of Child Psychology,* Vol. 1. New York, NY: Wiley.

Piaget, J. and B. Inhelder. (1971). *The Psychology of the Child.* New York: Basic Books.

Raffini, J. P. (1993). *Winners Without Losers: Structures and Strategies for Increasing Student Motivation to Learn.* Boston, MA: Allyn and Bacon.

Raywid, M.A., and L. Oshiyama. (2000). "Musings in the Wake of Columbine: What Can Schools Do?" *Phi Delta Kappan* 1(6), 444–449.

Rosenfield, D., R. Folger, and H. Adelman. (1980). "When Rewards Reflect Competence: A Qualification of the Over-Justification Effect." *Journal of Personality and Social Psychology,* 39(3), 368–376.

Rosenshine, B. and R. Stevens. (1986). "Teaching Functions." In M. C. Wittrock (ed.), *Handbook of Research on Teaching,* 3rd. Ed. New York: Macmillian.

Rotter, J. (1966). "Generalized Expectations for Internal versus External Control of Reinforcement." *Psychological Monographs,* 1, 609.

Rotter, J. (1975). "Some Problems and Misconceptions Related to the Construct of Internal versus External Control of Reinforcement." *Journal of Consulting and Clinical Psychology,* 43, 56–67.

Rowling, J. K. (1998). *Harry Potter and the Sorcerer's Stone.* New York, NY: Scholastic.

Ryan, K. (1970). *Don't Smile Until Christmas: Accounts of the First Year of Teaching.* Chicago, IL: University of Chicago Press.

Schnitzer, S. (1993). "Designing an Authentic Assessment." *Educational Leadership,* 50(7), 32–35.

Shrigley, R. L. (1985). "Curbing Student Disruption in the Classroom—Teachers Need Intervention Skills." *National Association of*

Secondary School Principals Bulletin. 69(7), 26–32.

Sigel, I. E. and R. R. Cocking. (1977). *Cognitive Development from Childhood to Adolescence: A Constructivist Perspective.* New York: Holt, Rinehart and Winston.

Skinner, B. F. (1974). *About Behaviorism.* New York: Knopf.

Stipek, D. J. (2001). *Motivation to Learn: Integrating Theory and Practice.* 4th ed. Needham Heights, MA: Allyn and Bacon.

Strachota, B. (1996). *On Their Side: Helping Children Take Charge of Their Learning.* Greenfield, MA: Northeast Foundation for Children.

Sylwester, R. (1997). "The Neurobiology of Self-Esteem and Aggression." *Educational Leadership,* 54(5), 75–80.

Toffler, A. (1970). *Future Shock.* New York, NY: Random House.

U.S. Census Bureau, (2000). *Who's Minding the Kids? Child Care Arrangements,* Fall, 1995.

U.S. Department of Education and U.S. Department of Justice. (2000). *2000 Annual Report on School Safety.* Retrieved from http://www.ed.gov/offices/OESE/SDFS/annrept00.pdf on 4/27/02.

U.S. Department of Education, (1999). *Dropout Rates in the United States: 1997.* Table 5, National Center for Educational Statistics: Washington, D.C.

U.S. Department of Health and Human Services, Administration on Children, Youth, and Families. (2001). *Child Maltreatment 1999.* Washington, DC: U.S. Government Printing Office.

U.S. Department of Justice, (1999). *Uniform Crime Reports for the United States, 1998.* Federal Bureau of Investigation: Washington, D.C.

U.S. Department of Labor. (2002). "Employment Characteristics of Families in 2001." *Employment Characteristics of Families Summary.* Retrieved from http://stats.bis.gov/news.release/famee.nr0.htm, on 4/20/2002.

Valentine, M. R. (1999). *How to Deal With Discipline Problems in the Schools.* Dubuque, IA: Kendall/Hunt Publishing Company.

Von Glasersfeld, E. (1981). "The Concepts of Adaption and Viability in Radical Constructivist Theory of Knowledge." In I. E. Sigel, Brodinsky, and Golinkoff (eds.), *New Directions in Piagetian Theory and Practice.* Hillside, NJ: Lawrence Eribaum Associates.

Vorrath, H. and L. Brendtro. (1985). *Positive Peer Culture.* Hawthorne, NY: Aldine du Gruyter.

Ward, W. A. (2000) *PEOPLESMART,* Berret-Koehler Publ.

Wesley, D. C. (1998). "Eleven Ways to Be a Great Teacher." *Educational Leadership,* 55(5), 80–82.

White, R. (1959). "Motivation Reconsidered: The Concept of Competence." *Psychological Review,* 66, 297–333.

Withall, J. (1969). "Evaluation of Classroom Climate." *Childhood Education,* 45(7), 403–408.

APPENDIX A

The Components of a Successful Learning Environment

Definitions of Success/Failure Ratio, Motivation, and Self-Esteem

SUCCESS/FAILURE RATIO

1. The success/failure ratio is a measure of an individual's self-worth as determined by the ratio of their successful experiences to their failure experiences.
   a. S/F > 1 denotes many more successful experiences than failure experiences.
   b. S/F < 1 denotes many more failure experiences than successful experiences.

MOTIVATION

1. Motivation is a measure of an individual's will to initiate and to put forth effort in activities from which some gain is sought.
2. Motivation is defined as the Expectation of Success multiplied by Value.
3. $M = E \times V$
   a. Expectation of Success is the belief an individual has that they can attain a desired goal.
   b. Value is the importance of the goal to the individual.
4. Motivation can be intrinsic or extrinsic.
   a. Intrinsic Motivation is defined as an Internal Locus of Control multiplied by an Internal Value Structure.
   b. Intrinsic Motivation = Internal Locus of Control × Internal Value Structure.
      1) An individual has an Internal Locus of Control when the individual's expectation of success is dependent upon factors within the individual's control (i.e. effort, ability).
      2) An Internal Value Structure exists when the outcomes valued by the individual are independent of the participation of others (i.e. competence, interest).
   c. Extrinsic Motivation is defined as an External Locus of Control multiplied by an External Value Structure.
   d. Extrinsic Motivation = External Locus of Control × External Value Structure.
      1) An individual has an External Locus of Control when the individual's expectation of success is dependent upon factors outside the individual's control (i.e. luck, type of teacher).
      2) An External Value Structure exists when the outcomes valued by the individual are dependent on the participation of others (i.e. rewards, show superiority).

SELF-ESTEEM

1. Self-Esteem is defined as the sum of Significance, Competence, Virtue, and Power.
2. SE = S + C + V + P
   a. Significance is an individual's belief that she is respected, liked, and trusted by people who are important to her.
   b. Competence is an individual's sense of mastery in tasks that she values.
   c. Virtue is an individual's perceived feeling of worthiness as a result of her ability and willingness to help others.
   d. Power is an individual's perception that she exerts control over important aspects of her environment.
3. Motivation can be Pro-Social or Distorted.
   a. Pro-Social Self-Esteem is self-esteem obtained through socially acceptable means.
      1) $SE_{ps} = S_{ps} + C_{ps} + V_{ps} + P_{ps}$
   b. Distorted Self-Esteem is self-esteem obtained through antisocial means.
      1) $SE_{d} = S_{d} + C_{d} + V_{d} + P_{d}$

APPENDIX B

The Professional Decision Making Matrix

Authority Base	Success/Failure Ratio		Motivation				Self-Esteem							
	>1	<1	I.L.C	E.L.C	I.V.S	E.V.S	S_{PS}	S_D	C_{PS}	C_D	V_{PS}	V_D	P_{PS}	P_D
Referent (influence through respectful, trusting, caring relationships)														
Expert (influence through expert pedagogy)														
Legitimate (influence through title)														
Coercive (influence through rewards/ punishments)														

Key:
I.L.C. = internal locus of control; E.L.C. = external locus of control; I.V.S. = internal value structure; E.V.S. = external value structure
S_{PS} = significance pro-social; C_{PS} = competence pro-social; V_{PS} = virtue pro-social; P_{PS} = power pro-social
S_D = significance distorted; C_D = competence distorted; V_D = virtue distorted; P_D = power distorted

APPENDIX C

Teacher Individual Management Action Plan (TIMAP)

Teacher Individual Management Action Plan

Student's Name ____________________

1. What is the specific behavior that the student exhibits, and why is this behavior a discipline problem warranting intervention?

2. What names or labels do I use when referring to the student, or how am I thinking about this student?

3. How does this student perceive my use of authority?

4. What are the possible functions or goals of the behavior being exhibited, using S/F Ratio, motivation, and self-esteem?

5. How have I attempted to increase the likelihood that this student will experience a successful learning environment?

6. How have I provided this student with opportunities for self-control by using nonverbal and verbal interventions, as well as logical consequences? Are there further opportunities for self-control that can be provided for this student?

7. What further strategies will I use to maintain and reestablish a successful learning environment for the student?

8. What interventions will I use to gain the cooperation of this student in reestablishing a successful learning environment, while protecting a successful learning environment for all students?

APPENDIX D

Anecdotal Records

Student Name: ______________________

Phone Number:______________________

DATE	STUDENT BEHAVIOR and RESPONSE TO INTERVENTION	TEACHER ACTION	STUDENT SIGNATURE

APPENDIX E

Hierarchy of Interventions

	ALL STUDENTS	STUDENTS EXHIBITING COMMON DISCIPLINE PROBLEMS	STUDENTS EXHIBITING CHRONIC DISCIPLINE PROBLEMS
maximum opportunities for student self-control least disruptive to the learning environment least confrontational teachers have many remaining interventions	**Prevention: Establishing Successful Learning Environments** S/F > 1 Intrinsic Motivation internal locus of control internal value structure Pro-Social Self-Esteem significance competence virture power	**Prevention: Establishing Successful Learning Environments** S/F > 1 Intrinsic Motivation internal locus of control internal value structure Pro-Social Self-Esteem significance competence virture power	**Prevention: Establishing Successful Learning Environments** S/F > 1 Intrinsic Motivation internal locus of control internal value structure Pro-Social Self-Esteem significance competence virture power
		Level 1: Reestablishing Successful Learning Environments S/F > 1 Intrinsic Motivation internal locus of control internal value structure Pro-Social Self-Esteem significance competence virture power	**Level 1: Reestablishing Successful Learning Environments**
		Level 2: Pro-Active Interventions change instructional pace boosting interest redirecting behavior	**Level 2: Pro-Active Interventions**
		Level 3: Nonverbal Interventions planned ignoring signals proximity touch	**Level 3: Nonverbal Interventions**

(continued)

	Level 4: Verbal Interventions use students' name inferential statements questions I-statements demands	**Level 4: Verbal Interventions**
teachers have fewer remaining interventions	**Level 5: Applying Consequences** "you have a choice"	**Level 5: Applying Consequences**
most confrontational most disruptive to the learning environment minimum opportunities for student self-control		**Level 6: Chronic Disruptive Behavior** teacher/student conf.: authentic questions goal attainment behavior: Goal, Plan, Do, Check student self-monitoring first teacher/parent-guardian conference contracting for behavioral change anecdotal record keeping: student participation referral to professionals inside school conditional removal from class second teacher/parent-guardian conference referral to professionals outside school

Subject Index

Author Index